Compensation for Wrongful Convictions

I0888323

This book presents a comprehensive comparative analysis of the substantive and procedural aspects of compensation for wrongful convictions in European countries and the USA, as well as the standard derived from the case law of the European Court of Human Rights. The collection draws comparative conclusions as to the similarities and differences between selected jurisdictions and assesses the effectiveness of the national compensation schemes. This enables the designing of an optimum model of compensation, offering accessibility and effectiveness to the victims of miscarriages of justice and being acceptable to jurisdictions based on common law, and civil law traditions, as well as inquisitorial and adversarial types of criminal process. Moreover, the discussion of the minimum European standard as established in the case law of the European Court of Human Rights enables readers to identify how the Strasbourg Court can contribute to strengthening the compensation scheme. The book will be essential reading for students, academics and policymakers working in the areas of criminal law and procedure.

Wojciech Jasiński is Professor and co-founder of the Digital Justice Center, Faculty of Law, Administration and Economics, University of Wrocław, Poland.

Karolina Kremens is the Director and co-founder of the Digital Justice Center at the Faculty of Law, Administration and Economics, University of Wrocław, Poland.

Routledge Contemporary Issues in Criminal Justice and Procedure

Series Editor **Ed Johnston** is a Senior Lecturer in Law, Bristol Law School, University of the West of England (UWE), UK.

The Law of Disclosure
A Perennial Problem in Criminal Justice
Edited by Ed Johnston and Tom Smith

Challenges in Criminal Justice
Edited by Ed Johnston

Probation, Mental Health and Criminal Justice
Towards Equivalence
Edited by Charlie Brooker and Coral Sirdifield

In Defense of Juveniles Sentenced to Life
Legal Representation and Juvenile Criminal Justice
Stuti S. Kokkalera

Fair Trial Rules of Evidence
The Case Law of the European Court of Human Rights
Jurkka Jämsä

A Recent History of Homicide Investigation
Changes and Implications for Criminal Justice in England and Wales
Sophie Pike

Compensation for Wrongful Convictions
A Comparative Perspective
Edited by Wojciech Jasiński and Karolina Kremens

Efficiency and Bureaucratisation of Criminal Justice
Global Trends
Edited by Ed Johnston and Anna Pivaty

See more at https://www.routledge.com/Routledge-Research-in-Legal-History/book-series/CONTEMPCJP

Compensation for Wrongful Convictions

A Comparative Perspective

Edited by
Wojciech Jasiński and Karolina Kremens

Routledge
Taylor & Francis Group
LONDON AND NEW YORK

First published 2023
by Routledge
4 Park Square, Milton Park, Abingdon, Oxon OX14 4RN

and by Routledge
605 Third Avenue, New York, NY 10158

Routledge is an imprint of the Taylor & Francis Group, an informa business

This book is a result of the research project no 2017/26/E/HS5/00382 funded by the Polish National Science Centre entitled 'Compensation for Wrongful Deprivation of Liberty. Theory and Practice'. It came about within the framework of Academic Excellence Hub – Digital Justice Center carried out under Initiative of Excellence – Research University at the University of Wrocław.

British Library Cataloguing-in-Publication Data
A catalogue record for this book is available from the British Library

Library of Congress Cataloging-in-Publication Data
Names: Jasiński, Wojciech, editor. | Kremens, Karolina, editor.
Title: Compensation for wrongful convictions : a comparative perspective / edited by Wojciech Jasiński and Karolina Kremens.
Description: Abingdon, Oxon [UK] ; a New York, NY : Routledge, 2023. | Series: Routledge contemporary issues in criminal justice and procedure | Includes bibliographical references and index. |
Identifiers: LCCN 2022047746 | ISBN 9781032134741 (hardback) | ISBN 9781032134765 (paperback) | ISBN 9781003229414 (ebook)
Subjects: LCSH: Compensation for judicial error. | Government liability. | Reparation (Criminal justice) | Compensation for judicial error--Europe. | Compensation for judicial error--United States.
Classification: LCC K5560 .C66 2023 | DDC 345/.0122--dc23/eng/20230206
LC record available at https://lccn.loc.gov/2022047746

ISBN: 978-1-032-13474-1 (hbk)
ISBN: 978-1-032-13476-5 (pbk)
ISBN: 978-1-003-22941-4 (ebk)

DOI: 10.4324/9781003229414

Typeset in Galliard
by Taylor & Francis Books

Contents

Tables

Contributors

Wojciech Jasiński Ph.D., habil., is Professor and co-founder of the Academic Excellence Hub – Digital Justice Center at the Faculty of Law, Administration and Economics, University of Wrocław, Poland. He works also in the Research and Analyses Bureau of the Polish Supreme Court and is a Member of the Legal Expert Group of Stefan Batory Foundation, one of the leading Polish NGOs. In 2011 Wojciech was awarded a French Government Scholarship (Université Paris 1 Panthéon-Sorbonne) and in 2015 a Minister of Science and Higher Education Scholarship for Outstanding Young Researchers. He lectured at the City University of London, UK (2010, 2012), Universidad de Castilla-La Mancha, Toledo, Spain (2013, 2014, 2016), Universidade de Santiago de Compostela, Spain (2017) and the University of Bologna (2019). He participated in national and international research projects financed inter alia by the Polish National Science Centre, European Commission and European Cooperation in Science and Technology (COST). Currently he is leading a Polish team in a project entitled "Facilitating mutual recognition: Analytics and Capacity building Information Legal EXplainable tool to strengthen cooperation in the criminal matter (FACILEX) under EU Justice Programme 2021. Wojciech Jasiński publishes in Polish and English on various aspects of criminal procedure, law of evidence and human rights in criminal proceedings. His habilitation book entitled *Illegally Obtained Evidence in Criminal Proceedings* was awarded first prize in the competition for the most useful law book for the judicial system's practice in 2019 organized by Wolters Kluwer Poland.

Karolina Kremens, LL.M. Ph.D., habil., is Director and co-founder of the Academic Excellence Hub – Digital Justice Center at the University of Wrocław, Poland. Before joining the Center, she worked for almost ten years as an Assistant Professor at the Department of Criminal Procedure (University of Wroclaw) where she was teaching national, comparative and international criminal procedure. She also worked in the past as an Associate Prosecutor in one of the District Prosecutor's Offices in Wrocław, Poland. Her book *Powers of the Prosecutor in Criminal Investigation: A Comparative Perspective* was published by Routledge in 2021. In 2016 she was awarded the Fulbright Scholarship (University of Connecticut Law School, USA), in 2006 the Edward Barry McDougall Scholarship (University of

Ottawa, Canada) and in 2017 the Scholarship for Outstanding Young Scholars (Polish Minister of Higher Education). She lectured at Bologna (Italy), Exeter (UK), Aberystwyth (UK) and Toledo (Spain) Universities among others. In 2022/2023 as a recipient of Bekker Scholarship (National Academy of Academic Exchange – NAWA) she will be leading a project entitled 'Gender-Sensitive Criminal Process' at the University of Ottawa, Canada. She has led numerous national and international research projects including 'Reasonable Search – Between Effective Investigation and Rights of Individual' funded by the Polish National Science Centre (NCN) and 'Knowledge, Advisory and Capacity Building Information Tool for Criminal Procedural Rights in Judicial Cooperation' (CROSSJUSTICE) awarded by the European Commission (as a leader of Polish team). Her research interests focus on the impact of new technologies on criminal justice systems, gendered perspectives on criminal process as well as on comparative and international criminal procedure.

Anna Helena Albrecht studied law at the Westfälische Wilhelms University in Münster, Germany, and received her doctorate with a thesis on substantive criminal law in 2006. After her legal clerkship, she expanded her research focus as a post doc researcher to include criminal procedural law and comparative criminal law. A research stay at the University of Birmingham, UK, funded by the Alexander von Humboldt Foundation followed. In 2015, she was appointed to a junior professorship in criminal law at the University of Potsdam, Germany. Since 2021, she has held a full professorship there and her research focuses on criminal law, criminal procedural law, media law and comparative criminal law.

Dorota Czerwińska is a Research and Teaching Assistant, as well as a Ph.D. candidate at the Department of Criminal Procedure at the Faculty of Law, Administration and Economics, University of Wrocław, Poland. She also works as a criminal defence lawyer. She is involved as an investigator in research projects financed by the Polish National Science Center, the European Commission and the European Cooperation in Science and Technology. She also acts as the principal investigator in the research project funded by the Polish National Science Centre 'Optimum Model of Plea Bargaining. Between Efficiency and Justice'. Her research focuses mainly on Polish and comparative criminal procedure, especially the instruments of negotiated justice.

Simona Drukteinienė is Professor of Private Law at the Law School of Mykolas Romeris University, Vilnius, Lithuania. She studied law at Vilnius University and in 2002 obtained a Master of Laws degree. She completed and defended her thesis on public liability at Mykolas Romeris University, Lithuania in 2008. Her spheres of interest include tort law, contract law, public liability and personality rights issues. Simona is also a practicing lawyer and a partner in the litigation department of the law firm WALLESS. She is also a recommended arbitrator of Vilnius Court of Commercial Arbitration. Since 2010, Simona has been participating in the annual European tort law project organized by the

European Centre of Tort and Insurance Law (ECTIL) together with the Institute for European Tort Law, as well as in other projects on various specific issues of tort law organized by the Institute for European Tort Law. She is a member of the committee supervising the Civil Code of the Republic of Lithuania appointed by the Minister of Justice. In 2021, Simona was appointed to the International Centre for Settlement of Investment Disputes (ICSID) Panel of Arbitrators by the Government of the Republic of Lithuania for a period of six years.

Nina Holvast is an Interdisciplinary Researcher with an education in law and criminology (both University of Leiden). She obtained her doctorate from the University of Amsterdam. Since 2017 she has worked at the Erasmus School of Law (Rotterdam), where she is currently Associate Professor at the Department of Law, Society and Crime. Her research focuses on the functioning of courts and the legal profession. Holvast has also been studying procedures to overturn wrongful convictions since 2018. Holvast has been an academic visitor of the Judicial Institute of University College London and the Centre for Socio-Legal Studies at the University of Oxford. She has also been a member of the editorial board of the Dutch and Flemish journal of empirical research on law, *Action/Recht der Werkelijkheid*, and is currently a board member of *Erasmus Law Review*.

Artur Kowalczyk is a Research and Teaching Assistant and a PhD candidate at the Department of Criminal Procedure at the Faculty of Law, Administration and Economics, University of Wrocław, Poland. He has completed his judicial training at the Polish National School of Judiciary and Public Prosecution and deals with criminal cases as an assessor at the District Court in Milicz, Lower Silesia. He participates in the research project on compensation for wrongful deprivation of liberty financed by the Polish National Science Centre. His research focuses mainly on Polish and comparative criminal procedure, with particular regard to German-speaking countries.

Sjarai Lestrade is Associate Professor of Criminal (Procedural) Law at Radboud University, Nijmegen, the Netherlands. In 2018 she obtained her doctorate on the criminalisation of human trafficking. Her research and teaching focus both on criminal law and criminal procedure law and the impact of international and European law on national law. Her research interests also include the influence of social and technological development on criminal (procedural) law. Lestrade writes the half-year chronicle Criminal Law in the Dutch law journal (*Nederlands Juristenblad – NJB*). She is an annotator for the Dutch ECHR Updates and Criminal Law Updates and a member of the editorial board on ECHR jurisprudence for the journal *Delikt & Delinkwent*. Lestrade is also deputy judge in the District Court of Gelderland.

Simone Lonati is an Italian Attorney and Associate Professor of criminal procedure at Bocconi University, Milan, where he teaches Italian criminal procedure and European criminal procedure. He also teaches at the Postgraduate

Specialization School for Legal Professions at Bocconi University, Milan, and at Pavia University. He is a member of the editorial boards of several legal journals and he is a member of the Panel of Expert Evaluators appointed by the Italian Ministry of Education in the legal sciences area. He is also a member of the European Law Institute (ELI) and of the European Criminal Law Academic Network (ECLAN). Lonati is author of two monographs, *Il diritto dell'accusato a "interrogare o fare interrogare" le fonti di prova a carico* (Giappichelli Editore 2008) and *Il procedimento penale davanti al tribunale in composizione monocratica: aspetti problematici e soluzioni interpretative* (Giappichelli Editore 2012), of a number of contributions to collective volumes and of numerous articles appearing in both Italian and international legal journals. His work and research agenda focuses on the protections and guarantees granted to individuals and legal entities under investigation or charged with a criminal offence under Italian and European law. The crucial issue in this area of criminal procedure concerns the balance between the effectiveness and efficiency of criminal prosecution and the rights of the defendant, which are often enshrined in constitutional rules or international treaties. He was given the Excellence in Research Award by Bocconi University in 2013.

Joost Nan is a full Professor of Criminal (Procedural) Law at the Erasmus School of Law (Erasmus University, Rotterdam). He studied criminal law in Leiden (2003), after which he took up employment as a lawyer in a general practice. He subsequently specialized in criminal proceedings, particularly in Supreme Court proceedings. In 2011, he obtained his doctorate in Tilburg on the lex certa principle. Joost has been a university lecturer in criminal law and criminal procedural law at the Erasmus School of Law since 2013. He currently specializes in criminal procedural law in general, legal remedies (including the extraordinary remedy of revision) and financial and economic crime. In his practice, which he keeps on the side, he is chiefly occupied with criminal cassation proceedings.

Juan Carlos Ortiz-Pradillo is Professor of Civil and Criminal Procedure at the Complutense University in Madrid. His research focuses mainly on cybercrime and digital evidence, criminal justice and fundamental rights. His legal studies also focus on international judicial cooperation, whistleblowing and negotiated justice, as well as arbitration and mediation in civil and commercial matters. He is author of seven books and has published more than 80 articles in legal journals and books (in Spanish, English and Italian). Professor Ortiz-Pradillo has been a visiting scholar at the San José (Costa Rica), Florence (Italy), Lisbon (Portugal), Wroclaw (Poland), Liège (Belgium) and Valparaíso (Chile) Universities. He has conducted several research projects and has taken part in more than a dozen national and European research projects, as well as given courses and participated in conferences in various countries. In addition to his academic career, Professor Ortiz-Pradillo has broad experience in training courses for police, prosecutors, judges and magistrates in collaboration with the Spanish Council of the Judiciary and the Ministry of Justice. He is also an External Consultant of the American Bar Association Rule of Law Initiative (Branch Office in Perú) for the training of Peruvian judges and prosecutors in the fields of bribery and corruption. Juan Carlos Ortiz-Pradillo was also been Chairman of the Arbitration Court of the Chamber of Commerce of Toledo (2016–2020).

Hannah Quirk is Reader in Criminal Law at King's College London. Her research interests develop her previous work as a Case Review Manager at the Criminal Cases Review Commission, investigating claims of wrongful conviction and sentencing. Dr Quirk is an Academic Fellow of the Honourable Society of the Inner Temple. She sits on the editorial boards of *The Criminal Law Review* and *The Wrongful Conviction Law Review*. Her book *The Rise and Fall of the Right of Silence* was published by Routledge in 2016. She is a trustee of Transform Justice and the Sentencing Academy.

Meghan J. Ryan is a Gerald J. Ford Research Fellow, Altshuler Distinguished Teaching Professor and Professor of Law at the Southern Methodist University Dedman School of Law in Dallas, Texas. She is also a Co-Director of the Tsai Center for Law, Science, and Innovation. Professor Ryan writes and teaches at the intersection of criminal law and procedure, torts and law and science. Her current research focuses on the impact of evolving science, technology and cultural values on criminal convictions and punishment, as well as on civil remedies. Professor Ryan received her AB, magna cum laude, in Chemistry from Harvard University and her JD, magna cum laude, from the University of Minnesota Law School. Professor Ryan clerked for the Honorable Roger L. Wollman of the United States Court of Appeals for the Eighth Circuit. She also practiced law in the trial group of the Minneapolis-based law firm Dorsey & Whitney LLP, where she focused on commercial and intellectual property litigation, as well as on white-collar defense and compliance. Additionally, Professor Ryan has conducted research in the areas of bioinorganic chemistry, molecular biology and experimental therapeutics at the Mayo Clinic and the University of Minnesota.

Ulf Stridbeck LL.D, was Professor in Criminal Law, Head of the Department of Public and International Law, Faculty of Law, University of Oslo, Norway, 2014–2017 and Professor Emeritus from 1 January 2020. He has conducted research in criminal procedure law and is specially focused on miscarriages of justice. He has also published scientific articles on forensic psychology. He is the founder and the Editor-in-Chief the *Norwegian Criminal Law Journal.* Since 2003 he has been a member of the Executive Board of the Nordic Network for Research on Psychology and Law (NNPL).

Małgorzata Wąsek-Wiaderek graduated from the John Paul II Catholic University of Lublin and the Catholic University of Leuven, Belgium (LL.M.) and gained a PhD and habilitation in law at the John Paul II Catholic University of Lublin. Since 2015 she has been the Head of Department of Criminal Procedure and Professor at the Faculty of Law, Canon Law and Administration, the John Paul II Catholic University of Lublin. Since 2018 she has also been judge of the Supreme Court (Criminal Chamber). She was nominated by the Polish

Government as ad hoc judge of the European Court of Human Rights in 2014–2016 and was a member of the Codification Commission of Criminal Law from 2009 to 2016. Her research focuses mainly on Polish and comparative criminal procedure, human rights in criminal proceedings and European cooperation in criminal matters. She has authored over 100 publications on criminal procedural law, protection of human rights in the criminal proceedings and judicial cooperation in criminal matters in the European Union. She has led three national research projects funded by the former Scientific Research Committee and (currently) the National Science Centre of Poland; she has also participated in several international research projects.

Introduction

Wojciech Jasiński and Karolina Kremens

It is an obvious although unpleasant truth that it is impossible to eliminate errors from the criminal justice system. The reconstruction of facts and their evaluation in criminal proceedings is always prone to certain risks. They may result from flawed reasoning used to argue in criminal proceedings, from the application of imperfect methods of proving guilt when relying on witnesses or from putting too much trust in scientific evidence that can sometimes be misleading. The risks also stem from cognitive imperfections of judges, both lay and professional. And despite lawmakers putting a great deal of effort into improving codes and rules that aim to reduce mistakes, practice shows that errors are, nevertheless, inevitable. They are especially hurtful when they result in deprivation of liberty, and frequently result in the imprisoned individual being held in poor conditions.

In response to such errors, states have built various systems that help to reverse wrongful convictions and that allow incarcerated individuals to clear their name. In recent years, also thanks to successful campaigns to exonerate the innocent undertaken by NGOs such as the Innocence Project, wrongful convictions have been at the centre of a vivid academic examination, which includes a comparative analysis.[1] As there is no common approach to revision in criminal matters, laws allowing the revision of conviction in favour of the accused are available through various procedures under the criminal or administrative frameworks.[2]

1 See e.g. C. Hoyle and M. Sato, *Reasons to Doubt. Wrongful Convictions and the Criminal Cases Review Commission* (Oxford University Press 2019); B. Forst, *Errors of Justice: Nature, Sources and Remedies* (Cambridge University Press 2004); C.R. Huff and M. Killias (eds.), *Wrongful Conviction: International Perspectives on Miscarriages of Justice* (Temple University Press 2010); C.R. Huff and M. Killias (eds.), *Wrongful Convictions and Miscarriages of Justice: Causes and Remedies in North American and European Criminal Justice Systems* (Routledge 2013); M. Naughton, *The Innocent and the Criminal Justice System: A Sociological Analysis of Miscarriages of Justice* (Palgrave Macmillan 2013); M. Naughton, *Rethinking Miscarriages of Justice: Beyond the Tip of the Iceberg* (Palgrave Macmillan 2007); R. Nobles, D. Schiff, *Understanding Miscarriages of Justice: Law, the Media and the Inevitability of a Crisis* (Oxford University Press 2000).

2 See the recent analysis of remedies for wrongful convictions in comparative perspective concerning the Netherlands, Belgium, France, England and Wales, Poland, Spain, Italy, Germany and Sweden in 'Special Issue: Towards a European Right to Claim

DOI: 10.4324/9781003229414-1

But if it is acknowledged that the mistakes are inescapable and that wrongful convictions resulting in imprisonment may happen and may eventually be reversed, it is almost a natural consequence to search for an effective mechanism to compensate those wrongfully deprived of liberty as a result of wrongful conviction. Since the right to liberty protects us all from having our freedom arbitrarily taken away states are specifically called upon to adequately respond to errors resulting in deprivation of liberty. Moreover, a mechanism allowing for the elimination and compensation of such errors is a necessary condition to legitimize the criminal justice system. If the power to do justice as exercised by the state must be respected by individuals, a mechanism for compensating damage resulting from a defective functioning of the criminal justice system should be adopted. If the system lacks such a mechanism, or if such a mechanism is ineffective, the social trust in criminal justice and the moral legitimacy of the state to investigate, prosecute and punish are likely to erode. Compensating damage suffered by the wrongfully incarcerated is also crucial from the individual perspective. Despite not being the only remedy accessible to victims of judicial errors, it nevertheless seems to be decisive in providing a chance to return to a life disrupted by a malfunctioning of the criminal justice system.

Taking into account the significance of compensation for wrongful conviction, also for the legitimization of the criminal justice system, it is not surprising that a right to compensation has also been recognized and explicitly provided at the international level. According to Article 14(6) of the International Covenant on Civil and Political Rights (ICCPR)

> when a person has by a final decision been convicted of a criminal offence and when subsequently his conviction has been reversed or he has been pardoned on the ground that a new or newly discovered fact shows conclusively that there has been a miscarriage of justice, *the person who has suffered punishment as a result of such conviction shall be compensated according to law*, unless it is proved that the nondisclosure of the unknown fact in time is wholly or partly attributable to him.[3]

Similar guarantees are provided in Article 3 of Protocol No. 7 of the European Convention on Human Rights (ECHR)[4] and further interpreted by the European Court of Human Rights (ECtHR).

However, the crucial question is how the compensation system for those that suffered miscarriages of justice that resulted in conviction should operate. From the individual and systemic perspective an effective compensation mechanism

Innocence? Normative and Practical Reflections on Remedies for Overturning Wrongful Convictions' (2020) *4 Erasmus Law Review* 13.

3 International Covenant on Civil and Political Rights of 16 December 1966, United Nations, Treaty Series, vol. 999, p. 171, emphasis added.

4 Protocol no. 7 to the Convention for the Protection of Human Rights and Fundamental Freedoms of 22 November 1984, *Council of Europe*, European Treaty Series, vol. 117, p. 33.

should be carefully designed and put into practice in every state. This book aims to provide a comprehensive comparative analysis of the substantive and procedural aspects of the compensation schemes in countries chosen for that purpose. It also discusses the standard derived from the case law of the ECtHR and critically assesses whether and to what extent it may serve as an incentive to raise the level of protection afforded at the national level. The analysis of compensation schemes functioning in countries of distinct legal and social backgrounds focuses on the identification of regulations or practices that best serve to effectively remedy the damage caused by wrongful conviction. Building a collective volume of this kind seems necessary since, to date, the issue of compensation for wrongful conviction has not been analysed from the broader comparative perspective.[5] That seems surprising, considering the academic interest in the phenomenon of wrongful convictions and their causes discussed above. Thus, the objective of this book is to fill that gap and offer an in-depth analysis of the most important remedy accessible to the victims of miscarriages of justice.

The analysis in this volume concerns the theory and practice of compensating for wrongful convictions in nine jurisdictions. The choice of countries was determined by the variety of compensatory proceedings models offered by those states and the distinct historical paths leading to it. The focus of the book is on European countries. It considers six countries from Western Europe (England and Wales, Germany, Italy, Spain, the Netherlands and Norway) and two states from Central and Eastern Europe (Lithuania and Poland). However, an analysis of the law in the USA is also offered in order to provide the reader with a wider perspective and to contrast it with European approaches to compensating the wrongfully convicted. This choice should not be considered as incidental, since the phenomenon of wrongful convictions is debated most extensively in the USA. The selection of European countries is intended to encompass both the long-established democracies and countries that have relatively recently emerged from the communist regime, to establish whether the approach towards compensatory mechanisms is in any way dependent on that factor. The research design also aspires to validate the differences between states representing the common law system and the Continental model. This is done with in order to ascertain whether the adversarial-inquisitorial dichotomy of the systems of criminal process had any impact on shaping the compensation procedures in these countries.

The methodology adopted for this book focuses on the comparative method. It is believed that this will allow distinct perspectives and different resolutions to the problem that all societies encounter to be shown. One of the established methods of research and a proven way of constructing works in comparative law is to start by presenting separate reports for each of the chosen countries.[6] According to this

5 See a recent article analysing issues of international law: J.D. Mujuzi, 'The Right to Compensation for Wrongful Conviction/Miscarriage of Justice in International Law' (2019) 2 *International Human Rights Law Review*, 215–244.

6 K. Zweigert and H. Kötz, *Introduction to Comparative Law* (Clarendon Press 2011), p. 43.

approach, the objective reports, free from critical evaluation, should be presented as a preliminary step before making an actual comparison.[7] This is a generally accepted method of presenting comparative research in the field of criminal procedure.[8]

Based on these methodological assumptions each chapter within this volume, except for the last one, provides an analysis of the law and practice of the compensation for wrongful conviction in a different country. The analysis covers the evolution of the mechanisms for compensation and the discussion behind their adoption. The reception of such mechanisms both in practice and in scholarly writings is also discussed. Where available the relevant statistical data has been given to provide a more in-depth analysis of how often damages are awarded and the average amount thereof. The assessment of the existing legal frameworks and their advantages and disadvantages is presented but the focus remains on the accessibility and effectiveness of the compensatory mechanisms.

The decision to study the compensation for wrongful conviction from a comparative perspective requires some difficult choices to be made regarding priorities between possible topics and problems that might be considered for further discussion. There are numerous questions that can be posed. What are the grounds for compensation for wrongful conviction that justify awarding damages? What are the limitations of the right to compensation? Who is entitled to claim compensation for wrongful conviction? What type of procedure is adopted for the claims? How do the theoretical and practical approaches to the method of calculating compensation differ? What remedies against the decision on compensation are available? What are the main advantages and shortcomings of the existing provisions and practice of compensation for wrongful convictions? The editors faced a hard task in choosing the ones that are crucial for the assessment of national compensation schemes. However, since only what is comparable can be compared, instead of leaving the narrative to the authors within their chapters, a questionnaire was prepared in advance. This limited the risk of some elements of the presented systems being overlooked. It also helped to organize the presentation of each system in an analogous manner and kept the structure of the analysis comprehensible. This technique also forced each author to explicitly acknowledge the lack of certain mechanisms or institutions that the questionnaire asked for. In other words, if the institution did not exist at all in a certain system, had the question not been put in the questionnaire the author of a chapter would probably not have referred to its non-existence.

The structure of each of the chapters devoted to the nine chosen jurisdictions was based on the following issues:

1 Origins and development of compensation for wrongful conviction.
2 Sources of law regulating compensation for wrongful conviction.

7 ibid, pp. 43–44.

8 See e.g. C.M. Bradley, *Criminal Procedure: A Worldwide Study* (Carolina Academic Press 1999), M. Delmas-Marty and J.R. Spencer (eds.), *European Criminal Procedures* (Cambridge University Press 2012); R. Vogler and B. Huber (eds.), *Criminal Procedure in Europe* (Duncker & Humblot 2008).

3 Grounds for compensation for wrongful conviction.
4 Procedure for claiming compensation.
5 Method of calculating the amount of compensation.
6 The recourse claims of the state against persons who caused a wrongful conviction.
7 The practice of compensating the wrongfully convicted.
8 The evaluation of the national mechanism for the compensation for wrongful conviction.

This structure allows comparative conclusions to be drawn as to the similarities and differences between selected jurisdictions and the effectiveness of the national compensation schemes to be assessed. The latter offers some insight into what rules and practices serve and safeguard the legitimate interests of the victims of miscarriages of justice.

Admittedly, the uniform structure of the chapters carries risks. The most obvious one being that the uniformization may provoke authors to neglect topics relevant from the national perspective. Another risk might be that the common framework could lead to misunderstandings and misrepresentations of the technicalities of national provisions. Also, the conceptualization is to some extent biased by the structure of the systems best known to the editors. While being aware of these pitfalls, it should be emphasized that in comparative analysis there is no 'view from nowhere'.[9] The structure adopted in order to compare what is comparable is always at least to some extent tainted by certain conceptual frameworks. Since there is no ideal method available, if the risks mentioned here have been neutralized this is only thanks to the discussions between the authors and editors in the process of the preparation of the chapters for which we are very grateful.

The peculiarities of national compensation schemes also left imprints on the chapters. Although their structure is similar, the descriptions of the national legal frameworks or the emphasis on certain points differ. In some cases, the issues pertaining to substantive law are highlighted, in others the focus remains on procedure. Also the terminology used is sometimes slightly different as determined by the respective national legal regimes. This is the consequence of affording the authors discretion as to the shape of their respective chapters.

Apart from a discussion about the national legal systems, the book also focuses on international law standards, particularly on the minimum European standard as established in the ECHR and the case law of the ECtHR. This focus is justified as the Council of Europe human rights protection system, characterized by the judicial activism performed by the judges of the ECtHR, offers much more effective protection than that provided by the UN human rights bodies. The reference to international law serves as a background for comparative analysis. On the one hand, it allows the identification of the common minimum denominator limiting the discretion of the states in shaping the compensation schemes. On the other hand, the focus on international standards also aims at detecting whether and how the Strasbourg Court can contribute to strengthening the effectiveness of national

9 See: T. Nagel, *A View from Nowhere* (Oxford University Press 1986).

laws and practice. Therefore, this volume offers a comprehensive analysis of how the right to compensation provided primarily by Protocol no. 7 of the ECHR is interpreted and whether, and to what extent, the Strasbourg Court is willing to play an active role in shaping the scope of this right.

This book concludes with a final chapter that uses the country-by-country analysis to compare the substantive and procedural aspects of national legal frameworks regarding compensation for wrongful conviction. It offers a global view on the similarities and differences between the legal systems researched as well as identifiable trends regarding the compensation for wrongful conviction. In this consideration special emphasis is placed on the accessibility and effectiveness of the existing schemes. The analysis aims at identifying the optimal shape of provisions regarding compensation for wrongful conviction which may maximize the remedial effect for the victims of miscarriages of justice.

This book has been prepared as part of the research project entitled 'Compensation for Wrongful Deprivation of Liberty. Theory and Practice' generously funded by the Polish National Science Centre (project no. 2017/26/E/HS5/00382). The project, led by Wojciech Jasiński, comprised of three other scholars: the second editor of this volume – Karolina Kremens – and two fellow researchers and doctoral students – Dorota Czerwińska and Artur Kowalczyk – who also contributed to this book with a chapter on Poland. As editors we are very grateful for Dorota's and Artur's commitment, their constant support, inspiring ideas and hard work throughout the last four years. We would also like to express our gratitude to all authors of the chapters collated in this volume, who accepted the invitation to take part in this project and provided detailed reviews and assessments of domestic compensation schemes. This task demanded not only conducting a legal analysis, but also acquiring and processing statistical data or studying case law. A significant proportion of this research has not been done before, or at least has been updated to offer the reader the most up-to-date knowledge possible about the national legal systems. We are also grateful that this study was warmly welcomed by Routledge. We believe that the book fills an important gap in studies of the widely understood phenomenon of wrongful convictions and may serve as an inspiration for various stakeholders with an influence on the shape of national compensation laws. Lastly, we are grateful to Kamil Sobański, Student Research Assistant in the Digital Justice Center at the Faculty of Law, Administration and Economics at the University of Wrocław, for his invaluable help in editing the book.

Bibliography

Bradley CM, *Criminal Procedure: A Worldwide Study* (Carolina Academic Press 1999)

Delmas-Marty M and Spencer JR (eds.), *European Criminal Procedures* (Cambridge University Press 2012)

Forst B, *Errors of Justice: Nature, Sources and Remedies* (Cambridge University Press 2004)

Hoyle C and Sato C, *Reasons to Doubt. Wrongful Convictions and the Criminal Cases Review Commission* (Oxford University Press 2019)

Huff CR and Killias M (eds.), *Wrongful Conviction: International Perspectives on Miscarriages of Justice* (Temple University Press 2010)

Huff C, and Killias M (eds.), *Wrongful Convictions and Miscarriages of Justice: Causes and Remedies in North American and European Criminal Justice Systems* (Routledge 2013)

International Covenant on Civil and Political Rights of 16 December 1966, United Nations, Treaty Series, vol. 999

Mujuzi JD, 'The Right to Compensation for Wrongful Conviction/Miscarriage of Justice in International Law' (2019) 2 *International Human Rights Law Review*

Nagel T, *A View from Nowhere* (Oxford University Press 1986)

Naughton M, *Rethinking Miscarriages of Justice: Beyond the Tip of the Iceberg* (Palgrave Macmillan 2007)

Naughton M, *The Innocent and the Criminal Justice System: A Sociological Analysis of Miscarriages of Justice* (Palgrave Macmillan 2013)

Nobles R, Schiff D, *Understanding Miscarriages of Justice: Law, the Media and the Inevitability of a Crisis* (Oxford University Press 2000)

Protocol no.7 to the Convention for the Protection of Human Rights and Fundamental Freedoms of 22 November 1984, Council of Europe, *European Treaty Series*, vol. 117

'Special Issue: Towards a European Right to Claim Innocence? Normative and practical reflections on remedies for overturning wrongful convictions' (2020) 4 *Erasmus Law Review* 1–106

Vogler R and Huber B (eds.), *Criminal Procedure in Europe* (Duncker & Humblot 2008)

Zweigert K and Kötz H, *Introduction to Comparative Law* (Clarendon Press 2011)

1 Compensation for wrongful convictions in England and Wales

Hannah Quirk

1 Introduction

There are three clear phases in the evolution of compensation mechanisms in England and Wales[1] for wrongful convictions: the *ex gratia* scheme (until 2006); the first statutory scheme (1988); and the 2018 revised scheme. The various policies have been shaped by political considerations, domestic legislation, judicial decisions, and international treaty obligations. At the heart of the much of the controversy is the contested and chameleon-like definition of a miscarriage of justice.[2] As Lord Bingham observed, whilst miscarriage of justice is a 'very familiar' term, it has 'no settled meaning'.[3] The term has been applied to situations ranging from detentions and arrests that do not lead to charge, to the wrongly convicted factually innocent.[4] In the context of compensation, the courts held that 'miscarriage of justice' has an autonomous meaning which is narrower than in other contexts,[5] but even this proved difficult to agree upon. Legislative intervention has made the definition clearer, but the policy less fair and a case is pending before the European Court of Human Rights.[6]

1 Scotland has a different appellate test and has both the statutory and *ex gratia* schemes, see https://www.gov.scot/publications/miscarriage-of-justice-compensation-claim-form. Northern Ireland cases are dealt with by the Department of Justice in Belfast, other than where the case involves questions of national security or protected information (D. Holder, 'An End to Miscarriages of Justice?' 14 March 2014, available at http://rightsni.org/2014/03/an-end-to-miscarriages-of-justice/#_ftn5, last accessed 16 May 2022). There is no information on the Department of Justice website.

2 H. Quirk, 'Identifying Miscarriages of Justice: Why Innocence in the UK is not the Answer' 2007, 70(5), *Modern Law Review* 759–777, 761; R. Nobles and D. Schiff, *Understanding Miscarriages of Justice: Law, the Media, and the Inevitability of Crisis* (Oxford University Press, 2000).

3 *R. (on the application of Mullen) v Secretary of State for the Home Department* [2004] UKHL 18; [2005] 1 A.C. 1.

4 C. Walker, 'Miscarriages of Justice in Principle and Practice' in C. Walker and K. Starmer, *Miscarriages of Justice: A Review of Justice in Error* (Blackstone Press, 1999) 31.

5 *R (on the application of Ali) v Secretary of State for Justice* [2013] EWHC 72 (Admin), para. 4.

6 That of Sam Hallam and Victor Nealon.

DOI: 10.4324/9781003229414-2

2 Appellate process

Those convicted of less serious offences at the magistrates' court have an automatic right of appeal by means of a re-trial in the Crown Court before a judge and two lay magistrates.[7] Appeals against conviction in the Crown Court (the more serious cases, determined by a jury) require leave (permission) from the Court of Appeal, and must be based on legal argument or new evidence. The appeal must be lodged within 28 days of conviction unless permission is granted for an 'out of time' appeal. Sentences come into effect immediately and are not deferred pending appeal so wrongly convicted people may have spent time in prison before their convictions are quashed but they are not eligible for compensation as this is seen as the system working correctly.

The Court of Appeal does not use the term 'miscarriage of justice' when quashing convictions. It does not re-try cases and it makes no finding of innocence. It considers whether the jury's verdict would have been the same if it had heard the new evidence or argument. If it is not certain that the jury would have convicted, then the appeal must be allowed. The test has altered over the years,[8] but the sole criterion now applied is whether the Court thinks a conviction is 'unsafe'.[9] Unsafety is another term that 'does not lend itself to precise definition'.

> In some cases unsafety will be obvious, as (for example) where it appears that someone other than the appellant committed the crime and the appellant did not, or where the appellant has been convicted of an act that was not in law a crime, or where a conviction is shown to be vitiated by serious unfairness in the conduct of the trial or significant legal misdirection, or where the jury verdict, in the context of other verdicts, defies any rational explanation. Cases however arise in which unsafety is much less obvious: cases in which the court, although by no means persuaded of an appellant's innocence, is subject to some lurking doubt or uneasiness whether an injustice has been done.[10]

The Court decided that it can only receive one appeal against conviction.[11] To gain a re-hearing, an unsuccessful appellant must apply to the Criminal Cases Review Commission (CCRC). This was the first, state-funded body in the world set up to examine and investigate claims of wrongful conviction.[12] It can refer a conviction back to court if it considers that there is a 'real possibility' that it will be found to be unsafe. The Court will then consider the appeal as normal. The CCRC also considers any request for assistance by the Secretary of State in relation to the use of the Royal Prerogative of Mercy and it can recommend the issuing of

7 Magistrates' Courts Act 1980, s. 108.

8 See R. Pattenden, *English Criminal Appeals 1844–1994: Appeals Against Conviction England and Wales* (Clarendon Press, 1996).

9 Criminal Appeal Act 1968, s. 2, as amended by Criminal Appeal Act 1995, s. 2(1)(a).

10 *R. v Criminal Cases Review Commission Ex p. Pearson* [1999] 3 All E.R. 498.

11 *R. v Pinfold (Terence Joseph)* [1988] Q.B. 462.

12 https://ccrc.gov.uk; C. Hoyle and M. Sato, *Reasons to Doubt: Wrongful Convictions and the Criminal Cases Review Commission* (Oxford University Press, 2019).

a free pardon under the Royal Prerogative where it sees fit,[13] but pardons are rarely issued now. It is only this last, very small, group of 'exceptional'[14] appeals of those pardoned or granted an appeal via the CCRC having either lost their first appeal or not previously appealed that is eligible, even in principle, for compensation. Such a process inevitably takes a long time; usually several years.

3 Origins and development of compensation for wrongful convictions

'For as long as anyone can remember',[15] the Home Secretary had the power in exceptional circumstances to make *ex gratia* payments out of public funds to individuals following a wrongful conviction. Over the years, criteria were developed to determine such payments. Eligibility was limited to those who had spent time in custody and had subsequently: received a free pardon; had their conviction quashed on a second appeal following a referral by the Home Secretary; or had their conviction quashed by the Court of Appeal or the House of Lords following an 'out of time' appeal[16] as described above. Beyond that, the criteria used by the Home Secretary were opaque,[17] and reasons were not given for decisions.[18] Judicial interpretation provided some assistance 'though clarification of entitlement seems to have rarely favoured the applicant.'[19] The courts initially deemed that, as the payments were made under the Royal Prerogative, the Secretary of State was not obliged to give reasons and his decisions were unreviewable so long as he acted in accordance with his own guidelines and acted fairly in his decision-making.[20] This was reversed,[21] but few cases succeeded[22] and, it was claimed, the outcomes were unpredictable and inconsistent.[23]

13 Criminal Appeal Act 1995, s. 16. A pardon releases a person from the effect of a penalty or a consequence of a sentence, the conviction is not quashed as this can only be done by the courts.

14 M. Naughton, 'Redefining Miscarriages of Justice: A Revived Human-Rights Approach to Unearth Subjugated Discourses of Wrongful Criminal Conviction' (2004) 45 *British Journal of Criminology* 165–182, 165.

15 J. R. Spencer, 'Compensation for Wrongful Imprisonment' (2010) 11 *Criminal Law Review* , 803–822, 805.

16 Mr Douglas Hurd, *Hansard*, HC, vol. 87, col. 689, 29 November 1985, cols 691–692.

17 *R v Secretary of State for the Home Department, ex parte Harrison* [1988] 3 All ER 86.

18 *R v Secretary of State for the Home Department, ex parte Chubb* [1986] Crim LR 809.

19 N. Taylor, 'Compensating the Wrongfully Convicted' (2003) 67 *Journal of Criminal Law* 220–236, 224.

20 *R v Secretary of State for the Home Department, ex parte Chubb* [1986] Crim LR 809.

21 *R. v Secretary of State for the Home Department ex parte. Harrison* [1988] 3 All E.R. 86.

22 *R. v Secretary of State for the Home Department ex parte. (Tawfick)* [2001] A.C.D. 28, 171. The Home Affairs Committee gave details of the *ex gratia* payments made between 1972 and 1981. (Home Affairs Committee, *Report on Miscarriages of Justice.* 1981–82. HC 421. See also *Government Reply to the Sixth Report from the Home Affairs Committee Session 1981–82 HC 421 Miscarriages of Justice* Cmnd 8856 April 1983.

23 JUSTICE, *A Report by JUSTICE: Compensation for Wrongful Imprisonment* (JUSTICE, 1982), 8–9.

The International Covenant on Civil and Political Rights (ICCPR) 1966 made providing compensation for miscarriages of justice an obligation under international law. The ICCPR was signed on 16 September 1968 and ratified by the UK on 20 May 1976. A statutory scheme was not established until over a decade later, however. In 1985, the Home Secretary confirmed that he would be prepared to pay compensation where this was required by international obligations. He added that he would also continue to pay compensation to those who had spent time in custody following a wrongful conviction or charge, where he was satisfied that this had resulted from serious default on the part of a member of a police force or of some other public authority. He added that, in principle, he was prepared to pay compensation in further exceptional circumstances, such as where facts emerged at trial, or a first appeal, that 'completely exonerate the accused person' who had spent time in custody. He was not prepared to pay compensation 'simply because at the trial or an appeal the prosecution was unable to sustain the burden of proof beyond a reasonable doubt in relation to the specific charge that was brought'.[24] This approach was adopted and applied by subsequent Home Secretaries[25] until the abolition of the *ex gratia* scheme in 2006.[26] It was held later that serious default by a public authority did not include the trial judge.[27] A judicial mistake in a summing up or a mistaken ruling as to admissibility would not constitute exceptional circumstances[28] nor, more surprisingly, would judicial misconduct.[29] At the time, Walker described the schemes as 'niggardly in their scope [and] grossly inefficient in their operation';[30] this proved to be their zenith, however.

The government argued that the *ex gratia* scheme fulfilled its international commitments and, in many ways, it far exceeded those obligations. The ICCR Treaty required a legal *right* to compensation, however, rather than merely the possibility of a goodwill payment made *ex gratia* ('by favour'). The UK was under pressure from the United Nations Human Rights Committee[31] and there had been judicial comment about its failure to give statutory effect to the Treaty.[32] It

24 Mr Douglas Hurd, Home Secretary, HC Deb., 29 November 1985, cols 691–692.

25 See *In re McFarland* [2004] UKHL 17, para. 8; *R v Secretary of State for the Home Department, ex parte Mullen* [2004] UKHL 18, para..29.

26 J. R. Spencer 'Compensation for Wrongful Imprisonment', (2010) 11 *Criminal Law Review* 803–822, 805.

27 *R. v. Secretary of State for the Home Department, ex parte Garner and others, The Times*, 3 May 1999.

28 *R. v. Secretary of State for the Home Department, ex parte Garner and others, The Times*, 3 May 1999.

29 *R (on the application of John Henry Taylor) v Secretary of State for the Home Department* (2002) EWHC Admin 2761.

30 C. Walker, 'The Agenda of Miscarriages of Justice' in C. Walker and K. Starmer (eds.), *Miscarriages of Justice: A Review of Justice in Error* (Blackstone Press Ltd, 1999), 3–30, 23.

31 See P. Ashman, 'Compensation for Wrongful Imprisonment' (1986) 136 *New Law Journal*, 497.

32 See N. Taylor, 'Compensating the Wrongfully Convicted' (2003) 67 *Journal of Criminal Law* 220–236, 222, and Lord Steyn's speech in *R v Secretary of State for the Home Department, ex parte Mullen* [2004] UKHL 18.

was also argued that compensation for wrongful imprisonment should not be left to ministerial discretion, particularly as the minister concerned was also responsible for the police who may have caused the wrongful conviction.[33] Members of the House of Lords took advantage of a Bill that provided a statutory scheme for compensating victims of crime to propose one for the wrongly convicted, which the government accepted.[34]

Section 133 of the Criminal Justice Act 1988 (CJA 1988) provides in almost identical terms to Article 14(6) ICCPR that:

> when a person has been convicted of a criminal offence and when subsequently his conviction has been reversed or he has been pardoned on the ground that a new or newly discovered fact shows beyond reasonable doubt that there has been a miscarriage of justice, the Secretary of State shall pay compensation for the miscarriage of justice to the person who has suffered punishment as a result of such conviction or, if he is dead, to his personal representatives, unless the non-disclosure of the unknown fact was wholly or partly attributable to the person convicted.

The government resisted amendments to the Bill to remove the 'beyond reasonable doubt' requirement and to include the more generous provisions of the *ex gratia* scheme. The CJA 1988 did not define a miscarriage of justice and this question consumed a great deal of judicial attention (discussed below). The categories eligible for the statutory provision are drawn much more narrowly than under the *ex gratia* scheme, for example, there is no scope for payments for those whose wrongful treatment by the state had been remedied at or before a first appeal. Eligibility was restricted to those whose convictions had been quashed or set aside following an appeal made out of time, or a referral by the Home Secretary (later the Criminal Cases Review Commission).[35] They were narrowed again in 2008 by an amendment that provided a conviction is not to be considered reversed unless and until the prosecution has decided not to proceed with a retrial.[36]

In 2006, Charles Clarke, then Home Secretary, announced that the *ex gratia* scheme was to be closed to new applicants with immediate effect in order 'to modernise and simplify the system, and to bring about a better balance with the treatment of victims of crime'.[37] As it was an entirely discretionary scheme, he could do so without consultation.[38] He also announced that, presumably not

33 HL Deb 27 October 1982 vol. 435 cc. 483–485.

34 Mr Douglas Hurd, *Hansard, HC*,18 January 1988, vol. 145, col. 688.

35 Section 133(5) of the CJA 1988, as amended by para. 16(4) of schedule 2 to the Criminal Appeal Act 1995.

36 Subsection (5A) was inserted by the Criminal Justice and Immigration Act 2008, s. 61 (5).

37 HC Deb, 19 April 2006, c14WS.

38 *R. (on the application of Niazi) v Secretary of State for the Home Department* [2007] EWHC 1495 (Admin); [2007] A.C.D. 75; [2008] EWCA Civ 755.

coincidentally, the assessor had decided that, with immediate effect, he would take greater account of any criminal convictions of and conduct by the applicant which contributed to the circumstances leading to the miscarriage of justice when determining the level of non-pecuniary compensation to be awarded. Compensation in respect of legal costs would also be assessed by reference to a less generous scheme. Mr Clarke sought to go further by making the criteria for quashing convictions more restrictive,[39] but these plans were dropped. The Home Secretary's responsibility in this area was transferred to the Justice Secretary when the Ministry of Justice was created in 2007.

The judiciary also narrowed the entitlement for compensation. One of the first challenges to the statutory scheme was brought by Nicholas Mullen. His convictions for terrorism-related offences were quashed based on the security services having arranged his illegal removal from Zimbabwe to the UK to stand trial[40] but his application for compensation was rejected. The House of Lords was unanimous in refusing the appeal, but the judges differed in their reasoning. For the purposes of the scheme, Lord Steyn favoured a 'narrow' definition of miscarriage of justice that referred only to the conviction of the factually innocent. In contrast, Lord Bingham adopted a 'wider' definition which included cases in which something had gone seriously wrong with the trial process, resulting in an improper conviction.[41]

Subsequent cases avoided addressing this conflict, until the Supreme Court convened a nine-member panel to take 'a fresh look' at defining miscarriages of justice for the purposes of compensation in the case of *Adams*.[42] By a narrow majority it held that eligibility should extend beyond the factually innocent to include cases '[w]here the fresh evidence is such that, had it been available at the time of the trial, no reasonable jury could properly have convicted the defendant'.[43]

39 *Quashing Convictions: Report of a Review by the Home Secretary, Lord Chancellor and Attorney General*, September 2006.

40 *R v Mullen* [1999] EWCA Crim 278.

41 *R v Secretary of State for the Home Department, ex parte Mullen* [2004] UKHL 18.

42 *Adams*, para. 85 per Lord Hope. See also para. 177 (Lord Kerr). For further discussion, see C. Hoyle, 'Compensating Injustice: The Perils of the Innocence Discourse' in J. Hunter, P. Roberts, S. Young, and D. Dixon (eds.) *The Integrity of Criminal Process: From Theory to Practice* (Hart, 2016).

43 In *Adams* the Court identified four models of successful appeal:

- Category 1: Where the fresh evidence [on which the appeal was based] shows clearly that the defendant is innocent of the crime of which he has been convicted.
- Category 2: Where the fresh evidence is such that, had it been available at the time of the trial, no reasonable jury could properly have convicted the defendant.
- Category 3: Where the fresh evidence renders the conviction unsafe in that, had it been available at the time of the trial, a reasonable jury might or might not have convicted the defendant.
- Category 4: Where something has gone seriously wrong in the investigation of the offence or the conduct of the trial, resulting in the conviction of someone who should not have been convicted. *Adams*, para.37 per Lord Phillips (referring to the decision of Dyson LJ in *Queen (Adams) v Secretary of State for Justice* [2009] EWCA Civ 1291, para.19).

Despite a lengthy judgment, there was a disappointing lack of clarity in the court's reasoning and no consideration of the underlying principles of compensation. No authority was cited for Lord Phillips' assumption that the primary objective of section 133 is to provide for payment of compensation to those convicted and punished for crimes that they did not commit; and that a subsidiary objective is to not provide compensation to those who have been convicted and punished for a crime that they did commit.[44] There is clearly a political argument to be made for such a position, but it is difficult to marry with established principles of the presumption of innocence and the rule of law.[45] Shortly after *Adams*, the High Court further narrowed the test in *Ali*[46] to '[h]as the claimant established, beyond reasonable doubt, that no reasonable jury (or magistrates) properly directed as to the law, could convict on the evidence now to be considered?'.[47]

The government was unhappy with the continuing litigation in this area. Draft legislation was introduced almost immediately that further restricted eligibility for compensation to cases in which, 'if and only if the new or newly discovered fact shows beyond reasonable doubt that the person was innocent of the offence'.[48] This provoked outrage from those who thought it 'an affront to our system of law',[49] and counter to the 'golden thread'[50] that runs through English criminal law, that it is the duty of the prosecution to prove the defendant's guilt. In response, the proposed wording was amended, replacing the requirement of innocence with the condition 'if and only if the new or newly discovered fact shows beyond reasonable doubt that the person did not commit the offence'.[51] Despite efforts by the government to explain this change in wording,[52] it is largely a distinction without a difference.

44 *Adams*, para. 37 per Lord Phillips.

45 H. Quirk and M. Requa, 'The Supreme Court on Compensation for Miscarriages of Justice: Is It Better that Ten Innocents Are Denied Compensation than One Guilty Person Receives It?' (2012) 75 *Modern Law Review*, 387–400, 400.

46 *R (on the application of Ali) v Secretary of State for Justice* [2013] EWHC 72 (Admin).

47 Ibid para. 41.

48 Anti-Social Behaviour, Crime and Policing Bill (HC Bill 7), s. 132(1) (as originally introduced), 9 Oct.

49 Baroness Kennedy of the Shaws QC, *Hansard*, House of Lords, Anti-Social Behaviour, Crime and Policing Bill, 22 January 2014, col. 673. See also JUSTICE, *Anti-Social Behaviour, Crime and Policing Bill. Written evidence to the Joint Committee on Human Rights and the Public Bill Committee* (June 2013) para. 56. Human Rights Select Committee, *Legislative Scrutiny: Anti-social Behaviour, Crime and Policing Bill* (9 Oct. 2013), para. 156, available at https://files.justice.org.uk/wp-content/uploads/2018/04/06170441/0218037-BROCHURE-Justice-Pro-Bono-brochure-Supporting-Exonerees_07-standard-00000002.pdf

50 *Woolmington v DPP* [1935] AC 462.

51 CJA 1988, s. 133(1ZA), inserted by Anti-social Behaviour, Crime and Policing Act 2014, s. 175(1).

52 *Hansard, HC Debates*, 4 February 2014, vol. 575, col. 163 *et seq.*

4 Procedure for claiming compensation

Successful appellants who meet the narrow criteria (or their relatives if they have died) are entitled to make a claim to the Ministry of Justice for compensation for their wrongful conviction.[53] The decision as to eligibility is determined by the Secretary of State.[54] This is one of the few areas of criminal justice decision-making reserved to a politician. Almost every other function has been delegated to the courts or administrative bodies to demonstrate political independence and to comply with human rights obligations.[55] Applications for compensation must be made within two years, although the Secretary of State has discretion to extend this in exceptional circumstances.[56] In keeping with the parsimonious approach, the guidance makes clear that not being aware of the scheme would not usually count as exceptional circumstances.[57]

The application requires the completion of a form that is available online,[58] or can be submitted on paper to the Ministry of Justice. There is no information about legal aid (which is no longer available for the procedure) or getting assistance with completing the form and the guidance is contradictory. The form consists of 13 pages (4 of which are equality and diversity questions, 1 contains the privacy notice). The 2018 JUSTICE Report criticised the complexity of the form – but the examples it cites are not on the current iteration which appears straightforward.[59] The decision-making process is purely administrative. The process has to abide by common law rules of fairness, but the rules give such leeway that it would be very difficult to challenge a decision.

5 Calculating the amount of compensation

The assessment of the amount of compensation to be awarded is determined by an Independent Assessor appointed by the Justice Secretary, Dame Linda Dobbs DBE has held this role since April 2016. The amount of an award is wholly a matter for the Assessor; the Secretary of State is required to accept the award

53 https://www.gov.uk/claim-compensation-for-miscarriage-of-justice
54 S. 133(3).
55 H. Quirk, 'Prisoners, Pardons and Politics: *R* (*On the Application of Shields*) v *Secretary of State for Justice*' (2009) *Criminal Law Review* 648–651; J. R. Spencer, 'Compensation for Wrongful Imprisonment', (2010) 11*Criminal Law Review* 803, 807, 819–820; H. Quirk and M. Requa, 'The Supreme Court on Compensation for Miscarriages of Justice: Is It Better that Ten Innocents Are Denied Compensation than One Guilty Person Receives It?' (2012) 75 *Modern Law Review* 387–400, 395.
56 Section 133(2).
57 The application procedure is set out athttps://hmctsformfinder.s3.amazonaws.com/forms/guidance/index.htm#footnote2
58 https://assets.publishing.service.gov.uk/government/uploads/system/uploads/attachment_data/file/1041755/Claim_compensation_for_miscarriage_of_justice_form.pdf
59 JUSTICE, *Supporting Exonerees: Ensuring Accessible, Consistent and Continuing Support* (2018), available at https://justice.org.uk/supporting-exonerees-ensuring-accessible-continuing-and-consistent-support

made by the Assessor.[60] There is now statutory guidance,[61] but it is still unclear how calculations are arrived at. The case of *O'Brien* and *Hickey* predates the current scheme but still appears to be good law. In that case, Lord Justice Auld noted that the Independent Assessor's role is an administrative, rather than judicial, one. Matters are dealt with on paper and in private, and awards are confidential to the claimant. The assistance of a Home Office instructed accountant may be sought. The Assessor has limited means of testing the facts relied upon by a claimant. There is no testing of the claimant's case other than by the Assessor who, in addition to attempting to award a fair sum for any suffering, also has a responsibility to safeguard public funds.[62]

In *Mattan* it was noted that the calculation was not straightforward:

> Various torts bear some relevance to an assessment of appropriate compensation for a miscarriage of justice – for example, wrongful arrest, malicious prosecution, false imprisonment, assault, person injuries, defamation and, it has been suggested, misfeasance in public office – but none is capable of reflecting comprehensively what a court might award in a the [sic] case of a miscarriage of justice simpliciter. Accordingly, in my view, an assessor, whilst having regard to the level of awards made in respect of various torts, should seek to make one overall award which reflects the overall wrong which has been done by reason of the miscarriage of justice.[63]

In determining the amount of compensation, the Assessor marks the hardship caused by a wrongful charge or conviction irrespective of whether there may be grounds for a claim of civil damages against those responsible for the miscarriage of justice. The Assessor is directed to apply principles 'analogous to those governing the assessment of damages for civil wrongs',[64] taking account of pecuniary and non-pecuniary loss. The Home Office Note begins with the general statement:

> A decision to pay compensation … does not imply any admission on the part of the Secretary of State of legal liability (other than a legal duty to pay compensation under the terms of section 133). Such decisions are not based on considerations of liability for which there are appropriate remedies at common law. The payment is made in recognition of the hardship caused by a wrongful charge or conviction and notwithstanding that the circumstances may give no ground for a claim of civil damages.[65]

60 Criminal Justice Act 1988, s. 133(4).
61 Criminal Justice Act 1988, s. 133(4A).
62 *The Independent Assessor v Michael O'Brien, Vincent Hickey, Michael Hickey* [2004] EWCA Civ 1035.
63 Cited in *ibid.* at [8].
64 Home Office "Note for Successful Applicants", first issued in 1957, re-issued in June 1997, cited in *The Independent Assessor v Michael O'Brien, Vincent Hickey, Michael Hickey* [2004] EWCA Civ 1035 at [8].
65 *Ibid.* at [32].

Non-pecuniary loss is not susceptible to precise arithmetical calculation; Sam Hallam's father killed himself while he was incarcerated; women may be too old to have children by the time they are released. It covers features such as loss of liberty, loss of family and social life, reputational damage and emotional suffering and anguish caused by the experience of imprisonment, (it is roughly equivalent to general damages recoverable on proof of an actionable civil wrong). In assessing the amount appropriate to compensate for suffering, harm to reputation or similar, the assessor shall take account of: the seriousness of the offence of which the person was convicted and the severity of the punishment resulting from the conviction; the conduct of the investigation and prosecution of the offence; and 'any other convictions of the person and any punishment resulting from them'.[66]

In a controversial decision,[67] the House of Lords held that the Assessor could make deductions from lost outgoings to include the living expenses that claimants would have incurred had they not been in prison, such as food and accommodation expenses. The reasoning was that to award the claimants the full amount of their notional lost earnings with no deduction except tax, would leave them financially better off than if they had earned the money as free men. The total amount of compensation payable under section 133 for a person's loss of earnings or earnings capacity in respect of any one year must not exceed the earnings compensation limit, which is set at an amount equal to 1.5 times the median annual gross earnings according to the latest figures published by the Office of National Statistics at the time of the assessment.

Deductions may be made from the total amount of compensation for any actions of the person that the assessor considers directly or indirectly caused, or contributed to, the overturned conviction; and other criminality and conduct of the applicant from the overall award.[68] Having considered these matters, in exceptional circumstances, the assessor may determine that the amount of compensation payable under section 133 is to be a nominal amount.[69] The rationale for this is problematic. It has nothing to do with contributory negligence, the mechanism by which civil awards may be reduced for any responsibility that claimants bear for their own loss. The assumption is that those who are not 'ideal victims' have either been harmed less (presumably because prison is not a new experience for them), or they are just less deserving of sympathy. This is not necessarily true. Those imprisoned for offences against children or a high-profile terrorist attack occupy very different places in the prison social hierarchy from armed robbers for example. Also the compensation is for the wrongful deprivation of liberty and censure, not a subjective test of how unpleasant the defendant found the experience.

66 Criminal Appeal Act 1995, s. 28 inserting a new s. 133(4A) into the Criminal Justice Act 1988.

67 *R. (on the application of O'Brien) v Independent Assessor* [2007] UKHL 10; [2007] 2 A.C. 312.

68 Section 133A(3).

69 Section 133A(4).

Overall compensation is now capped at £500,000 for those who served less than 10 years in prison and £1,000,000 for those who spent more than 10 years in prison (s. 133A(5)). When a conviction is quashed, the individual is released from court with just £46 and a travel warrant. They receive none of the resettlement support that a properly sentenced offender receives such as day release from prison, or a probation officer. There is no automatic assistance with accommodation, benefits, medical or psychological needs.[70] The only state support available is that provided by the Royal Courts of Justice Advice Bureau.[71] Successful appellants are not eligible for state benefits as they have not paid National Insurance contributions whilst in prison. They may be homeless, unemployed (often unemployable), with a range of medical and mental health conditions. In 2010, the coalition government abandoned the work started by the previous administration on identifying the unmet medical needs of those who have suffered a miscarriage of justice due to the financial climate.[72]

In addition to the statutory scheme, civil remedies can be sought on grounds such as trespass, false imprisonment, assault and/or battery, malicious prosecution, negligence and misfeasance in public office. These were better suited to the 'old fashioned' miscarriages of justice achieved through police violence. Improvements in police training and the evidential safeguards introduced by the Police and Criminal Evidence Act 1984 mean that physical abuse of suspects is almost unheard of now. Even those cases were notoriously difficult to establish due to evidential difficulties and the passage of time. In one of the most notorious judgments ever delivered, Lord Denning stopped the civil action of the Birmingham Six against the police for assault saying that:

> If the six men win, it will mean that the police were guilty of perjury, that they were guilty of violence and threats, that the confessions were involuntary and were improperly admitted in evidence, and that the convictions were erroneous ... This is such an appalling vista that every sensible person in the land would say: "It cannot be right that these actions should go any further".[73]

The Justice Secretary does not normally publish details of individual awards or give any information about individual applications or awards. Data collated by the human rights group JUSTICE, shows that compensation for miscarriages of justice has virtually disappeared.[74]

70 JUSTICE, *Supporting Exonerees: Ensuring Accessible, Consistent and Continuing Support* (2018), available at https://justice.org.uk/supporting-exonerees-ensuring-accessible-continuing-and-consistent-support

71 See Royal Courts of Justice Advice Bureau, available at www.rcjadvice.org.uk/miscarriages-of-justice (last accessed 25 March 2018).

72 https://hansard.parliament.uk/Commons/2010-11-23/debates/10112333000020/MiscarriagesOfJustice

73 *McIlkenny v. Chief Constable of the West Midlands* [1980] QB 283, [1980] 2 All ER 227, [1980] 2 WLR 689 1980 at 323D.

74 Drawn from JUSTICE, *Supporting Exonerees: Ensuring Accessible, Consistent and Continuing Support* (2018), available at https://files.justice.org.uk/wp-content/up

Table 1.1 Compensation for miscarriages of justice until 2013

Year	*Applications Received*	*Applications Granted*	*S. 133*	*Ex gratia*	*Paid (£m)*
2006–7	39	29	24	5	12.4
2007–8	40	12	10	2	8.4
2008–9	38	7	7	0	12.7
2009–10	37	1	1	0	12.1
2010–11		1	1	n/a	11.3
2011–12		10	10	n/a	13.2
2012–13		1	1	n/a	1.3

JUSTICE was unable to obtain data about the amount paid out since 2013, but another journalist found that trend accelerating.[75]

Table 1.2 Compensation for miscarriages of justice since 2013

Year ending 31 March	*Applications Received*	*Applications Granted*	*Compensation Awarded (£m)*
2013–14	45	5	3.5
2014–15	43	2	2.7
2015–16	29	2	0.6
2016–17	51	1	0.1
2017–18	36	0	0.1
2018–19	59	0	0
2019–20	98	3	0.1

6 Human rights challenges

The UK does not have a written constitution. Challenges have been made arguing that the compensation policy breaches the Human Rights Act 1998, which gave domestic effect to the European Convention on Human Rights (ECHR). The Supreme Court was unanimous that Article 6(2) was not engaged because the right to compensation was not conditional on proof of innocence by a claimant.[76] The matter was reconsidered after the latest restrictions ('s. 133(1ZA)')

loads/2018/04/06170441/0218037-BROCHURE-Justice-Pro-Bono-brochure-Supporting-Exonerees_07-standard-00000002.pdf

75 J. Robins '"Shameful': Just £10,000 Paid Out to Victims of Wrongful Conviction in Two Years', 23 October 2020, available at https://www.thejusticegap.com/shameful-just-10000-paid-out-to-victims-of-wrongful-conviction-in-three-years

76 (*R (on the application of Adams) v Secretary of State for Justice* [2011] UKSC 18), as refined in *R (on the application of Ali) v Secretary of State for Justice* [2013] EWHC 72 (Admin); [2013] 1 W.L.R. 3536.

were introduced in 2013. Sam Hallam's conviction for murder was quashed after seven years in prison as photographs found on his mobile phone 'significantly undermined' the prosecution evidence. Victor Nealon's conviction for attempted rape was quashed after 17 years in prison, as a sample obtained from the victim's clothing showed no trace of his DNA, but a full profile from an unknown male. Their respective claims for compensation were refused by the Justice Secretary on the ground that the fresh evidence on which their appeals were based did not show beyond reasonable doubt that they had not committed the offences. Their appeals were dismissed by the UK Supreme Court which held (by four to three) that Article 6(2) was engaged in compensation cases, but (by five to two) that the definition of miscarriage of justice in s. 133(1ZA) is compatible with Article 6(2). Once criminal proceedings have terminated, the only continuing relevance of Article 6(2) is to prohibit a public authority from suggesting that the acquitted defendant should have been convicted, which s. 133(1ZA) does not.[77]

The UK Supreme Court condemned the ECtHR's reasoning in *Allen*,[78] claiming that it was the first time that the domestic courts had to grapple with Strasbourg jurisprudence that was 'not just wrong but incoherent'.[79] This resulted in the neologism '*Hallam* grounds'[80] being applied to cases where a domestic court departs from a Strasbourg decision due to dissatisfaction with Strasbourg's reasoning, disagreement with its conclusions, or concerns with the consequences of its implementation.

It is fair to say that the positions of both the UKSC and the ECtHR lack clarity.[81] Nealon and Hallam have filed their applications with the ECtHR. Lord Mance questioned whether this area of law is one where uniformity of approach between countries is critical. He and Baroness Hale thought that cases after *Allen* suggested that the ECtHR may be moving towards the UKSC's limited view. Lord Reed thought the UKSC knew that its construction of the ECHR was out of step with established ECtHR decision-making; and that it was clear that the ECtHR would find section 133(1ZA) to violate Article 6(2).

7 Conclusion

In the 1990s and early 2000s significant monetary settlements were made to victims of miscarriages of justice. The Birmingham Six were eventually awarded compensation ranging from £840,000 to £1.2m each.[82] Whilst no amount of

77 *R (Hallam and Nealon) v Secretary of State for Justice* [2019] UKSC 2, [2019] 2 W. L.R. 440.

78 *Allen v United Kingdom* (Application no. 25424/09), (2013) 63 E.H.R.R. 10 (ECHR).

79 *R (Hallam and Nealon) v Secretary of State for Justice* [2019] UKSC 2, [2019] 2 W. L.R. 440, [90].

80 Lewis Graham, 'Taking Strasbourg Jurisprudence into Account' (2022) 2 *European Human Rights Law Review* 163–172.

81 H. Quirk 'Compensation for Miscarriages of Justice: Degrees of Innocence', 79(1) *The Cambridge Law Journal* 4–7.

82 J. Robins, 'Birmingham Six Member Paddy Hill on Why the Challenges Facing the Wrongly Convicted are More Severe than Ever' *The Independent*, 12 March 2016.

money could make up for the lost years, opportunities, and psychiatric harm that they had suffered,[83] it could assist with their everyday needs and in accessing treatment. From leading the way in responses to miscarriages of justice by setting up the CCRC, England and Wales have purposely become one of the worst performers when it comes to payment of compensation to victims of miscarriages of justice. Refusing compensation to most of those who have their convictions quashed creates the impression that the state is not liable for these errors, that the individual is unworthy of sympathy, and perhaps should be considered fortunate to have escaped conviction. The emphasis on establishing factual innocence before compensation will be awarded is reflective of increasingly punitive and populist attitudes in the criminal justice system. Quirk and King argue that 'the restrictions in compensation have mirrored and magnified the deterioration of defendants' rights and the presumption of innocence in statutory and policy changes over the last 25 years'.[84] Kent Roach contends that a 'factual innocence model' presents a threat to due process commitments. He suggests that its growing strength 'is related to the rise of a punitive and populist form of victims' rights, which seems only prepared to recognize the rights and the humanity of the clearly innocent'.[85] Hoyle contrasts the focus on victims of crime in the UK with the (current) lack of focus on victims of miscarriages of justice. She questions whether the latter are now regarded as 'yesterday's problem'.[86]

The government has promised compensation for the hundreds of sub postmasters wrongly convicted in what has become known as the Post Office Scandal – the largest miscarriage of justice the country has ever seen.[87] This appears to be as a result of its position as a majority shareholder in Post Office Ltd rather than due to any desire to compensate the hundreds of men and women who were wrongly convicted. This case has achieved an unusual degree of public attention. If the Hallam appeal succeeds in Strasbourg, this might provoke a reconsideration of the 'strictly and unequivocally defined'[88] policy.

The requirement to demonstrate innocence presents an almost insuperable hurdle for most appellants. It is most difficult for those who have been convicted

83 See BBC News, 'No Amount of Compensation is Enough' (19 April 2006).

84 H. Quirk and C. King, 'Justice Denied? Compensation for Miscarriages of Justice' in Lennon, King and McCartney (eds.), *Counter-terrorism, Constitutionalism and Miscarriages of Justice* (Bloomsbury, 2018) 269–286.

85 K. Roach, 'Defining Miscarriages of Justice in the Context of Post-9/11 Counter-Terrorism' in G. Lennon, C. King and C. McCartney (eds.), *Counter-terrorism, Constitutionalism and Miscarriages of Justice* (Bloomsbury, 2018) 187–207.

86 C. Hoyle, 'Victims of the State: Recognizing the Harms Caused by Wrongful Convictions' in M. Bosworth, C. Hoyle and L. Zedner (eds.), *Changing Contours of Criminal Justice* (Oxford University Press, 2016).

87 D. Ormerod and H. Quirk, 'The Post Office Miscarriage of Justice. Editorial' (2021) 7 *The Criminal Law Review* 509–512; N. Wallis, *The Great Post Office Scandal: The Fight to Expose a Multimillion Pound Scandal Which Put Innocent People in Jail* (Bath Publishing, 2021).

88 *R. (Kay) v Secretary of State for Justice* [2021] EWHC 2125, [2021] A.C.D. 117, DC at [66].

solely on a disputed confession (such as conflict-related cases from Northern Ireland) or by a 'credibility contest' between complainant and defendant (as in historical sexual abuse cases). Under the current rules, were the Birmingham Six to be released today, they would not be entitled to compensation.[89] The new compensation rules, essentially invert Blackstone's ratio being more concerned that 'it is better that ten innocent people are denied compensation to ensure that one guilty person does not receive it'.[90] Hoyle argues that the effect of sub-section 1ZA is to undermine the presumption of innocence and to create a two-tier system of acquittals[91] – those *deserving* and those *undeserving* of compensation. In practice, there is only one tier; the number eligible for compensation is statistically insignificant.

Bibliography

Ashman, P., 'Compensation for Wrongful Imprisonment' (1986) 136 *New Law Journal* 497–498.

BBC News, 'No Amount of Compensation is Enough' (19 April 2006).

Government Reply to the Sixth Report from the Home Affairs Committee Session 1981–82 HC 421 Miscarriages of Justice Cmnd 8856 April 1983.

Graham, L., 'Taking Strasbourg Jurisprudence into Account', (2022)2 *European Human Rights Law Review*. 163–172.

Holder, D., 'An End to Miscarriages of Justice?', 14 March 2014, available at http://rightsni.org/2014/03/an-end-to-miscarriages-of-justice/#_ftn5, last accessed 16 May 2022.

Home Affairs Committee, *Miscarriages of Justice: Sixth Report from the Home Affairs Committee, Session 1981–82* (H.M. Stationery Office, 1982).

Hoyle, C., 'Victims of the State: Recognizing the Harms Caused by Wrongful Convictions' in M. Bosworth, C. Hoyle and L. Zedner (eds.), *Changing Contours of Criminal Justice* (Oxford University Press, 2016).

Hoyle, C., 'Compensating Injustice: The Perils of the Innocence Discourse' in J. Hunter, P. Roberts, S. Young and D. Dixon (eds.), *The Integrity of Criminal Process: From Theory to Practice* (Hart, 2016).

Hoyle, C. and M. Sato, *Reasons to Doubt: Wrongful Convictions and the Criminal Cases Review Commission* (Oxford University Press, 2019).

Hurd Mr Douglas, *Hansard, HC*, Vol. 87, col. 689, 29 November 1985, cols 691–692.

Hurd Mr Douglas, *Hansard, HC*, 18January 1988, vol. 145 col. 688.

JUSTICE, *A Report by JUSTICE: Compensation for Wrongful Imprisonment* (JUSTICE, 1982), 8–9.

89 JUSTICE, *Anti-Social Behaviour, Crime and Policing Bill. Written evidence to the Joint Committee on Human Rights and the Public Bill Committee* (June 2013) para. 56.

90 H. Quirk and M. Requa, 'The Supreme Court on Compensation for Miscarriages of Justice: Is It Better That Ten Innocents Are Denied Compensation than One Guilty Person Receives It' (2012) 75 *Modern Law Review* 387–400, 395.

91 C. Hoyle, 'Compensating Injustice: The Perils of the Innocence Discourse' in S. M. Young, J. Hunter, P. Robertsand D. Dixon (eds.), *The Integrity of Criminal Process: From Theory into Practice* (Hart, 2016).

JUSTICE, 'Anti-Social Behaviour, Crime and Policing Bill. Written evidence to the Joint Committee on Human Rights and the Public Bill Committee' (June 2013) para. 56. *Legislative Scrutiny: Anti-social Behaviour, Crime and Policing Bill* (9 Oct. 2013), available at https://files.justice.org.uk/wp-content/uploads/2018/04/06170441/0218037-BROCHURE-Justice-Pro-Bono-brochure-Supporting-Exonerees_07-standard-00000002.pdf

JUSTICE, 'Supporting Exonerees: Ensuring Accessible, Consistent and Continuing Support' (2018), available at https://justice.org.uk/supporting-exonerees-ensuring-accessible-continuing-and-consistent-support/1980

Naughton, M., 'Redefining Miscarriages of Justice: A Revived Human-Rights Approach to Unearth Subjugated Discourses of Wrongful Criminal Conviction' (2004) *British Journal of Criminology* 45, 165–182.

Nobles R. and D. Schiff, *Understanding Miscarriages of Justice: Law, the Media, and the Inevitability of Crisis* (Oxford University Press, 2000).

Ormerod D. and H. Quirk, 'The Post Office Miscarriage of Justice. Editorial', (2021) 7 *The Criminal Law Review* 509–512.

Pattenden, R., *English Criminal Appeals 1844–1994: Appeals Against Conviction England and Wales* (Clarendon Press, 1996).

Quashing Convictions: Report of a Review by the Home Secretary, Lord Chancellor and Attorney General (Office for Criminal Justice Reform, September 2006).

Quirk, H., 'Identifying Miscarriages of Justice: Why Innocence in the UK is not the Answer', (2007) 70(5) *Modern Law Review*, 759–777, 761.

Quirk, H., 'Prisoners, Pardons and Politics: *R (On the Application of Shields) v Secretary of State for Justice*' (2009) *Criminal Law Review* 648–651.

Quirk, H., 'Compensation for Miscarriages of Justice: Degrees of Innocence', (2012) 79(1) *The Cambridge Law Journal* 4–7.

Quirk H. and C. King, "Justice Denied? Compensation for Miscarriages of Justice" in G. Lennon, C. King and C. McCartney (eds.), *Counter-terrorism, Constitutionalism and Miscarriages of Justice* (Bloomsbury, 2018) 269–286.

Quirk H. and M. Requa, 'The Supreme Court on Compensation for Miscarriages of Justice: Is It Better that Ten Innocents Are Denied Compensation than One Guilty Person Receives It?' (2012) 75 *Modern Law Review* 387–400.

Roach, K., 'Defining Miscarriages of Justice in the Context of Post-9/11 Counter-Terrorism' in G. Lennon, C. King and C. McCartney (eds.), *Counter-terrorism, Constitutionalism and Miscarriages of Justice* (Bloomsbury, 2018) 187–207.

Robins, J., 'Birmingham Six Member Paddy Hill on Why the Challenges Facing the Wrongly Convicted are More Severe than Ever', *The Independent*, 12 March 2016.

Robins, J., '"Shameful": Just £10,000 Paid Out to Victims of Wrongful Conviction in Two Years', 23 October 2020, available at https://www.thejusticegap.com/shameful-just-10000-paid-out-to-victims-of-wrongful-conviction-in-three-years

Spencer, J. R., 'Compensation for Wrongful Imprisonment', (2010) 11 *Criminal Law Review* 803–822, 805.

Taylor, N., 'Compensating the Wrongfully Convicted' (2003) 67 *Journal of Criminal Law* 220–236, 224.

Walker, C., 'Miscarriages of Justice in Principle and Practice' in C. Walker and K. Starmer, *Miscarriages of Justice: A Review of Justice in Error* (Blackstone Press Ltd, 1999) 31–62.

Walker, C., 'The Agenda of Miscarriages of Justice' in C. Walker and K. Starmer (eds.), *Miscarriages of Justice: A Review of Justice in Error* (Blackstone Press Ltd, 1999), 3–30, 23.

Wallis, N., *The Great Post Office Scandal: The Fight to Expose a Multimillion Pound Scandal Which Put Innocent People in Jail* (Bath Publishing, 2021).

Table of cases

Allen v United Kingdom (Application no. 25424/09), (2013) 63 E.H.L.R.R. 10 (ECHR).
In re McFarland [2004] UKHL 17.
McIlkenny v. Chief Constable of the West Midlands [1980] QB 283, [1980] 2 All ER 227, [1980] 2 WLR 689.
Queen (Adams) v Secretary of State for Justice [2009] EWCA Civ 1291.
R *(Hallam and Nealon) v Secretary of State for Justice* [2019] UKSC 2, [2019] 2 W.L.R. 440.
R *(on the application of Adams) v Secretary of State for Justice* [2011] UKSC 18), as refined in.
R *(on the application of Ali) v Secretary of State for Justice* [2013] EWHC 72 (Admin), para. 4.
R *(on the application of Ali) v Secretary of State for Justice* [2013] EWHC 72 (Admin).
R *(on the application of Ali) v Secretary of State for Justice* [2013] EWHC 72 (Admin); [2013] 1 W.L.R. 3536).
R *(on the application of John Henry Taylor) v Secretary of State for the Home Department* (2002) EWHC Admin 2761.
R *v Mullen* [1999] EWCA Crim 278.
R *v Secretary of State for the Home Department, ex parte Chubb* [1986] Crim LR 809.
R *v Secretary of State for the Home Department, ex parte Chubb* [1986] Crim LR 809.
R *v Secretary of State for the Home Department, ex parte Harrison* [1988] 3 All ER 86.
R *v Secretary of State for the Home Department, ex parte Mullen* [2004] UKHL 18.
R. *(Kay) v Secretary of State for Justice* [2021] EWHC2125, [2021] A.C.D. 117, DC at [66].
R. *(on the application of Mullen) v Secretary of State for the Home Department* [2004] UKHL 18; [2005] 1 A.C. 1.
R. *(on the application of Niazi) v Secretary of State for the Home Department* [2007] EWHC 1495 (Admin); [2007] A.C.D. 75; [2008] EWCA Civ 755.
R. *(on the application of O'Brien) v Independent Assessor* [2007] UKHL 10; [2007] 2 A.C. 312.
R. *v Criminal Cases Review Commission Ex p. Pearson* [1999] 3 All E.R. 498.
R. *v Pinfold (Terence Joseph)* [1988] Q.B. 462.
R. *v Secretary of State for the Home Department Ex ex p.arte (Tawfick)* [2001] A.C.D. 28, 171.
R. *v. Secretary of State for the Home Department, ex p.arte Garner and others, The Times*, 3 May 1999.
The Independent Assessor v Michael O'Brien, Vincent Hickey, Michael Hickey [2004] EWCA Civ 1035.
Woolmington v DPP [1935] AC 462.

2 Compensation for wrongful convictions in Germany

Anna Helena Albrecht

1 Origins and development of compensation for wrongful conviction

Compensation for wrongful conviction is considered one of the requirements of a fair trial[1] and is attributed an important role in enforcing the fundamental rights of the accused person in criminal proceedings.[2] In German law it is a specific manifestation of general state liability law, which has its roots in the *Allgemeines Landrecht für die Preußischen Staaten* (General State Laws for the Prussian States) of the late 18th and 19th centuries and is largely shaped by judicial law.[3] This general state liability law has a dual structure, differentiating between state liability for unlawful state action and claims for compensation after lawful state action.[4] This dichotomy is also reflected in the claims for compensation for wrongful conviction.

1.1 Development and material scope of the compensation for wrongful conviction according to the StrEG

The first precursors of provisions providing explicitly for compensation after wrongful conviction in Germany could already be found in a few of the German states of the 19th century.[5] Their background is seen in the enlightenment-based belief that the state shall compensate for the material harm suffered by persons who have been subjected to criminal proceedings through no fault of their own.[6] In 1876, the *Deutscher Juristentag*[7]

1 H Böing, 'Das Recht des Beschuldigten auf Entschädigung für unschuldig erlittene Haft' in H Jescheck (ed.), *Deutsche Landesreferate zum IX. Internationalen Kongreß für Rechtsvergleichung in Teheran 1974* (De Gruyter 1974) 73, 79.
2 S Friehe, *Der Verzicht auf Entschädigung für Strafverfolgungsmaßnahmen* (Duncker & Humblot 1997) 2.
3 H-J Papier and F Shirvani in F-J Säcker et al. (eds.), *Münchener Kommentar zum Bürgerlichen Gesetzbuch* (8th ed., CH Beck 2020) § 839 paras 1, 8 with further details and references.
4 For an overview see e.g. Papier and Shirvani (n 3) § 839 para 7 et seq.
5 Böing (n 1) 73, 74, also with an overview of further historical development; D Meyer, *StrEG* (11th ed., Carl Heymanns Verlag 2020) Einleitung para 14.
6 Meyer (n 5) Einleitung para 14.
7 The *Deutsche Juristentag* is a periodic conference of lawyers from Germany who discuss issues of legal policy, among other things.

DOI: 10.4324/9781003229414-3

in Salzburg also agreed that in the event of acquittal or withdrawal of the charge, the person concerned was to be adequately compensated for the detention on remand she had suffered, if the imposition or prolongation of the detention on remand was not her fault. However, corresponding regulations were not included in the *Reichsjustizgesetze* of the 1870s (including the *Reichsstrafgesetzbuch* [Criminal Code of the German Reich] and the *Reichsstrafprozessordnung* [Code of Criminal Procedure of the German Reich]). After unsuccessful legislative initiatives in 1882, 1886 and 1894, the Reichstag finally passed the *Gesetz betreffend die Entschädigung der im Wiederaufnahmeverfahren freigesprochenen Personen* (Act on Compensation for Persons Acquitted after Reopening of Proceedings after Final Judgment; StHaftEntSchG) in 1898, thus providing compensation for executed criminal detention.[8] The *Gesetz über Entschädigung für unschuldig erlittene Untersuchungshaft* (Act on Compensation for Innocently Suffered Pre-trial Detention; UHaftEntschG)[9] finally codified a claim for compensation for material harm caused by innocently suffered detention on remand. However, the prerequisites for the corresponding claims were very restrictively framed, presupposing, for example, that innocence had been established or at least every suspicion had been dismissed in the judicial proceedings (§ 1 (1) sentence 2 StHaftEntSchG, § 1 (1) UHaftEntschG). The practical significance of these acts therefore remained low.[10]

As for the Federal Republic of Germany, this state of the law remained largely unchanged until the year 1971, when the *Gesetz über die Entschädigung für Strafverfolgungsmaßnahmen* (Act on Compensation for Punitive Measures; StrEG)[11] came into force and now regulates in one unified act compensation for both consequences of conviction and certain other criminal prosecution measures, including detention on remand.[12] The need to change the existing law arose because the aforementioned prerequisites for compensation could not be reconciled with the presumption of innocence, which had been guaranteed since 1949 by the *Grundgesetz*[13] (Basic Law, i.e. the German Constitution; abbr. GG) and since 1953 in Germany by Art. 6 (2) ECHR.[14] With German reunification, the territorial scope of application of the act was extended to the territory of the former German Democratic Republic.[15]

8 *Reichsgesetzblatt* (Reichs Law Gazette; abbr. RGBl). 1898 I, 345.
9 RGBl 1904 I, 321.
10 Meyer (n 5) Einleitung para 17.
11 *Bundesgesetzblatt* (Federal Law Gazette; abbr. BGBl) 1971 I, 157; available at www.gesetze-im-internet.de/streg (accessed 26 December 2021).
12 The further description of the current legal situation will only explain those provisions that relate to the compensation of the consequences of wrongful convictions. However, since the provisions of §§ 5 et seq. StrEG referred to in this context do not distinguish between the consequences of a conviction and of other compensatable measures, in accordance with the general terminology of the law the term 'measure' will be used instead of 'conviction'.
13 Available at https://www.gesetze-im-internet.de/gg (accessed 26 December 2021).
14 Legislative materials, *Bundestagsdrucksache* (German parliament's Printed Paper; abbr. BT-Drs.) VI/460, 5; VI/1512, 1 et seq.; Meyer (n 5) Einleitung para 19; Friehe (n 2) 49 et seq.
15 Art 8 of the *Vertrag zwischen der Bundesrepublik Deutschland und der Deutschen Demokratischen Republik über die Herstellung der Einheit Deutschlands* (Unification Treaty); Meyer (n 5) Einleitung para 26.

Since its enactment, the law has undergone only minor changes, in particular to take account of the currency transition to the euro and to the changing economic realities.[16] After the introduction of the euro, the fixed amount for compensation for non-material harm was increased from €11 to €25 in 2009[17] and again to €75 in 2020[18] per day of imprisonment.

The primary objective of compensation under the StrEG is restitution and compensation for material as well as non-material harm.[19] Compensation for the wrongful conviction *per se* is not provided. In this respect, it is assumed that the reversal of the judgment in the public retrial would suffice.[20]

The grounds for the liability do not lie in the state's wrongdoing in a narrow sense. The StrEG grants compensation for lawful state actions, i.e. (*ex ante*) lawfully ordered and executed acts of criminal justice, even if they subsequently (*ex post*) turn out to be unlawful.[21] In its nature, the claim under the StrEG is a specific, statutorily regulated form of a so-called *Aufopferungsanspruch*.[22] Such a claim arises when the non-material legal rights to life, health and freedom of a citizen are directly impaired by – not necessarily unlawful – state action, resulting in a so-called *Sonderopfer*, an extraordinary sacrifice, which places a comparatively greater burden on the individual than on other members of the general public.[23] In the context of criminal proceedings, it is presumed that in general a citizen has to accept disadvantages caused by investigative measures of the prosecuting authorities, because such measures, which are in the general interest in criminal prosecution, can in principle impact all citizens.[24] In contrast, the burdens for which the StrEG provides compensation are classified by the act as a *Sonderopfer* that the person concerned is forced to bear and that extends beyond that of the general public.[25]

However, in accordance with legislative intent[26] and prevailing opinion,[27] compensation under the StrEG must also be paid for measures that are unlawful

16 Meyer (n 5) Einleitung para 26; K-H Kunz, in C Knauer et al. (eds), *Münchener Kommentar zur StPO 3–2* (CH Beck 2018) StrEG Einleitung para 31 et seq.

17 *Zweites Gesetz zur Änderung des Gesetzes über die Entschädigung für Strafverfolgungsmaßnahmen* (StrEGÄndG 2) of 30 July 2009, BGBl. I 2009, 2478.

18 *Drittes Gesetz zur Änderung des Gesetzes über die Entschädigung für Strafverfolgungsmaßnahmen* (StrEG) (StrEGÄndG 3) of 30 September 2002, BGBl. I 2020, 2049.

19 Kunz (n 16) Einleitung para 18; Meyer (n 5) Einleitung para 24.

20 (Critical) Kunz (n 16) § 7 para 7.

21 Kunz (n 16) Einleitung para 31.

22 BT-Drs. VI/1512, 1; BGHZ 60, 302, 304 et seq.; 72, 302, 305; 103, 113, 116; Kunz (n 16) Einleitung para 31; L Meyer-Goßner and B Schmitt, *Kommentar zur StPO* (63rd ed., CH Beck 2020) Vorb. StrEG para 1; more detail in Friehe (n 2) 118 et seq.

23 See Papier and Shirvani (n 3) § 839 para 98 et seq. with further references.

24 BGHZ 100, 335, 338; 103, 113 Kunz (n 16) Einleitung para 31; I-M Killinger, *Staatshaftung für rechtswidrige Staatshaftung für rechtswidrige Untersuchungshaft in Deutschland und Österreich im Lichte von Art. 5 Abs. 5 EMRK* (C.F. Müller 2020) 30.

25 BGHZ 60, 302, 304; Kunz (n 16) Einleitung para 31.

26 BT-Drs. VI/460, 6.

27 BGHZ 72, 302, 305 et seq.; BGH, MDR 1993, 740; OLG Karlsruhe, Justiz 1988, 87; Meyer-Goßner and Schmitt (n 22) Vorb. StrEG para 1; Meyer (n 5) Einleitung,

from the outset. They then exist alongside the claims of the convicted person from general official fault-based liability under § 839 *Bürgerliches Gesetzbuch* (German Civil Code; abbr. BGB)[28] in conjunction with Art. 34 (GG) or from Art. 5 (5) ECHR.

1.2 Other claims for compensation and repayments

§ 839 BGB lays down the civil servant's liability for an intentional or negligent breach of official duty, which is transferred to the state under the conditions of Art. 34 GG. The prerequisites for official liability are, however, high. A considerable restriction results in particular from § 839 (2) BGB, according to which in cases in which an official breaches her official duties in a judgment in a legal matter she is only liable if the breach of duty consists of a criminal offence. But in this context the prerequisites for a reopening of proceedings according to §§ 359 no. 3 and 364 *Strafprozessordnung*[29] (Code of Criminal Procedure; abbr. StPO) and thus the preconditions for liability according to § 1 StrEG are also important, because they also refer to a breach of official duties. In such cases, the convicted person will seek a reopening of the criminal proceedings not just to erase the stigma of the criminal conviction. She in fact must do so because the claim under § 839 BGB is according to paragraph 3 subsidiary to legal remedies that avert the harm, which include an application for a reopening of the proceedings.[30] Moreover, the procedural rules of criminal proceedings are more favourable. In civil procedure, the burden of proof lies with the plaintiff and thus the convicted person,[31] whereas in retrial proceedings under § 369 StPO and in the main hearing according to § 244 (2) StPO, the establishment of the facts has to be conducted *ex officio*. It also seems easier to produce new favourable evidence which justifies a reopening under § 359 no. 5 StPO than to prove a breach of official duty on the part of the official. This applies if a panel of judges (which is the case in German criminal proceedings in all proceedings in which a sentence of more than two years was expected) passed a judgment. For if a panel of judges has held the official act to be lawful, then, according to case law, individual responsibility on the part of the individual judges is to be negated.[32]

The situation is similar regarding a claim for unlawful deprivation of liberty under Art. 5 (5) ECHR. An undertaking based on this claim does not eliminate

paras 35, 53 et seq.; dissenting OLG Düsseldorf, decision of 28 August 2000–2 Ws 226/00; Kunz (n 16) Einleitung para 31.

28 Available at https://www.gesetze-im-internet.de/bgb (accessed 26 December 2021).

29 Available at https://www.gesetze-im-internet.de/stpo (accessed 26 December 2021).

30 Killinger (n 24) 68; Papier and Shirvani (n 3) § 839 para 391.

31 RGZ 164, 15, 20; A Teichmann in Stürner (ed.), *Jauernig Bürgerliches Gesetzbuch* (18th ed., CH Beck, 2021) § § 839 para 31.

32 BGHZ 17, 153, 158; 27, 338, 343; BGHZ 97, 97, 107; BGHZ 117, 240, 250; Papier and Shirvani (n 3) § 839 para 348; H Steege and C Muthers in B Dauner-Lieb and W Langen (eds.), *BGB Schuldrecht* (4th ed., Nomos Verlag 2021) § 839 para 257 et seq.

the conviction *per se*; moreover, the statutory determination of the lump sum of €75 per day in § 7 (3) StrEG of deprivation of liberty is not directly applicable. Some courts orientate themselves towards this sum also in the case of compensation according to Art. 5 (5) ECHR,[33] whereas other courts set the monthly compensation with reference to the compensation practice of the ECtHR at a much lower level of €500.[34] It can be assumed that it is for these reasons that liability under § 839 BGB as well as Art. 5 (5) ECHR with regard to compensation for wrongful conviction is of low practical significance; it will therefore not be further examined.

Claims for repayment of fines and procedural costs are based on general law of unjust enrichment according to §§ 812 et seq. BGB and § 14 *Einforderungs- und Beitreibungsanordnung*[35] (Claim and recovery order; abbr. EBAO) as *lex specialis* to the StrEG.[36] A claim for reimbursement of expenses is laid down in §§ 465, 467 StPO, which takes precedence over claims under the StrEG.[37]

1.3. Special statutory cases of compensation for wrongful convictions

Apart from these general regulations, there are acts in German law that regulate an entitlement to compensation for specific cases of conviction and criminal prosecution measures incompatible with (current) law and justice.

The *Bundesgesetz zur Entschädigung für Opfer der nationalsozialistischen Verfolgung* (Federal Act on Compensation for Victims of National Socialist Persecution; abbr.: BEG)[38] of 1956, which came into force retroactively in 1953, regulated compensation for victims of National Socialist persecution and persons considered equivalent to them by law (§ 1 BEG). Convictions were set aside by way of legislative general cassation without necessity to nullify convictions in separate proceedings,[39] i.e. immediately through the act itself, and compensation must be paid by the federal and state governments for damage to life, limb and health, freedom, property, assets and professional and economic advancement, in particular in the form of one-off payments, allowances and therapeutic procedures (§§ 15 et seq. BEG). The reasoning behind the act can be found in its preamble: it shall be recognised that the persons concerned have suffered injustice through their persecution, that the resistance they offered out of their convictions or for reasons of faith and conscience was a service to the welfare of the German people

33 E.g. OLGR Celle 2007, 303, 304.
34 E.g. OLG Koblenz MDR 2018, 866; OLG Hamm, decision of 14 November 2014 – I-11 U 16/14 –; for a brief overview see Killinger (n 24) 136 et seq.
35 Available at www.verwaltungsvorschriften-im-internet.de/bsvwvbund_13072011_430022R52002009EBAO.htm (accessed 26 December 2021).
36 Meyer (n 5) Einleitung para 61a; Kunz (n 16) Einleitung para 53.
37 Meyer (n 5) Einleitung para 56 et seq.
38 Act of 29 June 1956, BGBl. I 559, 562.
39 Regarding the term see E Pohlreich, 'Haftentschädigung, Rehabilitierung und Begnadigung als Mechanismen zur Unrechtskorrektur bei strafgerichtlichen Verurteilungen' [2021] 69 *Jahrbuch des öffentlichen Rechts* 233, 236.

and state and that democratic, religious and economic organisations were unlawfully harmed by the National Socialist oppression. In order to close the gaps in compensation left by the BEG, some of the *Länder* (federal states) have enacted supplementary legislation, such as the Berlin *Gesetz über die Anerkennung und Versorgung der politisch, rassisch oder religiös Verfolgten des Nationalsozialismus* (Act on the Recognition and Provision for Persons Persecuted by National Socialism on Political, Racial or Religious Grounds; abbr. PrVG).

Consequently, in 1992, after German reunification and almost forty years later, the Federal German legislator wanted to address judicial injustice in the GDR in a corresponding manner through the *Gesetz über die Rehabilitierung und Entschädigung von Opfern rechtsstaatswidriger Strafverfolgungsmaßnahmen im Beitrittsgebiet* (Law on the Rehabilitation and Compensation of Victims of Unlawful Criminal Prosecution Measures in the Acceding Territory, short: *Strafrechtliches Rehabilitierungsgesetz*; abbr. StrRehaG).[40] The aim of the act was to provide rehabilitation and satisfaction to all victims of a politically motivated criminal prosecution measure or otherwise of a judicial decision that was contrary to the rule of law and the Constitution, to facilitate rehabilitation in relation to the prevailing law and to increase the general compensation for imprisonment, which was perceived to be inappropriately low, at least in such cases.[41]

The StrRehaG therefore stipulates the prerequisites under which acts of injustice of a criminal nature that were committed in the Soviet Zone of Occupation in Germany, the German Democratic Republic and East Berlin between 8 May 1945 and 2 October 1990 can be declared unlawful and annulled and under which reparations must be made to the victims. The law therefore provides for the possibility of individual rehabilitation.[42] § 1 of the StrRehaG sets out the right to have decisions that are incompatible with fundamental freedoms and the rule of law annulled on application. § 6 of the act provides a right of reimbursement of fines paid, procedural costs and necessary expenses, § 16 to social compensation benefits, § 17 to financial compensation to the amount of currently €306.78 per month and § 18 to financial support benefits. Victims of imprisonment who are particularly disadvantaged in their economic situation can claim a special allowance of currently €330 per month under § 17a. § 22 provides for benefits for surviving dependants.

This category of extraordinary compensation mechanisms also includes the *Gesetz zur strafrechtlichen Rehabilitierung der nach dem 8. Mai 1945 wegen einvernehmlicher homosexueller Handlungen verurteilten Personen* (Act on the Criminal Rehabilitation of Persons Convicted of Consensual Homosexual Acts after 8 May 1945; StrRehaHomG) from 2017 onwards.[43] The penalisation of consensual sexual acts among men of sexual age was only successively restricted after 1945 and completely abolished as late as 1994. § 1 StrRehaHomG annulled the

40 Act of 29 October 1992 (BGBl. I 1814), in force since 4 November 1992.
41 Legislative materials, BT-Drs. 12/1608 2.
42 Pohlreich (n 39) 233, 236.
43 Act of 17 July 2017, BGBl. 2017 I 2443, in force since 22 July 2017.

respective convictions by way of general cassation.[44] On application lodged by the convicted person or a relative, the public prosecutor's office is to declare that the judgment has been annulled and issue a certificate of rehabilitation (§ 3 StrReheHomG). Furthermore, § 5 StrRehaHomG entitles the persons concerned to compensation from the federal government to the amount of €3,000 per annulled sentence and €1,500 per commenced year of deprivation of liberty. The objective of the act is to rehabilitate the convicted persons and to eliminate the stigma of the conviction based solely on their sexual orientation.[45]

2 Sources of law regulating compensation for wrongful conviction

State liability is grounded in constitutional law, in particular the *Rechtsstaatsprinzip*, i.e. the rule of law in Art. 20 (3) GG and the guarantees of judicial protection and property (Art. 19 (4) and Art. 14 GG).[46] For instance, the rule of law principle is the source of the obligation of the state to assume responsibility for unlawful state action, *inter alia* by eliminating its unlawful consequences or, if that is not possible, at least compensating for them.[47] Furthermore, state liability is explicitly laid down in Art. 34 GG. The latter stipulates that if a person, in the exercise of a public office entrusted to her, violates her official duty she bears towards a third party, as a rule the state or the public body is liable for this violation.

Apart from this, the compensatory mechanisms relevant in this context are regulated on the ordinary statutory, sub-constitutional level: by the StrEG, which is complemented in its application by the implementing regulations of the *Länder*, and § 839 BGB. As specific manifestations of state liability law, the provisions are to be classified as public law, in the same way as the latter. However, in the event of disputes, it is the civil courts that are called upon to decide (Art. 34 sentence 3 GG, § 40 (2) sentence 1 *Verwaltungsgerichtsordnung*)[48] (Code on Administrative Court Proceedings; abbr. VwGO). The reasons behind this are historical, in particular the fact that at the time of the development of this exceptional power of the civil courts, they, unlike the administrative courts, were fully judicially independent and thus better suited to provide sufficient judicial protection.[49] Moreover, according to § 8 StrEG the decision on whether compensation is to be granted under the StrEG is still to be taken in the criminal proceedings (for further details see below).

In accordance with the continental tradition of German law, the provisions of the StrEG are rather detailed, so the case law is mainly concerned with further concretising the statutory provisions.

44 Pohlreich (n 39) 233, 236.
45 Legislative materials, BT-Drs. 18/12038, 11.
46 Papier and Shirvani (n 3) § 839 para 1.
47 Papier and Shirvani (n 3) § 839 para 2.
48 Available at https://www.gesetze-im-internet.de/vwgo (accessed 26 December 2021).
49 H-J Papier and F Shirvani in T Maunz, R Herzog et al. (eds), *Grundgesetz Kommentar* (95th supplement of July 2021, CH Beck) GG Art. 34 para 306.

3 Grounds for compensation for wrongful convictions

3.1 Prerequisites to compensation according to § 1 StrEG

According to the central provision of § 1 StrEG on compensation for the impact of a conviction, anyone who has suffered harm as a result of a conviction by a criminal court shall be compensated out of the state treasury, insofar as the conviction is eliminated ("*Fortfall*"), or mitigated in criminal proceedings at a retrial or otherwise after it has become final. The term 'conviction' in this case means the determination of criminal guilt in criminal proceedings, irrespective of the sentencing.[50] A conviction is therefore also given in the case of a guilty verdict where the person has been given a warning with sentence reserved or the court has dispensed with imposing a penalty (cf. § 465 (1) sentence 2 StPO).[51] Convictions include those by penal order.[52]

An elimination of a conviction is to be assumed if the finding of guilt and sentence is completely reversed,[53] i.e. when the guilty verdict is overturned and the accused person is acquitted,[54] but also if the proceedings are discontinued.[55] In contrast, it is not sufficient for the conviction to be set aside and instead a *Maßregel der Besserung and Sicherung* (measure of reform and prevention, i.e. preventive corrective measure) pursuant to §§ 61 et seq. *Strafgesetzbuch*[56] (Penal Code; abbr. StGB) to be imposed (cf. § 1 (2) StrEG).[57]

Whether a conviction has been mitigated is determined by a comprehensive comparison of the new sentence with the original sentence.[58] The material result, not its legal reasoning, is decisive.[59] In view of the unrestricted wording in this respect, the requirements of § 1 (1) StrEG are to be assumed even if the mitigating result is exclusively based on the prohibition of *reformatio in peius* in the reopened proceedings as laid down in § 373 (2) StPO.[60] Assessments vary as to whether a mitigation is given if a custodial sentence of identical length is imposed but its execution is suspended on probation.[61]

As § 1 (1) StrEG itself stipulates, an elimination or mitigation of a conviction can be effected within a retrial. German law allows a reopening of proceedings after a final judgment in favour of the convicted person (§ 359 StPO), under

50 BGHSt 14, 391, 393; Meyer (n 5) § 1 para 19.
51 Kunz (n 16) § 1 para 9.
52 Meyer (n 5) § 1 para 6 et seqq.; Meyer-Goßner and Schmitt (n 22) StrEG § 1 para 1.
53 Meyer (n 5) § 1 para 23.
54 Kunz (n 16) § 1 para 12.
55 K Marxen and F Tiemann, *Die Wiederaufnahme in Strafsachen* (3rd ed., C.F. Müller 2014) para 563.
56 Available at https://www.gesetze-im-internet.de/stgb (accessed 26 December 2021).
57 Meyer (n 5) § 1 para 23.
58 OLG München, StV 1984, 471, 472; OLG Nürnberg, NStZ-RR 2012, 223, 224; Meyer-Goßner and Schmitt (n 22) StrEG § 1 para 3.
59 Meyer (n 5) § 1 Rn 27; Kunz (n 16) § 1 para 15.
60 Meyer (n 5) § 1 para 28; for further details see Pohlreich (n 39) 233, 241.
61 Affirmative Kunz (n 16) § 1 para 13; negative Marxen and Tiemann (n 55) para 564; Meyer (n 5) § 1 paras 15, 27, 30.

narrower conditions, however, and also to the disadvantage of the convicted person (§ 362 StPO). Reopening in favour of the sentenced person, as relevant in this context, is admissible:

> 1. if a document produced as genuine, to his detriment, at the main hearing was false or forged;
> 2. if a witness or expert, when giving testimony or an opinion to the convicted person's detriment, was guilty of intentional or negligent breach of the duty imposed by the oath or of intentionally making a false, unsworn statement;
> 3. if a judge or lay judge who participated in reaching the judgment was guilty of a culpable breach of his official duties in relation to the case, unless the violation was caused by the convicted person himself;
> 4 if a civil court judgment on which the criminal judgment is based is quashed by another final judgment;
> 5. if new facts or evidence were produced which, independently or in connection with the evidence previously taken, tend to support the defendant's acquittal or, upon application of a more lenient criminal provision, a lesser penalty or a fundamentally different decision on a measure of reform and prevention;
> 6. if the European Court of Human Rights has held that there has been a violation of the European Convention on the Protection of Human Rights and Fundamental Freedoms or of its Protocols and the judgment was based on that violation.[62]

§ 363 StPO rules out a reopening of proceedings for the 'purpose of imposing another penalty on the basis of the same criminal provision' or 'for the purpose of mitigating the penalty due to diminished responsibility'.[63] And § 364 sentence 1 StPO stipulates that with the exemption of § 362 no. 6 '[a]n application for the reopening of proceedings which is to be based on an allegation of an offence shall be admissible only if a final conviction has been made for this offence or if criminal proceedings cannot be commenced or conducted for reasons other than lack of evidence'.[64] Thus, insofar as the grounds for reopening under § 359 StPO, i.e. no. 1–3, are founded on a criminal offence such as forgery of documents, false testimony, accepting bribes or judicial perversion of justice, the application for reopening is only admissible if the offender has been convicted of the offence by a final court decision, unless reasons other than a lack of evidence precluded the initiation or conduct of criminal proceedings. Other ways than a retrial by which a final conviction can be eliminated or mitigated within the meaning of § 1 (1) StrEG are the reversal of a decision by the *Bundesverfassungsgericht* (Federal

62 Translation by *Gesetze im Internet*, available at https://www.gesetze-im-internet.de/englisch_stpo/englisch_stpo.html#p2198 (accessed 27 December 2021).

63 Translation by *Gesetze im Internet*, available at https://www.gesetze-im-internet.de/englisch_stpo/englisch_stpo.html#p2198 (accessed 27 December 2021).

64 Translation by *Gesetze im Internet*, available at https://www.gesetze-im-internet.de/englisch_stpo/englisch_stpo.html#p2198 (accessed 27 December 2021).

Constitutional Court) following a constitutional complaint against the decision according to § 95 (2) *Bundesverfassungsgerichtsgesetz*[65] (Act on the Federal Constitutional Court; abbr. BVerfGG) or the application of § 357 StPO.[66] The latter states that

> [i]f the judgment is quashed in favour of one defendant on account of a violation of the law occurring upon application of criminal law and if that part of the judgment which was quashed also affects other defendants who have not filed an appeal on law, then the court shall give its decision as if these persons had also filed an appeal on law.[67]

In addition, in practice as well as in academia, an application for *restitutio in integrum* in the periods for appeals against judgments or objections against penalty orders is also favoured.[68] In administrative fine proceedings, the StrEG is to be applied *mutatis mutandis* according to § 46 (1) *Gesetz über Ordnungswidrigkeiten* (Act on Regulatory Offences; abbr. OWiG).

Since the harm caused by the conviction is to be compensated, it is not necessary for the sentence imposed to have been enforced.[69] However the obligation to pay compensation is limited. It only arises if the elimination or mitigation of the conviction is effected in criminal proceedings after the decision has become final. It therefore does not extend to an alteration in the course of ordinary appeal proceedings.[70] According to § 2 StrEG, the person concerned can claim compensation for the execution of detention on remand or criminal prosecution measures mentioned in paragraph 2. Furthermore, an annulment of the sentence due to amnesty or clemency does not give rise to a claim.[71] The same applies to modifications that exclusively concern the execution of the sentence, such as the subsequent suspension of the execution, which leave the legal force of the sentence unaffected.[72] And finally, the scope does not extend to the elimination of convictions by way of law, such as in the aforementioned cases of general cassation.[73]

65 Available at www.gesetze-im-internet.de/bverfgg (accessed 27 December 2021).
66 BT-Drs. VI/460, 6 et seq.; OLG Stuttgart, NJW 1997, 206; Meyer-Goßner and Schmitt (n 22) StrEG § 1 para 2; Meyer (n 5) § 1 para 4 et seq., 10; Kunz (n 16) § 1 para 22.
67 Translation by *Gesetze im Internet*, available at https://www.gesetze-im-internet.de/englisch_stpo/englisch_stpo.html#p2198 (accessed 27 December 2021).
68 BayObLGSt 1986, 25; Meyer-Goßner and Schmitt (n 22) StrEG § 1 para 2; Kunz (n 16) StrEG § 1 para 21; Pohlreich (n 39) 233 (240); dissenting Meyer (n 5) § 1 para 11.
69 Kunz (n 16) § 1 para 37.
70 BT-Drs. VI/1512, 2; Meyer (n 5) § 1 para 12, 13; Kunz (n 16) § 1 para 32; Meyer-Goßner and Schmitt (n 22) StrEG § 1 para 2; Pohlreich (n 39) 233, 240
71 BT-Drs. VI/1512, 2; Meyer (n 5) § 1 para 12; Kunz (n 16) § 1 para 32 et seq.
72 OLG Hamm, EUGRZ 1986, 546, 547 et seq.; Pohlreich (n 39) 233, 240.
73 Meyer, § 1 para 13; Pohlreich (n 39) 233, 240.

3.2 Mandatory exclusion and discretionary denial of compensation according to §§ 5, 6 StrEG

Furthermore, § 5 StrEG provides reasons for which compensation is mandatorily excluded, and § 6 StrEG stipulates reasons for which compensation may be denied in whole or in part at the court's discretion, both for consequences of conviction and other criminal prosecution measures. The reasons mentioned in these provisions can mostly be understood as a manifestation of the civil law principle that (contributory) responsibility of the injured party excludes or reduces a claim for compensation as laid down in § 254 BGB, adapted to the specific situation of criminal proceedings. The list is understood to be exhaustive.[74] In contrast to the initial versions of the law on compensation and in accordance with the presumption of innocence, any remaining doubts about the guilt of the person concerned are no longer to the detriment of the convicted person, but to the detriment of the state treasury.[75]

The right to compensation for deprivation of liberty is mandatorily excluded pursuant to § 5 (1) no. 2 StrEG if a custodial correctional measure is ordered or if such an order is dispensed with solely because the purpose of the measure has already been achieved by the deprivation of liberty. These are, for example, cases in which the reopening leads to an acquittal due to incapacity, for instance, and instead detention within the framework of a correctional measure is ordered; however it is then questionable whether the new decision represents any mitigation at all.[76] For if at the same time a deprivation of liberty is imposed for preventive purposes or if such an order is dispensed with only because of the custodial sentence imposed, the deprivation of liberty resulting from the original conviction is or would be covered by the final result of the proceedings or can be (informally) credited.

More significant for cases of wrongful conviction and the cause of many court decisions is the ground for exclusion under § 5 (2) sentence 1 StrEG. Under this provision, compensation is also excluded if and to the extent that the accused has caused the criminal prosecution deliberately or through gross negligence. § 5 (2) sentence 2 StrEG explicitly exempts cases where the accused did not testify to the matter or refrained from lodging an appeal. In addition, exclusion is not applicable if the accused flatly denies the offence[77] or fails to present exculpatory evidence.[78] The conduct which may lead to an exclusion may be an action as well as an omission.[79] Whether it was carried out before, during or after the alleged offence is irrelevant.[80] A prerequisite is that the convicted person has entirely or at least

74 Kunz (n 16) § 5 para 2 et seq.; Meyer (n 5) Vor § 5 paras 3, 6, 13; Pohlreich (n 39) 233, 240.

75 See also Böing (n 1) 73, 89; Pohlreich (n 39) 233, 238.

76 BGH StraFo 2010, 87 et seq.; OLG Karlsruhe, NStZ-RR 2005, 255 (256); KG Berlin NStZ-RR 2013, 192; Kunz (n 16) § 5 para 10.

77 KG Berlin, decision of 20 March 2000–4 Ws 41/00; Kunz (n 16) § 5 para 88.

78 OLG Düsseldorf NStZ 1984, 108; Meyer-Goßner and Schmitt (n 22) StrEG § 5 para 7.

79 Kunz (n 16) § 5 para 33; Meyer (n 5) § 5 para 38.

80 BayObLG 1973, 1938, 1939; OLG Stuttgart NStZ 1981, 484 with further references; Kunz (n 16) § 5 para 33; Meyer-Goßner and Schmitt (n 22) StrEG § 5 para 7.

substantially contributed to the measure or its continuation.[81] The conduct is not causal if the measure would have been imposed even without it[82] or if it is at least predominantly based on witness statements[83] or serious failures of the prosecution authorities.[84] An erroneous handling of the case by the authorities can disrupt the causal connection.[85] Deliberate causation is assumed if the accused person is willingly aware of the measure as a possible consequence of her acts or omissions,[86] and gross negligence is assumed if she has to an exceptional degree neglected the diligence that a reasonable person in the same situation would exercise in order to protect herself from harm caused by the prosecution measure.[87]

Since the application of § 5 StrEG leads to the mandatory exclusion of the claim, the provision is to be interpreted narrowly and a strict standard is to be applied regarding the fulfilment of its requirements.[88] If it is doubtful whether the requirements for an exclusion are met, such an exclusion must be ruled out.[89]

§ 6 (1) no. 1 StrEG leaves it to the discretion of the court to deny compensation in whole or in part if the accused person has caused the criminal prosecution by untruthfully incriminating herself in substantial points or in contradiction to her later statements or by withholding substantial exonerating circumstances although she has made a statement on the accusation. This therefore refers to the conduct of the accused person within the framework of the criminal proceedings in her role as the accused, while conduct before, after or outside the criminal proceedings can only be subject to § 5 (2) StrEG.[90] The accused person has incriminated herself in accordance with this provision if she has made any statements at all in breach of the truth, for example, if she has given a false confession. A contradiction in the accused person's statement is only sufficient if it concerns essential aspects of the case.[91] Acts other than express or implied statements, such as interference with witnesses or other evidence, are not covered.[92] A denial of compensation due to the withholding of exonerating circumstances presupposes that the person

81 Kunz (n 16) § 5 para 33.
82 KG StraFo 2009, 129,130; OLG Karlsruhe NStZ-RR 2005, 255,256; Meyer-Goßner and Schmitt (n 22) StrEG § 5 para 7.
83 BGHR StrEG § 5 Abs. 2 S. 1 Fahrlässigkeit, grobe 4; OLG Düsseldorf, StV 1988, 446; OLG Köln, StraFo 2001, 146; Kunz (n 16) § 5 para 37.
84 BGH NStZ-RR 2017, 264; KG NStZ-RR 2012, 30, 31.
85 BGH NStZ-RR 2021, 217 et seq.; K Cornelius in J Graf (ed.), *Beck'scher Online-kommentar StPO* (41st ed., CH Beck 2021) StrEG § 5 para 8, 11.
86 KG Berlin, decision of 20 August 1999–1 AR 553/99–4 Ws 132/99; Kunz (n 16) § 5 para 56.
87 Settled case law, e.g. BGH StraFo 2008, 352; StraFo 2010, 87 et seq.
88 BGH StraFo 2010, 87; OLG Karlsruhe NStZ-RR 2005, 255 et seq.; KG Berlin StraFo 2009, 129,130; NStZ-RR 2012, 30, 31; Cornelius (n 88) StrEG § 5 para 19; Kunz (n 16) § 5 para 38.
89 Meyer (n 5) § 5 para 38.
90 BVerfG, NJW 1996, 1049, 1050; Kunz (n 16) § 6 para 5; Meyer (n 5) § 6 para 8 et seq.
91 BVerfG, NJW 1996, 1049, 1050; OLG Köln StraFo 2002, 337; Kunz (n 16) § 6 para 8 et seq.; Meyer (n 5) § 6 paras 8, 11 et seq.
92 Meyer (n 5) § 6 para 15.

concerned was aware of a significant exonerating circumstance, recognised or negligently failed to recognise its significance and withheld this circumstance when as a suspect at least in part making a statement on the case.[93] Examples include the non-disclosure of the actual perpetrator[94] or the withholding of an alibi,[95] however neither a general denial of the offence nor a temporary silence constitute grounds for a refusal.[96] Whether defence counsel advised the accused person to such defence conduct is irrelevant.[97] The conduct must have caused the imposition of the measure. Contributory causation is sufficient as long as the cause is essential.[98] Accordingly, a denial under § 6 StrEG is precluded if the measure would have been imposed regardless of the accused's statement.[99]

According to § 6 (1) no. 2 StrEG, the court may also refuse compensation if in the retrial the person originally convicted is not convicted of a criminal offence or the proceedings against them have been discontinued only because she acted in a state of incapacity or because a procedural impediment such as statutory limitation or permanent unfitness to stand trial prevailed. It is considered equivalent to the procedural impediment if a conviction in the retrial is precluded only by the prohibition of *reformatio in peius*.[100] The discretion as a rule only arises if it is established that without these grounds the accused person would have been convicted or detained.[101] As far as the discontinuation of the proceedings is concerned, however, the prevailing opinion weakens this standard by letting it suffice that at the stage of the proceedings when the procedural impediment is established, a conviction appears at least more probable than not and no circumstances are recognisable that stand in the way of a determination of guilt in accordance with the rules of procedure.[102]

Finally, § 6 (2) StrEG places compensation at the discretion of the court if the court applies the provisions applicable to a juvenile and thereby takes into account a deprivation of liberty suffered. The provision is based on the same rationale as §

93 OLG Düsseldorf StV 1984, 108, 109; 25.6.2013–2 Ws 275/13; OLG Stuttgart MDR 1984, 427; Meyer-Goßner and Schmitt (n 22) StrEG § 6 para 4 with further references.

94 Meyer-Goßner and Schmitt (n 22) StrEG § 6 para 4.

95 OLG Hamm, decision of 15 October 2013–5 RVs 96/13, 5 Ws 380–381/13, KG Berlin GA 1987, 405; Kunz (n 16) § 6 para 10.

96 KG Berlin, decision of 20 March 2000–4 Ws 41/00; Kunz (n 16) § 6 para 10 et seq.; stricter with regard to a temporal silence Meyer (n 5) § 6 para 9.

97 OLG Düsseldorf NStZ-RR 1996, 223; Meyer-Goßner and Schmitt (n 22) StrEG § 6 para 4.

98 KG Berlin, StraFo 2009, 129, 130; OLG Brandenburg, decision 5 December 2007–1 Ws 273/07; Kunz (n 16) § 6 para 5; Meyer (n 5) § 6 para 11.

99 OLG Düsseldorf 25.6.2013–2 Ws 275/13; OLG Oldenburg, StraFo 2005, 384; Kunz (n 16) § 6 para 5.

100 OLG Stuttgart NJW 1977, 641; cf also VGH Sachsen NJW 2019, 2077; Kunz (n 16) § 6 para 39.

101 OLG Zweibrücken NStZ 1986, 129; OLG Hamm NStZ-RR 1997, 127; Kunz (n 16) § 6 para 23; Meyer (n 5) § 6 para 31.

102 BGH NStZ 2000, 330; OLG Frankfurt a. M. NStZ-RR 2002, 246; OLG Hamm NStZ-RR 2010, 224; Kunz (n 16) § 6 para 23.

5 (1) no. 2 StrEG, that the deprivation of liberty is materially covered by the outcome of the proceedings but adapts it to the special situation of juvenile criminal proceedings and in this respect takes precedence over this provision.[103] It allows the youth court to decide more flexibly on the crediting of deprivations of liberty.

4 Scope and calculation of the amount of compensation

If a claim for compensation is established on the merits, the state owes compensation for both material and non-material harm as required by § 7 StrEG, which lays down the scope of the state's liability. Under § 7 (1) and (2) StrEG, material harm exceeding €25 shall be compensated as well as non-material harm in the case of deprivation of liberty on the basis of a court decision. For this non-material harm, § 7 (3) StrEG stipulates compensation by means of a fixed lump sum of €75 for each day or part thereof of executed deprivation of liberty, regardless of the circumstances of the individual case. § 7 (4) StrEG excludes compensation for any harm that would have occurred without the criminal prosecution measure.

The notion of damages for pecuniary loss is taken from civil law and, correspondingly, its determination also follows the rules of civil law, in particular §§ 249 et seq. BGB.[104] It includes any deterioration of the accused's economic situation which can be quantified in material terms. This entails disadvantages in career and income, including loss of earnings and loss of profit, which could have been expected in the ordinary course of events or in the particular circumstances of the case.[105] The damages are calculated by comparing the financial situation that has arisen as a result of the measure with the hypothetical financial situation that would have existed without its imposition.[106] The accused person should therefore be placed in the same position as she would have been in if the damaging event, in this case the conviction, had not occurred.[107] However, an entitlement to the rectification of consequences, e.g. by way of public rehabilitation, or in *rem restitution* is not provided for.[108] The compensation is usually made by way of capital payment, but can also be paid in the form of an allowance, for example in the case of continuing disadvantages.[109] Beyond the minimum limit in § 7 (2) StrEG, the harm which has been adequately caused by the prosecution measure is to be compensated in full;[110] a maximum limit does not exist.[111] However, only

103 Kunz (n 16) § 6 para 42; Meyer (n 5) § 6 para 42.
104 BGHZ 63, 203, 205; 65, 170, 173; 106, 313, 315.
105 Kunz (n 16) § 7 para 8; for a detailed list of potential heads of damage see *inter alia* Meyer (n 5) § 7 para 17 et seq.
106 S Grommes, in J Graf (ed.), *Beck'scher Onlinekommentar OWiG* (32nd ed., CH Beck 2021) § 7 para 11; Meyer (n 5) § 7 para 11.
107 Instead of many Meyer (n 5) § 7 para 11.
108 Kunz (n 16) § 7 para 7.
109 Kunz (n 16) § 7 para 19.
110 OLG Celle, NJW 2004, 3347; Kunz (n 13) § 7 para 8.
111 Kunz (n 16) § 7 para 17.

those material harms which are adequately causally based on the conviction or the execution of the sentence are to be compensated, and no indirect harms.[112] The expenses for the defence that were necessary for the elimination of the judgment insofar as they are not covered by the procedural costs decision, as well as the costs for the lodging of the claim according to the StrEG, including the necessary lawyers' fees, may also be claimed.[113]

The obligation to pay damages for both pecuniary and non-pecuniary loss is reduced if the court partially denies compensation pursuant to § 6 StrEG. Also, the person concerned is obliged to avert or at least minimise the harm as far as is possible and reasonable, and a contributory fault with regard to the occurrence and extent of the damage may be taken into account.[114] In addition, expenses saved may be deducted insofar as damage and advantage are connected, e.g. costs for accommodation and food in relation to compensation for detention, but not costs of defence.[115]

5 Procedure for claiming compensation

Anyone who has suffered harm because of a criminal conviction, if the conviction in the retrial or otherwise, after it has become final, which is overturned or mitigated in criminal proceedings is entitled to claim compensation for wrongful conviction according to § 1 StrEG. § 11 StrEG extends this claim to persons to whom the person was obliged to provide maintenance if they have been deprived of maintenance as a result of the prosecution measure. Also, the claims are inheritable as of the time they arise.

The compensation procedure under the StrEG consists of two stages. In the main hearing within the course of the retrial, the criminal court decides *ex officio* and within the framework of the decision or judgment concluding the proceedings whether a ground for the obligation to compensate exists (the so-called *Grundverfahren*, § 8 StrEG). If the decision cannot be made in the main hearing, the court may decide outside the hearing (§ 8 (1) sentence 2 StrEG), which, contrary to the statutory classification as an exception, is widely used in practice.[116] The criminal court only declares whether, in principle, an obligation to compensate

112 S Beukelmann, 'Kausalitätsschwächen der Haftentschädigung' [2018] NJW Spezial 632; Meyer (n 5) § 7 para 12.

113 Part I B II 2. g. of the implementing regulations of the Land Brandenburg to give an example of those of the *Länder*, BGHZ 65, 170; OLG Brandenburg, decision of 29 January 2020 – 4 U 172/19; OLG Hamm, decision of 29 January 2021 – I-11 U 41/20; Meyer-Goßner and Schmitt (n 22) StrEG § 7 paras 5, 6; H Vordermayer et al, *Handbuch für den Staatsanwalt* (6th ed., Carl Heymanns Verlag 2019) part G, § 7 StrEG, para 75 et seq.

114 BGH NJW 1988, 1141; Meyer-Goßner and Schmitt (n 22) StrEG § 7 para 1; Kunz (n 16) § 7 para 98.

115 OLG Düsseldorf StraFo 2007, 35, 36; Meyer-Goßner and Schmitt (n 22) StrEG § 7 para 1. For details see e.g. Part I B II 2. B. of the implementing regulations of Brandenburg.

116 (Critical) Marxen and Tiemann (n 55) para 580; Meyer (n 5) § 8 para 18 et seqq.

arises and determines the person entitled to compensation and the measures for which compensation is to be paid.[117] It does not address the scope of the claim and nor consequently the questions of whether and to what extent harm has been caused and whether it has been adequately caused by the measure.[118] If the person entitled then files a claim for compensation, the amount of compensation is assessed in a judicial administrative procedure[119] (the so-called *Betragsverfahren*, § 10 StrEG). In practice, the average duration of the procedure is 15 months.[120]

The details of the procedure are governed by two different regulatory regimes. With the *Grundverfahren* still being part of the reopened criminal proceedings, in general the provisions of criminal procedural law apply. German criminal proceedings are inquisitorially shaped, and the main hearing is subject to the principles of orality, immediacy and publicity. In addition to the accused person and the deciding court, the public prosecutor's office participates. The accused is assisted by a defence counsel if she has chosen one or if the court has appointed counsel in the case of a mandatory defence pursuant to § 140 StPO. Such cases of mandatory defence are, *inter alia*, if the main hearing at first instance is to be held at the *Oberlandesgericht* (Higher Regional Court), the *Landgericht* (Regional Court) or the *Schöffengericht* (courts with lay judges), and thus all cases in which a custodial sentence of more than two years is to be expected (cf. § 25 *Gerichtsverfassungsgesetz* – Courts Constitution Act; abbr. GVG), if the accused person is charged with a *Verbrechen*, a serious offence which is punishable by a minimum term of imprisonment of one year (§ 12 StGB), if the accused person is in detention on remand or if the assistance of defence counsel appears necessary due to the severity of the offence, to the factual or legal difficulty or if it is evident that the accused person cannot defend herself.

Against the court's decision in the *Grundverfahren*, a *sofortige Beschwerde* (immediate appeal) pursuant to §§ 304, 311 et seq. StPO may be filed within one week of notification of the decision according to § 8 (3) StrEG,[121] irrespective of whether the decision on the merits of the case can be and is challenged by means of *Berufung* (appeal) or *Revision* (appeal on points of law).[122]

117 OLG Düsseldorf, NStZ-RR 1996, 287; Meyer-Goßner and Schmitt (n 22) StrEG § 8 para 1.

118 BGHZ 63, 209; OLG Düsseldorf, NStZ-RR 1996, 287; Kunz (n 16) § 7 para 3; Meyer (n 5) Vor §§ 8–9 StrEG para 9.

119 S Forkert-Hosser, in K Miebach and O Hohmann (eds), *Wiederaufnahme in Strafsachen* (CH Beck 2016) chap. L para 108; Meyer (n 5) Vor §§ 10–13, para 1; Meyer-Goßner and Schmitt (n 22) StrEG § 10 para 1.

120 A Hoffmann and F Leuschner, 'Rehabilitation und Entschädigung nach Vollstreckung einer Freiheitsstrafe und erfolgreicher Wiederaufnahme' online publication available at https://www.krimz.de/fileadmin/dateiablage/E-Publikationen/BM-Online/bm-online11.pdf (accessed 27 December 2021) 47.

121 OLG Frankfurt NJW 1074, 202; OLG Düsseldorf JMBlNW 95, 250; Kunz (n 16) Einleitung para 29.

122 Meyer (n 5) Einleitung para 22; Forkert-Hosser (n 119) chap. L para 98.

The *Betragsverfahren* is subject to the provisions of §§ 10 to 13 StrEG and to the regulations of administrative procedure and civil law.[123] To initiate this stage, the person entitled to compensation must apply within six months to the public prosecutor's office that last conducted the investigation in the first instance (§ 10 (1) sentence 1 StrEG). According to sentence 3, the public prosecutor's office must instruct the person entitled about the right and the time limit for filing the application; pursuant to sentence 4, the six-month time limit begins with the service of the instruction. If the entitled person culpably fails to raise the claim within the time limit, the claim is excluded. Also, even if the instruction is not provided, the claim is excluded under § 12 StrEG at the latest after one year since the legally binding determination of the obligation to pay compensation. *Restitutio in integrum* cannot be granted.[124]

The application is not required to be in any particular form.[125] It must specify the nature and extent of the disadvantages for which compensation is sought, and provide evidence.[126] The application must 'indicate the claim of the entitled person in such concrete terms that it enables the competent judicial administrative authority to immediately enter into an initial examination of the claim'.[127] However, case law emphasises that the substantive requirements must not be set too high. For example, the amount of damages does not always have to be quantified and isolated heads of damages can be supplemented, even after the expiry of the time limit.[128] The lack of some information regarding the claim or evidence is also not detrimental. In this respect, the person concerned can be required to provide the missing information.[129] The requirements with regard to compensation for deprivation of liberty are even lower. This is because the amount of compensation is determined by the duration of the imprisonment, which is specified in the decision on the grounds for compensation within the *Grundverfahren*, and the statutory provision of § 7 (3) StrEG. The claim must therefore be raised, but otherwise not further substantiated.[130]

The decision within the *Betragsverfahren* falls within the competence of the *Land* judicial administration according to § 10 (2) sentence 1 StrEG, more precisely and depending on the delegation, as a rule on the director of the public prosecutor's office at the *Landgericht* or the *Oberlandesgericht*.[131] The authority is

123 BGH NJW 1976, 1218, 1219; Meyer (n 5) § 10 para 1.
124 BGHZ 108, 14, 19 et seq.; OLG Nürnberg, NStZ-RR 2003, 62; Kunz (n 16) § 10 para 9.
125 Meyer (n 5) § 10 para 13.
126 BGHZ 108, 14, 19 et seq.; OLG Nürnberg, NStZ-RR 2003, 62; Kunz (n 16) § 10 para 9.
127 BGHZ 108, 14, 19 et seq.; OLG Nürnberg, NStZ-RR 2003, 62; Meyer (n 5) § 10 para 13; Schütz, StV 2008, 52.
128 Meyer (n 5) § 10 para 13.
129 BGHZ 108, 14, 19 et seq.; OLG Nürnberg, NStZ-RR 2003, 62; Kunz (n 16) § 10 para 9 et seq.
130 Kunz (n 16) § 10 para 13.
131 The latter is the case *inter alia* in Brandenburg, see Part I B. of the implementing regulations of Brandenburg; for an overview of the allocation of decision-making responsibility in the different *Länder* see Hoffmann and Leuschner (n 120) 15 et seqq.

bound by the court's decision in the *Grundverfahren*.[132] With regard to the further prerequisites for compensation and its extent, the person entitled to compensation in accordance with the general rules of civil procedure must explain and prove, for example, the harm, its extent and its causation by the measure,[133] whereby the latter is often indicated *prima facie*.[134] The person must also show what actions she has taken to mitigate the harm.[135] If the person is not able to quantify the damages, she must present and prove valid bases for an estimate.[136] The details of the procedure are regulated differently in the *Länder* by the respective implementing regulations.[137] Usually, it is regulated that the respective authority verifies the information provided by the person concerned in her application and, if necessary, carries out its own investigations, if necessary with the assistance of the police.[138] *Ex officio* investigations will not be carried out.

Due to the division of the proceedings into the two aforementioned stages, legal counsel must be re-authorised for the *Betragsverfahren*.[139] If the applicant cannot raise the necessary means due to her personal economic situation, has no other means of obtaining help which she can reasonably be expected to accept and if such recourse does not appear to be wilful, she may avail herself of advisory assistance through a lawyer in accordance with § 1 *Beratungshilfegesetz* (Advisory Assistance Act; abbr. BerHG).

The person entitled to compensation may bring a civil action against the decision in the *Betragsverfahren* before the *Landgericht* (Regional Court) within three months (§ 13 StrEG).

6 The recourse claim of the state against persons who caused wrongful conviction

Claims to which the person compensated is entitled against third parties because their illegal actions brought about the prosecution measure will according to § 15 (2) StrEG pass to the state treasury up to the amount of the compensation paid. The entity obliged to pay compensation under the StrEG may also demand, in application of the basic principle of § 255 BGB, that the entitled party cedes to it congruent claims for damages against third parties for culpable breach of

132 BGHZ 103, 113, 115; OLG Dresden, OLG-NL 1996, 216; Meyer-Goßner and Schmitt (n 22) StrEG § 8 para 1; Meyer (n 5) Vor §§ 10–13, para 5.
133 BGHZ 103, 113, 117; OLG Schleswig NJW-RR 2004, 599 (600); Forkert-Hosser (n 119) chap. L para 134; Kunz (n 16) § 7 para 13.
134 Kunz (n 16) § 7 para 14.
135 OLG Schleswig NJW-RR 2004, 599; *Meyer* StrEG § 7 para 56; Forkert-Hosser (n 119) chap. L para 134.
136 BGH NJW 1977, 957, 960; OLG Schleswig, NJW-RR 2004, 599, 601; *Meyer* StrEG § 7 para 57.
137 As an example see Part II B. II. no. 2.g. of the implementing regulations of Brandenburg.
138 Meyer StrEG § 10 para 16; Kunz (n 16) § 10 para 22.
139 Forkert-Hosser (n 119) chap. L para 116; Meyer (n 5) § 10 para 9; Meyer-Goßner and Schmitt (n 22) StrEG § 10 para 3.

contract.[140] The state can therefore pursue any claims for damages under civil law by the wrongfully convicted person against a third party that led to the imposition or even prolongation of the measure. Examples of the unlawful acts referred to are a false criminal report, a false incriminating statement or a breach of official duty.[141] However, no relevant case law is apparent in this respect, so that it can be assumed that such recourse is at best rare in practice.

7 The practice of compensating the wrongfully convicted

Neither the frequency with which claims for such compensation are brought and granted nor their amount can be clearly determined, because the nationwide statistical record ceased in 1995. For the year 1994, eight cases of compensation according to § 1 StrEG were registered, which amounted to a rounded compensation sum of 66,000 Deutschmarks (approx. €34,000).[142] A study on rehabilitation and compensation after successful retrial over the years 1990 to 2016 found – albeit with a narrowly defined and thus small study group (see below) – compensation sums of between €2,380 and €412,141, resulting in an average sum of €96,055; compensation for non-material harm averaged €63,900 (between €1,975 and €63,900), while that for material harm averaged €131,281 (between €534 and €398,116).[143]

Currently, the *Statistisches Bundesamt* (Federal Statistical Office) records both reopenings and proceedings for compensation under the StrEG. In 2020, the courts completed 1,285 proceedings that were initiated by an application for a reopening, in 932 cases ruling in favour of the accused person within the meaning of § 359 StPO;[144] however, it is not noted whether they were successful.[145] From 2014 to 2020, between 3,706 and 4,120 proceedings for compensation under the StrEG were pending at the public prosecutor's offices per year.[146] However, as the statistics from 1994 and a comparison with the figures on reopenings already indicate, these numbers also include proceedings aimed at compensation for procedural measures such as detention on remand.[147] The already mentioned study concerning the years 1990–2016 has identified 29 cases in which 31 innocent persons were sentenced to imprisonment.[148] It was based, however, on an interpretation of a wrongful conviction that is narrower than the prerequisites for a claim for restitution under the StrEG: only those persons who were acquitted after a retrial were counted.[149] The mitigation of a sentence was therefore not included.

140 BGH NStZ 1989, 479; Meyer-Goßner and Schmitt (n 22) StrEG § 7 para 11.
141 Kunz (n 16) § 15 para 5.
142 Kunz (n 16) Einleitung para 86.
143 Hoffmann and Leuschner (n 120) 50.
144 Statistisches Bundesamt, Fachserie 10, Reihe 2.3, 2020, 24, 62, 82.
145 F Leuschner et al., 'Imprisoned But Innocent: Wrongful Convictions and Imprisonments in Germany, 1990–2016' [2019] *66 Crime and Delinquency* 687, 691.
146 Statistisches Bundesamt, Fachserie 10, Reihe 2.6, 2020, 13, 129.
147 F Leuschner et al. (n 145) 687, 691.
148 F Leuschner et al. (n 145) 687, 695.
149 F Leuschner et al. (n 145) 687, 695.

The estimates for erroneous sentences (not necessarily to the detriment of the accused person) are considerably higher, ranging from 'rather in the lower single-digit percentage or per mille range'[150] to a not inconsiderable[151] or even a 'high' number[152] or at least 20 per cent.[153] With regard to the amounts of compensation, the informative value of statistical records without further data might be limited anyway, because the amounts of damages for pecuniary loss strongly depend on the circumstances of the individual case and on damages for non-pecuniary loss for which the mentioned statutory lump sum applies. The increase in the lump sum was always preceded by criticism of it being too low;[154] whether this will continue after the last, significant increase in 2020 remains to be seen. In any case, it is four times more than the sum of €500 per month that some courts awarded, before the increase of the lump sum, on considerations of equity for violations of Art. 5 (5) ECHR.[155] Since the extent of the compensation for material loss complies with general principles of civil law, it is, as far as can be seen, generally accepted. However, it is considered particularly challenging that the person concerned must prove the causality of wrongful conviction for the harm (see below).

Accordingly, the specific case law on the amount of compensation under the StrEG is not very extensive. Compensation for material harm is largely determined by the general civil law jurisdiction and the lump sum to compensate for non-material harm does not really leave room for concretising case law.

8 The evaluation of the national mechanism of the compensation for wrongful convictions

Compensation for wrongful convictions – under the StrEG as well as in general – is seldom discussed, either in public or in academia.[156] The rare criticism focuses on three aspects in particular: the proceedings, the provisions for exclusion and denial of compensation in §§ 5 and 6 of the StrEG and the nature and amount of compensation.

8.1 Evaluation of the proceedings

The division into the two stages of the *Grundverfahren* and the *Betragsverfahren* or even three stages if the decision in the latter is appealed to the civil court, which

150 A Mosbacher, 'Das Ideal richterlicher Wahrheitsfindung und die Betrübnisse des wirklichen Lebens. Richterliche Schuldfeststellung und die Gefahr des Fehlurteils' [2015] *9 Forensische Psychiatrie, Psychologie, Kriminologie*, 82, 86.
151 R Eschelbach in J Graf (ed.), (n 85) § 261 para 9.2; A Sickor, 'Von den Gebrechen des reformierten Strafverfahrens' [2015] StV, 516, 521.
152 J Schwenn, 'Fehlurteile und ihre Ursachen – die Wiederaufnahme im Verfahren wegen sexuellen Mißbrauchs' [2010] StV, 705, 706.
153 A Geipel in K Miebach and O Hohmann (eds.), *Wiederaufnahme in Strafsachen* (CH Beck 2016) chap. A para 100.
154 Cf. T Schaefer, 'Entschädigung für Strafverfolgungsmaßnahmen' [2009] NJW 344.
155 OLG Hamm, decision of 14 November 2014 – I-11 U 16/14; OLG Koblenz, decision of 18 April 2018 – 1 W 144/18.
156 Schaefer (n 154) 344.

are conducted by different authorities, are subject to differing regulations and involve several short time limits. This process is criticised for being lengthy, tedious and complicated.[157] Moreover, those affected consider the requirement of an application for the *Betragsverfahren* itself to be unjust, as it requires the wrongly convicted to take the initiative and puts the onus on her to enforce her claim. Instead, the state, as the originator of the wrongful conviction, should be obliged in this respect as well.[158] Furthermore, the burden of proof with regard to the amount of damages is considered to place a considerable burden on the wrongfully convicted person and leads to considerable frustration on her part.[159] Quantifying and proving the value of individual items of material harm, for example furnishings, possibly after several years of imprisonment, is time-consuming and often no longer possible. Moreover, proving causality, especially for the loss of a job, or even the impediment to professional progress, is considered particularly difficult.[160] It is also feared that the public prosecutor's office, which decides on the amount of compensation in the *Betragsverfahren*, and the police, who support the public prosecutor's office in the necessary investigations, are not sufficiently independent and impartial[161] or at least are not perceived as such by the person concerned due to the antagonism in the previous proceedings.[162] However, the procedure is also acknowledged as tried and tested and it is pointed out that the obligation to instruct counteracts its complexity.[163] Nor has any fundamentally different alternative yet been proposed. As the criminal court already decides on the merits of the claim, it would seem obvious that it should also decide on the amount of the claim. Such a decision following the rules of civil law would not be unique in German criminal proceedings, since according to § 403 StPO, the victim of a crime or her heir may, in the criminal proceedings, bring a property claim against the accused person arising out of the offence, the so-called *Adhäsionsverfahren* (adhesion proceedings). A decision of the criminal court on the compensation claim in full would deviate from the special allocation of cases of state liability to the civil courts. On the one hand, the historical rationale for this special allocation to the civil courts (see above) would also apply to criminal courts and is considered outdated now anyway. On the other hand,

157 J Baumann, 'Kritische Bemerkungen zum Gesetz über die Entschädigung für Strafverfolgungsmaßnahmen' in H Luttger (ed.), *Festschrift für Ernst Heinitz* (De Gruyter 1972) 705, 707; Hoffmann and Leuschner (n 120) 75, 84; Killinger (n 24) 31, 43; Meyer (n 5) Einleitung para 23.

158 Hoffmann and Leuschner (n 120) 74.

159 Forkert-Hosser (n 119) chap. L para 134 et seq.

160 Instead of many S Beukelmann, 'Kausalitätsschwächen der Haftentschädigung' [2018] NJW Spezial, 632; Forkert-Hosser (n 119) chap. L paras 135, 137; Hoffmann and Leuschner (n 120) 84 et seqq.

161 Regarding the public prosecutor's office Forkert-Hosser (n 119) chap. L para 120; Marxen and Tiemann (n 55) para 584; regarding the police H Dahs, *Handbuch des Strafverteidigers* (8th ed., Dr. Otto Schenk 2015), para 341; with reservations Kunz (n 16) § 10 para 22; Meyer (n 5) § 10 para 16.

162 Killinger (n 24) 43.

163 Meyer (n 5) § 10 para 23.

according to § 2 StrEG, compensation is also to be granted for other measures in proceedings that the public prosecutor's office discontinues and in which consequently a joint decision by a criminal court would not be possible. A comprehensive decision on the claim under § 1 StrEG would thus result in a procedural divergence with regard to the assessment of the amount.

8.2 Evaluation of the grounds for exclusion or denial of compensation

There is sporadic criticism of the fact that untruthful or contradictory statements by the accused person can lead to the complete or partial loss of the claim under §§ 5 (2), 6 (1) no. 1 StrEG. A false self-incrimination could serve as a defence against the suspicion of a more serious criminal offence. The adverse consequence amounted to a burden of truth on the accused person or a 'penalty for lying'.[164] A negligent contradictory statement because of which under § 6 (1) no. 1 StrEG the court may refuse compensation in whole or in part could already be given if the accused person expressed herself in an unclear or ambiguous manner.[165] And because according to this provision the non-disclosure of a material exonerating circumstance can also justify such a denial, the accused person had only the choice between a complete statement and complete silence if she wanted to preserve her entitlement to compensation in full. She could, however, have a legitimate interest in not revealing a circumstance that was exonerating but, from her point of view, worthy of concealment.[166] It should be borne in mind that the determination of whether a claim under § 5 StrEG is excluded or the decision under § 6 StrEG as to whether the claim is to be denied is still to be taken by the court in the *Grundverfahren* and thus in the reopened criminal proceedings themselves. It is therefore quite conceivable that the concern about preserving a claim for compensation may affect the convicted person's freedom to make a statement in the retrial or, conversely, that concern about the disclosure of previously concealed exculpatory circumstances may lead to a loss of the claim. The objections therefore suggest at least a restrictive interpretation of the requirements of §§ 5 (2), 6 (1) no. 1 StrEG, which takes into account the right to effective defence and the freedom of self-incrimination and therefore, for example, leaves the person concerned room to withhold circumstances that would incriminate herself or relatives.[167] The discretionary provision of § 6 StrEG permits the court to take into account considerations of reasonableness, as is also done in the parallel provision of § 467 (3) sentence 2 no. 2 StPO on the reimbursement of costs.[168]

164 Baumann (n 157) 705, 712.
165 Baumann (n 157) 705, 713.
166 Baumann (n 157) 705, 713 et seq.
167 Cf. Meyer (n 5) Vor § 5 para 15.
168 L Niesler in J Graf (ed.), (n 85) § 467 para 10; restrictively S Grommes in C Knauer et al. (eds), *Münchener Kommentar zur StPO 3–1* (CH Beck 2019) § 467 para 18; Meyer (n 5) § 6 paras 19, 29.

8.3 Evaluation of the extent of compensation

By its very nature, the lump sum for the deprivation of liberty does not take into account the special circumstances of the individual case, such as a particular sensitivity of the person detained or the length and circumstances of the detention.[169] Those affected see this derogation from the otherwise individual determination of the amount of damages as an undue privilege of the state.[170] However, it also prevents differentiations that do not appear to be appropriate, for example on the basis of the social status of the person concerned, and thus serves to ensure equality.[171] And neither the person concerned who is under the burden of proof nor the proceedings are encumbered with a dispute about the individual amount of compensation for non-pecuniary loss, which is hardly quantifiable anyway.[172] Accordingly, the enforcement and determination of the claim does not seem to raise any problems in practice.[173] This is also indicated by a comparison with compensation for pecuniary loss. In the aforementioned study on compensation for wrongful convictions in the years 1990 to 2016, it was shown that compensation for non-material harm for executed imprisonment was always applied for, while damages for pecuniary loss were only applied for in half of the cases; moreover, proceedings for compensation of non-material harm alone took an average of two months, compared to proceedings in which damages for pecuniary loss were additionally sought taking an average of two years.[174] Also, more extensive claims for damages for non-pecuniary loss may be brought on the basis of other legal grounds, which admittedly have higher prerequisites (see 1) b)).[175]

The stipulation of the minimum limit for the compensation of the material loss, however, appears – even if due to the effort involved in the proceedings – to be an inappropriate state privilege which is also alien to the claim based on a general *Aufopferungsanspruch*.[176] It particularly affects those persons who have the least financial means,[177] and it appears particularly inappropriate when the cause of a claim for damages is a wrongful criminal conviction. The aforementioned fact that applications for compensation of pecuniary losses are filed much less frequently could suggest that the general civil law requirements for proving material harm pose a very high bar for claimants under the StrEG. It should be noted that the vast majority of these applications covered in the study mentioned were successful; the actual compensation paid, however, often fell significantly short of what was demanded.[178]

169 Böing (n 1) 73, 87; Hoffmann and Leuschner (n 120) 77 et seq.; Kunz (n 16) § 7 para 83; Meyer (n 5) § 7 para 66; Pohlreich (n 39) 233, 242.
170 Hoffmann and Leuschner (n 120) 77 et seq.
171 BT-Drs. VI/1512, 3; BR-Drs. 151/09, 4; Kunz (n 16) § 7 para 83; critical Meyer (n 5) § 7 para 66.
172 Böing (n 1) 73, 87; Kunz (n 16) § 7 para 83.
173 Hoffmann and Leuschner (n 120) 46.
174 Hoffmann and Leuschner (n 120) 47 et seq.
175 Kunz (n 16) § 7 para 83; Pohlreich (n 39) 233, 242.
176 Baumann (n 157) 705, 709.
177 Meyer (n 5) § 7 para 66.
178 Hoffmann and Leuschner (n 120) 46, 50, 79 et seq.

Furthermore, the deduction of expenses saved, for example in relation to accommodation and food, is widely acknowledged in jurisdiction as well as literature as being in accordance with general principles of civil law,[179] while considered an impertinence and a further inappropriate privilege of the state in its liability by those affected.[180]And finally, it is doubtful whether the reversal of the judgment in a public main hearing and the payment of a sum of money will suffice, perhaps some other form of public rehabilitation, for example by public notification, would be more appropriate.[181]

9 Conclusions

In principle, it appears that the German legislator has found an appropriate and pragmatic solution to compensate wrongfully convicted persons. Why it is of little importance in practice would be worth exploring further. However, the impression is given that this process is too pragmatic and too technical to adequately address persons who have been wrongfully convicted on a personal level and accommodate their psychological distress caused by the wrongful conviction and – where relevant – imprisonment. In this respect, it could help not only to lower the requirements for determining the amount of damages and causation, but also to conduct the entire compensation procedure *ex officio* and to create a mechanism for public rehabilitation, for instance by means of public announcement of the annulment or mitigation of the judgment. The *Rechtsstaat* also proves its worth when it publicly stands by (even only *ex post*) erroneous decisions and their corrections.

Bibliography

BaukelmannP, 'Anmerkung zu LG Frankfurt, Urteil vom 29.06.1983–1982/4 0 78/83' [1985] *Neue Zeitschrift für Strafrecht* 30

Baumann J, 'Kritische Bemerkungen zum Gesetz über die Entschädigung für Strafverfolgungsmaßnahmen' in Luttger H (ed.), *Festschrift für Ernst Heinitz* (De Gruyter 1972) 705

Beukelmann S, 'Kausalitätsschwächen der Haftentschädigung' [2018] *Neue Juristische Wochenschrift Spezial* 632

BGHR StrEG § 5 Abs. 2 S. 1 'Fahrlässigkeit, grobe'

Böing H, 'Das Recht des Beschuldigten auf Entschädigung für unschuldig erlittene Haft' in Jescheck H (ed.), *Deutsche Landesreferate zum IX. Internationalen Kongreß für Rechtsvergleichung in Teheran 1974* (De Gruyter 1974)

Cornelius K, in Graf J (ed.), *Beck'scher Onlinekommentar StPO* (41st ed., CH Beck 2021) StrEG § 5

Dahs H, *Handbuch des Strafverteidigers* (8th ed., Dr. Otto Schenk 2015)

179 P Baukelmann, 'Anmerkung zu LG Frankfurt, Urteil vom 29.06.1983–2/4 0 78/83', in: NStZ 1985, 30; Kunz (n 16) § 7 para 90 et seq.

180 Hoffmann and Leuschner (n 120) 77.

181 Kunz (n 16) § 7 para 7; Pohlreich (n 39) 233, 241 et seq. See also Hoffmann and Leuschner (n 120) 68 et seq., 86 et seq.

Eschelbach R, in Graf J (ed.), *Beck'scher Onlinekommentar StPO* (41st ed., CH Beck 2021) § 261

Forkert-Hosser S, in Miebach K and Hohmann O (eds.), *Wiederaufnahme in Strafsachen* (CH Beck 2016) chap. L

Friehe S, *Der Verzicht auf Entschädigung für Strafverfolgungsmaßnahmen* (Duncker & Humblot 1997)

Geipel A, in Miebach K and Hohmann O (eds.), *Wiederaufnahme in Strafsachen* (CH Beck 2016) chap. A

Grommes S, in Graf J (ed.), *Beck'scher Onlinekommentar OWiG* (32nd ed., CH Beck 2021) § 7

Grommes S, in Knauer C et al. (eds.), *Münchener Kommentar zur StPO 3–1* (CH Beck 2019) § 467

Hoffmann A and Leuschner F, '*Rehabilitation und Entschädigung nach Vollstreckung einer Freiheitsstrafe und erfolgreicher Wiederaufnahme*' online publication available at https://www.krimz.de/fileadmin/dateiablage/E-Publikationen/BM-Online/bm-online11.pdf; (accessed 27 December 2021)

Killinger I-M, *Staatshaftung für rechtswidrige Staatshaftung für rechtswidrige Untersuchungshaft in Deutschland und Österreich im Lichte von Art. 5 Abs. 5 EMRK* (C.F. Müller 2020)

Kunz K-H, in Knauer C *et al.* (eds.), *Münchener Kommentar zur StPO 3–2* (CH Beck 2018) StrEG Einleitung

Leuschner F *et al.*, 'Imprisoned but Innocent: Wrongful Convictions and Imprisonments in Germany, 1990–2016' [2019] 66 *Crime and Delinquency* 687

Marxen K and Tiemann F, *Die Wiederaufnahme in Strafsachen* (3rd ed., CF Müller 2014)

Meyer D, *StrEG – Kommentar zum Gesetz über die Entschädigung für Strafverfolgungsmaßnahmen* (11th ed., Carl Heymanns Verlag 2020)

Meyer-Goßner L and Schmitt B, *Kommentar zur StPO* (63rd ed., CH Beck 2020) StrEG § 1

Mosbacher A, 'Das Ideal richterlicher Wahrheitsfindung und die Betrübnisse des wirklichen Lebens. Richterliche Schuldfeststellung und die Gefahr des Fehlurteils' [2015] 9 *Forensische Psychiatrie, Psychologie, Kriminologie* 82

Niesler L, in Graf J (ed.), *Beck'scher Onlinekommentar StPO* (41st ed., CH Beck 2021) § 467

Papier H-J and Shirvani F, in Maunz T, Herzog R et al. (eds.), *Grundgesetz Kommentar* (95th supplement of July 2021, CH Beck) GG Art. 34

Papier H-J and Shirvani F, in Säcker F-J et al. (eds.), *Münchener Kommentar zum Bürgerlichen Gesetzbuch* (8th ed., CH Beck 2020) § 839

Pohlreich E, 'Haftentschädigung, Rehabilitierung und Begnadigung als Mechanismen zur Unrechtskorrektur bei strafgerichtlichen Verurteilungen' [2021] 69 *Jahrbuch des öffentlichen Rechts* 233

Schaefer T, 'Entschädigung für Strafverfolgungsmaßnahmen' [2009] *Neue Juristische Wochenschrift* 344

Schütz W, 'Der Anspruch nach dem StrEG im Zivilprozeß' [2008] *Strafverteidiger* 52

Schwenn J, 'Fehlurteile und ihre Ursachen – die Wiederaufnahme im Verfahren wegen sexuellen Mißbrauchs' [2010] *Strafverteidiger* 705

Sickor A, 'Von den Gebrechen des reformierten Strafverfahrens' [2015] *Strafverteidiger* 516

Steege H and Muthers C, in Dauner-Lieb B and Langen W (eds.), *BGB Schuldrecht* (4th ed., Nomos Verlag 2021) § 839

Teichmann A, in Stürner R (ed.), *Jauernig Bürgerliches Gesetzbuch* (18th ed., CH Beck, 2021) § 839

Vordermayer H et al., *Handbuch für den Staatsanwalt* (6th ed., Carl Heymanns Verlag 2019)

Table of cases

BGHZ 100, 335
BGHZ 103, 113
BGHZ 60, 302
BGHZ 72, 302
BGH, MDR 1993, 740
OLG Karlsruhe, Justiz 1988, 87
OLG Düsseldorf, decision of 28 August 2000 – 2 Ws 226/00 –
RGZ 164, 15
BGHZ 17, 153
BGHZ 27, 338
BGHZ 97, 97
BGHZ 117, 240
OLGR Celle 2007, 303
OLG Koblenz MDR 2018, 866
OLG Hamm, decision of 14 November 2014 – I-11 U 16/14 –
BGHSt 14, 391
OLG München, StV 1984, 471
OLG Nürnberg, NStZ-RR 2012, 223
OLG Stuttgart, NJW 1997, 206
BayObLGSt 1986, 25
OLG Hamm, EUGRZ 1986, 546
BGH StraFo 2010, 87
OLG Karlsruhe, NStZ-RR 2005, 255
KG Berlin NStZ-RR 2013, 192
KG Berlin, decision of 20 March 2000–4 Ws 41/00 –
OLG Düsseldorf NStZ 1984, 108
BayObLG 1973, 1938
OLG Stuttgart NStZ 1981, 484
KG StraFo 2009, 129
OLG Karlsruhe NStZ-RR 2005, 255
OLG Düsseldorf, StV 1988, 446
OLG Köln, StraFo 2001, 146
BGH NStZ-RR 2017, 264
KG NStZ-RR 2012, 30
BGH NStZ-RR 2021, 217
KG Berlin, decision of 20 August 1999 – 1 AR 553/99–94 Ws 132/99
BGH StraFo 2008, 352
KG Berlin StraFo 2009, 129
BVerfG, NJW 1996, 1049
OLG Köln StraFo 2002, 337
OLG Düsseldorf StV 1984, 108

OLG Düsseldorf 25.6.2013 – 2012 Ws 275/13
OLG Stuttgart MDR 1984, 427
OLG Hamm, decision of 15 October 2013 – 5 RVs 96/13, 5 Ws 380–381/13 –
KG Berlin GA 1987, 405
KG Berlin, decision of 20 March 2000 – 4 Ws 41/00 –
OLG Düsseldorf NStZ-RR 1996, 223
KG Berlin, StraFo 2009, 129
OLG Brandenburg, decision 5 December 2007–1 Ws 273/07 –
OLG Düsseldorf 25.6.2013–2012 Ws 275/13 –
OLG Oldenburg, StraFo 2005, 384
OLG Stuttgart NJW 1977, 641
VGH Sachsen NJW 2019, 2077.
OLG Zweibrücken NStZ 1986, 129
OLG Hamm NStZ-RR 1997, 127
BGH NStZ 2000, 330
OLG Frankfurt a. M. NStZ-RR 2002, 246
OLG Hamm NStZ-RR 2010, 224
BGHZ 63, 203
BGHZ 65, 170
BGHZ 106, 313
OLG Celle, NJW 2004, 3347
OLG Brandenburg, decision of 29 January 2020 – 4 U 172/19 –
OLG Hamm, decision of 29 January 2021 – I-11 U 41/20 –
BGH NJW 1988, 1141
OLG Düsseldorf StraFo 2007, 35
OLG Düsseldorf, NStZ-RR 1996, 287
BGHZ 63, 209
OLG Frankfurt NJW 1074, 202
OLG Düsseldorf JMBlNW 95, 250
BGH NJW 1976, 1218
OLG Nürnberg, NStZ-RR 2003, 62
BGHZ 108, 14
OLG Dresden, OLG-NL 1996, 216
OLG Schleswig NJW-RR 2004, 599
BGH NJW 1977, 957
OLG Schleswig, NJW-RR 2004, 599
BGH NStZ 1989, 479
OLG Hamm, decision of 14 November 2014 – I-11 U 16/14
OLG Koblenz, decision of 18 April 2018 – 1 W 144/18

3 Compensation for wrongful convictions in Italy*

Simone Lonati

1 Miscarriages of justice and redress

Criminal procedure inevitably faces the risk that some of the key stages and the final outcome of a trial may be fallacious. Moreover, there is always some degree of error in any human judgment. But a shortcoming in the justice system is an intolerable eventuality, considering that its consequences are largely irreparable, especially when it has compromised the defendant's fundamental human rights to dignity and personal liberty. It is an eventuality to which the state must respond by eliminating, where still possible, the negative consequences that the victim of the error continues to suffer and by ensuring financial compensation in proportion to the damages suffered.

The Italian code of criminal procedure (hereinafter CCP)[1] outlines two different compensation schemes: one covering cases where the defendant has been placed under wrongful detention on remand during criminal proceedings, and the other where it is conclusively found that a person was wrongfully convicted by a final judgment.[2]

* The author wishes to thank Davide Attanasio and Alessandro Nascimbeni for their valuable work on this chapter.

1 The Italian code of criminal procedure was introduced by d.P.R. 22 September 1988, no. 447, and came into force in 1989.

2 With regard to miscarriages of justice, according to a traditional scholarship opinion, a distinction must be made between miscarriages of justice *stricto sensu* and *lato sensu*: the first describes cases of wrongful final convictions (Articles 643ff CCP); the second refers to cases of wrongful preventive detention (Articles 314ff CCP). A reference to this approach is made by Maria Lucia Di Bitonto, 'L'errore giudiziario nelle carte dei diritti fondamentali in Europa' in Luca Lupária Donati (ed), *L'errore giudiziario* (Giuffrè 2021), 65; Elga Turco, *L'equa riparazione tra errore giudiziario e ingiusta detenzione* (Giuffrè 2007), 2. The study of miscarriages of justice relating to a final judgment of conviction cannot disregard the detailed analyses of the matter by scholarship. In these terms, see *inter alia* C. Ronald Huff and Martin Killias (eds), *Wrongful convictions: international perspectives on miscarriages of justice* (Temple University Press 2008); C. Ronald Huff and Martin Killias (eds), *Wrongful convictions and miscarriages of justice. Causes and remedies in North American and European criminal justice systems* (Routledge 2013); David T. Johnson, *The culture of capital punishment in Japan* (Palgrave Macmillan 2020), 61ff; Geert-Jan Alexander Knoops, *Redressing miscarriages of justice: practice and procedure in national and international criminal law cases* (Brill 2007); Allison D. Redlich and John Petrila (eds), 'Special

DOI: 10.4324/9781003229414-4

The cases of wrongful detention on remand eligible for compensation are regulated by Article 314 CCP, which distinguishes between 'material injustice' in the first paragraph and 'procedural injustice' in the second paragraph. In the event of a material injustice, the right to compensation is triggered by a judgment of acquittal at the outcome of the proceedings, while in the case of a procedural injustice the right to compensation is triggered if, at the time detention on remand was ordered, the requirements set forth in Articles 273 and 280 CCP had not been met, regardless of the final outcome of the trial itself.

Compensation for miscarriages of justice in the strict sense – namely, the ones arising from an exoneration upon judicial review of a final judgment of conviction – is regulated by Articles 643ff CCP. Unlike the compensation scheme provided for wrongful detention on remand, the former necessarily depends on a favourable outcome of the judicial review requested by the person convicted.

The concept of 'miscarriage of justice' is therefore defined through different statutory provisions resting on different requirements. Nevertheless, their basic rationale represents a common thread that is based on the principles of inviolability of personal liberty (Article 13 Italian Constitution)[3] and presumption of innocence (Article 27, paragraph 2 Italian Constitution).[4] Said constitutional values guide the interpretation of Article 24, para 4 Constitution, which places on the legislator the burden of identifying the means of redress for miscarriages of justice in such a way as to remedy any damage suffered by a person within the sphere of his/her personal liberty.

In the Italian constitutional system, compensation for miscarriages of justice is to be understood as a solidaristic remedy, whereby the damage suffered by a person unlawfully detained or convicted (and later exonerated following judicial review) must be compensated by the state, so that the individual sacrifice is shared by the entire community.[5] In accordance with Article 2 Constitution, in order to ensure the protection of inviolable human rights,[6] the Italian Republic requires the fulfilment of the mandatory duties of political, economic and social solidarity.

issue: The age of innocence: Miscarriages of justice in the 21st Century' (2009) 27 *Behav. Sci. & L.* 297.

3 The Italian Constitution was approved by the Constituent Assembly on 22 December 1947, promulgated by the Provisional Head of State Enrico De Nicola on the following 27 December and published on the same day in the *Official Gazette* no. 298, extraordinary edition. It entered into force on 1 January 1948.

4 Paolo Troisi, *L'errore giudiziario tra garanzie costituzionali e sistema processuale* (Cedam 2011), 103ff.

5 Corte cost, 11 June 2008 (entered 20 June 2008), no. 219, [2008] Giur. cost. 2456, with comment by Maria Grazia Coppetta, 'Riparazione per l'ingiusta detenzione: una declaratoria di incostituzionalità dirompente?', *ibid.* 2476, acknowledging, with reference to the provisions laid down for wrongful preventive detentions, the solidaristic purpose of the remedy. See also Antonio Balsamo, 'Riparazione per ingiusta detenzione' in Adolfo Scalfati (ed), *Prove e misure cautelari. Le misure cautelari*, in Giorgio Spangher (directed by), *Trattato di procedura penale* (vol. II, Utet 2008), 519.

6 Among which there is the right to personal liberty expressly defined in Article 13 Constitution as inviolable, thus falling among those rights enshrined in Article 2 Constitution. See Paolo Barile, *Diritti dell'uomo e libertà fondamentali* (Il Mulino 1984), 113.

Given this common constitutional framework, it must be said that the compensation scheme most frequently applied in practice is the one covered by Articles 314 and 315 CCP, namely for wrongful detention on remand. According to official data from the Ministry of Justice, in 2019 the total expenditure for compensation in cases of wrongful detention on remand amounted to approximately €43.5 million, while with reference to compensation for wrongful conviction under Article 643 CCP, the total amount incurred in 2019 was about €5.2 million.[7] In total between 1992 and 2021, the number of cases of wrongful detention on remand amounted to 30,017, for a total public expenditure of approximately € 819 million, compared to 214 cases of wrongful conviction arising from judicial review, for a total of approximately €76 million.[8]

For the purposes of this volume, the present chapter will mainly, even if not exclusively, deal with the topic of miscarriages of justice *stricto sensu*. Firstly, the matter will be analysed in light of the relevant constitutional and supranational principles necessary to understand the different theories regarding the legal nature of the remedy; subsequently, a description of the provisions laid down in the Italian CCP on the compensation schemes for miscarriages of justice resulting from a wrongful final conviction will be provided, focusing on legislative requirements, bars to compensation, proceedings and criteria for compensation; finally, some concluding remarks will be made.

7 Corte dei conti, *Equa riparazione per ingiusta detenzione ed errori giudiziari* (Delib. n. 15/2021/G, 16 September 2021), 41ff. In 2019 compensation due to wrongful pre-trial detention accounted for 89 per cent of the total payments made (about €48.6 million). The data show that in 2020 the total amount spent due to miscarriages of justice decreased to approximately €44 million. According to the organisation Errorigiudiziari.com a sharp decline in both cases and spending was also registered in 2021 probably due (also) to fewer cases being considered by courts because of the pandemic. See Benedetto Lattanzi and Valentino Maimone, 'Errori giudiziari e ingiusta detenzione, tutti gli ultimi dati aggiornati' (*errorigiudiziari.com*, 25 March 2022) <www.errorigiudiziari.com> accessed 22 May 2022. With specific reference to compensation for wrongful detention on remand the latest data published by the Ministry of Justice show indeed a decrease in the total amount spent and in the number of orders issued: from €36.9 million (750 orders) in 2020 to €24.5 million (565 orders) in 2021. See Ministero della Giustizia, *Misure cautelari personali e riparazione per ingiusta detenzione: dati anno 2021. Relazione al Parlamento ex L. 16 aprile 2015, n. 47* (Update April 2022), 25ff, available at <www.giustizia.it> accessed 23 May 2022.

8 The data regarding cases of wrongful conviction arising from judicial review refer to the time period between 1991 and 2021. See Lattanzi and Maimone, 'Errori giudiziari e ingiusta detenzione, tutti gli ultimi dati aggiornati' (n 7). The same statistical survey, albeit updated to 2019, can also be found in Benedetto Lattanzi and Valentino Maimone, 'Ingiusta detenzione in Italia, un'analisi', in Lupária (n 2), 963ff; Benedetto Lattanzi and Valentino Maimone, 'Innocenti e invisibili: quante vittime della giustizia sfuggono alle statistiche' (*errorigiudiziari.com*, 4 October 2021) <www.errorigiudiziari.com> accessed 8 March 2022. It should be noted that the same authors consider these statistical data undervalued since the number of victims of miscarriages of justice in Italy over the past 30 years is estimated to amount to 50,000. This statistical discrepancy is the result of a large number of so-called 'invisible innocents' in the Italian justice system. On this matter, see also: Viviana Lanza, 'Ingiusta detenzione, ogni anno oltre duecento invisibili' (*Il Riformista*, 9 January 2022) <www.ilriformista.it> accessed 13 March 2022.

2 Miscarriages of justice eligible for compensation in light of constitutional and supranational principles

Before addressing the compensation regime laid out in the Italian CCP, it is worth briefly analysing the relevant constitutional and supranational principles.

In Italy, in Article 24, para 4, the Constitution places on the legislator the burden of establishing the conditions and procedures for redressing miscarriages of justice. Therefore, the constitutional text does not explicitly state the interested party's right to apply for compensation against miscarriages of justice but simply transfers to the legislator the duty to concretely identify the compensation scheme rules and eligibility conditions.

From the very start, the generic scope of Article 24 paved the way for a debate on its exact scope of application, namely whether the provision also covered cases of wrongful detention on remand. According to an initial interpretation,[9] the miscarriage of justice covered by the constitutional rule strictly amounted to a wrongful final conviction found upon judicial review. Leaning on the programmatic nature of Article 24, para 4 Constitution – which, as mentioned, places on the legislator the burden of identifying the compensation scheme rules and eligibility conditions – the first legal commentators believed that this approach necessarily stemmed from the absence, in the Italian CCP in force at the time, of a specific rule regarding redress for wrongful detention on remand. In fact, the only statutory reference was deemed to be Article 571 CCP, which provided solely for compensation against a wrongful final conviction found upon judicial review.[10]

The constitutional conception of miscarriage of justice in the strict sense was, however, left behind with the entry into force of the new code of criminal procedure, which, as previously noted, in Articles 314 and 315 CCP, also provides for compensation in cases of wrongful detention on remand. With the new provisions, therefore, there remains no doubt that the wording of Article 24, para 4 Constitution should be construed as also covering wrongful preventive measures.[11] This new interpretation ought to also be supported on the basis of other joint constitutional standards binding the state – namely Articles 2, 3 and 13 Constitution – whereby the state has the duty to protect and guarantee inviolable human rights (Article 2

9 For a more detailed analysis of the matter see Troisi (n 4) 172ff; Turco (n 2) 41ff; *Dig. disc. pen.* (4th edn, 1997), vol XII, 330ff.

10 The narrow interpretation of the constitutional concept of 'miscarriage of justice' was also supported by the Constitutional Court. See Corte cost, 15 January 1969 (entered 24 January 1969), no. 1, in *Dejure.* Originally, the legal remedy envisaged in Article 571 of the former CCP was not based on the wrongfulness of the conviction, which had resulted in an infringement of the individual's liberty, but on the state of need of the unjustly convicted and the consequent intervention of the state took the form of a 'charitable action'. Later, Law 23 May 1960, no. 504, amended Articles 571–574 CCP and added Article 574 *bis* to the former CCP, recognising for the first time the compensation for judicial error as a subjective right. This approach has been maintained in the new CCP that came into force in 1989. See, on this, Marcello D'Aiuto, 'La riparazione dell'errore giudiziario', in Lupária (n 2) 726–727.

11 In these terms, Corte cost, 18 July 1996 (entered 25 July 1996), no. 310, [1996] Giur. cost. 2557. In this case, the Court held that Article 314 CCP constitutes a fulfilment of the constitutional provision.

Constitution), including personal liberty (Article 13 Constitution), and to redress any injury to a right that qualifies as inviolable.[12] The foregoing must also be read jointly with Article 27, para 2 Constitution, which enshrines the principle of presumption of innocence until final conviction.[13]

The constitutional guarantees thereby outlined, as a whole, impose: firstly, that any restrictions to personal liberty at the pre-trial stage be sought solely as an extreme remedy; and secondly, that monetary relief be awarded when, at the outcome of a trial, it is found that a preventive measure falls within the cases set forth in Article 314 CCP (material and procedural injustices).

At a supranational level – unlike the Italian constitutional framework – the matter of miscarriages of justice eligible for compensation is regulated by different provisions depending on whether the case regards a wrongful final conviction or a wrongful detention or arrest.[14] Specifically, the ECHR, in Article 5 § 5, states that anyone who has been placed under arrest or detention in violation of the provisions of the precedent paragraphs of the same Article is entitled to claim compensation.[15] While miscarriages of justice relating to a wrongful conviction are regulated by Article 3, Protocol No. 7 ECHR, which states a right to compensation when a final conviction is overturned in the light of new or newly discovered facts, provided that the non-disclosure of the new facts is not attributable to the accused.

The matter at hand is also regulated by the International Covenant on Civil and Political Rights: Article 9 § 5, in even broader terms compared to the ECHR provisions, provides for a right to compensation for any person who has been the victim of unlawful arrest or detention, while Article 14 § 6 – correspondingly to Article 3, Protocol No. 7 ECHR – provides for a right to compensation in the event of a wrongful conviction.

In light of the aforementioned constitutional and supranational principles, some significant discrepancies should be highlighted. Firstly, it can easily be observed that the supranational laws distinguish between the regulation of wrongful convictions and the regulation of unlawful detentions or arrests, while the Italian Constitution makes an explicit overall reference to both types of miscarriages of justice in Article 24, para 4 Constitution. In terms of nomenclature, the supranational regulations are formulated in such a way as to directly grant the individual a subjective right to compensation, whereas the wording of the Constitution places the burden of regulating the matter (including the eligibility requirements to apply for compensation) on the legislator.

12 Corte cost, 11 June 2008 (entered 20 June 2008), no. 219 (n 5).

13 See Troisi (n 4) 180–181 and Balsamo (n 5) 626; as well as D'Aiuto (n 10) 722, where the author highlights that the presumption of innocence principle covers criminal proceedings in their entirety, in the context of which the Court, by correctly applying the assessment criteria set forth by the law, must prevent miscarriages of justice.

14 Di Bitonto (n 2) 63ff.

15 More generally, Article 5, § 5 ECHR – protecting the right to liberty and security of person – details a number of exceptions to the prohibition to restrict the fundamental principle of personal liberty (Article 5, § 1 ECHR), as well as a number of procedural guarantees for the person placed under arrest or detention (Article 5, § 2, 3 and 4 ECHR). See also Turco (n 2) 46ff.

Furthermore, it is important to underline that, at a supranational level, the conduct of the interested party may constitute a bar to compensation only in cases of wrongful conviction (i.e. Articles 3, Protocol No. 7 ECHR and 14 § 6 of the International Covenant on Civil and Political Rights), while in the Italian CCP the accused's conduct is also taken into account in cases of wrongful detention on remand (Article 314, para 1 CCP). With specific reference to this last case, note should be taken of the broader scope of the supranational terminology ('arrest' and 'detention') compared to that of the Italian code, which only mentions 'preventive custodial detention measures'. This lexical difference inevitably redounds to the scope of application of the above rules: the conventional scope of application, as regulated, seems to cover a wider range of cases where personal liberty is in fact restricted.[16]

3 The legal basis of compensation for wrongful detention and wrongful conviction

In order to address the rules set forth by the Italian CCP we must first analyse the legal nature of the remedy. This issue does not merely have dogmatic relevance, but also practical consequences in relation to the criteria used for the attribution of liability for the injury suffered by the interested party. Hence, for example – as will be explained in further detail below – should compensation for miscarriages of justice be qualified as a remedy having the same nature as compensation for damages, then the criteria set forth in Article 2043 Italian civil code[17] for civil wrongs should apply.

This matter has been subject to three main interpretations.[18] In accordance with a first and more dated opinion,[19] building on the unlawfulness of the judgment or order issued by the judiciary, compensation for miscarriages of justice would stem from a state liability for civil wrongs. In these terms, the remedy would have the same nature as the one underlying tort liability. This approach, however, does not seem convincing and, specifically, two points of criticism have been levelled at it. The first builds on the remedy's legal basis, which, unlike tort liability under Article 2043 Italian civil code, does not amount to a civil wrong: that is because the court's decision cannot be such. Rather, the remedy stems from the solidaristic principle expressed in Article 2 Constitution, whereby the state undertakes to protect – even by awarding redress – inviolable human rights.[20] The

16 Paola Spagnolo, 'La riparazione per ingiusta detenzione: verso una tutela sostanziale del diritto alla libertà personale' (2017) 11 La legislazione penale <www.lalegislazionepenale.eu> accessed 9 March 2022, 3.

17 The Italian civil code was enacted by Royal Decree no. 262 of 16 March 1942 and entered into force on 21 April of the same year.

18 For a detailed overview of the matter see Turco (n 2) 2ff; and more recently Elga Turco, 'Riparazione per l'ingiusta detenzione', in Angelo Giarda and Giorgio Spangher (eds), *Codice di procedura penale commentato* (Wolters Kluwer 2017), 3609ff.

19 For a review of the case law and scholarship in support of this theory, see once again Turco (n 2) 3.

20 See Balsamo (n 5) 638.

second point of criticism regards the subjective elements of tort liability, which, as known, require either the wilful misconduct or negligence of the tortfeasor. Based on this approach, however, the right to compensation should be excluded every time the court's 'error' was neither malicious nor negligent.

On the basis of these criticisms, another interpretation was developed, which tends to place the remedy within the context of compensation for a lawful act.[21] In particular, this theory rests on the assumption that the interested party – given the harm caused to his/her personal liberty – has a personal public-law claim that the state has a duty to settle. Thus, the liability framework thereby invoked is the one of state liability for a lawful act.[22] Once again, this position has not been immune to criticism.[23] The legal basis of the right to compensation for miscarriages of justice does not *necessarily* stem from a lawful act: in fact, Article 314, para 2 CCP – which regulates cases of procedural injustice – includes a number of orders issued against the law.[24] Furthermore, unlike compensation for lawful state action (e.g. expropriation for public interest), in redressing miscarriages of justice there is no divergence between the interest of the person seeking compensation for the injury suffered and that of the state. Indeed, the latter evidently has no interest in having the individual's personal liberty unlawfully restricted; on the contrary, the objective of the court is to adopt decisions that are compliant with the law and with constitutional guarantees.

The third and last interpretation more adequately supports the autonomous nature of the remedy, defined as a *tertium genus* (or third type) compared to the models of damages for civil wrongs and of compensation for lawful acts.[25] Based on this last interpretation the legal basis for compensation should be solely found in the solidaristic purpose of the remedy, which aims to balance out the prejudice incurred by the interested party. The state's obligation to settle the individual's subjective claim, in other words, would directly rest on the provisions set forth in Articles 2, 13, 24, para 4 and 27, para 2 Constitution,[26] which, as previously noted, impose on the state a duty to hold individuals harmless against an unlawful deprivation of their personal liberty.[27] From this perspective, by providing for a compensation regime, it seems that the legislator has decided to transfer the risk of ascertaining the miscarriage of justice from the individual to the entire community.[28]

Having clarified what might be the legal basis of compensation for miscarriages of justice, we now look into the provisions laid out in the Italian code of criminal procedure.

21 See also Corte cost, 11 June 2008 (entered 20 June 2008), no. 219 (n 5). In approximately similar terms, Cass pen, sez. un., 30 October 2008 (entered 29 January 2009), no. 4187, [2009] Resp. civ. prev. 777. See also Turco (n 2) 9ff.
22 For a reference to this matter see Troisi (n 4) 252–253.
23 See Turco (n 2) 13–14.
24 *Dig. disc. pen.* (V aggiornamento, 2010), 489.
25 Supporting this theory Turco (n 2) 14ff.
26 *Dig. disc. pen.* (n 24) 489.
27 On this matter see also *Dig. disc. pen.* (n 9) 320.
28 Again *Dig. disc. pen.* (n 24) 489.

4 The relevant statutory framework: the provisions of the Italian code of criminal procedure

The Italian CCP, as noted, provides for two separate compensation schemes for wrongful convictions, on the one hand, and wrongful detention, on the other. The first case is regulated by Chapter IX of the code of criminal procedure on appeals and concerns miscarriages of justice found upon judicial review (Articles 643ff CCP); the second case – regarding detention on remand measures – is regulated by Chapter IV (Articles 314–315 CCP).

In the following sections, in line with the purpose of this volume, particular attention will be paid to the former compensation scheme, namely the one related to wrongful convictions.

4.1 Redressing wrongful convictions under Article 643 CCP

The original compensation regime for miscarriages of justice is the one currently regulated by Article 643 CCP,[29] whereby a person whose conviction has been quashed following judicial review is entitled to apply for compensation for the injury suffered, in proportion to the duration of any term of imprisonment[30] and to the impact of the wrongful conviction on the individual and his/her family.[31]

A mandatory requirement for the application of the above compensation scheme is *res judicata*: the judgment of conviction must be final. This requirement alone is, however, insufficient to trigger a right to compensation.

Indeed, it is also necessary that the judicial review[32] on application by the interested party leads to the conviction being quashed.[33] Only at the outcome of the judicial review is the miscarriage of justice – albeit innate in the judgment of

29 On this matter see *Dig. disc. pen.* (n 9) 319ff, as well as D'Aiuto (n 10) 717ff.

30 It is not, however, necessary for the sentence to have been enforced; see Paolo Tonini, *Manuale di procedura penale* (Giuffrè 2019), 1005–1006.

31 On the criteria used to determine the compensation amount see below section 4.4.

32 Under Article 643, para 1 CCP the right to apply for the compensation derives from an acquittal coming from the legal remedy *ex* Article 630 CCP (judicial review). Under the latter article, the grounds for judicial review are established exhaustively and are all aimed at resolving the antinomy between the fact underlying an irrevocable judgment of conviction and the material content of new data that reveal the injustice of that sentence. Therefore, other legal remedies aimed at removing unfair judgments, i.e. the extraordinary appeal in cassation for error of fact (Article 625 *bis* CCP) and the so-called 'European judicial review' where concluded not with an acquittal but with a lighter sentence, seem to be excluded. See, *inter alia*, D'Aiuto (n 10) 727–728; with specific attention to the former legal remedy, see Mitja Gialuz, *Il ricorso straordinario per cassazione* (Giuffrè 2005), 390; with a different view Michele Caianiello, 'La riapertura del processo ex art. 625 bis c.p.p. a seguito di condanna della Corte europea dei diritti dell'uomo' (2009) *Cass. pen.* 1465, 1472.

33 Article 643 CCP does not require that the exoneration following judicial review be granted on a specific ground: it may be the result of an acquittal under Article 530 CCP or of a dismissal under Articles 529 and 531 CCP.

conviction – formally acknowledged by the judiciary, thereby making the person unlawfully convicted and later exonerated eligible for compensation.[34]

Lastly, under paragraph 3 of Article 643 CCP, the right to compensation is excluded when the term of imprisonment has already been deducted from the sentence to be served for another crime. The reason behind this choice clearly resides in the intent to avoid the interested party from benefitting twice from the acknowledgement of a miscarriage of justice.[35]

4.2 The bars to compensation: malice and gross negligence

The Italian code of criminal procedure establishes a bar to the right to compensation in case of wrongful conviction. In particular, the right to compensation is denied when the interested party, acting with malice or gross negligence, has caused the miscarriage of justice.[36]

Regarding the definition of malice, according to the prevailing case law,[37] which supports a broader notion than the one typically applied in criminal law, the malicious intent is defined as conduct that is consciously and deliberately liable to create the 'danger to community' requirements.[38] What is considered relevant, therefore, is that the person deliberately engages in conduct that is concretely liable to mislead the court, such as in cases of false self-accusation, or of actions aimed at suborning a witness, expert or interpreter, or of a deliberate failure to self-defend against a slanderous accusation for unlawful purposes.[39]

34 See D'Aiuto (n 10) 723–724 and Troisi (n 4) 109.

35 Turco (n 2) 254–255.

36 This limitation applies both to wrongful conviction and wrongful detention but with a different scope of application: it applies to the latter not only in the case where the interested party has directly caused the miscarriage of justice but also where he/she has *contributed* to causing it. In other words, the contribution – namely contribution to the miscarriage of justice – is deemed relevant solely in relation to wrongful detention, while Article 643 CCP only takes into account conduct that directly causes the miscarriage of justice. Said distinction, according to some authors, rests on the belief that the elements grounding preventive measures – gathered for the most part outside of the proceedings – are more liable to corruption than those that are put together during the course of the proceedings. See Alida Montaldi, 'Riparazione per l'ingiusta detenzione', in Mario Chiavario (coordinated by), *Commento al nuovo codice di procedure penale* (Utet 1990), 321; for a different opinion, see *Dig. disc. pen.* (n 9) 342.

37 See Balsamo (n 5) 673–674, addressing, by way of example, the case of a person who self-incriminates him/herself or fraudulently produces evidence against his/her defence.

38 *Ex multis* Cass pen, sez. un., 13 December 1995 (entered 9 February 1996), no. 43, [1996] Cass. pen. 2146, with comment by Paola Felicioni, 'Condizioni ostative al diritto alla riparazione per ingiusta detenzione ed esercizio del diritto di difesa: spunti problematici', *ibid.* 2156.

39 D'Aiuto (n 10) 734. The author affirms that the notion of malice intent established by case law is distinct from that set out in Article 43 of the Italian criminal code, in having great regard to the suitability of the conduct to mislead and not to the mere

With specific reference to the concept of negligence, the boundaries are traced by Article 43 Italian criminal code (hereinafter CC),[40] which describes the negligent psychological coefficient as the expectation, not the intention, to cause the event, which therefore takes place by reason of the negligent and reckless conduct of the person or by violation of laws, regulations, orders or rules.[41] Negligence, by express provision of the law, must also be gross and thus amount to significantly negligent conduct.[42] In case law this concept has been identified in the defendant's conduct at trial as being characterised by significant imprudence or, indeed, gross negligence, such as in the case of an inert or malicious defence or in the inactivity of the technical defence accompanied by a breach of the defendant's duty to supervise the defence counsel's work.[43]

In addition, further attention should be paid to the temporal scope of application of the bars to compensation, so as to understand whether the personal conduct prior to the knowledge of the proceedings and, therefore, to the qualification as suspect/accused may be included therein. Even in this regard, the prevailing case law chooses to extend the scope of application of the bars to compensation: the Italian Court of Cassation has on several occasions stressed that 'gross negligence' also includes any conduct put in place before knowledge of the pending proceedings.[44]

prediction and intention of the event. In this sense, a notion of intent deriving from contract law is applied.

40 The Italian criminal code was issued by Royal Decree 19 October 1930, no. 1398, and entered into force on 1 July 1931.

41 Cass pen, sez. un., 13 December 1995 (entered 9 February 1996), no. 43 (n 38).

42 *Ibid.*

43 D'Aiuto (n 10) 734–735. In this regard a case law trend to include in the concept of 'gross negligence' the choice made by the suspect to exercise his/her right to remain silent (or to refuse to answer questions or to answer by lying) during the interrogation of the suspect for the purpose of preventive measures should be noted. See, *inter alia*, Cass pen, sez. IV, 23 October 2015, no. 46423, Rv. 265287; Cass pen, sez. IV, 17 November 2011 (entered 23 February 2012), no. 7296, Rv. 251928; Cass pen, sez. IV, 10 June 2008 (entered 29 October 2008), no. 40291, Rv. 242755; Cass pen, sez. III, 17 February 2005 (entered 14 April 2005), no. 13714, [2006] Cass. pen. 3737; *contra*, more recently, Cass pen, sez. IV, 2 July 2021 (entered 16 September 2021), no. 34367, in *Dejure*. On this matter, see also Lattanzi and Maimone, 'Innocenti e invisibili: quante vittime della giustizia sfuggono alle statistiche' (n 8). The recent amendment of Article 314, para 1 CCP by Legislative decree 8 November 2021, no. 188, aims at hindering this judicial practice. In this sense, the first judgments seem promising. See, *inter alia*, Cass pen, sez. IV, 8 February 2022 (entered 15 March 2022), no. 8616, in *Dejure*.

44 D'Aiuto (n 10) 734–735. In these terms, see also Cass pen, sez. un., 26 June 2002 (entered 15 October 2002), no. 34559, [2003] Cass. pen. 57; Cass pen, sez. IV, 3 June 2010 (entered 24 September 2010), no. 34656, Rv. 248074; and Cass pen, sez. un., 28 November 2013 (entered 24 December 2013), no. 51779, [2014] Dir. giust. Of an opposite opinion some scholars: see for all Turco (n 2) 241–242. Along the same lines Elizabeth M.T. Di Palma, 'Dolo e colpa grave, cause ostative al sorgere del diritto soggettivo alla riparazione per ingiusta detenzione' (1997) Cass. pen. 814, 817.

4.3 Compensation proceedings

Under Article 645, para 1 CCP, the court that has jurisdiction to take cognisance of the claim is the appellate court that overturned the conviction, whose jurisdiction is, in turn, determined on the basis of the criteria outlined in Article 11 CCP.[45]

The application for compensation must be filed, under penalty of rejection, within two years of the judgment quashing the conviction (Article 645, para 1 CCP) becoming final or, in any case, within two years of when the judgment ordering the pre-trial dismissal of the charges is no longer subject to challenge or when the notice of discontinuance was served.

Furthermore, the application must be filed in writing and contain all documents deemed useful to prove eligibility for compensation. It may be filed in person by the interested party or by someone authorised through a power of attorney in accordance with Article 122 CCP.[46]

Under Article 644, para 1 CCP, the persons that have a standing to apply for compensation, in the event of the death of the interested party, are also the spouse, a next of kin relative, an affine to the first degree and a lineal relative by adoption. In this case, the amount of compensation cannot in any case exceed the amount that would have been determined in favour of the interested party.[47]

Once the application for compensation has been filed it must be notified, together with the order setting the date for the hearing, at least ten days before the hearing to the public prosecutor. It must also be notified, by the clerk's office, to the treasury secretary of the state legal advisory office of the district of the court having jurisdiction and served on all interested parties. According to the prevailing

45 See Article 633, para 1 CCP establishing that the court of jurisdiction over petitions for judicial review is determined under Article 11 CCP ('Jurisdiction for proceedings concerning magistrates'). In particular, the appellate court is identified on the basis of Article 11 CCP with respect to the district corresponding to the judge who issued the judgment on the merits that became final.

46 In the Italian legal system, when a personal act is to be performed in a criminal proceeding and the interested party cannot be present, the technical representation of the defence counsel is not sufficient. Indeed, it is necessary for the party to confer voluntary representation to the defence counsel or to another person of his/her trust, and this can only be done by means of a special power of attorney to perform a particular act.

47 This statutory provision – as expressly clarified by the Court of Cassation – also applies to cases of wrongful detention on remand by reference in Article 315, para 3 CCP to the rules on wrongful conviction. See, *ex plurimis*, Cass pen, sez. IV, 6 February 2019 (entered 15 May 2019), no. 20845, in *Dejure*. On this matter see also Corte cost, 13 December 2004 (entered 23 December 2004), no. 413, [2005] Cass. pen. 1551, which confirmed that the right to claim compensation in the case of the death of the suspect – against whom all charges have been dismissed – is transferred to the deceased suspect's heirs when, following the acquittal of any co-defendants, it is found that the deceased suspect would have also been acquitted had he/she been alive. On this matter see also Mariaivana Romano, 'Ambiti operativi della riparazione per ingiusta detenzione alla luce delle novità giurisprudenziali' (2010) Dir. pen. proc. 1496, 1500.

opinion, failure to give notice to the public prosecutor and to the treasury secretary is ground for application of the invalidity regime under Article 180 CCP (see Article 127, para 5 CCP), while the failure to notify the interested party – considered equivalent to the failure to serve summons to enter appearance on the defendant – is ground for absolute invalidity under Article 179, para 1 CCP.[48]

The proceedings, under Article 645, para 1 CCP, are held in chambers in accordance with the methods set forth in Article 127 CCP. The interested parties can file briefs and documents up to five days prior to the hearing. The main characteristics of the hearing are that the appearance in court of the interested parties is merely optional and the hearing is conducted behind closed doors. On this latter issue, it should be noted that the European Court of Human Rights[49] has found a violation of Article 6 § 1 ECHR in the Italian statutory provision that denies the interested parties' right to request an open-court hearing. Within the framework of the Italian compensation regime – as highlighted by the European Court – there is no exceptional circumstance that may justify the preclusion of an open-court hearing. Nevertheless, by reason of the application of the procedural rules laid down in Article 127 CCP, the current statutory framework still provides for a closed hearing (Article 127, para 6 CCP).[50]

During the preliminary investigation stage, the applicant has the burden of proving the grounds for his/her compensation claim; vice versa, the treasury secretary has the burden of proving any bars to compensation. Furthermore, should the documentary evidence adduced be insufficient, the court may, even *ex officio*, request the parties to supplement said documents for the purpose of deciding on the matter.[51]

Finally, the matter is decided upon by court order issued by the judging panel,[52] whereby the application may either be: i) held inadmissible on lack of standing or non-compliance with the two-year time limit set forth in Article 645 CCP; ii) rejected as unfounded (for example in the presence of any of the aforementioned bars to compensation); or iii) admitted. In this last case, the court shall determine the amount of compensation to be awarded and, where the applicant is in need and unable to support him/herself financially, it may award interim compensation in the form of an allowance. The interim compensation is directly enforceable and is borne by the Ministry of Economy and Finance. If the application is admitted, court fees are borne by the losing party – i.e. the public administration. However, when the Ministry of Economy and Finance has not

48 Of this opinion, Turco (n 2) 304; Balsamo (n 5) 686.

49 *Lorenzetti v. Italy*, App no. 32075/09 (ECtHR, 10 April 2012), available at <www.hudoc.echr.coe.int> accessed 22 May 2022. On this matter see also Sofia Mirandola, 'Un'altra camera di consiglio destinata a schiudersi' (2013) Cass. pen. 4043.

50 On this matter the Constitutional Court was also called to rule but it declared the petition inadmissible on grounds of lack of relevance; see Corte cost, 3 July 2013 (entered 18 July 2013), no. 214, [2013] Cass. pen. 4394.

51 Armando Macrillò, 'La riparazione per l'ingiusta detenzione cautelare', in Lupária (n 2) 792.

52 The panel is composed of three judges.

entered an appearance or when, despite entering an appearance, it has not challenged the application it cannot be considered a losing party and, therefore, cannot be ordered to reimburse court fees.[53]

Under Article 646, para 3 CCP, the court order must be notified to the public prosecutor and served on all interested parties, who, within 15 days of when the notice of entry of order was notified or served (Article 585, para 1, letter a) CCP), may lodge an appeal with the Court of Cassation. The decision of the Court of Cassation is final.

4.4 The criteria for determining the amount of compensation

The court order admitting the application for remedy, as noted, must also quantify the amount to be awarded by way of compensation in favour of the applicant[54] and specify the criteria used to calculate that amount.

The assessment of the judge – by reason of the difficulty in proving the precise *quantum* of the harm suffered by the person wrongfully detained or convicted – is not grounded on the objective criteria typically used to quantify compensation for damages. This approach rests on two arguments. The first concerns the nature of this type of remedy, the prevailing interpretation of which, as observed, tends to include it in the category of liability for lawful acts or, at the most, in a separate third category; it would, on the contrary, be difficult to include it in the category of liability for civil wrongs.[55] The second argument rests directly on the provisions of the Italian CCP on compensation for wrongful detention under Article 314, para 1 CCP, which expressly states that the interested person is entitled to equitable compensation, namely on the basis of equitable considerations, which take account, through a global evaluation, of all the elements necessary to assess the injury. This criterion – albeit expressly mentioned only in relation to cases of wrongful detention on remand – also applies to miscarriages of justice in the strict sense (Article 643 CCP),[56] coherently with the considerations underlying the preliminary project to the code of criminal procedure, whereby, despite a number of subsequent amendments, the criteria for the monetary quantification of the injury was in any case grounded on equitable principles.[57]

53 See, *inter alia*, Cass pen, sez. IV, 21 December 2018 (entered 7 February 2019), no. 5923, in *Dejure*. At the same time, if the application for compensation is not admitted the public administration cannot obtain the reimbursement of court fees if it has not entered an appearance or challenged said application.

54 Under Article 643, para 2 CCP the state redresses by awarding an amount or, under some circumstances, by setting a life annuity plan. Also, the beneficiary may, at his/her request, be placed in an institution at the state's expenses (e.g. care home or hospital).

55 See above section 3.

56 In these terms Troisi (n 4) 291ff; D'Aiuto (n 10) 742. It seems that of a contrary opinion is Turco (n 2) 102.

57 See Ministero della Giustizia, *Relazioni al progetto preliminare e al testo definitivo del codice di procedura penale* (GU no. 250, Ordinary Supplement no. 93, 24 October 1998). Some have highlighted how the absence of an explicit reference to equitable

The necessary resort to an equitable assessment also allows the assertion that, with specific reference to wrongful detention on remand, the court must take into consideration – despite Article 314 CCP containing no mention thereof – the duration of the wrongful detention, together with any personal and family-related consequences suffered.[58] The latter element, on the contrary, is expressly provided for in Article 643 CCP together with the duration of the sentence served.[59] Therefore, the compensation for wrongful conviction aims, on the one hand, at compensating personal and family-related consequences suffered, namely the suffering caused by imprisonment, the moral suffering caused by the injustice of the sentence, the damage caused to reputation and social life and any mental illness of family members caused by the situation,[60] on the other hand, it aims at compensating the limitation of personal liberty caused by the wrongful conviction.[61]

In the end, the main criteria to be used by the court is equity, in such a way to make an overall assessment of the pecuniary[62] and non-pecuniary[63] damage suffered by the interested party following an unlawful conviction, apart from a mere arithmetical calculation.[64] Clearly, the court shall provide an adequate and

compensation in the definitive wording of the CCP cannot be considered as a fortuity but as a specific legislative choice. Therefore, the *voluntas legis* would be aimed at differentiating the criteria for determining the amount of compensation, on the one hand, in the case of wrongful detention on the basis of the judge's *aequitas* and, on the other hand, in the case of wrongful conviction on the basis of objective assessment criteria typically used for the determination of pecuniary and non-pecuniary damages in the 'tort liability' model. See Troisi (n 4) 292ff; Elga Turco, 'Ingiusta detenzione e riparazione del danno esistenziale' (2008) Cass. pen. 4735, 4740.

58 This approach is validated by the generic reference in Article 315, para 3 CCP to the statutory rules on wrongful conviction, which must therefore be applied, *mutatis mutandis*, in their entirety.

59 See Balsamo (n 5) 691–692.

60 D'Aiuto (n 10) 741.

61 *Ibid.*, where the author underlines how the scope of compensation is extended to any judgment served: not only with regards to imprisonment but also in consideration of the duration of any accessory penalties or alternative measures to imprisonment and, by express legislative provision, to any form of internment, whether as an alternative to prison or as a security measure.

62 Actual loss (e.g. liability for damages, bankruptcy etc.) and loss of profits (e.g. failure to conclude contracts, disqualification from a profession or art, dismissal, loss of business or further prospects of career and study etc.).

63 Any type of moral, biological and existential damage resulting from the unfair conviction.

64 However, this does not mean that the court is prevented from resorting to compensatory criteria that limit its discretion. See Cass pen, sez. IV, 25 November 2003 (entered 22 January 2004), no. 2050, [2004] Giur. it. 1025. For further case law, see in general (even if referred to compensation for wrongful detention) Cass pen, sez. un., 9 May 2001 (entered 14 June 2001), no. 24287, [2001] Cass. pen. 2674; Cass pen, sez. III, 29 April 2003 (entered 2 July 2003), no. 28334, [2004] Cass. pen. 3329; and, more recently, Cass pen, sez. III, 1 April 2014 (entered 9 July 2014), no. 29965, in *Dejure*; Cass pen, sez. IV, 27 June 2019 (entered 12 July 2019), no. 30649, in *Dejure*.

logically congruous statement of reasons in relation to the specific case, as a corrective to the arbitrariness inherent in the judge's equitable intervention.[65]

5 Conclusions

In the face of the inherently fallacious nature of judging, the Italian criminal legal system provides for two main remedies against miscarriages of justice *lato sensu*: one aiming at compensating someone who has been wrongfully detained during criminal proceedings, the other covering cases of wrongful conviction. Data show that 99.4 per cent of the total cases of miscarriage of justice and 89 per cent of the total incurred compensation costs for the state in 2019 concerned cases of wrongful detention on remand.[66] Nevertheless, the miscarriages of justice *stricto sensu*, even if not characterised by large numbers, cannot be disregarded. Accordingly, the irreparable consequences resulting from a wrongful conviction represent one of the main tragedies of our criminal justice system and affect citizens' trust in the administration of justice.

From this perspective, the analysis carried out has shown how this compensation scheme represents a *post iudicatum* remedy provided for in the Italian legal system to alleviate the consequences of a wrongful conviction and as a necessary reaction to the unjust violation of the fundamental rights to dignity and personal freedom.[67]

In particular, on the basis of the constitutional and supranational principles examined, among the different theories developed on the legal nature of the remedy, the most appropriate one relies on its solidaristic purpose that is pursued through the transferral of the risk of ascertaining the miscarriage of justice from the individual to the entire community. This is particularly reflected in the approach adopted by case law with regard to the criteria for determining the amount of compensation, which, as examined, is mainly based on equity and entrusted to the court's overall assessment of damage – pecuniary and non-pecuniary – suffered by the wrongfully convicted individual.

Nevertheless, it is precisely in case law that the most problematic aspect of the right of compensation in the case of wrongful conviction has emerged. As observed, indeed, jurisprudence has adopted a broad notion of the concepts of malice and gross negligence, envisaged in the Italian criminal procedure code as bars to compensation for the wrongfully convicted, by including in the latter concept conduct committed before knowledge of a pending proceeding or covered by the right of defence. This case law approach risks seriously affecting the

65 See, *inter alia*, Cass pen, sez. III, 10 February 2004 (entered 18 May 2004), no. 23211, Rv. 229289; Cass pen, sez. IV, 3 June 1998 (entered 13 July 1998), no. 1744, Rv. 211646; more recently, on compensation for wrongful detention, Cass pen, sez. IV, 6 December 2016 (entered 10 February 2017), no. 6394, Rv. 269077; Cass pen, sez. IV, 2 July 2021 (entered 16 July 2021), no. 27474, Rv. 281513.

66 Lattanzi and Maimone, 'Ingiusta detenzione in Italia, un'analisi' (n 8) 963–964; Corte dei conti (n 7) 43.

67 D'Aiuto (n 10) 723.

concrete functioning of the legal institute with unacceptable consequences for people who have already been the victim of a wrongful conviction.

In this sense, the recent legislative intervention on Article 314 CCP goes in the right direction establishing that the defendant's exercise of his/her right to remain silent does not affect his/her right to compensation for wrongful detention on remand.[68] Accordingly, case law seems to have already correctly interpreted such new provision.[69]

Bibliography

Balsamo A, 'Riparazione per ingiusta detenzione' in Scalfati A (ed), *Prove e misure cautelari. Le misure cautelari*, in Spangher G (directed by), Trattato di procedura penale (vol. II, Utet 2008)

Barile P, *Diritti dell'uomo e libertà fondamentali* (Il Mulino 1984)

Caianiello M, 'La riapertura del processo ex art. 625 bis c.p.p. a seguito di condanna della Corte europea dei diritti dell'uomo' (2009) *Cass. pen.* 1465

Coppetta MG, 'Riparazione per l'ingiusta detenzione: una declaratoria di incostituzionalità dirompente?' (2008) *Giur. cost.* 2476

Corte dei conti, *Equa riparazione per ingiusta detenzione ed errori giudiziari* (Delib. n. 15/2021/G, 16 September 2021)

D'Aiuto M, 'La riparazione dell'errore giudiziario', in Lupária Donati L (ed), *L'errore giudiziario* (Giuffrè 2021)

Di Bitonto ML, 'L'errore giudiziario nelle carte dei diritti fondamentali in Europa' in Lupária Donati L (ed), *L'errore giudiziario* (Giuffrè 2021)

Di Palma EMT, 'Dolo e colpa grave, cause ostative al sorgere del diritto soggettivo alla riparazione per ingiusta detenzione' (1997) *Cass. pen.* 814

Dig. disc. pen. (4th edn, 1997), vol XII

Dig. disc. pen. (V aggiornamento, 2010), 489

Felicioni P, 'Condizioni ostative al diritto alla riparazione per ingiusta detenzione ed esercizio del diritto di difesa: spunti problematici' (1996) *Cass. pen.* 2156

Gialuz M, *Il ricorso straordinario per cassazione* (Giuffrè 2005)

Johnson DT, *The culture of capital punishment in Japan* (Palgrave Macmillan 2020)

Knoops GJA, *Redressing miscarriages of justice: practice and procedure in national and international criminal law cases* (Brill 2007)

Lanza V, 'Ingiusta detenzione, ogni anno oltre duecento invisibili' (*Il Riformista*, 9 January 2022) <www.ilriformista.it>

Lattanzi B and Maimone V, 'Ingiusta detenzione in Italia, un'analisi', in Lupária Donati L (ed), *L'errore giudiziario* (Giuffrè 2021)

Lattanzi B and Maimone V, 'Innocenti e invisibili: quante vittime della giustizia sfuggono alle statistiche' (errorigiudiziari.com, 4 October 2021) <www.errorigiudiziari.com>

Lattanzi B and Maimone V, 'Errori giudiziari e ingiusta detenzione, tutti gli ultimi dati aggiornati' (errorigiudiziari.com, 25 March 2022) <www.errorigiudiziari.com>

Macrillò A, 'La riparazione per l'ingiusta detenzione cautelare', in Lupária Donati L (ed), *L'errore giudiziario* (Giuffrè 2021)

68 See Article 4, para 1, letter b) Legislative Decree 8 November 2021, no. 188.

69 Cass pen, sez. IV, 8 February 2022 (entered 15 March 2022), no. 8616 (n 43).

Ministero della Giustizia, *Misure cautelari personali e riparazione per ingiusta detenzione: dati anno 2021. Relazione al Parlamento ex L. 16 aprile 2015, n. 47* (Update April 2022)

Ministero della Giustizia, *Relazioni al progetto preliminare e al testo definitivo del codice di procedura penale* (GU no. 250, Ordinary Supplement no. 93, 24 October 1998)

Mirandola S, 'Un'altra camera di consiglio destinata a schiudersi' (2013) *Cass. pen.* 4043

Montaldi A, 'Riparazione per l'ingiusta detenzione', in Chiavario M (coordinated by), *Commento al nuovo codice di procedure penale* (Utet 1990)

Redlich AD and Petrila J (eds), 'Special issue: The age of innocence: Miscarriages of justice in the 21st Century' (2009) 27 *Behav. Sci. & L.* 297

Romano M, 'Ambiti operativi della riparazione per ingiusta detenzione alla luce delle novità giurisprudenziali' (2010) *Dir. pen. proc.* 1496

Ronald Huff C and Killias M (eds), *Wrongful convictions: international perspectives on miscarriages of justice* (Temple University Press 2008)

Ronald Huff C and Killias M (eds *Wrongful convictions and miscarriages of justice. Causes and remedies in North American and European criminal justice systems* (Routledge 2013)

Spagnolo P, 'La riparazione per ingiusta detenzione: verso una tutela sostanziale del diritto alla libertà personale' (2017) 11 *La legislazione penale* <www.lalegislazionepenale.eu>

Tonini P, *Manuale di procedura penale* (Giuffrè 2019)

Troisi P, *L'errore giudiziario tra garanzie costituzionali e sistema processuale* (Cedam 2011)

Turco E, *L'equa riparazione tra errore giudiziario e ingiusta detenzione* (Giuffrè 2007)

Turco E, 'Ingiusta detenzione e riparazione del danno esistenziale' (2008) *Cass. pen.* 4735

Turco E, 'Riparazione per l'ingiusta detenzione', in Giarda A and Spangher G (eds), *Codice di procedura penale commentato* (Wolters Kluwer 2017)

Table of cases

Cass pen, sez. un., 13 December 1995 (entered 9 February 1996), no. 43, [1996] Cass. pen. 2146;

Cass pen, sez. IV, 3 June 1998 (entered 13 July 1998), no. 1744, Rv. 211646;

Cass pen, sez. un., 9 May 2001 (entered 14 June 2001), no. 24287, [2001] Cass. pen. 2674;

Cass pen, sez. un., 26 June 2002 (entered 15 October 2002), no. 34559, [2003] Cass. pen. 57;

Cass pen, sez. III, 29 April 2003 (entered 2 July 2003), no. 28334, [2004] Cass. pen. 3329;

Cass pen, sez. IV, 25 November 2003 (entered 22 January 2004), no. 2050, [2004] Giur. it. 1025;

Cass pen, sez. III, 10 February 2004 (entered 18 May 2004), no. 23211, Rv. 229289;

Cass pen, sez. III, 17 February 2005 (entered 14 April 2005), no. 13714, [2006] Cass. pen. 3737;

Cass pen, sez. IV, 10 June 2008 (entered 29 October 2008), no. 40291, Rv. 242755;

Cass pen, sez. un., 30 October 2008 (entered 29 January 2009), no. 4187, [2009] Resp. civ. prev. 777;

Cass pen, sez. IV, 3 June 2010 (entered 24 September 2010), no. 34656, Rv. 248074;

Cass pen, sez. IV, 17 November 2011 (entered 23 February 2012), no. 7296, Rv. 251928;

Cass pen, sez. un., 28 November 2013 (entered 24 December 2013), no. 51779, [2014] Dir. giust.;
Cass pen, sez. III, 1 April 2014 (entered 9 July 2014), no. 29965, in *Dejure*;
Cass pen, sez. IV, 23 October 2015, no. 46423, Rv. 265287;
Cass pen, sez. IV, 6 December 2016 (entered 10 February 2017), no. 6394, Rv 269077;
Cass pen, sez. IV, 21 December 2018 (entered 7 February 2019), no. 5923, in *Dejure*;
Cass pen, sez. IV, 6 February 2019 (entered 15 May 2019), no. 20845, in *Dejure*;
Cass pen, sez. IV, 27 June 2019 (entered 12 July 2019), no. 30649, in *Dejure*;
Cass pen, sez. IV, 2 July 2021 (entered 16 September 2021), no. 34367, in *Dejure*;
Cass pen, sez. IV, 2 July 2021 (entered 16 July 2021), no. 27474, Rv. 281513;
Cass pen, sez. IV, 8 February 2022 (entered 15 March 2022), no. 8616, in *Dejure*;
Corte cost, 15 January 1969 (entered 24 January 1969), no. 1, in *Dejure*;
Corte cost, 18 July 1996 (entered 25 July 1996), no. 310, [1996] Giur. cost. 2557;
Corte cost, 13 December 2004 (entered 23 December 2004), no. 413, [2005] Cass. pen. 1551;
Corte cost, 11 June 2008 (entered 20 June 2008), no. 219, [2008] Giur. cost. 2456;
Corte cost, 3 July 2013 (entered 18 July 2013), no. 214, [2013] Cass. pen. 4394;
Lorenzetti v. Italy, App no. 32075/09 (ECtHR, 10 April 2012).

4 Compensation for wrongful convictions in Spain

Juan Carlos Ortiz-Pradillo

1 Origins and development of compensation for wrongful conviction

The introduction and regulation of compensation for wrongful conviction mechanisms in Spain is directly related to the constitutional dimension of fundamental rights and how to compensate interferences in the core content of them, specifically when some interferences produce damage.

The current notion of the *social rule of law* and the consequent substantial consideration of fundamental rights are the fruit of a legal tradition that assumes, broadly speaking, that a State of Law (protector of individual rights) is a social State that develops public policies for the benefit of the common good, and this requires that the individual must bear certain sacrifices in favour of that common good. The legislator may occasionally deprive individuals of some element of that original content or even all the original content of their fundamental right when there are imperative circumstances that so require. But these *legitimate sacrifices* do not prevent the State from compensating if damage has occurred.

2 Sources of law regulating compensation for wrongful conviction

The rule of law proclaimed in the Spanish Constitution[1] (CE) requires that the public authorities adapt their actions to two essential principles: the principle of legality and that of patrimonial responsibility. As stated in Article 9.3 CE,

> The Constitution guarantees the principle of legality, the hierarchy of legal provisions, the publicity of legal statutes, the non-retroactivity of punitive provisions that are not favourable to or restrictive of individual rights, the certainty that the rule of law shall prevail, the accountability of public authorities, and the prohibition of arbitrary action of public authorities.

According to such premise, we must consider that it is the Constitution itself that recognises that the public authorities are subject to patrimonial responsibility. Specifically, it is regulated in Article 106 CE, which states the following:

1 *Constitución Española* (hereinafter, CE). *Spanish Official Journal* No. 311 29 December 1978. Permalink ELI: https://www.boe.es/eli/es/c/1978/12/27/(1)/con.

DOI: 10.4324/9781003229414-5

> 1. The Courts shall check the power to issue regulations and ensure that the rule of law prevails in administrative action, and that the latter is subordinated to the ends which justify it. 2. Private individuals shall, under the terms laid down by law, be entitled to compensation for any harm they may suffer in any of their property and rights, except in cases of force majeure, whenever such harm is the result of the operation of public services.

Therefore, what this article specifies is that if any damage to individuals occurs due to the actions of the public authorities, it must be compensated.

However, compensation in connection with actions by the administration of justice does not properly follow the rules of Article 106 CE, but the rules of Article 121 CE. The patrimonial responsibility of the State for the functioning of the administration of justice is regulated in Article 121 CE and in Articles 292 to 296 LOPJ.[2] Through it, compensation for damage that individuals may suffer unjustly because of actions or omissions of the courts is guaranteed. Article 121 CE states:

> Damages caused by judicial error as well as those arising from irregularities (irregular functioning) in the administration of justice shall give rise to a right to compensation by the State, in accordance with the law.

The expression 'in accordance with the law' is interpreted as meaning that Article 121 CE enshrines a right of legal configuration: it is not a fundamental right with essential and mandatory content that must be respected by the legislator, but it is a right that must be legally developed, so that the legislator acquires the capacity to regulate and develop the corresponding content on what is declared by the constituent power in Article 121 CE. In fact, the current legislation regulates three grounds or reasons for patrimonial liability of the State: a) judicial error, b) irregular functioning of administration of justice and c) unfair detention on remand (preventive custody).

This last ground is the most frequently applied and controversial in practice, and it was introduced in the LOPJ (Article 294) without being expressly included in the Constitution. Article 121 CE is completed and developed in the law, specifically in the LOPJ (Articles 292 and following), which establish the different ways by which the patrimonial responsibility of the State for the jurisdictional activity can be compensated.

3 Grounds for compensation for wrongful conviction

*3.1 Judicial error [*error judicial*] (Art. 292 LOPJ)*

The first ground of patrimonial liability of the State is judicial error. As we will see, pecuniary and non-pecuniary damage occasioned by judges and magistrates in the

2 Ley Orgánica 6/1985, de 1 de julio, del Poder Judicial (Organic Law of the Judiciary. Hereinafter, LOPJ).

exercise of their duties will give rise, where applicable, to State responsibility for a judicial error or the abnormal functioning of the administration of justice. However, under no circumstances may the injured parties bring actions against them directly.

The constitutional design of the State liability for errors of the public administration (and the administration of justice is part of the public administration) must be interpreted as what it is: a responsibility of the State and not a responsibility of the specific judge or magistrate causing the damage. This point is extremely important: anyone who considers that he/she has suffered damage caused by judges and magistrates in the exercise of their jurisdictional performance, far from lacking the means to obtain compensation, can stake their claim against the State.

The entry into force of the CE 1978, with its new guarantee of State liability for damage caused by judicial error or abnormal functioning of the administration of justice, did not mean the disappearance of the direct civil liability of the judge or magistrate, legally provided for in the legislation of 1870. This continued to exist – at least theoretically – in the Spanish system because the original version of the LOPJ of 1985 maintained this possibility in its Articles 411 to 413, conditioning it on the existence of 'intent or fault' of the judge or magistrate, but its application in practice was non-existent. The delivery of justice is the responsibility of the State, and therefore it is necessary to claim against the State and not against the judges. The LOPJ was amended in 2015 and the legislator repealed Articles 411 to 413 LOPJ, thus eliminating the direct civil liability of judges and magistrates.

The concept of 'judicial error' is very restrictive. In general terms, this must be a manifest, self-evident or stark mistake on the part of the judicial body. The Supreme Court has consistently and repeatedly held that the process for the recognition of a judicial error regulated in Article 293 LOPJ, as a result of the mandate contained in Article 121 CE, is not a third instance or a cassation 'in which the appellant may insist, before another Court, once again, on the criterion and position that was already rejected and rejected previously', but that this can only be successfully urged when the judicial body has made a mistake 'manifest and clear in the fixing of the facts or in the interpretation or application of the Law'.[3]

Not every possible mistake can be conceptualised as a ***judicial error***. This classification must be reserved for qualified and special cases in which a 'patent', 'indubitable', 'incontestable', 'flagrant' error is noted in the judicial decision, which has provoked 'illogical, irrational, grotesque or absurd factual or legal conclusions'. It also applies when the judicial body proceeds to interpret or apply the law and acts openly outside the legal channels, making an application of the law based on non-existent norms or understood out of all sense (manifestly illegal). In contrast, there is no judicial error 'when the Court maintains a rational and explainable criterion within the rules of legal hermeneutics', 'nor in the case of interpretations of the rule that, rightly or wrongly, obey a logical process'. In other words, this exceptional procedure cannot attack 'conclusions that are not

3 Supreme Court Judgment (Administrative Bench) 15 October 2021 Cassation No. 36/2020.

illogical or irrational', given that 'the declaration of judicial error does not try to correct a mistake, but the gross negligence of the judge'.[4]

According to Article 296.2 LOPJ, if the damage is the result of wilful misconduct or gross negligence on the part of the judge or magistrate, the State may compensate the injured party and, after that, it may demand, via administrative channels (administrative proceedings), that the responsible judge or magistrate reimburse the payment that was made, notwithstanding any disciplinary responsibility that might have been incurred, in accordance with the stipulations of this law.

Article 36 Law on the Legal Regime of the Public Sector (hereinafter, LRJSP)[5] determines the responsibility of the authorities and personnel for the service of the public administrations. Individuals shall directly require the public administration to pay compensation for the damage caused by the authorities and personnel of the service of the public authorities. And the administration concerned, where it has indemnified the injured, shall require its service or organ to be responsible for the liability of the injured party, or for negligence or serious negligence, prior to the corresponding procedure.

The administration concerned is the General Council of the Judiciary.[6] And the procedure for the requirement of liability of judges and magistrates, due to wilful misconduct or gross negligence, is ruled under the general provisions of the Law on the Common Administrative Procedure of the Public Administrations.[7]

Article 36 LRJSP also says that:

> For the requirement of such liability and, where appropriate, for quantification, the following criteria shall be weighted among others: the harmful outcome produced, the degree of culpability, the professional responsibility of the staff at the service of public administrations and their relationship with the production of the harmful outcome.

4 Supreme Court Judgments (Administrative Bench) 27 March 2006 Cassation No. 6/2004; 20 June 2006 Cassation No. 13/2004; 15 January 2007 Cassation No. 17/2004; 12 March 2007 Cassation No. 18/2004; 30 April 2008 Cassation No. 7/2006; 9 July 2008 Cassation No. 6/2007.

5 *Ley 40/2015, de 1 de octubre, del régimen legal del sector público* (Law on the Legal Regime of the Public Sector (hereinafter, LRJSP)). *Spanish Official Journal* (BOE) No. 236, 2 October 2015. Permalink ELI: https://www.boe.es/eli/es/l/2015/10/01/40/con.

6 The General Council of the Judiciary is a constitutional organ (ruled under the CE and LOPJ) with the role of governing the judiciary: the formation, modus operandi and governance of the courts and tribunals, the legal statute for tenured judges and magistrates and for the personnel in the employ of the judicial administration, the system of incompatibilities governing members of the General Council of the Judiciary and their functions, particularly with regard to appointments, promotions, inspections and the disciplinary system.

7 *Ley 39/2015, de 1 de octubre, del procedimiento administrativo común de las Administraciones Públicas* (Law on the Common Administrative Procedure of the Public Administrations (hereinafter, LPAC)). *Spanish Official Journal* (BOE) No. 236, 2 October 2015. Permalink ELI: https://www.boe.es/eli/es/l/2015/10/01/39/con.

And Article 296.2 LOPJ also specifies the following criteria: 'The detrimental result occasioned and the existence or otherwise of intent.'

*3.2 Irregular functioning of administration of justice [*funcionamiento anormal de la administración de justicia*] (Art. 292 LOPJ)*

The other legal ground for claiming compensation from the public administration for damage caused by the administration of justice is the irregular functioning of the legal services included in the structure of the administration of justice. Unlike these manifest and self-evident errors of the court (judging staff like judges and magistrates), the responsibility of the State for the irregular functioning of the administration of justice is the usual way to claim for compensation when, for example, there are undue delays in the procedure, loss or damage to goods in the custody of judicial bodies, suicide of a prisoner within a penitentiary institution, etc.

The main difference between the first ground (judicial error) and this second is that the concept of 'irregular functioning of the administration of justice' usually refers to the activity or omissions and failures of the judicial system in general, and not exclusively of judges and magistrates.[8]

In general, 'irregular functioning' is understood as any defect in the performance of the courts or tribunals, conceived as an organic complex in which different people, services, means and activities are integrated. The elements that must be given in order to be able to assess the patrimonial responsibility of the State, when the title of imputation is the irregular functioning of the administration of justice, are the following:

a The existence of effective, individualised and economically assessable damage.
b The existence of an irregular functioning of the administration of justice.
c The concurrence of the appropriate causal relationship between the operation or omission of the administration of justice and the damage caused in such a way that it appears as a consequence of it and therefore is attributable to the administration.
d The exercise of the claim action within a period of one year from the date of the production of the damage.

The purpose of this second legal ground is to give full effect to the right to equality in the provision of public services that falls within the competence of the public administration, since if a particular citizen is damaged by the provision of a public service, he/she must be compensated for the sacrifice that is caused to him.

In any case, the damage must be unlawful, in the sense that the citizen does not have the duty to bear it. The patrimonial liability for the functioning of the

8 Supreme Court Judgment (Civil Bench) 19 April 2022 Cassation No. 14/2021: 'only a judicial decision may be the subject of the procedure for declaring a judicial error. The erroneous actions and decisions of the court clerks may be included in the abnormal functioning of the administration of justice, in order to demand compensation for the damages suffered, but they cannot be classified as a judicial error insofar as they do not respond to the exercise of jurisdictional activity'.

administration of justice is not an objective liability defined exclusively by the wrongfulness of the damage. An irregularity is required in its functioning differentiated from the exercise of judicial power.[9]

Finally, the LOPJ remarks in both cases (judicial error or irregular functioning) that

> under no circumstances compensation will be awarded when the legal error or the irregular functioning of the justice was caused by wilful or unlawful conduct by the affected party (Art. 295 LOPJ) and that revocation or annulment of judicial decisions does not entail per se a right to compensation.
>
> (Art. 292.3 LOPJ)

*3.3 Unfair detention on remand [*prisión provisional indebida*] (Art. 294 LOPJ)*

This is the most controversial and criticised case for compensation. It applies to those who have been placed in detention on remand and then been acquitted or exonerated as not guilty, but in these concrete situations:

- Non-existence of the facts (also called 'objective non-existence'). This includes both absence of the facts or the absence of criminal dimension of the facts (the act does not constitute a crime).
- A non-suit writ or acquittal (*sobreseimiento,* withdrawal of the case) due to a lack of evidence against the defendant.

Compensation for unfair detention on remand is considered a special case of the patrimonial responsibility of the State regarding the administration of justice. In the case of judicial error, the claim must be preceded by a specific judicial decision that expressly recognises the error (Art. 293.1 LOPJ). However, in the case of unfair detention on remand, the injured party can directly address his compensation request to the Ministry of Justice so that the claim is processed through administrative channels (Art. 294.2 LOPJ), without the need for a judicial decision expressly declaring the existence of such an error. It is enough to have a judicial decision from which the inadmissibility of that precautionary measure is clearly deduced (not necessarily due to the non-existence of the imputed facts) since it is understood that the criminal process itself has evidenced the existence of the judicial error, so that another declaration to that effect is no longer necessary.

In this third case of patrimonial liability of administration, Spanish jurisprudence has played a very important role.[10] Until 2010, the courts had interpreted Article

9 Supreme Court Judgment (Administrative Bench) 28 September 2020 Cassation No. 123/2020.

10 Lucía Domínguez Ruiz, 'Indemnización por prisión preventiva injusta: evolución del artículo 294.1 de la LOPJ a la luz de la jurisprudencia nacional y europea' (2020) 2 *Justicia: Revista de Derecho Procesal*, 309–341.

294 LOPJ fairly broadly and considered that this provision protected the case of the so-called 'subjective non-existence' (the proof of non-participation in the facts of the person who has suffered the detention on remand), since it showed the lack of relationship of the subject with the imputed fact from which the adoption of the provisional detention measure derives. Nevertheless, the jurisprudence excluded from the application of Article 294 LOPJ the case of acquittal for lack of evidence of the participation of the subject in the commission of the criminal act.

However, and after two important judgments of the European Court of Human Rights (ECtHR)[11] in which the European court questioned whether the Spanish judicial authorities made a double and different interpretation of the same legal precept, the Supreme Court abandoned this extensive interpretation of Article 294 LOPJ and changed to a narrow and strict interpretation of it, in the literal sense of its terms, limiting its scope to the cases of claims of patrimonial responsibility with support in acquittal or final judgment for non-existence of the imputed fact. After the ECtHR *Tendam v. Spain* of 13 July 2010, the Supreme Court jurisprudence changed to a very narrow interpretation and declared that Article 294 LOPJ provides for compensation to those who have been remanded in custody and finally acquitted *only in the case of* non-existence of the facts he/she was charged with or when the judicial sentence declared that the defendant was not the perpetrator. That is, when it has been proved that someone else was the perpetrator or participated in the criminal action in another way,[12] but Article 294 LOPJ would not apply when the defendant was acquitted or declared innocent due to lack of evidence.

Fortunately, this rigorous and literal interpretation of Article 294 LOPJ has been modified based on a new doctrine of the Spanish Constitutional Court, which in 2019 declared the partial unconstitutionality of the literal wording of said Article 294 LOPJ. In its Judgment No. 8/2017, of 19 January 2017,[13] the Constitutional Court declared that the refusal to compensate when the accused had been acquitted by application of the principle *in dubio pro reo* violates the right to the presumption of innocence, since it emits suspicions about the guilt of the appellant and uses the reference to said right as an integrating element of the relationship of chance of the damage produced in the field of patrimonial responsibility, which is considered inappropriate, since in order to determine whether or not it concurs with the responsibility of the administration of justice for detention on remand, it cannot use arguments that directly or indirectly affect the presumption of innocence.

But it was not until Judgment No. 85/2019, of 19 June 2019,[14] that it expressly declared the unconstitutionality of two expressions of Article 294 LOPJ

11 *Puig Panella v. Spain* App no 1483/02 (ECtHR 25 April 2006) and *Tendam v. Spain* App no 25720/05 (ECtHR 13 July 2010).

12 Lorena Bachmaier Winter, Antonio del Moral García, *Criminal Law in Spain* (2nd edn, Wolters Kluwer, 2012) 273.

13 Constitutional Court Judgment 8/2017 of 19 January 2017 Appeal (*Amparo*) No. 2341–2012. *Spanish Official Journal* (BOE) No. 46, 23 January 2017.

14 Constitutional Court Judgment 85/2019 of 19 June 2019 Appeal (*Amparo*) No. 4314–2018. *Spanish Official Journal* (BOE) No. 177, 25 July 2019.

that should be eliminated: 'for non-existence of the imputed fact' and 'for this same cause' of Article 294.1 LOPJ.

The nullity of these two expressions has forced the Spanish courts to eliminate the differentiation between acquittal for objective non-existence and for subjective non-existence. Since this judgment of the Constitutional Court, any case of preventive detention followed by acquittal, including acquittal for lack of evidence or *in dubio pro reo,* must be considered as a case of compensation covered by Article 294 LOPJ.

The Supreme Court changed its jurisprudence and, at end of 2019, expressly applied the new doctrine of the Constitutional Court 'in a framework of congruence with the general theory of civil liability and with the warnings of material and temporal content contained in the last two paragraphs of the Constitutional Court Judgment 85/2019, as well as in those that have followed'.[15]

4 Procedure for claiming compensation

4.1 Administrative procedure

To claim compensation for any of the three cases established in the LOPJ, an application must be submitted by the affected person to the Ministry of Justice, through an administrative procedure in accordance with the Law on the Common Administrative Procedure of the Public Administrations (LPAC).

The procedure is not initiated *ex officio*, so it is required at the request of the interested party. The administrative procedure formalities shall be in accordance with the regulations for State patrimonial liability (Articles 66 and following LPAC). According to Article 66.1 LPAC, the application must contain:

- a Name and surnames of the interested party and, if applicable, of the person who represents him.
- b Identification of the electronic means, or in its absence physical place in which it wishes that the notification is practiced. In addition, interested parties may provide their email address and/or electronic device for the public administrations to notify them of the sending or making available of the notification.
- c Facts, reasons and petition claims in which the request is clearly specified. Moreover, the application must be accompanied by all allegations, documents and information deemed appropriate or any other means of proof, to certify the right to compensation and the causal relationship between the damage and the functioning of the public service.
- d Place and date.
- e Signature of the applicant or accreditation of the authenticity of his will expressed by any means.
- f Organ, centre or administrative unit to which it is addressed and its corresponding identification code.

15 See Supreme Court Judgments (Administrative Bench) No. 1348/2019, of 10 October 2019, and No. 1883/2019, of 20 December 2019.

In any case, the right to claim compensation expires one year from the date on which it could have been exercised; that is, from when the event that gave rise to the compensation occurred or the damaging effect was apparent. In the case of judicial error, the period shall begin from the date on which the error was declared by a specific judicial judgment; in the case of irregular functioning of the administration of justice, it begins from the time the damage claimed took place; and in the case of unfair detention on remand, from the date of the final acquittal or dismissal.

The administrative procedure includes the hearing of the interested party, but it can be waived if the applicant expresses his decision not to make claims or to provide new documents or justifications (Art. 82 LPAC). According to Article 91 LPAC, the resolution in the procedures in matters of patrimonial liability must declare the existence or otherwise of the causal link between the operation of the public service and the injury and, where appropriate, the assessment of the damage caused, the amount and the manner of the compensation, where appropriate, in accordance with the criteria to be calculated and paid out in accordance with Article 34 LRJSP.[16]

The resolution passed in the procedure at the Ministry ends the administrative process. If the express resolution has not been passed six months after the start of the procedure, the silence of the administration is considered negative: the request for compensation is rejected (Art. 91.3 LPAC). The party may, thus, appeal at the administrative bench of the jurisdiction – concretely, at the administrative chamber of the National Court.[17]

The applicant must also calculate the amount of compensation with a concrete economic assessment of the liability, and he/she is bound by the request made administratively. Nevertheless, the applicant can modify the amount made in his/her initial administrative request and add new and supervening circumstances that aggravate the harmful consequences (for instance, worsening of an illness contracted in prison). In any case, the passing of time is not a reason to request an increase in the sum.

16 Article 34.2 LRJSP says: 'Compensation shall be calculated on the basis of the assessment criteria laid down in the tax legislation, the compulsory expropriation and other applicable rules, with the prevailing market valuations being weighted, where appropriate. In cases of death or bodily injury, the assessment included in the scales of the existing rules on compulsory insurance and social security may be taken as a reference.' The legal criteria in the case of 'bodily injury' have been applied to State liability for wrongful conviction as 'non-pecuniary loss'. So, public administrations and courts of justice use the criteria and amounts ruled under Law 35/2015, of 22 September, Reforming the System for the Assessment of Damages Caused to People in Traffic Accidents. *Ley 35/2015, de 22 de septiembre, de reforma del sistema para la valoración de los daños y perjuicios causados a las personas en accidentes de circulación. Spanish Official Journal* «BOE) No. 228, 23 September 2015. Permalink ELI: https://www.boe.es/eli/es/l/2015/09/22/35. See Section 6.

17 The National Court (Audiencia Nacional) is not the Supreme Court. It is a court with three chambers (Criminal, Administrative and Labour). The administrative chamber competences are ruled by Article 66 LOPJ (for instance, administrative appeals against legal provisions and acts by ministers and state secretaries).

4.2 Specialities of the procedure for claiming compensation in case of judicial error

Firstly, and before requesting the compensation in the administrative process, the applicant needs a specific judicial decision (*title*) that expressly recognises the existence of the error. If the decision that is considered a judicial error is not final (*res judicata*), the affected party must use the legal remedies. A declaration of judicial error will not be possible against a judgment which is still subject to further appeals or remedies according to the legal system (Art. 293.1.f LOPJ). Once a judicial decision is final (*last instance* judicial decision), when no appeal or other remedy can be filed, it becomes *res judicata*, and it cannot be overruled. Then, the applicant can request the declaration of the judicial error from the Supreme Court Bench (Chamber) corresponding to the same jurisdiction as the body to which the error is attributed, using the *revision* remedy.

In criminal matters (wrongful conviction), the *revision* remedy is the mechanism established in Articles 954 and following of the Criminal Procedure Law[18] (LECrim). Article 954 LECrim establishes the following cases in which the revision of a criminal sentence with the effect of *res judicata* is appropriate:

a Where a person has been convicted by a final prison sentence which gave value to a document or testimony as evidence which was later declared to be false, the forced confession of the accused by violence or coercion or any other punishable act carried out by a third party, as long as these events are declared in a final decision in the criminal proceedings held for that purpose.
b Where a final criminal conviction sentencing one of the intervening magistrates or judges for the offence of malfeasance by virtue of a decision passed in the proceedings where the judgment was made whose review is claimed, without the ruling having been different.
c Where two final judgments have been passed on the same crime and accused.
d Where, after judgment, facts or evidence become known which, if they had been provided, would have determined acquittal or a less severe sentence.
e Where, after a pre-trial matter having been resolved by the criminal court, a final judgment is later passed by the non-criminal court competent to decide on the matter which is contradictory to the criminal judgment.

Once the criminal conviction has been annulled via Article 954 LECrim, the affected person can trigger the administrative procedure before the Ministry of Justice to claim for compensation. The decision of the revision remedy is the title to initiate the administrative proceedings.

Secondly, it must be pointed out that the judicial action for recognising the error must be requested, without fail, within three months of the date from which

18 The Spanish Criminal Procedure Code is the *Ley de Enjuiciamiento Criminal* (hereinafter, LECrim). Real Decreto de 14 de septiembre de 1882. *Spanish Official Journal* (Gaceta Oficial) No. 260, 17 September 1882. Permalink ELI: https://www.boe.es/eli/es/rd/1882/09/14/(1)/con.

the right could be exercised. No declaration of error may be made against a judicial decision until all appeals or legal remedies have been exhausted. Once the judicial error has been recognised by a judgment, the applicant may request compensation from the Ministry of Justice.

5 Legal aid

Article 119 of the Spanish Constitution grants legal aid to those who can demonstrate lack of sufficient financial means. That constitutional right is ruled under the Legal Aid Law (LAJG),[19] which regulates its procedure, amounts, etc. Legal aid can be claimed by Spanish citizens, nationals of other Member States of the European Union and any other foreign national with the right to legal aid in Spain if they can demonstrate insufficient means for litigation, and provided they are resident in Spain.[20]

Regardless of the existence of sufficient financial means or the nationality or residency status of the applicant, legal aid in Spain is automatically granted to:

- Victims of gender or domestic violence, human trafficking or terrorism, in any prosecutions linked to, arising from or being the consequence of their status as a victim.
- Children and adults incapacitated due to intellectual disabilities or mental health, when they have been victims of abuse or neglect.
- Any person in employment or in receipt of Spanish social security benefits pursuing or involved in employment proceedings.

Legal aid may cover the following legal costs: pre-trial legal advice, lawyer fees, court fees, costs of publishing announcements in official journals, deposits required for lodging certain appeals, experts' fees, affidavits, an 80 per cent reduction in the fees for notarial deeds and certificates from the land registry and translation and interpretation services.

In criminal matters, legal aid is available for all cases for all citizens, even foreigners, who can demonstrate insufficient means for litigation. It covers all proceedings. It includes appeals and enforcement of judgments, so it also includes the following administrative proceeding for claims of compensation for wrongful conviction.

19 *Ley 1/1996, de 10 de enero, de asistencia jurídica gratuita* (hereinafter, LAJG). Legal Aid Law 1/1996, of 10 January 1996. *Spanish Official Journal* (BOE) No. 11, 12 January. Permalink ELI: https://www.boe.es/eli/es/l/1996/01/10/1/con. Its implementing regulation is the Royal Decree 141/2021, of 9 March (*Real Decreto 141/2021, de 9 de marzo, por el que se aprueba el Reglamento de asistencia jurídica gratuita*). *Spanish Official Journal* (BOE) No. 59, of 10 March. Permalink ELI: https://www.boe.es/eli/es/rd/2021/03/09/141.

20 In immigration matters, all foreign citizens who can certify insufficient means for litigation, even if they do not reside legally in Spain, are entitled to free legal assistance in all proceedings relative to their application for asylum and the Foreigners Immigration Law, including preliminary administrative proceedings.

In order to verify that the applicant has insufficient means for litigation, the law regulates maximum incomes according to the IPREM (the Multi-Purpose Public Income Index – IPREM, as per its Spanish initials – which is established annually in the State Budget Act. In 2022, the IPREM was €579,02 per month or €8,106.28 per year in 14 payments. According to this, the maximum income of the applicant cannot exceed two and a half times the IPREM if the applicant is part of a family unit (less than four members) and three times the IPREM if the family unit comprises four or more people.

The proceeding and the application form for legal aid is processed by the legal guidance departments (*Servicio de orientación jurídica*) of the local bar association in the place where the court responsible for trying the main issue is located, or with the court of the place of residence of the applicant. People can check if they meet the requirements with an online tool at the webpage of the General Council of Spanish Bar Associations.[21]

6 Calculating the amount of compensation

On the one hand, and in the case of unfair detention on remand, Article 294.2 LOPJ says that '*Compensation will be determined considering the time they were remanded in custody and in view of the personal and family consequences.*' This is the only reference in Spanish legislation to how the authorities should calculate compensation in the case of wrongful deprivation of liberty, so one of the harshest criticisms is, indeed, the lack of an adequate legal basis for calculating the amount of compensation for the responsibility of the State.

Furthermore, the two legal criteria 'time' (period of deprivation of liberty) and 'personal and family consequences' (circumstances) are very broad and indeterminate criteria that have not been legally developed, nor are there objective tables or scales that quantify the damage. Therefore, the calculated amount differs widely from one case to another, since the authorities take refuge in the idea of the exceptionality and speciality of each specific case and so the amounts of compensation vary hugely.

For that reason, the Constitutional Court, in the aforementioned judgment No. 85/2019, of 19 June 2019,[22] has demanded the requirements and scope of compensation to be limited through the legislative intervention and, in its absence, through interpretations consistent with its purpose and the general theory of civil liability carried out by the administration and, finally, the judicial bodies.

On the other hand, and in cases of judicial error or irregular functioning of the administration of justice, Article 91 LPAC requires the administrative organ (Ministry of Justice) to assess the claim and fix the amount and the manner of the

21 See also the General Council of Spanish Lawyers website for further information (English translation available). The tool is available at: https://www.abogacia.es/en/servicios/ciudadanos/servicios-de-orientacion-juridica-gratuita.

22 Constitutional Court Judgment 85/2019, of 19 June 2019 Appeal (*Amparo*) No. 4314–2018. Spanish Official Journal (BOE») No. 177, 25 July 2019.

compensation, where appropriate, in accordance with the criteria of Article 34 LRJSP. As this article refers to provisions laid down, among others, 'in the scales of the existing rules on compulsory insurance and social security', administrative authorities and courts of justice have taken into account the criteria and amounts related to damages caused in traffic accidents.[23]

Nevertheless, those criteria and amounts are fixed for bodily or physical injuries and not for non-pecuniary damage. Therefore, compensation for damage caused by wrongful convictions follows the two criteria of Article 294.2 LOPJ.

As both criteria have wide margins of interpretation, the Supreme Court has been offering the lower courts, in its case law, a series of *guidelines* (standards or patterns) to take into consideration when calculating the amount of compensation. Despite the 'highly subjective component' of non-pecuniary damage, repeatedly recalled by jurisprudence, the Supreme Court has been setting certain patterns to guide the achievement of equitable treatment in each case and, at the same time, to avoid inequalities in the compensation of non-pecuniary damage.

For example, the Supreme Court has pointed out that it is necessary to consider the wages that have not been received, the period of imprisonment, the importance and significance of the harm both in the pure personal and professional order and the non-pecuniary damage suffered as a result of all this. Other relevant circumstances or guidelines are the age, health, civic conduct, imputed facts, criminal or prison records, rehabilitation of lost honourability, the social discredit and the greater or lesser probability of reaching the social oblivion of the fact, as well as the mark that the prison may have left on the personality or conduct of the one who has suffered it.

Irrespective, damage to someone's personality is something hardly quantifiable or measurable with a minimum of objectivity. How does one determine the anguish, anxiety, insecurity, restlessness, frustration, annoyance, irritation or fear that the environment in a prison usually entails?

It is true that administrative decisions of the Ministry of Justice in matters of State liability for wrongful conviction have considered those guidelines but when attending to specific circumstances, the daily amount differs a lot. Moreover, correction factors to such daily amounts are sometimes applied to fix the compensation, depending on the number of days spent in prison. The Supreme Court has ruled that 'moral damage cannot be assessed daily, but from a global perspective,

23 The sources of law related to compensation for traffic accidents are: the *Real Decreto Legislativo 8/2004, de 29 de octubre, por el que se aprueba el texto refundido de la Ley sobre responsabilidad civil y seguro en la circulación de vehículos a motor* (Royal Decree 8/2004, of 29 October, which approved the rewritten text of the Motor Vehicles Public Liability and Insurance Act). *Spanish Official Journal* (BOE) No. 267, 5 November. Permalink ELI: https://www.boe.es/eli/es/rdlg/2004/10/29/8, and the *Ley 35/2015, de 22 de septiembre, de reforma del sistema para la valoración de los daños y perjuicios causados a las personas en accidentes de circulación* (Law 35/2015, of 22 September, Reforming the System for the Assessment of Damages Caused to People in Traffic Accidents). *Spanish Official Journal* (BOE) No. 228, 23 September 2015. Permalink ELI: https://www.boe.es/eli/es/l/2015/09/22/35.

which, we add, must be done considering the allegations and justifications provided'.[24]

Since the undue prolongation of the stay in prison gradually aggravates the non-pecuniary damage, the compensation is progressive, so that a correction factor is introduced with which the daily base is increased each time a certain period elapses. But authorities decide almost discretionarily if the amount is based on a fortnightly, monthly or annual basis. There is no assessed rule.[25]

As an example, a person who has been in prison for around two years usually receives compensation of between €12,000 and €36,000. There is, therefore, no single and objective formula. Although a 'scale or schedule' for undue imprisonment is commonly spoken of (see below), there is substantial judicial discretion in the determination of compensation. In fact, the jurisprudence of the Third Chamber has gradually expanded the content of non-pecuniary damage: first, only the negative effect that the entry and stay in prison had on the *psyche* of the individual and that was concretised in the suffering of anguish, fear, insecurity, frustration or anxiety was considered compensable; later, from 1999, the Supreme Court was adding to the above the social discredit and the rupture with the environment of the individual.

As we can see, and despite the objectivity of the calculation rule, the analysed judgments of the Supreme Court included in the table do not show any uniform criteria in the determination of compensation, since they apply disparate daily bases and correction factors depending on the particular case.

For instance, in a recent case in Spain resolved by the Judgment of the Supreme Court (Administrative Chamber) of 22 September 2021, the applicant claimed

Table 4.1 Supreme Court case compensation

High Court judgment	*Correction factor (monthly)*	*Daily rate (base, €)*	*Number of days of imprisonment*	*Daily rate of compensation (€)*
30.6.1999	25%	24.04	234	61.15
13.11.2000	125%	60.10	28	74.04
20.1.2003	10%	12.02	946	70.76
26.1.2005	25%	36.06	237	88.32
21.3.2006	—	60.06	151	60.06

Source: Luna Yerga et al.[26]

24 Supreme Court Judgment (Administrative Bench) 20 December 2019 Cassation No. 3847/2018.

25 Supreme Court Judgment (Administrative Bench) 10 October 2019 Cassation No. 339/2019.

26 Montserrat De Hoyos Sancho, 'La indemnización de la prisión provisional tras sentencia absolutoria o auto de sobreseimiento libre: situación actual y propuestas' (2020) 1 *Revista de la asociación de profesores de derecho procesal de las universidades españolas*, 126–174.

compensation in the amount of €333,397.70 for the 326 days of detention on remand suffered. To arrive at this figure, the applicant quantified the damage as €200 per day, progressively increased to the sum of €1,862,53 per day, in addition to the damage suffered as a result of the prosecution. However, the Supreme Court declared that, according to the duration of the deprivation of liberty (10 months and 22 days), it considers it appropriate to set the compensation at the amount of €12,000, for all concepts of Article 294 LOPJ.

7 Evaluation of the national mechanism of the compensation for wrongful convictions

The obligation to compensate the innocent adequately for the harm resulting from imprisonment dissuades the State from keeping in prison or agreeing to restrictive measures against the freedom of persons without sufficient evidence. But the mechanism legally established in Spain to grant compensation for wrongful convictions (in all the three cases ruled under Articles 292–296 LOPJ) has been the subject of several criticisms due to the wide discretion of the authorities when fixing the amounts of compensation, the almost derisory nature of the amounts granted (sometimes, the daily compensation has been less than the national minimum wage) and the strict criteria for the handling of administrative procedures.

Similarly, and until the ruling of the Constitutional Court of 2019, not all people who have been acquitted or who have benefitted from the dismissal of the criminal procedure were compensated for the damage suffered by the detention on remand, but only those whose innocence had been sufficiently demonstrated. That is, those who had been released after suffering preventive detention were only entitled to compensation when the acquittal or dismissal had taken place due to the objective non-existence of the fact. Therefore, the cases of subjective non-existence had been left out of the scope of application of Article 294.1 LOPJ, not only in cases of lack of evidence, but also when the lack of participation had been proven.

However, the Constitutional Court has warned that not every case of detention on remand followed by acquittal will lead to compensation automatically, since everything will depend on how Article 294 LOPJ is legally configured, something that the legislator has not yet decided to improve. And when this happens, the Constitutional Court has also anticipated that

> the doctrine of this judgment not only respects the wide margins of legislative configuration or judicial interpretation in what affects the quantum compensation, but also does not prevent rejecting that there is in the specific case a right to compensation by virtue of the application of criteria of the general law of damages (such as the 'compensatio lucri cum damno' or the relevance of the victim's own conduct).[27]

27 Constitutional Court Judgment 41/2021, of 3 March. Appeal (Amparo) No. 1128-2018.

The doctrine has condemned all this confusion derived from the deficits of compensation for wrongful imprisonment and has advocated the need for an adequate regulatory framework to ensure effective compensation. Some scholars have also demanded a legal improvement of other cases in which acquitted citizens should also be compensated for the damage that could have been caused by other precautionary measures and investigating powers adopted throughout the course of the case. A revision of the legal system of procedural costs has also been demanded, since it is not fair to declare the costs *ex officio* (each party pays its fees) when the accused is finally acquitted and these are not imposed on the private prosecution. Although this is the system traditionally used in Spain, it does not seem in accordance with the necessary effects *ad extra* of the presumption of innocence that if a person is acquitted of the accusations that weighed on him he must assume the expenses incurred by his necessary participation, defence and representation in the case.[28]

Finally, it is important to note that the new Draft of Criminal Procedure Law of 2020[29] incorporates important changes that affect the compensation for wrongful conviction. In the new text, the compensation for sacrificial damage arising from unfair detention on remand is recognised in terms of a subjective right, also providing for the compensation regime that governs these cases, that is, the compensable cases and the criteria for fixing the quantum compensation. As the criteria and proceedings to claim for damage caused by wrongful convictions would follow the criteria for compensating unfair detention on remand (criteria of Article 294.2 LOPJ), this new text would be the main source of law to calculate and claim the compensation.

In addition, it is intended to introduce a special procedure for obtaining compensation for unfair detention on remand in the Code of Criminal Procedure itself: the 'special procedure for compensation for detention on remand followed by acquittal' – Articles 868 to 872 – where the admissibility and determination of the compensation for detention on remand will be decided by the criminal courts and will be governed by the criteria of the general theory of civil liability and the law of damages. The indemnifiable cases are those in which, after the detention on remand, there is a final acquittal or order of dismissal, without differentiating the reasons, and in addition, the damage to be compensated will be that actually suffered and provided that it did not result immediately or primarily from the conduct of the person under investigation.[30]

28 Montserrat De Hoyos Sancho, 'La indemnización de la prisión provisional tras sentencia absolutoria o auto de sobreseimiento libre: situación actual y propuestas' (2020) 1 *Revista de la asociación de profesores de derecho procesal de las universidades españolas*, 126–174.

29 The initial version of the Draft of Criminal Procedure Law of 2020 is available (only in Spanish) at: https://www.mjusticia.gob.es/es/AreaTematica/ActividadLegislativa/Documents/210126%20ANTEPROYECTO%20LECRIM%202020%20INFORMACION%20PUBLICA%20%281%29.pdf.

30 In greater detail, the novelties of the Draft of Criminal Procedure Law are described in Marien Aguilera Morales, 'La prisión provisional en el nuevo Anteproyecto de Ley de Enjuiciamiento Criminal' (2021) 3 *Revista de la asociación de profesores de derecho procesal de las universidades españolas*, 399–438.

Bibliography

Aguilera Morales M, 'La prisión provisional en el nuevo Anteproyecto de Ley de Enjuiciamiento Criminal' (2021) 3 *Revista de la asociación de profesores de derecho procesal de las universidades españolas*, 399–438.

Bachmaier Winter L, del Moral García A, *Criminal Law in Spain* (2nd edn, Wolters Kluwer, 2012) 273.

De Hoyos Sancho M, 'La indemnización de la prisión provisional tras sentencia absolutoria o auto de sobreseimiento libre: situación actual y propuestas' (2020) 1 *Revista de la asociación de profesores de derecho procesal de las universidades españolas*, 126–174.

Domínguez Ruiz L, 'Indemnización por prisión preventiva injusta: evolución del artículo 294.1 de la LOPJ a la luz de la jurisprudencia nacional y europea' (2020) 2 *Justicia: Revista de Derecho Procesal*, 309–341.

Luna Yerga A, Ramos González S, Marín García I, 'Guía de Baremos: valoración de daños causados por accidentes de circulación, de navegación aérea y por prisión indebida' (2006) 3 *Indret: Revista para el Análisis del Derecho*, 27.

Table of cases

Puig Panella v. Spain App no 1483/02 (ECtHR 25 April 2006).

Tendam v. Spain App no 25720/05 (ECtHR 13 July 2010).

Constitutional Court Judgment 8/2017 of 19 January 2017 Appeal (*Amparo*) No. 2341–2012.

Constitutional Court Judgment 85/2019 of 19 June 2019 Appeal (*Amparo*) No. 4314–2018.

Supreme Court Judgment (Administrative Bench) 27 March 2006 Cassation No. 6/2004.

Supreme Court Judgment (Administrative Bench) 20 June 2006 Cassation No. 13/2004.

Supreme Court Judgment (Administrative Bench) 15 January 2007 Cassation No. 17/2004.

Supreme Court Judgment (Administrative Bench) 12 March 2007 Cassation No. 18/2004.

Supreme Court Judgment (Administrative Bench) 30 April 2008 Cassation No. 7/2006.

Supreme Court Judgment (Administrative Bench) 9 July 2008 Cassation No. 6/2007.

Supreme Court Judgment (Administrative Bench) 10 October 2019 Cassation No. 339/2019.

Supreme Court Judgment (Administrative Bench) 20 December 2019 Cassation No. 3847/2018.

Supreme Court Judgment (Administrative Bench) 28 September 2020 Cassation No. 123/2020.

Supreme Court Judgment (Administrative Bench) 15 October 2021 Cassation No. 36/2020.

Supreme Court Judgment (Civil Bench) 19 April 2022 Cassation No. 14/2021.

5 Compensation for wrongful convictions in the Netherlands[1]

Joost Nan, Nina Holvast and Sjarai Lestrade

1 Introduction: origins and development of compensation for wrongful convictions

Ever since the nineteenth century there has been legislative talk about the right to compensation after a wrongful conviction. Although such a right was generally accepted and deemed fair, even by the legislator, it was not until 1926 that the current Code of Criminal Procedure (CCP) came into being in the Netherlands in which such a right was introduced. The academic discussion on this topic had an even broader focus, and also alluded to the issue of compensation for damages incurred after proceedings that did not – generally – end in any sort of conviction that could warrant pretrial detention.[2] In the case of detention on remand, compensation will only be awarded if that is fair, given the circumstances. The legislator was explicit in the opinion that an absolute right to compensation in those cases, which was advocated at the time by some scholars,[3] should be rejected. If the state handled the case correctly and in the public interest, liability was not always just. An actual right to compensation was always deemed just when a person's conviction was overturned after a revision procedure and no sanction was subsequently imposed. In that situation there was more reason to assume that the person involved was innocent. A more imperative right to compensation was therefore appropriate. In the current 'modernisation' of the entire CCP, the stipulations on compensation after a wrongful conviction will change somewhat, but no major alterations are expected. We will address the upcoming changes when and where appropriate.[4]

1 Authors wish to thank Vincent Boer, LLM, for his help on this contribution.

2 *Kamerstukken II* 1913/14, 286(3) (explanatory memorandum) 86–88 and 161. See for the background AJ Blok and LC Besier, *Het Nederlandsche Strafproces* (Haarlem: Tjeenk Willink 1925) I, pp. 276–285 and II pp. 536–538.

3 See the literature in the previous footnote.

4 All Dutch legislation can be found at: https://wetten.overheid.nl/zoeken. The draft of the new CCP is expected to be introduced as a bill to Parliament sometime in 2023. It will presumably take several years and numerous changes before the new CCP will come into effect (which has been predicted for 2026). For more on this legislative project see: https://www.rijksoverheid.nl/onderwerpen/nieuwe-wetboek-van-strafvordering.

DOI: 10.4324/9781003229414-6

In this chapter on the Dutch regulations on compensation after a wrongful conviction, we will define a wrongful conviction as a conviction for a crime resulting from regular or ordinary criminal proceedings that has subsequently been overturned after the extraordinary procedure of revision on the exclusive legal grounds of: 1) two convictions that cannot coexist, 2) a successful complaint to the European Convention on Human Rights (ECHR) as appropriate redress or 3) a *novum* (see Article 457 Section 1 CCP). Both factual or legal innocence and procedural errors could therefore constitute a wrongful conviction.[5] In the event of a successful revision application, the case will be tried before a 'fresh' *appellate* court which has had no dealings with the case (even if the original conviction came from a regional court). In short, the original verdict(s) can be upheld or quashed (depending on the ground, either by the Supreme Court or the appellate court). If the verdict is quashed, the appellate court gives its own ruling, whereby it cannot give a more severe sentence than the one that was originally given.

We will discuss the legal framework for compensation after a successful revision procedure (Section 2), the calculation of the amount of compensation (Section 3), the recourse claim of the state against persons who caused wrongful convictions (Section 4) and the practice of compensating the wrongfully convicted (Section 5). Subsequently we will evaluate the Dutch mechanism for compensation for wrongful convictions (Section 6). In Sections 2–4 we will focus on the specific entry in Article 539 CCP, because this will normally govern compensation to a large extent. The possibility to claim other damages based on civil law will be briefly mentioned in Section 3.2.

2 Legal framework

2.1 Background of the current legal framework

The Netherlands is party to the International Covenant on Civil and Political Rights (ICCPR). Article 14 Section 6 ICCPR gives the former suspect a right to compensation if their final conviction is reversed.[6] Article 3 of the Seventh Protocol to the ECHR provides a similar right. Since the Netherlands has not ratified that Seventh Protocol (because of the scope of the right to a review of a conviction by a higher tribunal), this provision has no effect and cannot be relied on to claim any compensation.

The most specific stipulations on compensation for a wrongful conviction can be found in the CCP. The mechanism was originally laid down in 1926 in Article

5 Compare Na Jiang, *Wrongful Convictions in China. Comparative and Empirical Perspectives* (1st edn, Springer 2016) Ch. 2.

6 It reads: 'When a person has by a final decision been convicted of a criminal offence and when subsequently his conviction has been reversed or he has been pardoned on the ground that a new or newly discovered fact shows conclusively that there has been a miscarriage of justice, the person who has suffered punishment as a result of such conviction shall be compensated according to law, unless it is proved that the non-disclosure of the unknown fact in time is wholly or partly attributable to him.'

481 CCP, regarding compensation for damages incurred because the former suspect underwent penalties, and the measure of placement under a hospital order (in case of insanity) and pretrial detention. The stipulation was later transferred to Article 480 CCP in the Reform of Revision in Favour of Former Suspects Act (2012).[7] In this transfer the scope of the provision was widened to also encompass other measures which led to deprivation of liberty, in addition to placement under a hospital order. The legislator believed the distinction could not be justified and made compensation possible in more cases. The legislator mentioned the measure of placement in a facility for repeat offenders (*inrichting voor stelselmatige daders*, ISD).[8] The Reform of Revision in Favour of Former Suspects Act also introduced Article 482 CCP, which dealt with the damages and legal fees paid by the former suspect to the victim. Those damages and fees could be reimbursed to the former suspect; reimbursement is paid by the state. Articles 480 and 482 CCP were merged in 2020, when several separately placed regulations on compensation were relocated and placed together in Article 539 CCP, without any changes except a technicality.[9]

The topic of compensation for a wrongful conviction is thus currently still regulated in the CCP. There is no stipulation in the constitution, nor is there any other specific regulation. There are the general regulations of civil law, especially undue payment and tort law, which could also be applied to state liability in case of a successful revision application and subsequent positive outcome for the former suspect (see especially Article 6:162 Civil Code).[10] This arrangement might change when the modernisation of the CCP has taken effect, which is expected to be in 2026. As of 2022, it appears that the stipulations in the new CCP will primarily deal exclusively with compensation after a wrongful conviction. In the current draft, it is impossible for the former suspect to start civil proceedings against the state for any claim which falls under the scope of Article 539 CCP and for other claims up to €25,000.[11] The role of civil law will thus be more limited. Compensation (claims) are and will be primarily a matter of public (in this case criminal) law.

7 See on the background and effectiveness of this act Joost Nan et al., *Victa vincit veritas?* (1st edn, Boom Juridisch 2018), Joost Nan et al., 'Evaluatie van de Wet hervorming herziening ten voordele' (2019) *Nederlands Juristenblad* 184.

8 *Kamerstukken II* 2008/09 32045 3 (explanatory memorandum) 42.

9 See further *ibid.* [2.2.1].

10 See briefly *ibid.* [3.2].

11 See the draft bill of the new CCP (*ambtelijke versie* July 2020) Article 6.6.1. The relevant provision, Article 6.6.6, will probably read (non-official translation): '1. If after the annulment of the irrevocable final judgment pursuant to Book 5, Title 8.1, no penalty or measure or the measure referred to in Article 37 CC is imposed, a compensation will be awarded in regard to the insurance and pre-trial detention as well as the punishment suffered and custodial measure. The allocation takes place insofar as there are grounds of fairness, taking all circumstances into account. 2. The request for compensation is submitted by the former suspect within five years after he has been able to take cognizance of the termination of the case'.

To the best of our knowledge, there is just one case law on this topic (see Section 5). We did not find any rulings from the Supreme Court.[12] We expect that the case law, if it does cover more than just a couple of cases, is of no real importance in interpreting the regulations. An exception to this may be the *Putten murder case*, which is discussed in more detail in Section 5. There are no statistical data on compensation claims of this sort available.

2.2 Grounds for compensation for wrongful convictions

2.2.1 Possibilities under the CCP

The possibilities covered in the CCP must be seen as the main options to claim compensation, especially Article 539 CCP. To sum up the possibilities included in Article 539 CCP: after a successful revision application has been made by the former suspect (regardless on which of the three exclusive grounds) and the conviction has subsequently been quashed and no sanction adjudicated, the former suspect has a right to compensation for the penalties that led to deprivation of liberty (Section 1) and can also try to claim damages for the pretrial detention that was applied (Section 2). In the proceedings in which the conviction was annulled, the appellate court can order the state to repay the damages the former suspect has paid to the victim (Section 3), as well as the legal fees the former suspect paid to the victim (Section 4). We will elaborate further on these options later in this section.

If, after revision, the original verdict is quashed and no sanction is adjudicated, the former suspect can claim the non-pecuniary damages incurred insofar as they relate to an earlier penalty, as well as measures which resulted in the deprivation of liberty.[13] Usually, the new trial will lead to an acquittal, but it is also possible that the conviction itself is upheld in the new trial, but that no sanction is imposed (see Article 9a Criminal Code (CC), *rechterlijk pardon*). If the text of Article 539 Section 1 CCP is interpreted according to the parliamentary explanation, it can be concluded that compensation is only possible for the undergoing of penalties and measures which led to a deprivation of liberty.[14] The relevant main penalties would then be imprisonment and detention. *Measures*, which are another type of sanction, which lead to a deprivation of liberty are placement under a hospital order (TBS or *terbeschikkingstelling*) and placement in a facility for repeat offenders (*plaatsing in een inrichting voor stelselmatige daders*).[15] If these sanctions are

12 But that is not extraordinary because an appeal to the highest Dutch criminal court is not possible in the specific compensation proceedings.

13 The former suspect's heirs can only claim material damages (see Article 539 Section 1 in conjunction with Article 533 Section 6 CCP).

14 See also AJ Blok and LC Besier, *Het Nederlandsche Strafproces* (Tjeenk Willink 1925) II, 538 and REP de Ranitz, *Herziening van arresten en vonnissen* (Tjeenk Willink 1977) 185.

15 On all criminal sanctions see HS Taekema and JS Nan, 'Principles of Dutch criminal law', in HS Taekema, AJ de Roo and C Elion-Valter (eds), *Understanding Dutch Law* (3rd edn, Boom juridisch 2020) para. 8.5.

not upheld and no other sanction followed due to a successful review of a criminal case, a claim for compensation can be made.[16] Undergoing a different sanction does not lead to a right to compensation. This is because restitution of deprivation of liberty is not possible, whereas a fine can be, which at the time was the only other main penalty.

It has been advocated to interpret Article 539 CCP in a wider manner and to see this stipulation as a possibility to claim compensation for all sanctions the former suspect had to undergo.[17] An appellate court also interpreted the article that way (regarding the penalty of suspension of the former suspect's driver's licence),[18] and this seems to be a more reasonable and practical interpretation. Otherwise, the former suspect has to start separate civil proceedings to claim the damages incurred due to the payment of a fine, executed community service, the confiscation of objects, etc, on the civil law basis of – in general – undue payment or tort law.[19] Certainly a fine would have to be repaid, confiscated items returned or restitution should take place. However, time spent on community service cannot be given back. Perhaps the damages incurred because of sanctions that do not lead to the deprivation of liberty do not legitimise a right to compensation (and there were far fewer sanctions around the turn of the nineteenth century).

This wider interpretation does not seem to be the leading one. This also becomes apparent from the stance taken by our current, 'modern' legislator, who appears to be holding on to the stricter interpretation.[20] In the future, under the new regulations in the CCP, the former suspect will be able to claim damages incurred to the amount of €25,000 because of the execution of those other sanctions in the same proceedings as for the sanctions which led to the deprivation of liberty. That claim is then based on the principle of fairness. However, a right to compensation will still not exist in the new legislation. For the damages exceeding €25,000, the former suspect will have to instigate civil proceedings.

As a consequence of the wording of Article 539 Section 1 CCP and the intention of the legislator, compensation for the sanctions the former suspect underwent and which led to deprivation of liberty is mandatory and damages should be awarded. The state is never exempt from liability. The only remaining question is what the amount of the compensation should be. This question will be answered on the basis of the principle of fairness and could, given the circumstances, result in very moderate damages being awarded, possibly zero. It is

16 In future a claim will also be possible if placement under a hospital order is imposed.

17 GAM Strijards, *Revisie: inbreuken en executiegeschillen betreffende het strafgewijsde* (Gouda Quint 1989) 285–286. See also JWHG Loyson 'De raadkamerprocedures in strafzaken' (2020) 14 *Praktijkwijzer Strafrecht* (3.14), who offers no substantiation of his wider view.

18 Court of Appeal Arnhem 28 March 1989, ECLI:NL:GHARN:1989:AD0697, *NJ* 1989/776.

19 Civil proceedings are deemed possible, AJA van Dorst, 'Herziening in strafzaken' in MF Attinger et al./PAM Mevis et al. (eds.), *Handboek Strafzaken*, (Wolters Kluwer 2021).

20 Explanatory memorandum new CCP (*ambtelijke versie* July 2020) 1069.

important to point out that the damages incurred because of the sanctions the former suspect underwent are not the same as the losses sustained because of the prosecution itself.

The damages incurred due to pretrial detention are a slightly different story. There is no right to compensation, but compensation could be awarded if that is deemed fair (see Article 539 Section 2 CCP). This will change in the planned new CCP. The former suspect will then also have a right to compensation for damages. It is doubtful whether the distinction between pretrial detention and the executed sanction which led to deprivation of liberty will lead to a very different approach in practice.[21] In this case, the principle of fairness forms the ground for awarding compensation (or leads to exemption of the state of liability) and for the determination of the amount. The regular provisions on compensation for pre-trial detention where no conviction follows (or for a crime on which the pretrial detention could be based) are to be applied accordingly. Compensation could, for instance, be denied or lowered if the former suspect acted in such a way that (prolonged) pretrial detention could be said to be their own fault. An example is freely confessing the crime or remaining silent when refuting the reasonable – or even grave – suspicions was possible, and could and would have resulted in earlier release.

Furthermore, the state can also be ordered to repay the damages that were awarded to the victim in the criminal proceedings, and which have already been paid by the former suspect (see Article 539 Section 3 CCP). This is not mandatory but optional. The same goes for the accompanying awarded legal fees that have been paid by the former suspect to the victim (see Article 539 Section 4 CCP). The idea was that the victim should not bear the burden in such matters. An exception was made if the victim was the cause of the wrongful conviction in the first place, for instance by making a false statement to the former suspect's detriment.[22] In such an extraordinary case, the request for reimbursement will be denied and the former suspect will have to address the former victim directly. The reimbursement can be ordered in the criminal proceedings after a successful revision application, in which no sanction is eventually imposed. It cannot and will not be ordered in the subsequent compensation proceedings. If the state is ordered to make these payments, the victim does not have to pay them to either the former suspect or the state. The stipulations are intended to make sure the victim does not end up out of pocket, except when the victim caused the wrongful conviction.[23]

These stipulations make it possible for the financial relationship between the former suspect and the victim to be settled in the verdict after a successful revision application, without the victim being involved and burdened. That is appropriate

21 MJA Duker, 'Niet-imperatieve toekenning bij onterecht ondergane verzekering en voorlopige hechtenis?' (2015) art. 480 Sv Archief Wetboek van Strafvordering AL Melai/MS Groenhuijsen et al. aant. 6.

22 *Kamerstukken II* 2008/09 32045 3 (explanatory memorandum) 25.

23 Ibid.

and efficient. There is one instance where this is not the case, where the victim is mostly to blame for the miscarriage of justice by making a false statement to the former suspect's detriment. When reimbursement by the state is not ordered, it is the former suspect who has to address such a former victim in civil proceedings. This will put a burden on the former suspect so perhaps it would be better if the state still had to compensate the former suspect and turn to the victim for reimbursement, for instance based on the right of recourse.[24] It seems fair to place the burden of redress on the state, under whose tutelage the judicial error occurred, even if the victim was mostly to blame. Currently, this is not possible. In the modernisation project, these stipulations will not be changed, but will be placed with the other stipulations on revision in favour of the former suspect, as it was when they were introduced (see Article 5.8.26 CCP).

The compensation of other costs, such as costs for legal representation (legal fees), other defence costs (for instance a hired expert to make a report) and costs for the attendance of court hearings, do not fall under the scope of Article 539. But the usual stipulations of Articles 529–538 CCP are applicable, so these costs could be reimbursed if they had not already been.[25] An important point is that the majority of these costs will only be reimbursed provided the criminal proceedings did not result in any sanction being adjudicated and the judicial pardon not being extended, and reimbursement is deemed fair. The scope of these provisions therefore more limited than that of Article 539 CCP.

2.2.2 Civil law as a residual category

Besides compensation based on Articles 529–539 CCP (especially in relation to the former suspect having to undergo a certain sanction or pretrial detention and reimbursement of the payments having to be made to the victim ex Article 539 CCP), there is the more general option of a claim for compensation based on undue payment or civil tort law (see Article 6:162 CC). These rules can be seen as complementary, as they allow other damages to be paid because of the state's obligation or liability in light of a revised conviction, *but only if these claims fall outside the scope of the provisions of the CCP.* An important category that can fall under this provision is that of restitution of damages and/or damages awarded in the case of sanctions the former suspect underwent that did not lead to a deprivation of liberty, such as financial penalties and measures. It could also be any illegal action of the state, for instance deprivation of liberty in violation of the

24 See also MJ Borgers and T Kooijmans *Het Nederlands strafprocesrecht* (10th edn, Wolters Kluwer 2021) 1080, footnote 635.

25 See for a rare example, Court of Appeal Leeuwarden 4 October 2002, ECLI:NL:GHLEE:2002:AE8349 and ECLI:NL:GHLEE:2002:AE8353. See for more on the topic of compensation after a criminal trial, NJ Kwakman, 'Schadecompensatie in het strafproces' (DPhil thesis, University of Groningen 2003) and NM Dane, 'Overheidsaansprakelijkheid voor schade bij legitiem strafvorderlijk handelen' (DPhil thesis, University of Leiden, 2009).

stipulations of the CCP of Article 5 ECHR.[26] Another category is non-pecuniary damages caused by the earlier prosecution and/or conviction itself, such as the burden of the conviction, damage to the reputation of the former suspect, missed business opportunities, etc.[27] They have to be damages beyond the hardship of the pretrial detention. For liability based on tort law, either the former suspect has to prove that the state acted illegally during the regular proceedings or the former suspect's innocence has to be evident from the verdict or case file.[28] An acquittal is not enough, as a verdict of not guilty does not always mean someone is innocent. In the case of a revised conviction, the chances that the subsequent verdict or documents prove innocence will be better than in normal proceedings. In the case of civil proceedings against the state for damages outside the scope of Articles 529–539 CCP, the usual provisions of civil procedural code are applicable.[29] In the new CCP, instigating such a civil proceeding will only be possible if the claim exceeds €25,000, according to Article 6.6.1 CCP. This means that the simpler claims can be handled by the criminal courts – which are more accessible – and the more complex cases by the civil courts.[30]

2.3 Procedure for claiming compensation under the CCP

Former suspects, or their heirs, are eligible to claim compensation (see Article 539 Section 1 CCP). If the amount claimed is at least €500, legal aid could be granted by the Legal Aid Board (*Raad voor Rechtsbijstand*). That is, if the former suspect's financial position is modest. Normally, a request for compensation would also contain a request for reimbursement of the legal fees in relation to the request. The standard amount that is awarded is €340 where no oral hearing is needed, and the compensation for the legal fees is doubled if such a hearing does take place. No court fee is levied on the former suspect for the request, even if the submission is altogether inadmissible or (largely) rejected.

Given the reference in Article 539 Section 1 CCP to Articles 533–536 CCP, the following procedural conditions and formalities apply. The request for compensation has to be filed within three months of the conclusion of the case (so after the reviewed verdict was given).[31] The competent court is the appellate court

26 Article 5 Section 5 ECHR gives a right to compensation in those cases.

27 See on Dutch civil law generally HN Schelhaas and HS Taekema, 'The outlines of Dutch private law', in HS Taekema, AJ de Roo and C Elion-Valter (eds), *Understanding Dutch Law* (3rd edn, Boom juridisch 2020). A useful website is http://dutchcivillaw.com.

28 See, among other authorities, Supreme Court 13 October 2006, ECLI:NL:HR:2006:AV6956, *NJ* 2007/432.

29 See further, M van Hooijdonk and P Eijsvoogel, *Litigation in the Netherlands: Civil Procedure, Arbitration and Administrative Litigation* (2nd edn, Wolters Kluwer 2009). The following websites could also be useful: http://dutchcivillaw.com and https://dutch-law.com/proceedings-netherlands.html.

30 Explanatory memorandum new CCP (*ambtelijke versie* July 2020) 1045.

31 In the new CCP this will be prolonged to five years, in alignment with civil law. See the draft bill of the new CCP (*ambtelijke versie* July 2020), Article 6.6.6 Section 2.

(criminal division) that has handled the case after revision, and that has given the latest verdict. If possible, the same panel of three judges should give a ruling on the request. The request has to be submitted on paper and signed by the former suspect, but no other formal conditions apply. If an oral hearing takes place (when it is deemed necessary by the court), it is held in public (not in camera). An oral hearing is not needed if the request and the (positive) outcome are clear. Also, the general regulations on Council chamber proceedings apply (*raadkamer*, see Articles 21–25 CCP). That is all proceedings other than the usual trial proceedings (in open court). During the 1990s, this type of proceeding was aligned with the requirements of Article 6 ECHR, which is sometimes applicable. Since a final determination of the civil rights of the former suspect takes place in the compensation proceedings, it seems safe to say the civil limb of the right to a fair trial is applicable.[32] The district attorney's office is the counterparty in the proceedings. The district attorney's office and the former suspect are both summoned in the case of an oral hearing. Attendance is not obligatory for the former suspect, who can be assisted or represented by legal counsel during the hearing and can also bring an interpreter, if necessary, but they are not provided by the court. The district attorney's office has to submit the relevant case file to the court and make it available to the former suspect and the attorney. Both the representative of the district attorney's office and the former suspect and/or the attorney are given a hearing and can thus make a statement. In contrast to normal criminal proceedings, the former suspect does not have the right to the last word (*laatste woord*).[33] Minutes of the hearing are made and signed by the clerk and then signed by the president of the chamber of judges or one of the other judges. The ruling itself has to be reasoned, dated and signed by the president of the chamber or one of the other judges and by the clerk; there is no time limit for the court to give a ruling. In the case of compensation proceedings, a ruling is generally given after six weeks. It is not possible to appeal against this type of ruling as the law does not provide for one (see Article 445 CCP).

The court has the general authority to give the necessary orders (see Article 23 Section 1 CCP). Witnesses and experts can be ordered to testify under oath, documents to be submitted by either party, etc. There is no formal process for the former suspect or the representative of the district attorney's office to call on expert witnesses, but both parties can ask the court to make use of its authority. The law does not provide for a burden of proof or any standard of proof. Since the request for compensation is submitted by the former suspect, it is up to this person to supply enough facts and circumstances and substantiate them with documents to stake the claim, at least concerning the outcome of the case ex Article 539 Section 1 CCP and the amount of compensation requested. The district attorney's office can rebut but also support the claim of the former suspect.

32 Compare *Kamerstukken II* 1991/92 22584 3 [1–11].

33 See, for instance, Supreme Court 28 May 1985, ECLI:NL:PHR:1985:AC8907, *NJ* 1985/909.

As previously stated, the claim is judged on the principle of fairness. The court is therefore not bound by the views of either party, even if they agree. Given all these characteristics, the proceedings could be said to be more inquisitorial in nature than adversarial.

3 The amount of compensation

The law only specifies that the calculation of the amount of compensation has to be done on the principle of fairness (again, see Article 539 Section 1 CCP). The law also stipulates that the living conditions of the former suspect are to be considered (Article 534 Section 2 CCP). Nothing further is stipulated. Furthermore, no practical guide is provided by the courts on this specific matter. There is, however, a general agreement drafted by the Dutch criminal judges which, among many other things (such as standard sanctions for the most common crimes), governs compensation for pretrial detention (*Oriëntatiepunten voor straftoemeting en LOVS-afspraken*). This agreement was drafted in order to have more uniformity in the outcome of the most common criminal cases and situations, but it does not have the status of a law. Judges can deviate from the given standards if the circumstances call for it. It makes sense that the claim of compensation is related to a successful revision, even though technically this type of request is not explicitly mentioned. The general compensation is currently €130 for any day spent in custody at a police station and €100 in jail on remand. Given the fact that compensation after a wrongful conviction is something quite different from being awarded compensation for pretrial detention when the normal criminal proceedings do not end with a conviction for which this detention was ordered, it is conceivable that different amounts will be requested and awarded. It is expected that the damages awarded will be (much) higher, depending on the circumstances of the case. However, the damages awarded could also be fairly moderate if the former suspect is to blame for the wrongful conviction.

The limited case law that has been published reveals substantial differences in the calculation of the damages awarded. The circumstances that influence the damages awarded that are mentioned by the courts are: the type of detention regime in which the former suspect served their detention (on average the regime after a conviction is deemed to be lighter than pretrial); the strong defamation effect after a final conviction (particularly in cases that received a lot of attention from the media); the duration of the detention (the longer the detention, the more impact is has on the lives of the former suspect); the life stage at which the former suspect was incarcerated; their family bonds.[34]

These circumstances can result in an amount of compensation which is close to the usual compensation for pretrial detention[35] or to a much higher amount. In

34 See more on this in Section 5, where the *Van Mechelen case*, the *Putten murder case* and the *Spelonk case* are discussed.

35 Court of Appeal's-Gravenhage 5 June 2003, ECLI:NL:GHSGR:2003:AF9801.

the infamous *Putten murder case*,[36] which received a lot of media attention, five times the usual amount of compensation for pretrial detention was awarded. In this case, two men were wrongfully convicted of manslaughter and rape.[37] In various other infamous wrongful conviction cases compensation was awarded to the former suspects not through a court case, but through a settlement with the state/prosecution office on the basis of civil state liability. the process for reaching such a settlement is not governed by any (procedural) rules. If both the former suspect and the state are in agreement on the liability of the state and the damages that are to be awarded, no court proceedings are necessary (which could be advantageous to both parties). If the media reports are to be believed, the amount of compensation awarded in those cases was related to that of the *Putten murder case*. However, since the details of the settlements were not made public, we are very much in the dark about the real numbers, as well as the circumstances that played a role in determining the amount of compensation.

4 The recourse claim of the state against persons who caused a wrongful conviction

The question arises whether the government as a party can claim for compensation against persons who caused a wrongful conviction. Can the government demand the costs of investigation and prosecution from the person who deliberately made a false statement? The legislator's point of departure is that the costs of preventive and repressive enforcement of criminal law may, as a matter of principle, not be charged to citizens and companies. The government does not consider the enforcement of law individually attributable. In addition, preventive and repressive enforcement should be equally applicable to everyone and should not be dependent on private contributions with regard to the costs. Enforcement should therefore, as a matter of principle, be financed by general state resources.[38] This starting point, which can be deduced from the current legal system, has however been questioned by the legislator itself. For example, in 2014 the legislator prepared a bill that provided for the payment of a contribution by convicted persons towards the costs of investigation, prosecution and trial.[39] The contribution concerned a fixed lump sum. However, this bill was withdrawn after criticism from, among others, the Council of State.[40] The Supreme Court has also ruled in its case law that costs for investigation cannot, as a matter of principle, be refunded

36 Court of Appeal Leeuwarden 4 October 2002, ECLI:NL:GHLEE:2002:AE8347; ECLI:NL:GHLEE:2002:AE8348; ECLI:NL:GHLEE:2002:AE8349; ECLI:NL:GHLEE:2002:AE8350; ECLI:NL:GHLEE:2002:AE8351 and ECLI:NL:GHLEE:2002:AE8352.

37 In a case in the Caribbean part of the Netherlands, *the Spelonk case*, amounts close to five times the usual compensation for detention were also awarded plus US$25,500 of compensation for loss of income.

38 See *Kamerstukken II* 2005/06, 30 526 3, pp. 5, 9. Furthermore, Supreme Court 22 April 2008, ECLI:NL:HR:2008:BB7077, *NJ* 2008, 468 m.nt. MJ Borgers.

39 See *Kamerstukken II* 2014/15 34067 3, pp. 1–2.

40 See *Kamerstukken II* 2017/18 34067 17.

through private law.[41] After all, these are costs incurred by the police in carrying out their public duty, which is to detect criminal offences. A recourse claim through private law would suggest an unacceptable interference with public law regulations, the same applies to costs as a result of a false declaration. However, the Supreme Court has formulated one exception to the rule. This is in the event that: 1) the person who made the report not only knew that the offence was not committed; but 2) also made the report for no other purpose than to harm the police; and 3) knew or should have understood at the time of the report that it would prompt or cause the police to take unnecessary investigative actions.[42] Under those circumstances, the government can still claim damages on the basis of tort law.

From this ruling of the Supreme Court it can be derived that an expert witness who makes a grave mistake will as a matter of principle also not be liable. We expect that a recourse claim for the damages which the state paid to the former suspect will accordingly suffer the same fate as the costs of the police investigation.

Although the state in general has no right to claim compensation against persons who caused a wrongful conviction, the filing of a false report does, of course, constitute a criminal offence. It is prohibited under Article 188 CC as a crime against public authority.[43] Consequently, the state is 'protected' against such behaviour.[44] The same goes for expert witnesses who deliberately make a false statement under oath and thus commit perjury (Article 207 Criminal Code), or for an expert witness deliberately filing a false report resulting in a falsehood (Article 225 Criminal Code).

The former suspect can claim damages incurred because of the false report from the person who thus caused the wrongful conviction, if the damages have not already been paid by the state. This is based on tort law. As the CCP offers the former suspect various more accessible routes, we do not expect the former suspect to claim damages from the person who caused the wrongful conviction.

5 The practice of compensating the wrongfully convicted

While the Dutch state regularly awards compensation for unlawful pretrial detention (in 2020 4,584 compensations were awarded totalling €5,681,219),[45] the cases in which compensation is awarded after a wrongful conviction appear to be

41 Supreme Court 14 February 2017, ECLI:NL:HR:2017:221, *NJ* 2017/140 m.nt. SD Lindenbergh and see also Supreme Court 15 May 2020, ECLI:NL:HR:2020:890, *NJ* 2020/269 m.nt. JW Zwemmer.

42 Supreme Court 14 February 2017, ECLI:NL:HR:2017:221, *NJ* 2017/140 m.nt. SD Lindenbergh [3.4.2–3.4.3].

43 Non-official translation: 'Section 188: Any person who reports or files a complaint of a criminal offence, knowing that such offence has not been committed, shall be liable to a term of imprisonment not exceeding one year or a fine of the third category.'

44 Compare HJ Smidt, *Geschiedenis van het Wetboek van Strafrecht (1881–1886): Deel II* (Tjeenk Willink 1881) 188.

45 Answers to Parliamentary questions 22 February 2021 3220575.

much rarer. This is because the total number of cases in which an application for revision is declared well-founded by the Dutch Supreme Court is quite limited. In the period October 2012 to December 2019, 55 cases were declared well-founded. In the five years before that, the numbers were somewhat higher with 114 well-founded cases.[46] Of those cases, a substantial proportion concerned relatively minor offences for which the former suspect did not serve any detention, such as mistaken identity in minor cases or not having car insurance. Therefore, it is unlikely that there were major damages to claim in these cases.[47] This means that the number of cases whereit has been possible to request substantial compensation is quite limited in recent years,. The courts do not keep records of these types of cases, so we are not able to provide the precise numbers. Not only does the number of cases appear to be limited and uncertain, the way in which the amount of compensation were calculated and the circumstances that were decisive are also indeterminate.

To provide some additional information on how compensation for wrongful conviction functions in practice, we conducted some research. First, we searched for all relevant verdicts which are publicly available via the website of the judiciary. A selection of all judgments is published on this website.[48] It publishes judgments in all the cases of the highest Dutch courts. If a case from a lower court has received media attention or is considered relevant case law, it is also published.[49] Additionally, we searched in the relevant legal literature databases, which include journals that publish relevant case law. This search only provided an output of four published verdicts (we will describe these verdicts below). We also conducted a media analysis where we searched for news articles about the compensation that was awarded in some renowned wrongful convictions. This was primarily conducted because we were familiar with the fact that in several cases compensation was awarded not via a court case, but through a settlement with the prosecution office. However, our search for published verdicts has not been comprehensive, it has only provided a selection. Nonetheless, these verdicts still provide an indication of how courts deal with compensation for wrongful conviction.

A case from 1989 provides some insight into how courts deal with the compensation for damages due to sanctions that did not result in deprivation of liberty. As mentioned, the legislator appears to interpret the criminal legislation in a manner that would not include compensation for other sanctions, such as community service or driving disqualifications (see Section 2.2.1). However, in this case[50] a former suspect was granted 2,000 guilders (which converts to €907) compensation for driving disqualifications based on Article 481 CCP. This case

46 For the numbers see NL Holvast, JS Nan and SMA Lestrade, 'Between legal certainty and doubt' (2020) 13(4) *Erasmus Law Review* 1, 8.

47 No precise numbers are available on the type of cases that were revised.

48 This is the website: www.rechtspraak.nl.

49 For the selection criteria see 'Besluit selectiecriteria uitsprakendatabank' at www.rechtspraak.nl.

50 Court of Appeal Arnhem 28 March 1989, ECLI:NL:GHARN:1989:AD0697, *NJ* 1989/776.

currently appears to be the only published case on these other sanctions and was, until recently, mentioned in legal commentaries on the legislation.[51]

Furthermore, in 2003 a case dealing with damages due to a violation of the European Convention on Human Rights, the *Van Mechelen case*[52], the Appellate Court of The Hague ruled that the court is not bound by the amount of compensation that the ECHR decided to be fair.[53] The court awarded substantially higher compensation than ruled by the ECHR. Compensation for legal fees was awarded in all published cases.

From the available case law, it remains rather unclear how the courts decide on the compensation and what circumstances play a decisive role in their decision. In the *Van Mechelen* case three men were each sentenced to 14 years' imprisonment for armed robbery and attempted murder. This case concerned the use of anonymous witnesses, which led to a violation of Article 6 ECHR. The civil appellate court subsequently judged that Van Mechelen would be acquitted if this evidence were to be disregarded in the criminal case.[54] In this case, the court awarded the former suspects compensation for the pretrial detention based on the general rules on pretrial compensation (then 150 guilders/€68 a day). For the post-trial detention, the court also referred to the pretrial detention rules as a guideline for deciding on the damages awarded for wrongful detention, but stated that these are not automatically applicable. On the one hand, the court saw reasons to moderate the amount of compensation; the detention regime after a conviction is usually lighter and there is no longer uncertainty about the duration of the detention. On the other hand, the defamation is stronger after a final conviction. The court also considered the fact that the main suspect spent 12 months in a penitentiary selection centre due to psychological problems.[55] Considering all the circumstances, the court awarded the main suspect a lump sum of €140,000 for the post-trial imprisonment. The court did not provide a calculation per day in the verdict, but this translates to 132 guilders (€60) per day, which is slightly less than the usual amount awarded for pretrial detention (being 150 guilders per day at the time).[56] However, a year earlier, in 2002, in the *Putten murder case* in which two men were wrongfully convicted for manslaughter and rape and spent six years and

51 MJA Duker, 'Schadevergoeding wegens andere onterecht ten uitvoer gelegde sancties?' (2007) Article 481 Sv Archief Wetboek van Strafvordering A.L. Melai/M.S. Groenhuijsen et al. aant. 6.

52 *Van Mechelen and others v. the Netherlands* App No. 21363/93 21364/93 21427/93 22056/93 (ECHR, 30 oktober 1997).

53 Court of Appeal's-Gravenhage 5 June 2003, ECLI:NL:GHSGR:2003:AF9801.

54 This was a civil law case because, at the time, it was not possible to have a case revised after a verdict by the ECHR. See Supreme Court 6 July 1999, ECLI:NL:HR:1999:ZD1603, *NJ* 1999/800. The CCP procedure was therefore not applicable.

55 At the time, penitentiary selection centres were special penitentiary centres specifically designed to observe suspects or convicts in order to provide psychological advice necessary for the (further) execution of a sentence.

56 The suspects were convicted on 4 February 1991 and set free on 25 April 1997; this is 2,272 days. 300,000/2,272 = 132.

eight months in prison, the criminal Appellate Court of Leeuwarden made rather different considerations in awarding compensation. Both wrongfully convicted persons in this notorious *case* received an amount of about €900,000 for the time of pre- and post-trial detention that they had wrongfully served.[57] The compensation amounted to five times the usual amount that is awarded as compensation for pretrial detention. The court also multiplied the usual amount of compensation by five for the pre- *and* the post-conviction phase. The court justified this decision by stating that the former suspects served detention for very serious and defaming crimes (rape and manslaughter) for which they may never be relieved of the stigma clinging to them. Furthermore, the fact that the former suspects were relatively young and were unable to spend time with their family and children or were unable to start a family was mentioned. In addition to compensation for detention that was served, the court also compensated the travel costs of family members.[58] In a more recent case (2014) in the Caribbean part of the Netherlands, the *Spelonk case*,[59] a rather similar calculation was made by the Joint Court of Justice of Aruba, Curaçao, Sint Maarten and of Bonaire, Saint Eustatius and Saba (based on the amounts of compensation common in the Dutch Caribbean). In that case, the court additionally awarded a suspect US$25,500 for loss of income. The former suspects in the *Spelonk case* had served seven years and ten months of wrongful detention. In addition to several reasons that are quite similar to those in the *Putten murder case*, the court also took into account the fact that the state had not shown any willingness to negotiate the granting of compensation, despite it being obvious that the former suspects were entitled to it given the way that the Netherlands had dealt with other wrongful conviction cases. This was considered an extra burden on the former suspect. Thus, while the crimes for which the former suspects were wrongfully committed were rather similar in seriousness in the *Van Mechelen*, the *Putten murder* and the *Spelonk* cases – although rape could be considered more defaming – and the time that they actually served also not vary much, the compensation that was awarded was very different. From the motivation provided in the verdicts, it is not clear what justified these differences. A possible difference, apart from the especially defaming effect of a rape conviction, which may have played a role in the *Putten murder case*, is the fact that the crimes in the *Van Mechelen case* were committed within a criminal environment, whereas those in the *Putten murder case* and the *Spelonk case* were not. Another possible and relevant difference is that the grounds for the errors in law differed. In the *Putten murder case* and the *Spelonk case* there was a 'novum' and the former suspects were deemed most likely innocent. In the *Van Mechelen case*, the ECHR had convicted the Netherlands of a violation of Article 6 ECHR. As a

57 Court of Appeal Leeuwarden 4 October 2002, ECLI:NL:GHLEE:2002:AE8347; ECLI:NL:GHLEE:2002:AE8348; ECLI:NL:GHLEE:2002:AE8349; ECLI:NL:GHLEE:2002:AE8350; ECLI:NL:GHLEE:2002:AE8351; ECLI:NL:GHLEE:2002:AE8352.

58 It also awarded certain legal fees.

59 Joint Court of Justice of Aruba, Curaçao, Sint Maarten, and of Bonaire, Sint Eustatius and Saba 11 October 2014, ECLI:NL:OGHACMB:2014:8, m.nt. T.M. Schalken (*Spelonk*).

result, the Dutch court 'only' judged that the suspect would have been acquitted if the evidence of the anonymous witnesses was disregarded.

The *Putten murder case* and the *Spelonk case* (referring to the Caribbean part of the Netherlands) appear to be the only revised murder cases in which compensation was awarded by the court. In several other infamous wrongful conviction cases (*the murder in Schiedam, Ina Post, Lucia de Berk* and the *Showbiz murder case*), the media also reported that substantial amounts of compensation were awarded to the former suspects. These compensations were not awarded by courts but through a settlement with the prosecution office, often accompanied by apologies for the course of events.[60] In the *Spelonk case,* the Joint Court of Justice of Aruba, Curaçao, Sint Maarten and of Bonaire, Saint Eustatius and Saba reasoned that a settlement would also have been an obvious way for the state to deal with the case, but since this had not happened the court ruled on the compensation. If the media are correct, the amounts of compensation awarded in the settled compensation cases are more or less in line with the *Putten murder case*, and all cases involved considerable amounts of money were.[61] However, as in Section 3, it is not known for what types of damages these compensations were awarded nor the reasons for and calculation of the compensation.

6 Conclusions

No real academic or professional discussion has taken place recently on the topic of compensation after a wrongful conviction.[62] It is just assume that such an option is available to the former suspect. Several important criminal cases have been revised over the years and some claims for compensation were made, but compensation for those errors is not a hot topic in the Netherlands – at least not legally; the media do report on them. The CCP has provided a route for the former suspect to claim compensation after a wrongful conviction since 1926. Currently this is codified in Article 539 CCP. The former suspect has a right to compensation for the penalties and measures undergone before the final conviction was overturned. Compensation for the pretrial detention will not be automatically awarded, only if and insofar as that would be fair. In upcoming legislation, a right to compensation will be extended to pretrial detention which the former suspect underwent. The claim is adjudicated by the same court – and preferably the same panel of judges – that eventually quashed the conviction and did not impose any sanction. The level of compensation has to be determined on the principle of fairness, given the circumstances of each case. Compensating a

60 We have contacted the lawyers involved, but due to confidentiality no further information could be given.

61 We have contacted several lawyers involved in these high-profile cases. One of the lawyers involved informed us that the settlement in question was indeed very considerable.

62 In contrast to the mechanism of revision itself, which is still under discussion, see NL Holvast, JS Nan and SMA Lestrade, 'Between legal certainty and doubt' (2020) *Erasmus Law Review* 13(4).

wrongfully convicted suspect has, and will continue to have, deep roots in the Dutch legal system.

In general, this system appears to be functioning adequately in compensating the most important aspects of wrongful conviction, although there is hardly any published case law. We believe that the system could be improved by stipulating in the law unequivocally that compensation is possible for damages incurred due to all sanctions that the former suspect had to undergo (and not just for the sanctions that led to a deprivation of liberty), without putting limits on the amount requested. This would give the former suspect a broader right to compensation and would make civil proceedings for the remainder of the damages unnecessary in all instances. That subsequent civil proceedings will be necessary in practice is doubtful. The *Putten murder case* in particular evidences that the courts are inclined to compensate the former suspect royally, even beyond the scope of Article 539 CCP, although the court was much more reticent in the *Van Mechelen case*. Furthermore, several high-profile cases have been settled out of court. We are critical of this, as this course of events is not transparent and frustrates the development of a uniform legal manner of dealing with compensation in serious wrongful conviction cases.

In circumstances where the alleged victim is to blame for the miscarriage of justice, we believe that the CCP should provide the option that the state reimburses the former suspect for damages and legal fees paid to the victim based on the later quashed conviction and addresses the victim for recourse. The current rules state that the former suspect has to do this by themself, but it would seem that the state should take on this responsibility. The criminal justice system did, after all, not filter out the falsities. This is irrelevant however asthere are no known cases where this was actually an issue. The state has only limited options against persons who caused a wrongful conviction.

Bibliography

Blok AJ and Besier LC, *Het Nederlandsche Strafproces* (Tjeenk Willink 1925).

Borgers MJ and Kooijmans T, *Het Nederlands strafprocesrecht* (10th edn, Wolters Kluwer 2021).

Dane NM, 'Overheidsaansprakelijkheid voor schade bij legitiem strafvorderlijk handelen', DPhil thesis, University of Leiden, 2009.

Duker MJA, 'Niet-imperatieve toekenning bij onterecht ondergane verzekering en voorlopige hechtenis?' in AL Melai and MS Groenhuijsen et al. (eds), *Wetboek van Strafvordering* (Kluwer 2015).

Duker MJA, 'Schadevergoeding wegens andere onterecht ten uitvoer gelegde sancties?' in AL Melai and MS Groenhuijsen et al. (eds), *Wetboek van Strafvordering* (Kluwer 2007).

Holvast NL, Nan JS and Lestrade SMA, 'Between legal certainty and doubt' (2020) *Erasmus Law Review* 13.

Jiang Na, *Wrongful Convictions in China. Comparative and Empirical Perspectives* (1st edn, Springer 2016).

Kwakman NJM, 'Schadecompensatie in het strafproces', DPhil thesis, University of Groningen, 2003).

Loyson JWHG, 'De raadkamerprocedures in strafzaken' (2020) *Praktijkwijzer Strafrecht* 14.
Nan JS et al., *Victa vincit veritas?* (1st edn, Boom Juridisch 2018).
Nan JS and others, 'Evaluatie van de Wet hervorming herziening ten voordele' (2019) *Nederlands Juristenblad* 184.
de Ranitz REP, *Herziening van arresten en vonnissen* (Tjeenk Willink 1977).
Schelhaas HN and Taekema HS, 'The outlines of Dutch private law' in HS Taekema, A de Roo and C Elion-Valter (eds), *Understanding Dutch law* (3rd edn, Boom juridisch 2020).
Smidt HJ, *Geschiedenis van het Wetboek van Strafrecht (1881–1886): Deel II* (Tjeenk Willink 1881).
Strijards GAM, *Revisie: inbreuken en executiegeschillen betreffende het strafgewijsde* (Gouda Quint 1989).
Taekema HS and Nan JS, 'Principles of Dutch criminal law' in HS Taekema, AJ de Roo and C Elion-Valter (eds), *Understanding Dutch Law* (3rd edn, Boom juridisch 2020).
van Dorst AJA, 'Herziening in strafzaken' in MF Attinger et al./PAM Mevis et al. (eds), *Handboek Strafzaken* (Wolters Kluwer 2021).
van Hooijdonk M and Eijsvoogel P, *Litigation in the Netherlands: Civil Procedure, Arbitration and Administrative Litigation* (2nd edn, Wolters Kluwer 2009).

Table of cases

Van Mechelen and others v. the Netherlands App no 21363/93 21364/93 21427/93 22056/93 (ECtHR, 30 October 1997).
Supreme Court 28 May 1985, ECLI:NL:PHR:1985:AC8907, *NJ* 1985/909.
Supreme Court 13 October 2006, ECLI:NL:HR:2006:AV6956, *NJ* 2007/432.
Supreme Court 6 July 1999, ECLI:NL:HR:1999:ZD1603, *NJ* 1999/800.
Supreme Court 22 April 2008, ECLI:NL:HR:2008:BB7077, *NJ* 2008, 468 m.nt. M.J. Borgers.
Supreme Court 14 February 2017, ECLI:NL:HR:2017:221, *NJ* 2017/140 m.nt. S.D. Lindenbergh.
Supreme Court 14 February 2017, ECLI:NL:HR:2017:221, *NJ* 2017/140 m.nt. SD Lindenbergh.
Supreme Court 15 May 2020, ECLI:NL:HR:2020:890, *NJ* 2020/269 m.nt. J.W. Zwemmer.
Court of Appeal Arnhem 28 March 1989, ECLI:NL:GHARN:1989:AD0697, *NJ* 1989/776.
Court of Appeal Leeuwarden 4 October 2002, ECLI:NL:GHLEE:2002:AE8347.
Court of Appeal Leeuwarden 4 October 2002, ECLI:NL:GHLEE:2002:AE8348.
Court of Appeal Leeuwarden 4 October 2002, ECLI:NL:GHLEE:2002:AE8349.
Court of Appeal Leeuwarden 4 October 2002, ECLI:NL:GHLEE:2002:AE8350.
Court of Appeal Leeuwarden 4 October 2002, ECLI:NL:GHLEE:2002:AE8351.
Court of Appeal Leeuwarden 4 October 2002, ECLI:NL:GHLEE:2002:AE8352.
Court of Appeal Leeuwarden 4 October 2002, ECLI:NL:GHLEE:2002:AE8353.
Court of Appeal's-Gravenhage 5 June 2003, ECLI:NL:GHSGR:2003:AF9801.
Joint Court of Justice of Aruba, Curaçao, Sint Maarten, and of Bonaire, Sint Eustatius and Saba 11 October 2014, ECLI:NL:OGHACMB:2014:8, m.nt. T.M. Schalken (*Spelonk*).

6 Compensation for wrongful convictions in Norway

Ulf Stridbeck

1 Short background about the Norwegian reopening model for wrongful convictions

Following the examples of England and Scotland, in 2004 Norway established the Norwegian Criminal Cases Review Commission (NCCRC),[1] which is an independent administrative body outside the court hierarchy, with the power to investigate and decide on the reopening of criminal cases.[2]

There are several grounds upon which the NCCRC may reopen a case: if there is compelling new evidence of relevance to the outcome of the case, a decision from an international court or improper behaviour by a law professional or others involved in the criminal case is determined. Section 391 of the Norwegian Criminal Procedure Act states:[3]

> In favour of the convicted person reopening of a case may be required:
>
> (1) when a judge, member of the jury, keeper of the records, police officer or official in prosecuting authority, prosecutor, defence counsel, expert or court interpreter has been guilty of a criminal offence in relation to the case, or a witness has given false evidence in the case, or a document that has been used in the case is false or forged, and it cannot be excluded that this has affected the judgment to the detriment of the person charged,
> (2) when an international court or UN human rights committee has in a case against Norway found that athe decision conflicts with a rule of international law that is binding on Norway, and it must be assumed that a new hearing

1 <www.gjenopptakelse.no/en/> accessed 19 July 2022.

2 See Ulf Stridbeck and Svein Magnussen (2011), Opening Potentially Wrongful Convictions – Look to Norway, *Criminal Law Quarterly*, Vol. 58: Iss. 2; Ulf Stridbeck and Svein Magnussen (2012) 'Prevention of Wrongful Convictions: Norwegian Legal Safeguards and the Criminal Cases Review Commission', *University of Cincinnati Law Review*: Vol. 80: Iss. 4, Article 15.

3 Lov om rettergangsmåten i straffesaker (Straffeprosessloven) LOV 22. mai 1981 nr. 25. [Norwegian Criminal Procedure Act, referred to as CPA], section 391, available at <http://www.ub.uio.no/ujur/ulovdata/lov-19810522-025-eng.pdf> accessed 19 July 2022.

DOI: 10.4324/9781003229414-7

> should lead to a different decision, or the procedure on which the decision is based conflicts with a rule of international law that is binding on Norway and there is reason to assume that the procedural error may have influenced the substance of the decision, and that a reopening of the case is necessary in order to remedy the harm that the error has caused.
>
> (3) When a new circumstance is revealed or new evidence is procured which seems likely to lead to an acquittal or summary dismissal of the case or to the application of a more lenient penal provision or a substantially more lenient sanction. In a case in which a custodial sentence, committal to compulsory mental health care pursuant to section 39 of the Penal Code, compulsory care pursuant to section 39 of the Penal Code or loss of civil rights is not imposed, new information or evidence that the person concerned should have presented at an earlier stage may not be produced.

The most frequent ground for reopening in favour of the convicted person is 'new evidence or new circumstances' (in 85 per cent of cases), followed by the special reason for reopening in section 392 second paragraph when special circumstances make it doubtful whether the judgment is correct (7 per cent) and an international court's decision (6 per cent). In a single case, there was a combination of grounds (2 per cent).[4]

Applications to the NCCRC for reopening can be made either in a convicted person's favour or to his/her detriment. It is extremely rare, if ever, that the public prosecutor's office, based on new evidence, including new technical analyses, requests that a final and conclusive judgment is reopened to the detriment of an acquitted person.[5] It is more common that the prosecutor requests that a case should be reopened in favour of a convicted person.

The NCCRC can be considered as a combination of an appeal court and the Innocence Project, well known in the US[6] and in some European countries,[7] where the responsibility for further investigation and the power to decide on reopening reside within the same body.

The Commission consists of five members and three deputies. Three of the five members have legal training, while the other two are laypeople. In addition, the NCCRC has its own investigative corps that investigates cases after an application for reopening has been received. The Commission has the legislative power to reopen cases and forward them to the courts. It has public financing and accepts all types of criminal cases.

4 Sixty-eight cases were considered. Jane Dullum, *Justisfeil i straffesaker. En analyse av saker behandlet av Kommisjonen for gjenopptakelse av straffesaker (Gjenopptakelseskommisjonen) i perioden 2004–2009*. [Errors of Justice in Criminal Cases. An Analysis of Cases Dealt with by the NCCRC in the Period 2004–2009] Oslo 2010, 46.

5 It has happened twice during the existence of NCCRC. In both cases, new advanced DNA analyses documented that the previously acquitted person was the perpetrator.

6 <innocenceproject.org> accessed 1 March 2022.

7 <euinnocencenetwork.org> accessed 1 March 2022.

The NCCRC receives around 170 applications annually, a number that is increasing. 2021 was an abnormal year; the Commission considered 223 cases and reopened 82 of them.[8] There was a clutch of cases triggered by the systemic and scandalous overlooking of European law regarding freedom of movement and social security benefits that had led to tens of custodial sentences and huge fines that the prosecuting authorities themselves eventually asked to be reopened. These social security cases are fraud cases, which is why that category was unusually large in 2021. The number of traditional cases with new acquittal evidence was as usual. In normal years the NCCRC reopens 20 cases. Only six murder cases have been reopened since 2004. Fifty-three cases of non-homicide violence have been reopened since 2004, 167 of economic crime and 40 of drug crime.[9]

As the decision on continued conviction or acquittal after the reopening is decided by a court – a different court from the one which convicted the person but at the same level – it is not within the NCCRC's mandate to take a position on the issue of compensation. When the NCCRC decides on reopening, they simply do not know what the legal outcome of the retrial will be. Eighty-three per cent of the new trials end with acquittal.[10] The other 17 per cent of new sentences are usually more lenient than the original sentence, since the courts often reach the same conclusion as the Commission. In such cases, the convicted person may be acquitted of some charges but convicted on others, thus receiving a new sentence for these. In cases where the court does not find the new evidence sufficient for acquittal on any charges they end up with the same verdict as in the original case.[11]

2 Origins and development of compensation for wrongful convictions

The Nordic countries introduced rules on compensation for wrongful prosecution and convictions at about the same time in the 1880s. In Norway, the rules on compensation for wrongful convictions have been formed in three stages. Norway got its first regulation in the Criminal Procedure Act of 1887.[12] It was strongly influenced by German regulation. The first Norwegian law only offered compensation for pecuniary loss. It was not until the new Criminal Procedure Act in 1981, which came into force in 1986, that rules on damages for non-pecuniary

8 NCCRC, *Annual Report 2021*, see <www.gjenopptakelse.no> accessed 19 July 2022.

9 ibid

10 Justis- og beredskapsdepartementet Ministry of Justice and Public Security, *Etterkontroll av kommisjonen for gjenopptakelse av straffesaker* [Evaluation of the Criminal Cases Review Commission] (2012) (report from a government-appointed working group chaired by Professor Ulf Stridbeck) [hereinafter *Evaluation of the Criminal Cases Review Commission*], 37.

11 *Evaluation of the Criminal Cases Review Commission*, 37.

12 Lov om Rettergangsmaaden i Straffesager (Opphevd) LOV-1887-07-01-5 [Act on the Procedure in Criminal Cases (Repealed)].

loss (redress) were introduced in Norway.[13] However, the 1981 Act was largely a continuation of the practice developed under the old law.

In 2003, a comprehensive revision of the compensation chapter in the Criminal Procedure Act was made.[14] The law came into force in 2004. The change in the law meant that those who had been affected by wrongful conviction had, to a greater extent than previously, legal claims for compensation for direct pecuniary consequences and non-pecuniary consequences. Recognition of compensation and legal claims became mandatory and in some limited areas standardized.[15]

This led to the question of whether compensation should be decided by a centralized administrative body as opposed to the decentralized procedure by a local court. Prior to 2004, the court that had previously taken a position on the question of guilt also decided on compensation.[16] In 2004 the decision on compensation was transferred to the *Statens Sivilrettsforvaltning* (State Civil Law Administration (SCLA)).[17] The SCLA is a governmental body that is responsible for a number of areas of civil law: guardianship, legal aid, compensation after prosecution and so on. The SCLA is also responsible for a number of state schemes that are of great importance to individuals in Norway. These schemes are intended to strengthen the rule of law and ensure the rights of the individual.

The aim of the reform was both to better ensure the accused's legal security, including ensuring that the rules were in accordance with the requirements of the European Convention on Human Rights (ECHR), and a desire to make the processing of compensation claims more efficient and less resource intensive.

The Norwegian Criminal Procedure Act chapter 31 provides rules (sections 444–451) on the right to compensation for wrongful investigation, prosecution and conviction. Society, not any particular individual, bears the economic consequences of the errors of justice.

Once the NCCRC has reopened the case, it is back on the normal criminal procedure track. If the person in the retrial is convicted again, he/she is sentenced again, and if s/he is acquitted, he/she may apply for compensation. In this case, the same rules apply as regular compensation cases in the event of acquittal on appeal.

13 Ken Uggerud, *Erstatning etter straffeforfølgelse* [Compensation after Prosecution], 1998, 23ff..

14 Act 10 January 2003, number 3. See also Johs. Andenæs and Tor-Geir Myhrer, *Norsk straffeprosess* [Norwegian Criminal Procedure], 4th ed. 2009, chapter 77.

15 There is standard compensation for stay in police custody. Wrongful custody of more than four hours is compensated by 1,500 NKR (€150) per day, Forskrift om standardsatser for oppreisning etter uberettiget strafforfølgning FOR-2003-12-12-1472 [Regulations on standard rates for redress after unjustified criminal prosecution], section 2.

16 Johs Andenæs and Tor-Geir Myhrer, *Norsk straffeprosess* [Norwegian Criminal Procedure], 4th ed. 2009, 612.

17 See <sivilrett.no> accessed 19 July 2022.

3 Sources of law (e.g. parliamentary acts, precedents) regulating compensation for wrongful convictions

The international source of law regulating compensation is Protocol No. 7 to the Convention for the Protection of Human Rights and Fundamental Freedoms.[18] The protocol has a special provision on compensation for wrongful conviction, Article 3:

> When a person has by a final decision been convicted of a criminal offence and when subsequently his conviction has been reversed, or he has been pardoned, on the ground that a new or newly discovered fact shows conclusively that there has been a miscarriage of justice, the person who has suffered punishment as a result of such conviction *shall be compensated according to the law or the practice of the State concerned*, unless it is proved that the nondisclosure of the unknown fact in time is wholly or partly attributable to him.[19]

Norway has incorporated the conventions on human rights into Norwegian law.[20]

The Criminal Procedure Act chapter 31 regulates compensation in criminal cases. The main rule is section 444, which states that a charged person is entitled to compensation from the state for pecuniary loss if he/she has been acquitted, if the investigation has been stopped or if he/she has been arrested or imprisoned in violation of the ECHR, Article 5 or the International Covenant on Civil and Political Rights (ICCPR), Article 9.[21] In cases where a person has been acquitted, he/she has a right to compensation for the damage the prosecution has caused him/her – regardless of the basis for the acquittal.[22]

> Section 444.
> Unless it is otherwise provided by section 446, a person charged is entitled to compensation by the State for any financial loss that the prosecution[23] has caused him aif he is acquitted bif the prosecution against him is discontinued cin so far as he has been arrested or detained in custody contrary to Article 5 of the European Convention on Human Rights or Article 9 of the UN International Covenant on Civil and Political Rights.
> A convicted person is also entitled to compensation for financial loss due to execution of a sentence that exceeds any sentence imposed after the case has been reopened.

18 European Convention on Human Rights <https://www.echr.coe.int/documents/convention_eng.pdf> accessed 19 July 2022.
19 My italics.
20 Lov om styrking av menneskerettighetenes stilling i norsk rett (menneskerettsloven) LOV-1999-05-21-30 [Act on strengthening the position of human rights in Norwegian law (Human Rights Act)].
21 <www.ohchr.org/en/professionalinterest/pages/ccpr.aspx> accessed 19 July 2022.
22 See the preparatory works of the Norwegian Criminal Procedure Act, Ot.prp. nr. 77 (2001–2002) 79.
23 'Prosecution' is the interrogation and the indictment. One could have written 'that the criminal process has inflicted on him'.

Even if the conditions for compensation for pecuniary loss, pursuant to section 444, are not fulfilled, the person charged shall, if it appears to be reasonable, be awarded damages for pecuniary loss resulting from special or disproportionate damage the prosecution has caused him/her.

> Section 445.
> Even if the conditions for compensation prescribed in section 444 are not fulfilled, the person charged shall, if it appears to be reasonable, be awarded compensation for financial loss resulting from special or disproportionate damage that the prosecution has caused him.

Section 445 sets out three conditions for compensation. First, the prosecution must have inflicted 'special or disproportionate harm' on the person. Second, this harm must have caused the person pecuniary loss. Third, it must appear reasonable to award the person compensation for the loss. If the cause, nature and consequences of the damage exceed what is usual in criminal proceedings, and compensation appears reasonable in light of the authorities' and the perpetrator's behaviour and the burdens imposed by the criminal proceedings, compensation shall be awarded. In some rare cases when 'it is proved that the nondisclosure of the unknown fact in time is wholly or partly attributable to him'[24] or the convicted assisted in the sentencing, for example by giving a false confession, the compensation may be reduced or cease to be payable. Compensation awarded pursuant to sections 444 and 445 may also be reduced or cease to be payable if the person charged has without reasonable grounds refused to give a statement to the police or withheld information about the case, has otherwise contributed to the conviction or has not helped to limit the damage. The SCLA must be careful when justifying the reduction. It can quickly become a violation of the presumption of innocence if it is argued that the acquitted person had exhibited conduct that contributed to the incorrect conviction. The voicing of suspicions regarding an accused's innocence is a violation of ECHR Article 6 No. 2.

4 Grounds for compensation for wrongful convictions

There are two grounds for compensation: compensation for pecuniary loss and compensation for non-pecuniary loss (redress).

4.1 Damages for direct pecuniary loss

To be able to file a claim for compensation for pecuniary loss (*condition sine quo non)*, the acquittal must be a final and conclusive judgment. This means the judgment is not final until the term of appeal has expired. There has to be a causal connection and adequacy between the wrongful conviction and damage suffered. If the pecuniary loss would have occurred in any case, the requirement of a causal

24 Convention for the Protection of Human Rights and Fundamental Freedoms, Article 3.

link would not have been met. The acquitted person has the burden of proving that he/she has suffered a loss due to the prosecution's decision not to proceed with the case or due to a wrongful conviction. It follows that it is incumbent upon the acquitted person to provide evidence of the loss and its amount.

The assessment of the *pecuniary loss* follows the general rules of tort law, such as lost earnings, travel expenses or loss of clients or customers. Determination of full compensation presupposes that liability has been established. The state has statutory strict liability for losses covered by the section.

If after reopening the new trial ends with a new sentence shorter than the first one, the convicted is entitled to compensation for the time the original punishment exceeded the new punishment.

4.2 Damages for non-pecuniary loss

The Criminal Procedure Act section 447 subsection 3 provides rules on damages for *non-pecuniary loss (redress)* if the accused has been subject to a custodial sentence, and then been acquitted after reopening. The acquitted person is entitled to damages for non-pecuniary loss determined after an individual specific assessment.

> A person who is acquitted after having served a custodial sentence is entitled to redress for humiliation or any other injury of a non-pecuniary nature. The amount thereof shall be determined according to the circumstances of the particular case.[25]

Variations from case to case, such as how stigmatizing the crime was, the length of the sentence and the individual circumstances of the convicted person, mean that damages for non-pecuniary loss are not standardized. For example, one year's imprisonment is not always compensated by the same amount of money: one year as part of a long sentence sometimes counts less than one year in a short sentence. In the case of damages for non-economic loss, the amount is calculated after a specific assessment of reasonableness. An appropriate amount shall be offered which appears reasonable for the suffering to which the acquitted person has been subjected. The size of the compensation varies from the purely symbolic patch on the wound for minor offences to very large amounts for serious legal errors. However, it is difficult to determine an amount for suffering that essentially cannot be measured in monetary terms. It has to be an overall assessment of the suffering the punishment has inflicted on the convicted person. As an illustration, in the Liland case (mentioned below) the Supreme Court justified the non-pecuniary loss of 10 million NOK (approximately €1.7 million) by the following:

> A significant amount of money may be suitable to mark society's assessment of the failure of the judicial system that has taken place. Pursuant to the Criminal Procedure Act, the decision shall be made at discretion. In determining, it must

25 CPA, section 447 subsection 3.

be taken into account that the conviction applies to very serious crimes. It must also be taken into account that the infringement has been extremely long-lasting.[26]

5 Procedure for claiming compensation

The case processing is a written procedure.[27] The acquitted person's claims for damages after wrongful conviction shall be presented to the police district[28] that investigated the case. The prosecution authority in that district shall comment on the case. This comment or statement, together with the case documents, must be sent to the SCLA. Based on the claim, the prosecution authority's statement and the case documents, a department director at the SCLA, after ordinary case processing, makes his/her decision. If necessary, the SCLA has the opportunity to obtain its own evidence. The decisions are detailed and reasoned. Moreover, they are public and can be read in anonymous form on Lovdata.no, a public website for all Norwegian court decisions.[29]

The SCLA's decisions cannot be appealed.[30] However, the Director of the SCLA can, ex officio or pointed out by the applicant, reconsider his/her decisions[31] if there is new and significant information of importance for the outcome of the case.

Besides the administrative process in the SCLA, there are two other ways in which compensation can be obtained. If the acquitted person is dissatisfied with the amount decided by the SCLA, he/she may take the compensation case to a court for a civil trial,[32] according to the rules in the Disputes Act,[33] where the state is sued by the exonerated person.

In cases where the exonerated person has been imprisoned for many years with great media attention, extensive public discussion and obvious errors of justice, the government may, to avoid a lawsuit, decide to award higher compensation than that offered by the SCLA. In this situation, the state enters into a settlement on the grounds of reasonableness. The decisive factors are how severe and stigmatizing the wrongful conviction has been. This is a political decision made by the Minister of Justice. In the Moen case[34] (mentioned below), the Minister of Justice

26 Supreme Court Judgment: Rt-1995–1131.
27 SCA, website; <https://www.sivilrett.no/erstatning-etter-strafforfoelgning.556839.no.html> accessed 19 July 2022.
28 CPA, section 449.
29 Lovdata.no is a Norwegian foundation that publishes judicial information about Norway.
30 CPA, section 449 first paragraph.
31 Public administration in Norway can always correct errors or mistakes. This will be a correction made by the same instance, not an appeal to a higher level.
32 CPA, section 449 second paragraph.
33 Lov om mekling og rettergang i sivile tvister (tvisteloven) LOV-2021–06–18–126 [Act on Mediation and Trial in Civil Disputes – The Dispute Act].
34 Borgarting Appeal Court Judgment: LB-2006-99831-1.

increased the damages for non-pecuniary loss. Formally, it was a settlement between Mr Moen and the state that ended with additional compensation.

In a case concerning damages subsequent to a prosecution, the person charged is entitled to free legal advice.[35] However, there is no formal right to a free trial. If the acquitted party's claim is upheld, the other party – the state – covers its own legal costs. As long as the lawsuit is reasonable, the state, like the other party, covers its own costs. However, when the acquitted person loses the case against the state, he/she has to pay the court fees.

6 Calculating the amount of compensation

There is no automatic or standardized payment of compensation. The acquitted person has to apply for it. Furthermore, the acquitted person must prove the pecuniary loss by means of invoices, tax claims, sick leave, medical certificates and anything else that can document the pecuniary consequences of the wrongful conviction.

The monetary value of non-pecuniary loss on the other hand is difficult to calculate. The assessment of the size of the non-pecuniary loss is based both on objective features of the wrongful conviction, such as the nature of the charge and the duration of the sentence, and the subjective consequences this has entailed, such as stigmatization. Where the objective circumstances of the case appear to be dominant in the violation, somewhat less emphasis is placed on the personal circumstances of the convicted person, especially with regard to the duration of the deprivation of liberty and the total violation.

7 The recourse claim of the state against persons who caused wrongful convictions

If a judge, lay judge, registrar, police officer, prosecutor, defence counsel, expert or court interpreter has committed a criminal offence in connection with a criminal case, it may be reopened according to CPA section 391 1. However, although such actions have been alleged in Norway, they have never yet been used as a basis for reopening a case.

If a court were to find that one of the actors mentioned has committed such an offence, he/she may be fined and possibly deprived of his/her position. However, the acquitted person will not get compensation directly from the criminal actor. That is, there is no possibility of making a recourse claim against persons who caused wrongful convictions in Norway. The acquitted person may claim compensation for damage from the state, in the ordinary way.

8 The practice of compensating the wrongfully convicted

Claims for compensation in reopened cases can result in large payments in serious cases. During the NCCRC's first eight years (2004–2011), the SCLA dealt with

35 CPA, section 450.

32 compensation cases. Some 54 million NOK (approximately €6.5 million) was paid out in this period, divided into 44 million NOK (approximately €5 million) after the SCLA's decision and 10 million NOK (approximately €1 million) after court proceedings. It is also divided into 16 million NOK (approximately €2 million) for pecuniary loss and 38 million NOK (approximately €4.5 million) for non-pecuniary loss.[36]

There are no detailed statistics since 2011. A rough overview would indicate that an average of four cases get compensation from the SCLA annually. As the NCCRC reopens about 15 cases annually, this means that roughly only a fifth of the acquitted claim compensation.

The leading case on compensation for wrongful conviction is the Liland case. The sentence was life imprisonment for killing two men with an axe. Per Liland served 14 years in prison and was subject to preventive non-custodial supervision for a further ten years. In 1995, he was acquitted.[37] The Supreme Court stated: 'Liland has been the victim of a miscarriage of justice in one of the worst ways imaginable, and has been deprived of a very large part of his life.'[38]

This case is the first known criminal case in Norway that considered non-pecuniary loss. The court calculated the amount based on the length of the sentence, if there were any special terms, special conditions the imprisonment underwent, the severity of the criminal act and the degree of reprehensibility in the actions of the police or prosecutors. With reference to the judgment: 'The violation is so extensive here, the unjust intervention in Liland's life so total, that one already approaches a maximum of injustice in relation to what money can repair or alleviate.'[39]

In addition, reprehensible treatment by the prosecuting authority and the police was a key element of assessment.[40]

In 1995 Liland received 10 million NOK (approximately €1.7 million) in non-pecuniary damages and 3 million NOK (approximately €0.5 million) in compensation for 14 years' imprisonment.[41]

In the Moen case (2005), his estate, after his death, received 20 million NOK (approximately €3 million) in non-pecuniary damages, after a settlement concerning compensation with the state, after reopening and acquittal for imprisonment for 18 years for two murders he had not committed.[42] The Minister of Justice also issued a public apology:

> I wish to make an unreserved apology to Fritz Moen and those who knew him and to his loved ones, for the injustice he was subjected to. There can be no excuses for the amount of suffering and injustice Fritz Moen was subjected to. This must be avoided in the future.

36 *Evaluation of the Criminal Cases Review Commission*, 39.
37 Supreme Court Judgment: Rt-1994–1149.
38 Supreme Court Judgment: Rt-1995–1131, 1135.
39 Supreme Court Judgment: Rt-1997–995, 999.
40 Supreme Court Judgment: Rt-1995–1131, 1136.
41 Supreme Court Judgment: Rt-1995–1131.
42 *Evaluation of the Criminal Cases Review Commission*.

9 Evaluation of the national mechanism for the compensation for wrongful convictions

Since the preparatory writing of the act in 2003,[43] there has not been any evaluation of the compensation model. Furthermore, there is no ongoing discussion about compensation for wrongful convictions in Norway.

As there has not been any public discussion on this topic, it can be considered as not sufficiently politically interesting. It is also possible that the SCLA is always on target, with the consequence that an evaluation is not necessary.

In my opinion, the Norwegian compensation model works well. Almost all of the acquitted who apply get more or less what they claim. However, only a very limited number of compensation cases – four to six annually out of more than 20 reopened cases – are brought before the courts every year. For some individuals, the most important thing may be to be found innocent and therefore pecuniary compensation is not necessary. Another explanation might be that very few serious cases with long sentences are reopened. Most of the cases are petty crimes with short sentences. For example, on average a murder case is only reopened once every three years. Forty per cent of the cases are reopened due to incorrect assessment of sanity. Many of these insanity cases are traffic cases: driving without a driver's licence or drink-driving. In these cases, the person has objectively performed the action but has not been subjectively liable since he/she was not fit to stand trial. Some of them concern fines as punishment. In many of these insanity cases, the convicted person has confessed to the crime, since he/she actually performed the action.

The size of the pecuniary compensation depends on what can be documented by pecuniary loss. Those amounts are probably correct. It is more difficult to assess the size of the non-pecuniary loss. Since the loss of freedom is impossible to put an economic value on – 'What is life worth?' – it is impossible to say when the non-pecuniary damages are adequate. Damages for non-pecuniary loss are also an expression of moral suffering, which is also difficult to put an economic value on. Moreover, the moral condemnation is both individual and dependent on the nature of the action. There is no objective norm for what the correct level of non-pecuniary damages should be. However, the leading cases of Liland and Moen provide guidelines for non-pecuniary damages.

Bibliography

Andenæs J and Myhrer T-G, *Norsk straffeprosess* [Norwegian Criminal Procedure], 4th ed. Universitetsforlaget (2009)

Dullum J, *Justisfeil i straffesaker. En analyse av saker behandlet av Kommisjonen for gjenopptakelse av straffesaker (Gjenopptakelseskommisjonen) i perioden 2004–2009.* [Errors of justice in criminal cases] Report Institutt for kriminologi og rettssociologi, Universitetet i Oslo (2010)

43 Ot.prp. nr. 77 (2001–2002).

Justis- og beredskapsdepartementet [Ministry of Justice and Public Security].,*Etterkontroll av kommisjonen for gjenopptakelse av straffesaker* [*Evaluation of the Criminal Cases Review Commission*] (2012)

Kommisjonen for gjenopptakelse av straffesaker, *Annual Report 2021*, <www.gjenopptakelse.no>

Stridbeck U and Magnussen S, 'Opening Potentially Wrongful Convictions – Look to Norway', *Criminal Law Quarterly*, (2011) Vol. 58: Iss. 2

Stridbeck U and Magnussen S, 'Prevention of Wrongful Convictions: Norwegian Legal Safeguards and the Criminal Cases Review Commission', *University of Cincinnati Law Review* (2012) Vol. 80: Iss. 4, Article 15

Uggerud K, *Erstatning etter straffeforfølgelse* [Compensation after Prosecution] Cappelen Damm Akademisk (1998)

Table of cases

Borgarting Appeal Court Judgment: LB-2006-99831-1
Supreme Court Judgment: Rt-1994–1149.
Supreme Court Judgment: Rt-1995–1131.
Supreme Court Judgment: Rt-1997–1995.

7 Compensation for wrongful convictions in Lithuania

Simona Drukteinienė

1 Origins and development of compensation for unlawful[1] conviction

It was not until 1990 that, having gained independence from the Soviet regime, Lithuania started developing modern tortious liability of the State.[2] Soviet law, which was introduced after the occupation of the Republic of Lithuania in 1944, did not accept the principle of public liability. Art. 486 of the Soviet Civil Code of 1964[3] (hereinafter the CC of 1964) indicated that the liability for unlawful conviction rests on the State irrespective of the fault of State officials, although special laws shall regulate the compensation mechanism. Under the authoritarian regime this norm remained inactive.

Immediately after the restoration of independence, the Lithuanian State started developing modern public liability rules. By the law of 1994 art. 485 the CC of 1964 was modified,[4] indicating that damage caused to a physical or legal person by unlawful actions of public organizations or State officials in the sphere of administrative governance shall be compensated according to the general liability rules. By the same law, art. 486 of the CC of 1964 was modified, replacing the word 'citizen' with the term 'physical person' as the victim[5] eligible for compensation and indicating in a new second part the right to non-pecuniary damages. Art. 486 of the CC of 1964 was modified again by the law of 1997. After modification, the norm stated that damage, including non-pecuniary damage, caused by unlawful conviction, detention, temporary apprehension or other procedural coercive measures shall be compensated in accordance with the rules established by the special law.

1 The term 'wrongful conviction' has the connotation of the element of fault. In Lithuania it is understood that this type of liability is strict; therefore, the term 'unlawful conviction' reflects the regulation better. For this reason, the term 'unlawful conviction' will be used throughout this chapter.
2 The terms 'tortious liability of the State', 'public liability' and 'state liability' are used as synonyms in this chapter and mean liability of the State for the damage caused by unlawful actions of public institutions and servants while exercising public functions.
3 *Official gazette*, 1964, no. 19–138.
4 *Official gazette*, 1994, no. 44–805.
5 The term 'victim' refers to the one who has suffered from tort. In this report the term 'victim' means a physical person who has suffered from wrongful conviction.

DOI: 10.4324/9781003229414-8

From November 1997 until 2002 the Law on Compensation for Damage Inflicted by Unlawful Actions of Interrogatory and Investigatory Bodies, the Prosecutor's Office and Court[6] was in force. It regulated issues of compensation for damage caused by unlawful actions of investigatory bodies, the prosecutor's office and courts, including compensation for unlawful conviction. The law stated that a person has the right to compensation for pecuniary and non-pecuniary damage caused by unlawful conviction, detention or temporary apprehension. Unlawful acts are breaches of laws by the court or other public officials, confirmed as such by decision of a court or other competent institution. A person shall seek compensation for damage in civil proceedings by filing the claim with the court. When the damage was caused by the court, the respondent shall be the Ministry of Justice of the Republic of Lithuania, and in other cases the institution whose officials have acted unlawfully.

The Civil Code of independent Lithuania[7] (hereinafter the CC) of 1 July 2001 introduced a modern regime of tortious liability for the damage caused by wrongs of public institutions. Art. 6.271 CC provides for the State and municipal liability for damage caused by State (municipal) institutions while exercising their public functions. Art. 6.272 CC governs State liability for damage caused by unlawful actions of State judiciary and law-enforcement institutions.

The newly introduced system of liability, set out in arts. 6.271–6.273 CC, abandoned the immunity principle of the State and established liability rules favourable to the victim. Art. 6.271 CC sets out the general tortious liability rules of the State; art. 6.272 CC is specifically designated for damage caused in the sphere of pretrial investigation and judiciary. Both norms indicate that the liable person is the State, not the individual institution. Art. 6.273 CC regulates who is the representative of the State in civil cases.

The Law on Compensation for Damage Inflicted by Unlawful Actions of Interrogatory and Investigatory Bodies, the Prosecutor's Office and Court of 1997 was replaced in 2002 by the new version of the Law on the Compensation for Damage Inflicted by the Unlawful Acts of Public Institutions and the Representation of the State and the Government of the Republic of Lithuania[8] (hereinafter the Law on the Compensation for Damage). The new CC in its three articles regulates all the main issues of public liability; thus the old version of the law of 1997 was no longer needed. The new version of the law of 2002 provides for the extrajudicial procedure of compensation for damage resulting from unlawful implementation of justice, the allocation and use of public finances for the compensation for damage and some issues of recourse by the State to its officers.

2 Sources of law regulating compensation for unlawful conviction

Compensation for unlawful conviction is regulated by art. 6.272 CC. This article governs State liability for damage caused by unlawful actions of State judiciary and law-enforcement institutions. Art. 6.272(1) CC stipulates:

6 *Official gazette*, 1997, no. 104–2618.
7 *Official gazette*, 2000, no. 74–2262; 2000, no. 77–0; 2000, no. 80–0; 2000, no. 82–0.
8 *Official gazette*, 2002, no. 56–2228.

> Damage resulting either from unlawful conviction, or unlawful detention as well as from unlawful temporary apprehension, or unlawful application of procedural coercive measures, or unlawful infliction of administrative penalty – arrest – shall be compensated fully by the state irrespective of the fault of the officials of preliminary investigation, prosecution or court.

The Law on the Compensation of Damage provides for the extrajudicial procedure of compensation of damage resulting either from unlawful conviction or unlawful temporary apprehension, as well as from unlawful detention, unlawful procedural coercive measures[9] or unlawful infliction of administrative penalty – arrest. The victim should address the Ministry of Justice with the request to compensate the damage within the period of three months after it became aware of the unlawfulness of the abovementioned measures. The Ministry of Justice should consider the application within three months. In the case of a positive decision by the Ministry of Justice the compensation offered may not exceed €10,000 in pecuniary damages and €5,000 in non-pecuniary damages. However, the amounts have been increased only recently.[10] Until 31 December 2022 the maximum amount in pecuniary damages was €2,900 and in non-pecuniary damages €1,500. If the person agrees with the positive decision of the Ministry of Justice, the agreement is signed by both parties. In the case of a negative decision or if the victim is not satisfied with the compensation offered, he may initiate the regular court proceedings.

Since 9 June 2021 by virtue on new article 2^1 of the Law on the Compensation of Damage the persons are entitled for compensation in pecuniary damages amounting to maximum 50 basic social benefits[11] for detention if the decision to terminate pretrial investigation or acquitting decision was adopted in their cases. In this instance, the person is not obliged to prove wrongfulness or unlawfulness of the State officials. The term to address the Ministry of Justice is one year after the decision to terminate pretrial investigation or announcement of the acquitting decision.

In both cases described above, the extrajudicial procedure is not compulsory. The victim may always address the court directly with the claim for compensation for damage. In the second case the victim is entitled to accept the compensation in pecuniary damages for detention and address the court for higher compensation in pecuniary damages and compensation in non-pecuniary damages. In this case the victim must prove all conditions of liability of the State, including unlawfulness.

The right to compensation is also regulated at the constitutional level. Article 30(2) of the Constitution[12] sets out that 'compensation for material and moral damage inflicted upon a person shall be established by law'. According to the

9 Procedural coercive measures include temporary apprehension, intensive care, house arrest, obligation to live apart from the victim and/or not to approach the victim closer than a specified distance, bail, seizure of documents, suspension of a special right, obligation to periodically register at a police station, written undertaking not to leave the place of residence, etc.

10 *Official gazette*, 2022, no. 56-2228.

11 Basic social benefit is social index periodically established by the Government of the Republic of Lithuania. Since 1 June 2022 one basic social benefit amounts to €46.

12 *Official gazette*, 1992, no. 33–1014.

consistent practice of the Constitutional Court of the Republic of Lithuania (hereinafter the Constitutional Court), the necessity to compensate damage is a constitutional principle.[13] In the ruling on the constitutionality of the Law on the Compensation for Damage of 1997, the Constitutional Court stated that art. 30 (2) of the Constitution does not allow for legal exceptions which would exclude compensation for pecuniary or non-pecuniary damage.[14] Therefore, when facing the question of compensation for damage, the courts have constitutional powers to compensate such damage by invoking the Constitution directly (including the constitutional principles of justice, legal certainty, proportionality, due process, equality and other constitutional provisions). Based on this explanation damages were awarded by the court to a person for the excessive duration of the penal case,[15] though art. 6.272 CC does not expressly set out the liability of the State for this type of unlawful act.[16]

Historically statutory law in Lithuania has been considered a primary or supreme legal source in the vein of the civil law tradition. However, the doctrine of judicial precedent was formulated for the first time by the Constitutional Court in 2006.[17] According to the constitutional doctrine, the courts must follow rules and principles adopted in the previous case law when deciding subsequent cases with analogous or very similar factual background. This rule applies both vertically – judicial precedents bind courts of lower instances – and horizontally – judicial precedents bind the court itself that has adopted the precedent. Judicial precedents can be deviated from, and new precedents can be formed only in exceptional circumstances.

Tortious State liability for unlawful conviction is regulated as part of civil liability, except for the extrajudicial compensation for damage, which falls under administrative law. Thus, case law is formed by the courts of general competence. According to art. 23(2) of the Law on Courts,[18] the Supreme Court of the Republic of Lithuania (hereinafter the Supreme Court), as the highest judiciary institution for cases of liability for unlawful conviction, forms the unified practice of courts of general competence while interpreting and applying laws. Therefore case

13 The ruling of 19 August 2006 of the Constitutional Court 'On the compensation for damage inflicted by unlawful actions of interrogatory and investigatory bodies, the prosecutor's office, and a court'. The texts of all rulings of the Constitutional Court are available in English at <http://www.lrkt.lt>.

14 The ruling of 19 August 2006 of the Constitutional Court 'On the compensation for damage inflicted by unlawful actions of interrogatory and investigatory bodies, the prosecutor's office, and a court'.

15 *A N v the Republic of Lithuania*, Supreme Court of Lithuania, 6 February 2007, case no. 3K-7–7/2007.

16 This ruling of the Constitutional Court was adopted on the constitutionality of the Law on the Compensation of Damage (version of 1997). However, the wording of the norm of the Law which was investigated by the Constitutional Court and the wording of art. 6.272(1) CC are identical. Thus, explanations by the Constitutional Court given in this ruling are relevant with regard to art. 6.272(1) CC.

17 See the ruling of 28 March 2006 of the Constitutional Court 'On the powers of the Constitutional Court to review its own decisions and dismiss the instituted legal proceedings, as well as on reviewing the financing of courts'.

18 *Official gazette*, 1994, No. 46–851; 2002, no. 17–649.

law, primarily that of the Supreme Court, is an important source for interpreting regulation regarding compensation for unlawful conviction.

3 Grounds for compensation for unlawful conviction

Art. 6.272(1) CC sets out the duty of the State to compensate for damage resulting from unlawful conviction. The norm states that the damage shall be compensated fully irrespective of the fault of the officials of preliminary investigation, prosecution institutions or court. The Commentary of the CC[19] and the scholarly writings on this provision argue that State liability under this article is strict.[20] However, according to the settled case law of the Supreme Court of Lithuania, exculpatory judgment shall not automatically result in compensation,[21] i.e. if a decision was overturned due to a different assessment of the evidence by the higher instance, this would not mean unlawfulness as the precondition of tort liability. Similarly, annulment of any other decision adopted in the penal or administrative procedures shall not *per se* mean unlawfulness as the precondition of public liability. Unlawfulness is established where the person was unlawfully convicted due to breaches of substantive or procedural criminal law. These breaches may be established either in penal proceedings by overturning the decision of the lower instance court (official) due to the breaches of norms of penal proceedings or in proceedings regarding compensation for damage.[22] Unsurprisingly, because of the difficulty of proving unlawfulness, case law where the person was awarded compensation is very scarce.[23]

19 Mikelėnas V (et al.), *Lietuvos Respublikos civilinio kodekso komentaras. Šeštoji knyga. Prievolių teisė (I)* [Commentary of the Lithuanian Civil Code. Sixth Book. Law of Obligations (I)] (Justitia 2003), 379 ff.

20 Selelionytė-Drukteinienė S, Valstybės deliktinės atsakomybės raidos tendencijos: daktaro disertacija [Developing trends of tort liability of the State: doctoral dissertation] Mykolas Romeris University 2008, 86, 208; for a summary see H Gabartas and L Šaltinytė, 'Lithuania', in: H Koziol and BC Steininger (eds), *European Tort Law 2008* (2009) 414, no. 35; Mikelėnas V, *Kailiukų bylos' pamokos: keli klausimai perskaičius Europos Žmogaus Teisių Teismo sprendimą byloje Jucys v Lietuva* [Lessons of the 'Case of Furs' or some Questions after Reading the Judgment of the European Court on Human Rights in the Case of *Jucys v Lithuania*] (no. 2(68) *Justitia* 2008), 6.

21 *R B v the Republic of Lithuania*, Supreme Court of Lithuania, 30 August 2013, case no. 3K-3–439/2013; *A D v the Republic of Lithuania*, Supreme Court of Lithuania, 30 November 2009, case no. 3K-3–534/2009.

22 *R B v the Republic of Lithuania*, Supreme Court of Lithuania, 30 August 2013, case no. 3K-3–439/2013.

23 There are a few cases by the Supreme Court of Lithuania and the Lithuanian Appeal Court where compensation was awarded due to unlawful conviction. See *A G and R G v the Republic of Lithuania*, Supreme Court of Lithuania, 5 February 2014, case no. 3K-3–4/2014; *K R v the Republic of Lithuania*, Supreme Court of Lithuania, 23 November 2005, case no. 3K-3–604; *A G and R G v the Republic of Lithuania*, Lithuanian Appeal Court, 21 May 2013, case no. 2A-336/2013; *T L v the Republic of Lithuania*, Lithuanian Appeal Court, 4 November 2013, case no. 2A-893/2013; *A Š v the Republic of Lithuania*, Lithuanian Appeal Court, 15 December 2009, case no. 2A-713/2009; *V P v the Republic of Lithuania*, Lithuanian Appeal Court, 22 September 2009, case no. 2A-562/2009; *D Š v the Republic of Lithuania*, Lithuanian

The other necessary preconditions for the State's duty to compensate damage are damage and a causal link between the unlawful acts and the damage.

4 Grounds of exemption of the State from liability for unlawful conviction

Theoretically all general grounds of exemption are applicable to the State, i.e. *force majeure*, third-party conduct, consent of the victim or risk assumption, state of necessity, self-defence and self-help (art. 6.253 CC). However, in practice the most important tool for limitation of liability is contributory negligence on the part of the victim.

Arts. 6.248(4) and 6.282(1) CC embody the principle of *volenti non fit iniuria*, meaning 'to one who volunteers, no harm is done'. Art. 6.248(4) CC, applicable both to contractual and tortious liability, reads:

> Where the creditor[24] is also at fault for the damage, the debtor's duty to compensate is reduced in proportion to the gravity of the creditor's fault, or the debtor may be exempted from civil liability.

Art. 6.282(1) CC, applicable to tortious liability, reads:

> If the victim's gross negligence contributed to causing or increasing damage, depending on the degree of the victim's fault (and on the degree of the fault of the person by whom the damage was caused, if any), the extent of the compensation can be reduced or the claim for the compensation rejected unless the laws provide for otherwise.

Thus, the State may be exempted from liability fully or in part if the person who has been unlawfully convicted impeded the process by calumniating himself, escaping from justice or otherwise.

5 Persons entitled to compensation for unlawful conviction

General tort law rules establish who may claim compensation for unlawful conviction. Arts. 6.263(1) and (2) CC set out the general rule of tortious liability. Art. 6.263(1) CC reads: 'Every person shall have the duty to abide by the rules of conduct so as not to cause damage to another by his actions (or omission).' Art. 6.263(2) CC further indicates: 'Any personal or property damage and, in the cases established by the law, non-pecuniary damage must be fully compensated by the liable person.'

By virtue of these norms, it is understood that the person who suffered from tort is eligible for compensation, i.e. he is the victim. The same is true with respect

Appeal Court, 4 August 2009, case no. 2A-447/2009. More case law can be found where compensation was awarded due to unlawful detention, temporary apprehension, other procedural coercive measures or lengthy trial of penal case.

24 The concept 'creditor' in the CC includes *inter alia* the tortious victim.

to damage caused by unlawful conviction, i.e. the person who has been unlawfully convicted is the victim eligible to claim compensation for damage.

As an exception to the general rule that the person directly affected by the tort shall be compensated, secondary victims may also be entitled to compensation for unlawful conviction in some cases. There are two grounds from which the right of secondary victims to compensation for damage may arise.

First, secondary victims may claim that due to the unlawful conviction of the primary victim, they suffered personal damage. Such claims of secondary victims are upheld in cases of death or serious injury of the primary victim. The right of secondary victims to claim compensation for damage suffered due to the death of the primary victim arises out of legislation – art. 6.284(1) CC sets out that dependants of the breadwinner (minor children, spouse, parents incapable of work or other factual dependants incapable of work), as well as any children born after his death, have the right to compensation for pecuniary and non-pecuniary damage. However, case law goes well beyond the literal wording of this norm in terms of the right to compensation for non-pecuniary damage. Other close relatives, such as grown-up children, parents of grown-up children, grandparents, grandchildren, brothers and sisters (whether minor or grown-up) are eligible for compensation for non-pecuniary damage suffered by the death of the primary victim. The fact of dependency is of no importance.[25] The right of secondary victims to compensation for damage in cases of serious injury to the health of the primary victim was established in case law of the Supreme Court[26] and is settled case law of Lithuanian courts.

Second, in the event of the death of the primary victim the question of inheritance of the right to compensation for damage arises. Art. 1.112(2) CC establishes that pecuniary rights shall be inherited. Art. 1.114(2) sets out that personal non-pecuniary rights may be transferred or inherited only in instances established by laws or if that does not contradict the nature of the values and principles of *bona fides* and is not limited by laws. Art. 5.1(3) CC states that personal non-pecuniary and pecuniary rights, inseparably connected to the person of the deceased (right to honour and dignity, to authorship, to author's name, inviolability of author's work, to the name of performer and inviolability of performance), the right to allowances and pensions shall not be inherited, except for instances established by laws. By virtue of these rules, the heirs of the deceased inherit the right to compensation for pecuniary damage suffered by the primary victim. However, the question whether they also inherit the right to compensation for the emotional sufferings by the primary victim himself prior to his death is far less clear. The right to compensation for non-pecuniary damage is closely connected to the person. Neither the laws nor legal doctrine answer the question whether such right is so closely connected to the person that it may not be inherited.

25 See e.g. *A A* and *G A v N J and AB 'Lietuvos draudimas'*, Supreme Court of Lithuania, 14 February 2005, case no. 3K-3–86/2005; *E P and V M v AB 'Karigė'*, Supreme Court of Lithuania, 26 September 2007, case no. 3K-3–351/2007.

26 See *L Z and others v Marijampolė Hospital*, Supreme Court of Lithuania, 18 April 2005, case no. 3K-7–255/2005.

In its ruling concerning the constitutionality of the Law on Compensation for Damage[27] in 2006 the Constitutional Court stated that the Constitution does not preclude the possibility that compensation for either pecuniary or non-pecuniary damage could be claimed by another person than the one who was injured.[28] The Constitutional Court also declared in the same ruling that the Constitution requires legal regulation to preclude the possibility of the State escaping its duty to compensate for damage resulting from the unlawful conduct of its institutions and officials, including those instances when it is impossible to compensate for the damage to the injured person due to his death, particularly when he died because of the unlawful conduct of State officials.

However, the Constitutional Court remained silent on the conditions which shall be satisfied by the secondary victims to be eligible for compensation. Thus, the position of the Constitutional Court was viewed as controversial by scholars. One author commented that this ruling added even more confusion to the issue.[29] Her position is that the right to inherit compensation for non-pecuniary damage should only be permissible under one of the following conditions: first, when the court has awarded compensation for non-pecuniary damage to the primary victim; second, when parties have determined the compensable amount for non-pecuniary damage; third, when the injured person has explicitly expressed his intention to invoke this right by referring to a court and there is sufficient evidence allowing a court to determine both that such a right exists and what the possible quantum of compensation would be.[30] Another author supported the ruling of the Constitutional Court, arguing that it would be feasible to recognize the right to inherit a claim for compensation for non-pecuniary damage and in so doing the following circumstances shall be taken into account: the importance of the value injured, the extent of negative consequences of the unlawful acts and other particular circumstances of the case.[31]

In 2014 the Supreme Court dealt for the first time with the issue of whether the right to claim compensation for non-pecuniary damage resulting from unlawful

27 The ruling of 19 August 2006 of the Constitutional Court 'On the compensation for damage inflicted by unlawful actions of interrogatory and investigatory bodies, the prosecutor's office, and a court'. As stated above in this chapter, the law was in force from 19 November 1997 until 7 June 2002 and regulated the issues of compensation for damage caused by unlawful actions of interrogatory and investigatory bodies, the prosecutor's office and court.

28 See ruling of 19 August 2006 of the Constitutional Court 'On compensation of damage inflicted by unlawful actions of interrogatory and investigatory bodies, the prosecutor's office and court'.

29 Volodko R, Teoriniai ir praktiniai neturtinės žalos instituto taikymo aspektai Lietuvos civilinėje teisėje: daktaro disertacija [Theoretical and practical aspects of the application of the institute of non-pecuniary damage in Lithuanian civil law: doctoral dissertation] Vilnius University 2009, 91 ff.

30 *Ibid.*, 87, 97–98, 434.

31 Cirtautienė S, *Neturtinės žalos atlyginimas kaip civilinių teisių gynimo būdas* [Compensation of Non-pecuniary Damage as a Legal Remedy] (Justitia 2008) 211.

conviction may be inherited.[32] The case concerned issues of unlawful imprisonment and conviction. The damage was claimed by the secondary victims – the spouse and daughter of the primary victim, who had been arrested and subsequently charged for an attempted rape. Three years later he was found guilty of robbery and sentenced to prison. Soon after that decision of the first-instance court he died while in prison pending an appeal. The experts concluded that he died of ischemic heart disease, which could have been aggravated by stress. Two years after his death, the prosecution decided to discontinue criminal proceedings against him on the grounds that he had committed no crime. The decision also noted that the criminal proceedings against the deceased involved numerous breaches of laws. The spouse and children of the primary victim each sought compensation of LTL 500,000 (€144,810) from the State as non-pecuniary damages for both the non-pecuniary damage that they suffered themselves and that suffered by their father/husband. The Supreme Court upheld the decision of the appeal instance court, which awarded both types of compensation. In addition, the Supreme Court took into consideration that the civil proceedings for compensation for damage were excessively long, as they lasted over twelve years, and decided to award each of the claimants[33] additional amounts of LTL 12,000 (€3,475) on these grounds. The decision of the Supreme Court was positively received by Lithuanian scholars.[34]

In 2016 the Supreme Court had another chance to rule on the issue of inheritance of the right to compensation for non-pecuniary damage suffered by the primary victim.[35] The case concerned the issue of compensation for damage resulting from unlawful detention. This case was initiated by the primary victim himself, who had been detained on the grounds of suspicion of committing a robbery of a substantial amount of money from the bank he worked at. The term of detention had been prolonged several times to approximately eight months until the appeal instance court annulled the final valid decision prolonging the detention. The court found that the mere suspicion of committing a crime is not a sufficient legal basis to impose detention as the most stringent coercive measure. Later the investigation against the claimant was terminated due to insufficient evidence of his involvement in the crime. The claimant argued that he had suffered pecuniary and non-pecuniary damage due to the unlawful detention. The claimant died during the civil proceedings. The heirs of the initial claimant – his wife and three minor children – stepped into the civil proceedings. The first-instance court awarded

32 *A G and R G v the Republic of Lithuania*, Supreme Court of Lithuania, 5 February 2014, case no. 3K-3–4/2014.

33 'Claimant' is the procedural term defining the person who has filed the claim with the court. In the analysed area the claimant may be either the primary victim who has been wrongfully convicted (or believes that he has been wrongfully convicted) or a secondary victim – a close relative of the primary victim who has suffered from unlawful conviction of the primary victim and is eligible for compensation under special rules.

34 See *Selelionytė-Drukteinienė/L Šaltinytė*, Lithuania, in: E Karner E/ Steininger BC (eds), *European Tort Law 2014* (de Gruyter 2015) 339, nos. 8–18.

35 *R T and others v the Republic of Lithuania*, Supreme Court of Lithuania, 30 September 2016, case no. 3K-3–399–687/2016.

compensation for both pecuniary and non-pecuniary damage. The court of appeal lowered the amount of pecuniary damages and rejected the claim for non-pecuniary damages. The Supreme Court disagreed with the findings of the appeal instance court regarding both the pecuniary and non-pecuniary damages. With respect to the latter, the Supreme Court analysed arts. 5.1(3) and 1.114 (2) CC and relied on the findings of the Constitutional Court in its ruling of 19 August 2006. Having analysed the jurisprudence of the European Court of Human Rights, the Supreme Court observed that, in principle, the possibility of inheriting the right to compensation for the non-pecuniary damage depends on whether the case had been initiated by the primary victim or by his heirs. In the latter case, the requirements of admissibility of the claim are more stringent, as the heirs must prove that the unlawful actions had a negative impact on them personally. The Supreme Court identified two reasons to allow succession of the right to compensation for non-pecuniary damage in this case. First, the claim was brought by the victim himself. The civil proceedings continued for six years due to circumstances beyond the control of the primary victim. Second, the initial claim explicitly stated that the alleged unlawful actions of the State institutions also had a negative impact on the victim's family.[36]

This decision of the Supreme Court shall be accepted favourably. However, it does not bring much clarity to the question of whether the fact that the claim was brought by the victim himself prior to his death and he had mentioned negative consequences of detention to his family in the claim were essential in recognizing the secondary victims' right to an award.

To sum up, dependants of the person who has been unlawfully convicted have the right to compensation for their own pecuniary damage and pecuniary damage suffered by the primary victim upon his death. They also have the right to compensation for their own non-pecuniary damage if the breadwinner suffered grave health impairments or died due to the unlawful conviction. Doctrine of the Constitutional Court, legal doctrine and case law also accept that secondary victims shall inherit the primary victim's right to compensation for his own non-pecuniary damage. However, the conditions on which inheritance shall be based still lack clarity.

6 Procedure for claiming compensation in court

6.1 Procedure before the first-instance court

There are no formal conditions for claiming compensation. Every person who believes he has suffered damage due to unlawful conviction may claim compensation. As stated above, the person who has suffered unlawful conviction may first ask for compensation in extrajudicial proceedings by filing the claim with the Ministry of Justice. If the person is not satisfied with the answer or decides not to avail himself of extrajudicial proceedings, he may file the claim directly with the court.

36 See comments on this decision by *Selelionytė-Drukteinienė S/ Šaltinytė L*, Lithuania, in: Karner E and Steininger BC (eds), *European Tort Law 2014* (de Gruyter 2015) 339, nos. 8–18.

Regular civil procedure rules apply for the claims of victims of unlawful conviction. According to art. 6.272(1) CC, the liable person is the State itself, not the institution. Art. 6.273(1) CC indicates that in cases of compensation for damage where the damage must be compensated by the State, it shall be represented by the government, or an institution authorized by the government. By virtue of this norm the Government of the Republic of Lithuania has adopted Decision no. 1054 of 29 September 2014 entitled On Appointment of the Representative of the State and the Government before Courts.[37] Item 3.23 of the Decision stipulates that save for the cases where damage has been inflicted by court or judge, in civil cases of compensation for damage where the damage must be compensated by the State, the State shall be represented in court by the institution the servants or employees of which have inflicted unlawful acts triggering liability of the State. Item 3.22.2 of the Decision indicates that in cases where damage has been inflicted by court or judge, the State shall be represented in court by the Ministry of Justice.

Courts of general competence deal with this type of cases.[38] All general rules of civil procedure established in the Code of Civil Procedure[39] (hereinafter CCP) apply. The process is the same as in other civil cases.

The case is initiated by filing the claim with the first-instance court. Courts of the first instance are district and regional courts, depending on the value of the dispute. District courts have competence to try all unlawful conviction cases, with the exception of cases where jurisdiction is granted to regional courts. Regional courts as the first-instance courts try cases where the value of the dispute exceeds €100,000 (the claim for the award of non-pecuniary damages is not included in this amount).

Cases concerning compensation of damage are considered civil cases, thus they are assigned to the civil cases division[40] of the court. Cases before the first-instance court are heard by one judge. The president of the court or the deputy may form a board of three judges, depending on the complexity of the case (art. 62(1) CCP). In practice this is done very rarely.

According to the main principle set out in art. 9(1) CCP, the court proceedings are public. Case materials can be classified or whole proceedings may be held in camera if this is justified by the need to protect personal life or to preserve state, professional or commercial secrets or when the court undertakes measures to reconcile the parties.

The participants to the proceedings are the claimant and the respondent. The claimant is the victim of wrongful conviction or, in certain circumstances,

37 Published on 6 October 2014 in the Register of Legal Acts, no. 2014–13674.

38 With regard to courts of special jurisdiction, there are five regional administrative courts and the Supreme Administrative Court of Lithuania. These courts hear disputes arising from administrative legal relations. Tort law cases arising out of damage caused by public authorities acting in their administrative capacity lie within the competence of administrative courts.

39 *Official gazette*, 2002, no. 36–1340. 2002, no. 42–0.

40 All courts of general competence comprise of two divisions – the civil cases division and the penal cases division.

secondary victims. The respondent is the State, represented by the institution whose actions are claimed by the claimant as unlawful or the Ministry of Justice.

The most important rights of the claimant and the respondent are the possibility to familiarize themselves with the documents of the case, present the evidence to the court, participate in the process of their investigation, present questions to other participants of the case, witnesses and experts, present arguments on all questions of the case, file requests, give oral or written explanations, contradict the requests and arguments of other participants of the case, appeal decisions of the court, make settlement agreements, etc.

Persons are eligible for legal aid if they satisfy the uniform criteria applied to all persons. No special schemes are applied to the victims of unlawful conviction. A citizen of the Republic of Lithuania or of a Member State of the European Union or a person who lawfully resides in Lithuania or other Member State of the European Union is eligible for legal aid if his assets and annual income do not exceed the level set by the government.

The judicial procedure is started by the victim by bringing the claim against the State. The representative(s) of the State have the duty to reply to the claim in writing within the term specified by the court, which shall not be shorter than 14 days and not longer than 20 days and is subject to extension upon the respondent's request to up to 60 days (art. 142(1) CCP). Preparation for the trial may be conducted orally by inviting the parties to the preliminary hearing (228 CCP) or in writing (227 CCP). In the latter case the parties exchange one round of written documents. The trial before the first-instance court is oral.

The process in civil proceedings is adversarial. General rules of evidence apply in cases on compensation for unlawful conviction. Thus, the claimant must prove the conditions of liability of the State – unlawful acts, damage and causation. The amount of damages must also be proved by the claimant, with the exception of non-pecuniary damages, which is established by the court. The State must prove grounds of exoneration if it relies on them and may also bring arguments denying the claimant's allegations as to the conditions of liability and amount of damages.

6.2 Appeal procedure

Any party to the proceedings who is not satisfied with the judgment of the first-instance court may bring an appeal. If a case was heard by a district court in the first instance, the case will be heard by a regional court in the appellate instance. If the court of first instance was a regional court, the dispute will be examined by the Court of Appeal of Lithuania.

The appeal shall be brought within 30 days of the decision of the first-instance court being announced (art. 307(1) CCP). The other parties to the proceedings shall reply to the appeal in writing within 20 days (art. 318(1) CCP).

Cases before the appeal instance court are heard either by one judge or by a panel of three judges (art. 62(3) CCP). If the value of the compensation in dispute does not exceed €2,000, the case is heard by one judge (art. 304(1) CCP). However, the president of the court or the president of the civil cases division of the court may form a board of three judges, depending on the complexity of the case (art. 304(1) CCP). Boards of three judges examine all other cases (art. 304 (1) CCP). At the suggestion of the judge assigned to the case, the chairmen of the court may form mixed boards of judges from the civil cases division and penal cases division of the court (art. 304(2) CCP).

The scope of appeal is unlimited with respect to the issues of legal or factual mistakes made by the first-instance court. However, the object of the appeal is the decision of the first-instance court, thus the appealing party must bring arguments demonstrating the unlawfulness and baselessness of the decision of the first-instance court (art. 306(1)(4) CCP).

The proceedings before the appeal instance court are written (art. 321(1) CCP), except for cases where the appeal instance court decides that oral proceedings are necessary (art. 322 CCP). Oral proceedings are rarely organized.

The decision of the appeal instance court comes into force on the day on which it is announced (art. 331(6) CCP).

6.3 Cassation procedure

A party not satisfied with the decision of the appeal instance court may file a cassation claim before the Supreme Court. However, the Supreme Court only hears cases on questions of law. A board consisting of three judges decides whether the claim has relevant ground for cassation. The term in which to present the cassation claim is three months after the decision of the appeal instance court comes into force (art. 345(1) CCP). If the claim is accepted by the Supreme Court, an opposite party must respond in writing within one month (art. 351(1) CCP).

Cases before the cassation instance court are heard by a board of three judges or by an extended composition of seven judges. Both may be either unitary or composed of judges from civil cases and criminal cases divisions (art. 62(4) CCP). The most complicated cases are heard by the plenary session of all judges of the Lithuanian Supreme Court (art. 357(1) CCP).

The proceedings before the cassation court are written, except for the cases where the Supreme Court decides that oral proceedings are necessary (art. 356(2) CCP). Oral proceedings are rarely organized.

7 Calculating the amount of compensation

The general provisions regulating compensation for damage apply to the calculation of compensation for unlawful conviction. Art. 6.251(1) CC, applicable both to contractual and tortious liability, and art. 6.263(2) CC, applicable to tortious liability, consolidate the principle of compensation for damage in full. Art. 6.251 (1) CC reads 'The damage[41] caused must be compensated in full, except in cases when limited liability is established by laws or a contract.' As indicated above, art.

41 The text itself mentions 'damages', however 'damage' is relevant.

6.263(2) CC stipulates that the inflicted damage must be 'fully compensated by the liable person'.

By virtue of these norms, pecuniary damage is always assessed *in concreto* based on the individual circumstances of the case. Pecuniary damages include compensation for lost income, expenses suffered for hiring a lawyer in the penal proceedings or other pecuniary losses which are closely linked with the unlawful conviction.

The amount of compensation for non-pecuniary damage is assessed on the basis of art. 6.250(2) CC, which provides that:

> the court in assessing the amount of non-pecuniary damage shall take into consideration the consequences of such damage sustained, the gravity of the fault of the person by whom the damage is caused, his financial status, the amount of pecuniary damage sustained by the victim, also any other circumstances of importance for the case, likewise the criteria of good faith, justice and reasonableness.

The list of criteria to be considered is non-exhaustive. Since the legislator has not determined the limits of the non-pecuniary damages or a special mechanism or formula for calculating them, the court has wide discretion to award just and full compensation for non-pecuniary damage to the victim. The Supreme Court has consistently held in its case law[42] that the courts need to take into account all criteria which are significant for the purposes of assessing compensable non-pecuniary damage; the courts should not overemphasize one single criterion. Firstly, the amount of compensation for non-pecuniary damage shall be determined by the interest which has been breached. Therefore, according to the Supreme Court, under certain circumstances, some criteria are more important than others. It is emphasized that in the case of breach of interests which are considered absolute – health and life – the key criteria shall be the consequences of the injury and the resulting moral suffering. The nature of the tortfeasor's and the victim's fault, their relationship and other subjective criteria are to be assessed only as far as they assist in determining the scope of negative legal consequences, not for punitive purposes.

According to the case law of the Supreme Court, the duration of unlawful conviction, mental suffering resulting from it, health impairments (if any), damage to reputation, etc. are the most important criteria when assessing the non-pecuniary damages for unlawful conviction.[43] The amount is calculated by the adjudicating authority on the basis of general tort liability principles. No tables or fixed sums are provided.

42 See e.g. *M V v UAB 'Algesa'*, Supreme Court of Lithuania, 15 February 2012, case no. 3K-3–35/2012; *R K and others v Kaunas Simonas Daukantas secondary school*, Supreme Court of Lithuania, 30 April 2012, case no. 3K-3–202/2012.

43 *K R v the Republic of Lithuania*, Supreme Court of Lithuania, 23 November 2005, case no. 3K-3–604/2005.

Amounts of compensation in non-pecuniary damages are pretty low in most cases. For example, LTL 20,000 (€5,792) was awarded to the heirs of an unlawfully convicted person to compensate for the deceased's suffering.[44] As discussed above, the person was unlawfully arrested, subsequently charged for an attempted rape, later for robbery, and was found guilty of the latter. The person was detained immediately after the first court decision and died in prison while pending an appeal. Two years later the prosecution decided to discontinue criminal proceedings against the deceased on the grounds that he had committed no crime. The decision also noted that the criminal proceedings against him involved numerous breaches of law and the only evidence against him was the fact that the victims allegedly recognized his car. The amount of compensation was assessed on the facts that detention and subsequent unlawful conviction for a grave crime of a person who had never been sentenced before caused severe emotional distress. LTL 30,000 (€8,688) and 20,000 (€5,792) were subsequently awarded to the spouse and daughter, respectively, of the unlawfully convicted person for their own mental suffering caused by the unlawful detention and conviction of their beloved one.

In another case LTL 8,000 (€2,316) was awarded in non-pecuniary damages to a person who had received a monetary penalty by the first-instance and appeal instance courts. The decision was overturned by the Lithuanian Supreme Court in renewed proceedings after eight months on the basis that a grave error of law had been made by the courts. The factors determining the amount of compensation were the gravity of the sentence (fine, not deprivation of liberty), period of proceedings after the decision of the first-instance court until the acquitting decision (eight months), the fact the sentence was suspended (the penalty in fact remained unpaid) and the magnitude of the mental suffering.[45]

LTL 10,000 (€2,896) was awarded in non-pecuniary damages to a person who had been unlawfully sentenced to three years' imprisonment. The imposition of the penalty was suspended, so in fact the person was not imprisoned. The person was a law student in a university abroad during the trial and conviction. Due to the unlawful coercive measure – written undertaking not to leave the place of residence and subsequent conviction – he suffered inconveniences and experienced mental suffering. The amount of compensation was later increased slightly, but did not exceed €6,000.[46]

As an exception worthy of mention is the case tried by the Supreme Court of Lithuania in 2020.[47] Compensation of €50,000 was awarded in non-pecuniary damages to a former judge due to unlawful criminal prosecution.[48] Penal proceedings

44 *A G and R G v the Republic of Lithuania*, Supreme Court of Lithuania, 5 February 2014, case no. 3K-3-4/2014.

45 *K R v the Republic of Lithuania*, Supreme Court of Lithuania, 23 November 2005, case no. 3K-3-604.

46 See case *D P v the Republic of Lithuania*, Supreme Court of Lithuania, 22 February 2018, case no. 3K-3-63-378/2018, where €6,000 was awarded in non-pecuniary damages for excessive unlawful detention.

47 *V S v the Republic of Lithuania*, Supreme Court of Lithuania, 2 July 2020, case no. 3K-3-210-695/2020.

48 The claimant did not bring the claim in pecuniary damages.

had ended in the criminal charges brought against her being dismissed. The facts of the case were as follows. The charges of abusing her position as judge were brought against her for an episode where the judge asked her secretary on the phone whether the secretary's sister, who was a doctor, could issue her daughter a sicknote. The doctor had issued the sicknote, as asked. The daughter was later charged with fraud for embezzling €96 of public funds because she had been given sick leave although she was not ill. The conversation of the judge had been recorded during a surveillance operation against the claimant's husband, also a judge, in a case against him for bribery. The penal proceedings took five years. The same year the charges were brought, the claimant was diagnosed with depression of average gravity. She did not work for approximately three years. Then she became a lawyer, but was struck off the list of lawyers because the first-instance court had found her guilty of abuse of office. As a result of the charges against her, she could not engage in work appropriate to her qualifications. The Supreme Court of Lithuania in the damages case found that officials breached the general duty of care because the surveillance operation and prosecution of the claimant were carried out in respect of conduct which was not even criminalized. The Supreme Court of Lithuania separately agreed that a number of other measures applied against the claimant were also unlawful. The court also agreed that an additional basis of State liability was the breach of the claimant's right to privacy by unlawful and disproportionate tapping of her telephone. In assessing the amount of compensation, the Supreme Court of Lithuania took into account that the claimant lost her good health, reputation and income, and was terrified as a result of her continuous persecution. An impeccable reputation was particularly important for her as a lawyer. Thus, the investigation against her had a significant negative effect on her ability to work as a lawyer. This precluded her from engaging in economic activities. The Supreme Court of Lithuania agreed that under those circumstances the unjustified criminal investigation against the claimant suggested that the award of non-pecuniary damages should be sufficiently high. However, the court stressed that the disciplinary charges against the claimant remained valid. The decision to dismiss the claimant from her office was taken by the Judiciary Council, on the grounds of breach of judicial ethics, and was later affirmed by the court. Consequently, the criminal charges against the claimant dismissed in 2015 did not mean that the claimant did not commit the misconduct which led to her disciplinary proceedings and dismissal from office.

As stated above, pecuniary damage is assessed *in concreto* based on the individual circumstances of the case. For example, income lost during the unlawful conviction is calculated on the basis of the amount earned before the conviction.

8 The recourse claim of the State against persons who caused unlawful conviction

Art. 6.280 CC 'The right of recourse against the person who caused damage' governs the issues of recourse. Part 1 of this article stipulates:

> A person who has compensated the damage caused by another person shall have the right of recourse against the person by whom the damage was caused in the amount equal to the paid compensation for damage unless a different amount is established by the laws.

However, due to specific regulation of the status of officers who may be responsible for unlawful conviction, art. 6.280(1) CC is not sufficient.

Art. 6.272(4) CC additionally sets out:

> Where the damage has been caused by intentional fault on the part of officials of pretrial investigation, prosecution, court officials or judges, the State, having compensated the damage, shall have the right of recourse against the officials concerned, within the procedure established by laws, of the sums in the amount provided for by laws.

This clause clearly states that the right of recourse may be exercised only in cases of intentional conduct of the judges, court officials or officials of criminal justice agencies conducting criminal investigation. The same rule is repeated in art. 5(1) of the Law on the Compensation for Damage.[49]

Such regulation reflects the high level of personal immunity granted to judges, prosecutors and other pretrial officers. In this regard art. 47(8) of the Law on Courts adds some ambiguity by setting out that the right of recourse towards judges may be exercised only in cases of their criminal action.

When actions of other State officials have triggered the liability of the State towards the victim, negligence is enough for their liability towards the State to arise. The recourse is capped at nine months' salary[50] and is full in cases of intentional conduct.

A person or persons who is (are) responsible for unlawful conviction may be sued by the State in a recourse action. It may be an officer of a criminal justice agency conducting a criminal investigation, prosecutor and/or the judge, depending on where the fault lies in particular. The main rule is that liability of officers is for personal fault. However, there is some case law stating that solidary liability may also be applied.[51]

Since the amendments in 2017 of the Law on the Compensation for Damage and in 2019 of the Law on Public Service, the State must exercise the right of recourse against the officials responsible for damage.

The survey carried out by the National Audit Office of Lithuania in 2016 showed that the exercise of the right of recourse was very poor (during the examined period

49 Until modifications that were carried out in December 2017, the right of recourse against these officials was capped at nine months' salary in cases of intentional conduct.

50 Art. 5(1) of the Law on the Compensation of Damage; art. 50(8) of the Law on the Special Investigations Service, *Official gazette*, 2000, no. 41–1162; art. 39(2) of the Law on Public Service, *Official gazette*, 2018, no. XIII-1370.

51 *The Republic of Lithuania v VL and others,* Supreme Administrative Court of Lithuania, 10 May 2016, case no. eA-458–261/2016.

of 2013–2015 only approximately 0.08 per cent of the compensation sums were recovered from the liable State officials).[52]

Recommendations provided by the National Audit Office of Lithuania included modification of a few laws by setting out the duty of the State to exercise the right of recourse after it has compensated the damage to a victim, and lifting the limitation of the right of recourse towards judges, prosecutors and other pretrial officers in cases of intentional conduct. Many of these recommendations were implemented. However, not enough statistical data exists to determine whether these legislative changes had an impact on the exercise of recourse.

9 The practice of compensating the unlawfully convicted

No statistics are available concerning the number of claims for unlawful conviction. All public liability claims fall under one category in the statistical data. In 2018, 2019 and 2020 approximately 100 new public liability claims were filed each year before the first-instance courts of general competence.[53] Cases of unlawful conviction are included in them. Only a few cases were tried by the Supreme Court and the Court of Appeal regarding unlawful conviction.[54]

10 An evaluation of the national mechanism for compensation for unlawful conviction

Lithuanian norms regulating compensation for damage for unlawful conviction are modern, thus naturally no legislative changes are anticipated, except for the recent initiative that took place to increase the maximum amounts of damages under the Law on the Compensation for Damage. However, though it is said that public liability for the wrongful convictions regime is strict, unlawfulness is the prerequisite of liability. Given the interpretation of unlawfulness in case law, whereby exculpatory decision does not automatically mean this condition, the person seeking compensation must prove deficiencies in the penal procedure to be eligible for reimbursement. This explains why case law awarding compensation is limited.

Bibliography

Cirtautienė S, *Neturtinės žalos atlyginimas kaip civilinių teisių gynimo būdas* [Compensation of non-pecuniary damage as a legal remedy] (Justitia 2008).

Gabartas H and Šaltinytė L, Lithuania, in: Koziol H and Steininger BC (eds), *European Tort Law 2008* (Springer 2009).

Mikelėnas V (et al.), *Lietuvos Respublikos civilinio kodekso komentaras. Šeštoji knyga. Prievolių teisė (I)* [Commentary of the Lithuanian Civil Code. Sixth Book. Law of Obligations (I)] (Justitia 2003).

52 The data comprise all instances of damage inflicted by the State to the private persons, including compensation for unlawful conviction.
53 https://www.teismai.lt/lt/visuomenei-ir-ziniasklaidai/statistika/106
54 See them named in fn 22.

Mikelėnas V, *Kailiukų bylos' pamokos: keli klausimai perskaičius Europos Žmogaus Teisių Teismo sprendimą byloje Jucys v Lietuva* [Lessons of the 'Case of Furs' or some Questions after Reading the Judgment of the European Court on Human Rights in the Case of *Jucys v Lithuania*] (no. 2(68) Justitia 2008).

Selelionytė-Drukteinienė S, Valstybės deliktinės atsakomybės raidos tendencijos: daktaro disertacija [Developing trends of tort liability of the State: doctoral dissertation] Mykolas Romeris University 2008.

Selelionytė-Drukteinienė S and Šaltinytė L, Lithuania, in: Karner E and Steininger BC (eds), *European Tort Law* 2014 (de Gruyter 2015).

Volodko R, Teoriniai ir praktiniai neturtinės žalos instituto taikymo aspektai Lietuvos civilinėje teisėje: daktaro disertacija [Theoretical and practical aspects of the application of the institute of non-pecuniary damage in Lithuanian civil law: doctoral dissertation] Vilnius University 2009.

Table of cases

The ruling of 28 March 2006 of the Constitutional Court 'On the powers of the Constitutional Court to review its own decisions and dismiss the instituted legal proceedings, as well as on reviewing the financing of courts'.

The ruling of 19 August 2006 of the Constitutional Court 'On the compensation for damage inflicted by unlawful actions of interrogatory and investigatory bodies, the prosecutor's office, and a court'.

A A and G A v N J and AB ' Lietuvosdraudimas', Supreme Court of Lithuania, 14 February 2005, case no. 3K-3–86/2005.

L Z and others v Marijampolė Hospital, Supreme Court of Lithuania, 18 April 2005, case no. 3K-7–255/2005.

K R v the Republic of Lithuania, Supreme Court of Lithuania, 23 November 2005, case no. 3K-3–604/2005.

A N v the Republic of Lithuania, Supreme Court of Lithuania, 6 February 2007, case no. 3K-7–7/2007.

E P and V M v AB ' Karigė', Supreme Court of Lithuania, 26 September 2007, case no. 3K-3–351/2007.

A D v the Republic of Lithuania, Supreme Court of Lithuania, 30 November 2009, case no. 3K-3–534/2009.

M V v UAB ' Algesa', Supreme Court of Lithuania, 15 February 2012, case no. 3K-3–35/2012.

R K and others v Kaunas Simonas Daukantas secondary school, Supreme Court of Lithuania, 30 April 2012, case no. 3K-3–202/2012.

R B v the Republic of Lithuania, Supreme Court of Lithuania, 30 August 2013, case no. 3K-3–439/2013.

A G and R G v the Republic of Lithuania, Supreme Court of Lithuania, 5 February 2014, case no. 3K-3–4/2014.

R T and others v the Republic of Lithuania, Supreme Court of Lithuania, 30 September 2016, case no. 3K-3–399–687/2016.

D P v the Republic of Lithuania, Supreme Court of Lithuania, 22 February 2018, case no. 3K-3–63–378/2018.

V S v the Republic of Lithuania, Supreme Court of Lithuania, 2 July 2020, case no. 3K-3–210–695/2020.

The Republic of Lithuania v V L and others, Supreme Administrative Court of Lithuania, 10 May 2016, case no. eA-458–261/2016.

A Š v the Republic of Lithuania, Lithuanian Appeal Court, 15 December 2009, case no. 2A-713/2009.

A G and R G v the Republic of Lithuania, Lithuanian Appeal Court, 21 May 2013, case no. 2A-336/2013.

D Š v the Republic of Lithuania, Lithuanian Appeal Court, 4 August 2009, case no. 2A-447/2009.

V P v the Republic of Lithuania, Lithuanian Appeal Court, 22 September 2009, case no. 2A-562/2009.

*T L v the Republic of Lithuan*ia, Lithuanian Appeal Court, 4 November 2013, case no. 2A-893/2013.

8 Compensation for wrongful convictions in Poland[1]

Dorota Czerwińska and Artur Kowalczyk

1 Introduction

Providing an effective mechanism for compensation for wrongful deprivation of liberty is essential in dealing with miscarriages of justice. Just and fair redress for pecuniary and non-pecuniary damage resulting from wrongful conviction and an effective legal path to claim it are conditions of the legitimation of the criminal justice system. If the state uses the power to deprive an individual of her freedom, it has to take full responsibility for the consequences of its misuse.

The aim of this chapter is to conduct an analysis of the Polish legal framework regarding both the scope of the state's civil liability for consequences of wrongful conviction and procedural aspects, as well as to assess its effectiveness and establish whether it requires any improvement.

2 Origins and development of compensation for wrongful conviction

The mechanism allowing for compensation of wrongful conviction has been available in Polish criminal law since the very beginning of Polish statehood. The first Polish Code of Criminal Procedure[2] of 1928 provided for detailed regulations in that regard. The Codification Commission, composed of the most prominent scholars and practitioners, argued that judicial errors are an inseparable part of criminal proceedings, hence the criminal courts are best suited to deal with wrongful convictions.[3]

According to the Code of Criminal Procedure (CCP) of 1928 the compensation for both pecuniary and non-pecuniary damage might have been awarded to a person who had been acquitted or convicted on the basis of 'a more lenient

1 This chapter has been developed as part of the project Compensation for Wrongful Deprivation of Liberty. Theory and Practice (Registration No. 2017/26/E/HS5/00382) financed by the National Science Centre, Poland.

2 *Code of criminal procedure* of 19 March 1928, Dziennik Ustaw 1928, nr 33, poz. 313 with amendments [hereinafter: CCP of 1928].

3 For a detailed history, see: Jan Waszczyński, *Odszkodowanie za niesłuszne skazanie i bezzasadne aresztowanie w polskim procesie karnym* (Wydawnictwo Prawnicze 1967) 24–26; Andrzej Bulsiewicz, *Proces o odszkodowanie za niesłuszne skazanie lub oczywiście bezzasadny areszt tymczasowy* (Towarzystwo Naukowe w Toruniu 1968) 17–21.

DOI: 10.4324/9781003229414-9

provision' as a result of the procedure for reopening proceedings. This term gave rise to serious doubts about whether it referred only to the legal classification of an act or to the leniency of the punishment as well. A relatively wide range of exemptions from the liability, such as in the case of acquittal despite circumstantial incriminating evidence, was also a matter of serious controversy. Thus, unless innocence has been proven, the court could easily dismiss a claim.[4]

After the Second World War the criminal justice system was influenced by the establishment of the communist regime in Poland. However, these changes did not affect the framework of compensation for wrongful conviction, at least on the normative level. The existing provisions remained in force, although they had no practical significance. The introduction of substantial changes followed the political breakthrough of 1956 and liberalisation of the regime.[5] The amendments regarding the liability of public authorities arising from wrongful deprivation of liberty included the introduction of compensation for wrongful detention on remand, the abolishment of all exemptions from the liability, an extension of the limitation period from three months to one year since the finality of the judgment granting the right to compensation and a shift from written, *in camera* proceedings towards an oral and public hearing. The new system of compensation was widely discussed by legal scholars.[6]

The case law regarding compensation for wrongful conviction was at that time greatly influenced by the guidelines of the Supreme Court from 1958[7] providing that the civil law should be used in the proceedings concerning compensation for wrongful conviction accordingly. It was also explicitly recognised that injuries that occurred at the time of serving a sentence, e.g. inflicted by prison officers, should be jointly compensated with the wrongful conviction. According to the Supreme Court's guidelines, 'the compensation should be granted for serving the penalty as it actually was enforced', not as it ideally should have been according to the law.

The Code of Criminal Procedure of 1969,[8] which replaced the one from 1928, did not bring any fundamental changes, except for adapting provisions on

4 Leon Peiper, *Komentarz do kodeksu postępowania karnego i przepisów wprowadzających tenże kodeks z dodatkowemi ustawami, rozporządzeniami i umowami międzynarodowemi w przedmiocie wydania prze-stępców przy szczegółowem uwzględnieniu przepisów kodeksu karnego i ustawy karnej skarbowej* (Leon Frommer Kraków 1933) 904–906.

5 *Act of 15 November 1956 on the liability of the State for damage caused by public officials*, Dziennik Ustaw 1956, nr 54, poz. 243.

6 Henryk Rajzman, 'Nowe przepisy o odszkodowaniu za niesłuszne skazanie lub oskarżenie' (1957) 3 Państwo i Prawo 539–547; Zbigniew Kubec, 'O zmianach w przepisach k.p.k. o odszkodowaniu za niesłuszne skazanie lub oskarżenie' (1957) 2 Nowe Prawo 63–66; Aleksander Kafarski, '*Postępowanie w sprawach o wynagrodzenie za niesłuszne skazanie*' (1959) 1 *Państwo i Prawo* 91–107; Jan Waszczyński, *Odszkodowanie za niesłuszne skazanie*, (n 3) 30–32; Andrzej Bulsiewicz, *Proces o odszkodowanie*, (n 3) 28–34.

7 Guidelines for the judiciary concerning application of articles 510–516 CCP, 729/58, (1958) Orzecznictwo Sądu Najwyższego, position 34.

8 *Code of Criminal Procedure of 19 April 1969*, Dziennik Ustaw 1969, nr 13, poz. 96 with amendments. This Code entered into force in 1970.

compensation to the terminology used in the Civil Code.[9] One of the major problems that remains unresolved to this day concerns the possibility of refusing compensation if the defendant had contributed to their wrongful conviction, for example by giving false statements or remaining silent about relevant circumstances.[10]

The democratic transition of the Polish system in 1989 and the 1990s enabled courts to quash convictions of the persons who were politically persecuted between 1944 and 1989 on the basis of a separate law passed in 1991.[11] It also allowed compensation to be claimed for both pecuniary and non-pecuniary damage by those whose convictions were quashed or their parents, spouses or children in the case of the death of the convict. These provisions are still in force and are applied frequently.

Under the Code of Criminal Procedure of 1997 (hereinafter: CCP),[12] which came into force on 1 September 1998, the rules for compensation for wrongful conviction were not amended fundamentally. The major changes were introduced in 2013[13] when the state's liability for wrongful conviction was extended to wrongful application of penal measures which may be imposed in addition to or in place of a penalty and the limitation period was extended to three years.[14] The reform entered into force on 1 July 2015, but only a few months later, in April 2016, it was overturned by the legislature and the former regulation was re-established.[15]

3 Sources of law regulating compensation for wrongful conviction

The compensatory mechanism is anchored in the Constitution of the Republic of Poland.[16] According to Article 41(5) of the Constitution, anyone who has been unlawfully deprived of their liberty shall have a right to compensation. There is also a more general provision of Article 77(1) of the Constitution granting the right to compensation for any harm done by any action of public authorities which

9 *Kodeks cywilny of 23 April 1964*, Dziennik Ustaw 1964, nr 16, poz. 93 with amendments. The Code is still in force.

10 Wiesław Daszkiewicz, 'Podstawy prawne wyłączenia odpowiedzialności państwa za szkodę wyrządzoną niesłusznym skazaniem' (1978) 11–12 *Nowe Prawo* 1599–1615.

11 *Act of 23 February 1991 on annulment of convictions whereby persons were persecuted for their activities aimed at achieving independence for Poland*, Dziennik Ustaw 1991, nr 34, poz. 149 with amendments.

12 *Code of criminal procedure of 6 June 1997*, Dziennik Ustaw 1997, nr 89, poz. 555 with amendments.

13 *Act of 27 September 2013 on the Amendment of CCP and other acts*, Dziennik Ustaw 2013, poz. 1247.

14 See on the new model of compensation Wojciech Jasiński 'Odszkodowanie i zadośćuczynienie za niesłuszne skazanie, wykonanie środka zabezpieczającego oraz niezasadne stosowanie środków przymusu po nowelizacji kodeksu postępowania karnego' (2015a) 9 *Prokuratura i Prawo* 49–79.

15 *Act of 11 March 2016 on the Amendment of CCP and other acts*, Dziennik Ustaw 2016, poz. 437.

16 *Constitution of the Republic of Poland of 2 April 1997*, Dziennik Ustaw 1997, nr 78, poz. 483 with amendments.

is contrary to law.[17] Due to the importance of the protected legal good (personal freedom), the right to compensation for unlawful deprivation of liberty has been regulated explicitly. This provision is also considered as a basis for special protection in comparison to damage caused by other types of acts by public authorities.[18] Although Article 41(5) of the Constitution provides only for compensation for the deprivation of liberty, omitting other forms of wrongful conviction, the statutory regulation also covers non-custodial penalties, such as community service or fines.

Generally, the model of compensation for wrongful conviction combines elements of civil and criminal procedure. Compensation for wrongful conviction is regulated in Chapter 58 of the CCP entitled 'Compensation for Wrongful Conviction, Detention on Remand or Arrest' and includes Articles 552–558. Hence, the claim for compensation for wrongful conviction is pursued under criminal procedure. However, the provisions of the Code of Civil Procedure[19] may be applied as well – but only to matters which are unregulated in CCP (Article 558 CCP). Yet, the right to compensation provided for in Chapter 58 CCP is considered to be a civil law remedy which is pursued in the specific proceedings before the criminal court.[20] It allows provisions rooted in civil law to be applied, such as those concerning the scope of pecuniary and non-pecuniary damage or consequences of the expiration of the limitation period.

The Polish legal system is a continental one, therefore court decisions are not a source of universally binding law.[21] Despite this fact, courts' judgments, and the Supreme Court's case law in particular, have a significant impact on the way both substantive and procedural provisions are interpreted in practice. One of the meaningful examples is the Supreme Court's resolution of 1999 establishing the state's liability for wrongful deprivation of liberty on a risk basis, which means that there is no need to prove the guilt of any public official responsible for its imposition.[22]

4 Grounds for compensation for wrongful conviction

The accused is entitled to compensation from the State Treasury for pecuniary and non-pecuniary damage resulting from a fully or partially served penalty which had

17 Paweł Wiliński, *Proces karny w świetle Konstytucji* (Wolters Kluwer 2011) 200.

18 See Paweł Sarnecki in Leszek Garlicki and Marek Zubik (eds) *Konstytucja Rzeczypospolitej Polskiej. Komentarz*, vol. II (Wydawnictwo Sejmowe 2016) 219.

19 *Code of Civil Procedure of 17 November 1964*, Dziennik Ustaw 1964, nr 43, poz. 296 with amendments.

20 Paweł Cioch, *Odpowiedzialność Skarbu Państwa z tytułu niesłusznego skazania* (Wolters Kluwer 2007) 91.

21 However, it is now clear that precedents in fact play a role in civil law systems as well. See e.g. Vincy Fon and Francesco Parisi, 'Judicial precedents in civil law systems: A dynamic analysis' (2006) 26 *International Review of Law and Economics* 519–535.

22 Resolution of the Supreme Court of 15 September 1999, I KZP 27/99, 1999 Orzecznictwo Sądu Najwyższego Izba Karna i Wojskowa 11–12, poz. 79. This resolution has been given within the context of wrongful detention on remand but the conclusion on the type of liability relates to wrongful deprivation of liberty as well.

been wrongfully imposed. However, the claim may only be pursued if the applicant was then acquitted or sentenced to a more lenient penalty as a result of reopening proceedings, hearing an appeal in cassation or an extraordinary complaint (Article 552 § 1 CCP). All these measures are of an exceptional nature and may be submitted against final judgments only in strictly limited situations.[23] These include flagrant errors of substantive or procedural law in the initial proceedings (in the case of cassation) and new circumstances that were discovered or took place after the court had given its ruling (in the case of reopening proceedings). These circumstances might be: new evidence implying the convict's innocence, a guilty verdict against a witness for perjury or a European Court of Human Rights (ECtHR) judgment determining the violation of human rights in the course of initial proceedings. The extraordinary complaint was introduced to the Polish legal system in 2018. It may be filed to the Supreme Court only by specific authorities, such as the Attorney General or Ombudsman.[24] This remedy is a subsidiary one – it is only admissible when no other legal measure is available. The grounds for extraordinary complaint involve an infringement of constitutionally protected human rights and freedoms, a flagrant violation of the law or a manifest contradiction between the facts found by the court and the evidence.[25]

The accused is also entitled to compensation if, after the reversal of conviction, the proceedings are discontinued due to circumstances not considered in the earlier proceedings (Article 552 § 2 CPC). It is therefore important whether these circumstances had already occurred at the time the judgment in a criminal case was handed down or appeared later.

When analysing the grounds for compensation for wrongful conviction in Poland, a few crucial points must be highlighted.

First – and in contrast to historical regulations – it is prohibited to differentiate between acquittal based on insufficient evidence and acquittal in cases in which the guilt of the defendant was unproven for other reasons.[26] The presumption of innocence determines that in both cases compensation should be awarded.

Second, the compensation may only be granted for a penalty that has been fully or partially enforced.[27] A conviction itself without serving the penalty is not

23 See more on grounds for cassation and reopening proceedings: Wojciech Jasiński and Karolina Kremens, 'The right to claim innocence in Poland' (2020) 4 *Erasmus Law Review* 44–45; Wojciech Jasiński and Karolina Kremens, *Criminal Law in Poland* (Kluwer Law International B.B. 2019) 274–278.

24 See Articles 89–95 of the *Act of 8 December 2017 on the Supreme Court*, Dziennik Ustaw 2018, poz. 5 with amendments.

25 Article 89 § 1 of the *Act of 8 December 2017 on the Supreme Court* (n 24). See more Wojciech Jasiński and Karolina Kremens, 'The right to claim innocence in Poland' (n 23) 45–46.

26 Judgment of the Supreme Court of 13 June 2002, V KKN 125/00, (2002) 9–10 Orzecznictwo Sądu Najwyższego Izba Karna i Izba Wojskowa, position 80; see Andrzej Bulsiewicz's commentary to this judgment: (2003) 5 Orzecznictwo Sądów Polskich, 269–271.

27 Paweł Cioch, *Odpowiedzialność Skarbu Państwa* (n 20) 144–145.

subject to compensation, which also applies to sentences that were suspended for any reason.[28] However, one may claim damages in such situations under general rules of the Civil Code concerning the state's liability for unlawful actions.

Third, the right to compensation covers all types of penalties: deprivation of liberty, community service and fines, but not penal measures which under certain circumstances may be imposed in addition to or in place of a penalty.[29] The same limitation applies to compensatory measures provided in criminal law. In fact, penal or compensatory measures may be equally or even more severe for an individual than the penalty itself.

Fourth, the compensation may also be awarded for wrongful imposition (and enforcement) of a security measure instead of a penalty (Article 552 § 3 CCP). Security measures are applied to prevent an offender who is incapable of bearing criminal responsibility from committing a prohibited act again. This includes people suffering from mental illnesses or sexual disorders or those addicted to alcohol or drugs.

Sometimes, the state may be exempt from the liability for wrongful conviction or such liability may be limited. If the convicted person had given a false report of a criminal offence or had given false testimony with the intention of misleading the court or law enforcement authority which led to conviction, the convicted person is not entitled to compensation (Article 553 § 1 CCP). This only relates to intentional false self-incriminations or false accusations resulting in wrongful conviction. The accused who simply exercised her right to defence must not be denied compensation.[30]

However, under Article 553 § 2 CCP the discussed exception is not extended to statements that had been given under the conditions defined in Article 171 § 4, 5 and 7 CCP, that is obtained by the use of force, illicit threating, chemical substances, technical means or even hypnosis in order to influence the interrogated person or to control the unconscious reactions of the body during the examination, as well as obtained by way of asking leading questions. The exception from the state's liability also does not apply when the damage or injury is a consequence of an abuse of power or a neglect of duty by a public official (Article 553 § 3 CCP). These provisions are incompatible or even contradictory. It is hard to imagine that the interrogated person has intentionally given a false statement but at the same time has been forced to testify.[31] It is either one or the other. It can

28 Judgment of the Court of Appeal in Białystok of 26 January 2010, II AKa 7/10, (2010) 10 Prokuratura i Prawo position 31.

29 Judgment of the Supreme Court of 1 April 2008, V KK 33/08, (2008) 1 Orzecznictwo Sądu Najwyższego w Sprawach Karnych, position 776. Such penal measures include: deprivation of public rights, driving ban, disqualification from specific positions and professions, prohibition on appearing in certain communities and locations or leaving a specific place of residence without the court's consent and restraining orders.

30 Judgment of the Supreme Court of 7 November 2005, III KK 177/05 (2006) 4 Orzecznictwo Sądu Najwyższego Izba Karna i Izba Wojskowa, position 34.

31 Wojciech Jasiński in Jerzy Skorupka (ed), *Kodeks postępowania karnego. Komentarz* (C.H. Beck 2021) 1461; Piotr Hofmański, Elżbieta Sadzik and Kazimierz Zgryzek, *Kodeks postępowania karnego. Komentarz*, vol. 3 (C.H. Beck 2012) 492.

be assumed that the legislator's purpose was to protect the defendant from the negative implications of public officials abusing their power but in such a case it cannot be stated that the false statements were given intentionally in the first place.

In the case of other forms of an applicant's contribution to wrongful conviction, the amount of compensation may be reduced correspondingly (Article 553 § 3 CCP). This can happen when the accused remained silent on relevant facts which could have prevented the conviction. It should be noted that the presumption of innocence and the right to remain silent protect the accused person from being forced to disclose information regarding the criminal act and their exercise cannot be treated as evidence of having committed the offence. However, none of these principles imply that the accused cannot suffer any kind of negative consequences of asserting the right to remain silent. If the accused decided not to disclose relevant facts which could have prevented the conviction, it can be seen as a contributory negligence and lead to the reduction of compensation.[32]

The claim for compensation has to be submitted within the one-year limitation period starting on the day the previous conviction was overturned (Article 555 CCP).

The grounds for compensation are regulated separately with regard to claims of a third person after the convict's death. The third person is entitled to compensation if she lost maintenance due to the wrongful conviction, provided that:

1 the originally convicted person was obliged to provide such maintenance by law,[33]
2 the originally convicted person effectively and continuously provided such maintenance, in so far as awarding damages is justified on an equitable basis.

Whether the person entitled to claim compensation is a relative of the initial victim of wrongful deprivation of liberty is irrelevant. The right to compensation is limited to the amount of the maintenance lost due to the deprivation of liberty of the deceased.[34] This right is an autonomous right of the person entitled to compensation as the original convict's right to compensation is not inheritable and expires with her death.[35] The third person's claim should be pursued within a limitation period of one year of the death of the deceased (Article 556 § 2 CCP).

32 Wojciech Jasiński in Jerzy Skorupka (ed), *Kodeks postępowania karnego. Komentarz* (n 31) 1462; *contra* Piotr Kruszyński, 'Z problematyki odszkodowania za niewątpliwie niesłuszne tymczasowe aresztowanie', in Janina Czapska *et al.* (eds), *Zasady procesu karnego wobec wyzwań współczesności. Księga ku czci profesora Stanisława Waltosia* (Wydawnictwo Prawnicze 2000) 284–285.

33 See Section III of *Family and Guardianship Code of 25 February 1964*, Dziennik Ustaw 1964, nr 9, poz. 59 with amendments.

34 Barbara Nita-Światłowska 'Podmiotowy i przedmiotowy zakres roszczenia odszkodowawczego wynikającego z art. 556 § 1 k.p.k.' (2016) 9 *Przegląd Sądowy* 17–19.

35 Piotr Hofmański, Elżbieta Sadzik and Kazimierz Zgryzek, *Kodeks postępowania karnego. Komentarz* (n 31) 504.

5 Procedure for claiming compensation

The compensation is awarded to the accused (Article 552 § 1 CCP). The use of the term 'accused' has raised criticism, as after having been acquitted the person entitled to compensation should not bear such a name which leads to further stigmatisation.[36] This remains inconsistent with the wording of Article 554 § 2a CCP, which uses the term 'applicant' when enlisting parties to the proceedings in which compensation is claimed (parties includes the applicant, the prosecutor and the State Treasury).

In the event of the death of the wrongfully convicted person other individuals are entitled to claim compensation limited to pecuniary damages (Article 556 § 1 CCP).

The applicant has the right to appoint a counsel (Article 556 § 3 CCP). The power of attorney granted by the applicant during her criminal process remains in force (Article 556 § 4 CCP). If the applicant proves inability to bear the costs of counsel without harm to the necessary maintenance of herself or her family, she may apply for legal aid (Article 78 § 1 CCP). In such a case, the counsel shall be appointed by the court. A refusal to appoint a counsel is subject to interlocutory appeal (Article 81 § 1a CCP).

The proceedings are initiated by the applicant's motion made in writing. The motion is deformalised and should include the name and address of the applicant, indication of the court, date and signature, as well as the statement as to the basis for the request. The applicant is not obliged to indicate the demanded damages nor to specify their pecuniary or non-pecuniary character. However, at a later stage the court may request that these are specified to properly direct the case. The application should also attach copies of the motion for other parties. The proceedings are free of charge (Article 554 § 4 CCP).

As mentioned before, compensatory proceedings are a specific type of criminal proceedings in which the rules of civil procedure may be applied to matters not regulated in the CCP. However, the scope of this application remains questionable. A broad interpretation of Article 558 CCP has been developed in the case law, where it is claimed that provisions of the Code of Civil Procedure may also be applied if certain matters are regulated in the CCP but its provisions cannot be applied in compensatory proceedings due to their specific features.[37]

The compensation claim is held before the Regional Court (*Sąd Okręgowy*)[38] of the circuit where the judgment of conviction was issued by the court of first instance. Like other judicial proceedings, these are, at least theoretically, of an

36 Stanisław Stachowiak, 'Odszkodowanie za niesłuszne skazanie, tymczasowe aresztowanie lub zatrzymanie w kodeksie postępowania karnego' (1999) 1 *Prokuratura i Prawo* 64.

37 Lech Krzysztof Paprzycki, in Lech Krzysztof Paprzycki (ed), *Kodeks postępowania karnego. Komentarz*, vol. 2 (Wolters Kluwer 2013) 460.

38 The Regional Court in Poland may be considered as the middle level of the judiciary. It is a court of first instance for serious offences and a court of appeal for judgments given by the District Court (Polish: *Sąd Rejonowy*).

adversarial nature. However, strong elements of the inquisitorial model are also present. This is a consequence of the model of Polish criminal procedure – the court may not only admit evidence presented by the parties but also take evidence on its own initiative.[39] Therefore, courts very often play an active role in evidentiary proceedings.

The role of the parties during proceedings is granted to the applicant, the prosecutor and the State Treasury (Article 554 § 2a). The latter only gained this status in 2019.[40] Their basic rights include: the right to call witnesses and other evidence, the right to participate in a hearing and the right to file an appeal against the court's judgment.

The prosecutor's role in compensatory proceedings remains unclear. Until 2019, the public prosecution service was customarily associated with acting in the state's interest, although there were no legal grounds to consider the prosecutor as a representative of the State Treasury. Since 2019, with the State Treasury having a separate representative, the prosecutor's role has become even more ambiguous. Considering that the public prosecution service acts in the public interest, the prosecutor should not be seen as a legal opponent to the applicant, as public interest usually requires that the harm resulting from wrongful conviction is compensated.[41]

The State Treasury is represented by the president of the court in which the final judgment imposing the penalty was issued (Article 554 § 2b CCP). This regulation is criticised by legal scholars as in some cases it leads to the State Treasury being represented by the president of the very same court which hears the case.[42] To ensure impartiality it is proposed to amend the law so that it designates another authority to represent the State Treasury. It may be, for example, the General Counsel of the Republic of Poland as a public official represents the State Treasury in civil proceedings.[43]

The procedure for claiming compensation reflects the course of standard criminal proceedings. If the motion meets formal requirements, the court sets the date of the hearing, notifies participants and delivers copies of the motion to the prosecutor and State Treasury. The court may summon witnesses and gather evidence requested by the applicant in the motion. The common practice of the courts is to

39 See Article 167 CCP.

40 See more on this amendment: Wojciech Jasiński, 'W kwestii zasadności uregulowania katalogu stron postępowania w przedmiocie odszkodowania za niesłuszne pozbawienie wolności' (2021b) 1 *Ruch Prawniczy, Ekonomiczny i Socjologiczny* 47–58.

41 According to Article 2 of the *Public Prosecution Service Act of 28 January 2016*, Dziennik Ustaw 2016, poz. 177 with amendments, public prosecutors' tasks are not only to prosecute offences but also – in more general terms – to uphold the rule of law.

42 Jerzy Skorupka, 'Sposób ukształtowania procedury karnej jako element oceny bezstronności obiektywnej (zewnętrznej) sądu' (2021) 7–8 Palestra 17–18.

43 Jerzy Skorupka, 'Sposób ukształtowania procedury karnej' (n 42) 18; Barbara Nita-Światłowska, 'Prokuratoria Generalna w postępowaniu karnym' in Leszek Bosek (ed), *Prawo i państwo. Księga jubileuszowa 200-lecia Prokuratorii Generalnej Rzeczypospolitej Polskiej* (Wydawnictwo Sejmowe 2017) 719–721.

use its discretion early at that stage of the process to include in the records of the case the file of the criminal proceedings in which the applicant was convicted and other documents gathered during her imprisonment.

The hearing is held in public in accordance with general rules of criminal process focused on presentation of evidence. The proceedings commence with the presentation of the motion by the applicant and close with final statements by the parties followed by the court's judgment. The central point of evidence-taking is the questioning of the applicant. Note that according to the rules of Polish criminal procedure the defendant during a regular criminal trial is interrogated as a unique source of evidence and not a witness (Article 175 § 1 CCP). The difference concerns the right to remain silent and the lack of criminal liability for false statements made by the accused person. Although during compensatory proceedings the applicant is usually questioned as a witness, some scholars argue that she should be treated like an accused person and should be provided with the right to refuse to testify to avoid self-incrimination.[44]

The burden of proof in compensatory proceedings is allocated between the applicant and the court, which was confirmed by the Supreme Court: 'The applicant should prove grounds for compensation and its amount. However, the court hearing the case, according to Article 2 § 2 CCP, should make efforts to provide that the basis for any kind of determination consists of true facts'.[45] According to the general rules of Polish criminal procedure, the court, bound by the principle of material truth, is obliged to verify all the important circumstances of the case even if the parties remain inactive (Article 2 § 2 and Article 366 § 1 CCP). The court has unlimited ability to act *ex officio* in gathering evidence (Article 167 CCP). This makes the proceedings concerning compensation claims more convenient for the applicant compared with the civil procedure, which imposes the burden of proof solely on the plaintiff.

The parties may submit an appeal against the judgment of the court of first instance (Article 444 § 1 CCP). Grounds for the appeal include the violation of substantive law, violation of procedural law in so far as it could have an impact on the judgment, an error of fact or awarding a manifestly disproportionate amount of compensation (Article 438 CCP). The Court of Appeal, which hears the case in a panel of three professional judges, may uphold, change or reverse the judgment or order a retrial.

The final judgment on compensation may only be challenged by an appeal in cassation or, to some extent, by a motion for reopening of proceedings. As

44 Romuald Kmiecik, 'Glosa do uchwały Sądu Najwyższego z dnia 11 września 1992 r. (I KZP 27/92)' (1995) 4 *Przegląd Sądowy* 86–88; see also Beata Bieńkowska, 'Glosa do postanowienia Sądu Najwyższego z dnia 5 lutego 1988 r., II KZ 3/88' (1989) 7–12 *Orzecznictwo Sądów Polskich i Komisji Arbitrażowych* 363.

45 Judgment of the Supreme Court of 4 November 2004, WK 19/04, (2004) 1 Orzecznictwo Sądu Najwyższego w Sprawach Karnych position 2011; see also: Judgment of the Supreme Court of 26 June 2019, III KK 289/18, LEX no. 2705800. However, in other judgments the Supreme Court stated that the applicant bears the burden of proof according to general civil law rule; see Decision of the Supreme Court of 6 May 2014, V KK 384/13, LEX no. 1463434.

previously mentioned, the appeal in cassation may only invoke a manifest violation of substantive or procedural law, whereas the proceedings can be reopened in exceptional situations when the judgment might have been influenced by an offence or the reopening is necessary in light of a decision given by an international authority (for example judgment of the ECtHR).[46]

6 Calculating the amount of compensation

The amount of compensation for wrongful conviction is awarded as an ordinary civil claim. The CCP does not contain any specific regulation regarding calculating the amount and refers to the general understanding of pecuniary and non-pecuniary damage under civil law. This means that the compensation is calculated individually after the evaluation of presented evidence.

The compensation covers material and non-material harm (Article 552 § 1 CCP). Under Article 361 § 2 CC, pecuniary damage shall equate to both substantial loss suffered and loss of reasonably expected profits. Any harm can be compensated as long as the causation link to the wrongful incarceration is established by the court. The substantial loss may include the loss of value of a company owned by the applicant. Loss of reasonably expected profits typically pertains to the loss of salary or business income during the time of incarceration. If the applicant proves that she could not achieve an income equal to what she had earned before the incarceration, the reduction of income after the incarceration can be covered as well. The amount of compensation for material damage shall be calculated by using the so-called differential method, that is by comparing the actual assets of the applicant with the hypothetical assets she would have possessed if the incarceration had not happened.[47]

The circumstances that have decisive influence on the amount of compensation vary depending on the type of damage: material or non-material.

Pecuniary damages are awarded in the amount equal to the suffered loss. This amount has to be explicitly proved by the applicant.[48] Not only the amount of loss but the causation link with the execution of the penalty have to be established on the basis of evidence. The amount of compensation shall be calculated with consideration of prices of the date of adjudicating (Article 363 § 1 CC). This is of importance if time has passed since the loss happened or prices suddenly increased. The compensation for the loss of income has to be calculated after considering the changed prices and income of society. If the compensation was calculated based on prices from decades ago, it would be insufficient to actually negate the harm.

46 Judgment of the Supreme Court of 12 June 2012, IV KO 10/12 (2012) 10 *Orzecznictwo Sądu Najwyższego Izba Karna i Izba Wojskowa*, position 109. See further Marcin Mrowicki, *Wznowienie postępowania karnego na podstawie rozstrzygnięcia Europejskiego Trybunału Praw Człowieka* (Biuro Rzecznika Praw Obywatelskich 2020) 192–195.

47 Judgment of the Supreme Court of 15 October 2020, II KK 16/20, LEX no. 3097169.

48 Decision of the Supreme Court of 24 April 2019, III KK 39/19, LEX no. 2686351.

Expressing the awarded damages in current prices allows its actual value to be maintained regardless of inflation.

On the other hand, damages for non-material harm are awarded in an appropriate amount, which should redress the harm and suffering caused by the execution of the wrongfully imposed punishment. Proper assessment of non-material harm and calculation of damages is a difficult task. There are no statutory guidelines as to how to perform it or which circumstances shall be considered. The harm should be assessed individually in the light of each individual case, and the case law identifies different factors as relevant.[49] These include the length of deprivation of liberty, the applicant's age, her family relations, damage to health caused by wrongful conviction, criminal record if any, especially previous incarceration, and the particular circumstances of the execution of the penalty, such as: overcrowded prison cell, traumatising experiences, prison violence, improper treatment by guards, involuntary exposure to cigarette smoke, lack of possibility to attend important family celebrations such as weddings or funerals and violation of some prisoner rights such as a right to be visited by family members. These aspects are difficult to assess *in abstracto* and the specific circumstances of the individual case always have to be considered. It is frequently emphasised that the amount of damages for non-pecuniary loss shall be adjusted to – and in any case shall not exceed – the living standard of society.[50] This approach has not been criticised in the literature, although the general view is that this criterion may only play an auxiliary role in setting the amount of compensation.[51] However, it may be questioned whether the purely personal and individual character of non-material harm is reconcilable with any factors other than those connected with the victim.

7 The recourse claim of the State Treasury against persons who caused wrongful convictions

According to Article 557 § 1 CCP, if pecuniary or non-pecuniary damage resulting from wrongful conviction was redressed, the State Treasury has a right to assert a recourse claim against a person who caused the conviction with her unlawful acts. The decision whether to assert this claim in civil lawsuit rests with the prosecutor or the authority entitled to represent the State Treasury (Article 557 § 2 CCP). If the prosecutor does not find any grounds to seek a recourse claim, it is stated in a written decision and communicated to the other authority entitled to pursue it.

49 Łukasz Chojniak, *Odszkodowanie za niesłuszne skazanie, tymczasowe aresztowanie lub zatrzymanie* (C.H. Beck 2013) 167; Paweł Cioch, *Odpowiedzialność Skarbu Państwa* (n 20) 115–116.

50 The most representative example is the widely cited Supreme Court decision of 22 January 2015, III KK 252/14, LEX no. 1640256.

51 Wojciech Jasiński, in Jerzy Skorupka (ed), *Kodeks postępowania karnego. Komentarz* (n 31) 1424; Katarzyna Wiśniewska, *Model odpowiedzialności Skarbu Państwa za stosowanie środków penalnych i procesowych wobec jednostki* (Krakowski Instytut Prawa Karnego 2020) 393–396.

The recourse claim may be brought against any person whose unlawful acts led to the wrongful conviction. They may constitute actions or omissions that are against the law and can take the form of a failure to fulfil legal duties during proceedings.[52] It is not specified in law which categories of persons may be sued by the State Treasury. Yet surely this group includes judges, prosecutors, police officers or other criminal justice agents.[53] Serious doubts, however, are raised as to the possibility of suing witnesses and expert witnesses, translators and interpreters. The opponents of including this group as potentially liable argue that there is no adequate causation link between their false testimony and issuing an unjust judgment.[54] Furthermore, the State Treasury is not responsible for the acts of those who do not act in their official capacity so they may not be held responsible by way of recourse claim.[55] However, other scholars claim that the latter argument is of no importance as the provision of Article 557 CCP does not limit the scope of people responsible by way of recourse to state employees. The adequate causation link between the false testimony and the wrongful conviction may not be ruled out because it is possible that such a testimony was treated by the adjudicating court as credible despite fulfilling all its duties in assessment of the evidence.[56]

Although the recourse claim is regulated in the CCP, it is rarely used in practice. Between September 1991 and December 2014 the prosecution service decided to bring only eight lawsuits out of 2,163 cases examined by the prosecutors for this purpose.[57] Lack of practical application of the provisions providing for the recourse claim is a subject of ongoing discussion among legal scholars, as well as the Ombudsman, Members of Parliament and even the mass media.[58] However,

52 Wojciech Jasiński, in Jerzy Skorupka (ed), *Kodeks postępowania karnego. Komentarz* (n 31) 1439. Some scholars claim such an action or commission has to be taken consciously in order to be perceived as unlawful (Dariusz Świecki, in Dariusz Świecki (ed), *Kodeks postępowania karnego. Komentarz*, vol. 2, (4th edn, Wolters Kluwer 2018) 766).

53 Wojciech Jasiński, in Jerzy Skorupka (ed), *Kodeks postępowania karnego. Komentarz* (n 31) 1439.

54 Dariusz Świecki, in Dariusz Świecki (ed), *Kodeks postępowania karnego. Komentarz*, vol. 2 (n 52) 766.

55 Zbigniew Gostyński and Ryszard Andrzej Stefański, in Ryszard Andrzej Stefański and Stanisław Zabłocki (eds), *Kodeks postępowania karnego. Komentarz*, vol. 3, (Wydawnictwo ABC 2004) 785.

56 Wojciech Jasiński, in Jerzy Skorupka (ed), *Kodeks postępowania karnego. Komentarz* (n 31) 1439; Jarosław Matras, in Katarzyna Dudka (ed), *Kodeks postępowania karnego. Komentarz*, Wolters Kluwer 2020, 1329–1330.

57 Paweł Czarnecki, 'Odpowiedzialność Skarbu Państwa za błędy wymiaru sprawiedliwości w sprawach karnych po 1 lipca 2015 r.' (2015) 2 *Internetowy Przegląd Prawniczy TBSP UJ 63*, tab. 1. However, the numbers include cases concerning damages not only for wrongful conviction but also for wrongful detention on remand and arrest, which are covered by the same legal regime in Poland.

58 In 2009 the Ministry of Justice responded to an interpellation of one MP that the reason for the lack of activity of prosecutors in the field of recourse claims is their inaccuracy and serious doubts regarding the conditions of their application (http://orka2.sejm.gov.pl/IZ6.nsf/main/517F80B7 accessed 5 February 2022). The Ombudsman asked the Ministry of Justice about this matter as long ago as 2014 (https://bip.brpo.gov.pl/sites/defa

this interest has not led to either legislative or practical change and the recourse claim remains absent from legal practice.

8 The practice of compensating the wrongfully convicted

The statistics provided by the public prosecution service only indicate a total number of cases regarding compensation under Chapter 58 CCP and the already mentioned Act of 1991 concerning compensation for annulled convictions from the communist times.[59] Furthermore, compensation for wrongful conviction is not distinguished from that awarded for wrongful detention on remand and arrest. Thus, these statistics do not provide insight into the number of claims for compensation for wrongful conviction. However, other publicly available statistical data refer to the number of persons who were awarded compensation for wrongful conviction, detention on remand and arrest as well as to their total sum (Table 8.1).[60]

Empirical studies show that claims for compensation for wrongful conviction are rare, especially in comparison to claims for compensation for wrongful detention on remand or arrest.[61] One of the reasons might be the fact that the risk of miscarriage of justice is a lot smaller with regard to final judgments on the merits of the case than in the case of decisions issued at an earlier stage of the proceedings.

ult/files/Do_MS_ws_%20dochodzenia_roszczen_regresowych_%20przys%C5%82uguja cych_Skarbowi_Panstwa.pdf, accessed 5 February 2022). The mass media took an interest in the subject in 2021 (Violetta Krasnowska, 'Państwo płaci, państwo płacą', *Polityka*, 25 May 2021). With regard to legal doctrine, see Łukasz Chojniak, *Odszkodowanie* (n 49) 208–209.

59 See the PK-P1K report of the National Prosecutor's Office available at https://www.gov.pl/web/prokuratura-krajowa/sprawozdania-statystyczne-za-2021-rok (accessed 4 May 2022).

60 See the long-term analysis of the Statistical Directory of the Justice System available at https://isws.ms.gov.pl/pl/baza-statystyczna/opracowania-wieloletnie/download,2853,33.html (accessed 22 November 2022). It is worth noting that the total amount of compensation awarded in 2021 was strongly influenced by the case of Tomasz Komenda which will be discussed herein below.

61 The amount of compensation for wrongful conviction constitutes less than 10 per cent of the total sum of compensation granted under the provisions of the Code of Criminal Procedure. This means than more than 90 per cent of the total sum was granted as compensation for wrongful detention on remand or arrest. Statistically, between 2009 and 2018 a total of 2,491 people were granted compensation for non-pecuniary damage resulting from manifestly wrongful detention on remand or arrest, whereas only 271 received it because of a wrongful conviction. See Katarzyna Wiśniewska, *Model odpowiedzialności* (n 51) 261–266. The number of awarded compensations varied in this period from 5 to 33 per year (*ibid* 264). According to another study, only 8 per cent of the motions for compensation heard in 2017 and 2018 in the selected courts concerned wrongful conviction, whereas 66 per cent involved wrongful detention on remand and 26 per cent referred to wrongful arrest. See Dorota Czerwińska and Artur Kowalczyk, 'Kryteria ustalania związku przyczynowego oraz rozmiaru szkody majątkowej i krzywdy wynikłej z niesłusznego pozbawienia wolności w świetle badań aktowych' (2021) 11–12 *Przegląd Sądowy* 150.

Table 8.1 Number of people awarded compensation and sum of compensation for wrongful conviction and wrongful detention on remand or arrest

	2016	*2017*	*2018*	*2019*	*2020*	*2021*
Total number of persons who were awarded compensation for wrongful conviction	70	27	12	12	11	6
Total sum of compensation for wrongful conviction (in Polish *złoty*)	2,727,817	1,033,600	846,300	204,178	477,500	12,388,000
Total number of persons who were awarded compensation for wrongful detention on remand or arrest	215	243	197	159	127	144
Total sum of compensation for wrongful detention on remand or arrest (in Polish *złoty*)	10,769,521	11,789,524	10,254,143	7,838,850	5,928,885	5,946,911

The other reason is a serious limitation of the right to compensation, which is only awarded subject to a previous judgment issued in cassation or reopened proceedings. However, such a limitation on the right to compensation is entirely justified by the value of legal certainty and the principle of *res judicata*.

As previously mentioned, there are no statutory guidelines as to the amount of compensation. It is decided by the court on a case-by-case basis. Thus, only empirical research may provide reliable insight into the amounts granted.[62] Their results showed different practices in various regions of Poland, as well as the evolution of the practice and the amounts awarded over recent decades. Many courts calculate the damages for non-pecuniary loss by multiplying the number of months or days of deprivation of liberty and a lump sum set by the court. The result of such an operation may then be adjusted to the individual circumstances of the case. The lump sums often differ between regions, although there are no formal grounds for this. This form of calculation was criticised both in the literature and case law, naming such an approach as schematic and contrary to the principle of individual compensation, which may lead to undervaluing the damage.[63] It may be argued that it promotes the constitutional principle of equality.[64] However, regional disproportions undermine this thesis.[65] According to one of the empirical studies, the compensation for non-pecuniary loss resulting from wrongful conviction or manifestly wrongful detention on remand in 2017 and 2018 was on average 436.03 PLN per day. The average varied regionally from 227 PLN to 816 PLN.[66] Older studies indicated the average amounts ranging from 33 to 66 PLN per day in 2008 and 2009 to 133 PLN in 2016.[67] In a 2012 study an average of 141.93 PLN per day of incarceration, varying regionally from 41 PLN to 333 PLN, was established.[68]

62 Such research has been conducted at least three times over the last decade: Dorota Czerwińska and Artur Kowalczyk, 'Kryteria ustalania związku przyczynowego' (n 61) 148–164; Katarzyna Wiśniewska, *Model odpowiedzialności* (n 51); Katarzyna Dudka and Bartłomiej Dobosiewicz, *Odszkodowanie za niesłuszne skazanie, tymczasowe aresztowanie lub zatrzymanie w praktyce orzeczniczej sądów powszechnych* (Instytut Wymiaru Sprawiedliwości 2012) 22–23.

63 Katarzyna Wiśniewska, *Model odpowiedzialności* (n 51) 402; Wojciech Jasiński, in Jerzy Skorupka (ed), *Kodeks postępowania karnego. Komentarz* (n 31) 1458–1459. Judgment of the Court of Appeal in Wrocław of 19 May 2016, II AKa 336/15, LEX no. 2057773.

64 See Katarzyna Wiśniewska, *Model odpowiedzialności* (n 51) 226–228.

65 Dorota Czerwińska and Artur Kowalczyk, 'Kryteria ustalania związku przyczynowego' (n 61) 158–159; Katarzyna Wiśniewska, *Model odpowiedzialności* (n 51) 420–421.

66 Dorota Czerwińska and Artur Kowalczyk, 'Kryteria ustalania związku przyczynowego' (n 61) 158–159.

67 Katarzyna Wiśniewska, *Model odpowiedzialności* (n 51) 402–403.

68 Katarzyna Dudka and Bartłomiej Dobosiewicz, *Odszkodowanie za niesłuszne skazanie* (n 62) 22. However, in this study – as opposed to those mentioned above – the average amount was calculated with regard to the compensation not only for the wrongful conviction and wrongful detention on remand but the arrest as well. As the arrest is a short-term deprivation of liberty, the amount calculated daily is significantly higher than in the case of a long-term incarceration, otherwise it would be economically insignificant.

Even though the courts tend to treat the average regional lump sums as a starting point for the compensation awarded in a particular case, the principle of individualisation is also observed. The empirical research showed examples of statistical anomalies consisting in granting higher compensation due to the particular circumstances of a case.[69]

It is even more difficult to provide general conclusions as to the practice of setting the amount of compensation for material harm as it totally depends on the size of the actual loss and lost income. One of the problems is the reduction of compensation by the amount of living expenses the applicant saved during incarceration. The proponents of this approach invoke the differential method of calculating damages for pecuniary loss. As was previously mentioned, this method is based on the comparison of the actual and hypothetical state of the applicant's assets. The hypothetical state is increased by the income the applicant would have gained if she had not been imprisoned. However, it shall also be diminished by the money the applicant would have spent on food or other goods that were provided by the state in prison. Such an approach was approved by the Supreme Court in 2000 and is widespread in practice, but strongly criticised by legal scholars.[70] The critics argue that this interpretation is morally unacceptable as it allows the state to effectively demand the wrongfully convicted person to repay the living expenses borne by the state during the unjustified incarceration.[71] What is more, it violates the constitutional requirement to fully compensate every unlawful deprivation of liberty.[72] According to empirical data, the practice of diminishing the pecuniary damages is another example of unjustified regional differences as it is applied unequally across the country.[73]

Other controversial issues are the approach to the loss of income from undeclared work and the possibility of compensating the expenses which were not borne by the convict herself but by her relatives, such as the costs of parcels, travel expenses for the purpose of visiting the prisoner as well as canteen money. Regarding the income from undeclared work, it is sometimes treated as illegal and thus unfit to compensate. Even if the court tends to acknowledge it, it is difficult to prove its amount.[74] As for the relatives' expenses clearly resulting from the wrongful conviction, in the case law one can find an opinion that they do not

69 Katarzyna Wiśniewska, *Model odpowiedzialności* (n 51) 403, 415.

70 Katarzyna Wiśniewska, *Model odpowiedzialności* (n 51) 224; Decision of the Supreme Court of 20 January 2000, I KZP 46/00, LEX no. 550515.

71 Katarzyna Wiśniewska, *Model odpowiedzialności* (n 51) 225–226; Judgment of the Court of Appeal in Wrocław of 29 December 2015, II AKa 404/15, LEX no. 2039642.

72 Katarzyna Wiśniewska, *Model odpowiedzialności* (n 51) 225–226; Judgment of the Court of Appeal in Wrocław of 29 December 2015, II AKa 404/15, LEX no. 2039642.

73 Dorota Czerwińska and Artur Kowalczyk, 'Kryteria ustalania związku przyczynowego' (n 61) 153–155; Katarzyna Wiśniewska, *Model odpowiedzialności* (n 51) 446–447.

74 Dorota Czerwińska and Artur Kowalczyk, 'Kryteria ustalania związku przyczynowego' (n 61) 153; Katarzyna Wiśniewska, *Model odpowiedzialności* (n 51) 438–440.

constitute part of the applicant's damage unless they came from her assets or were later reimbursed by the applicant.[75]

When discussing the practice of compensating the damage resulting from wrongful conviction in Poland, one cannot omit the landmark judgment in Tomasz Komenda's case.[76] In 2004 Komenda was sentenced to 25 years' imprisonment for the murder and rape of a 15-year-old girl, which took place on New Year's Eve 1996. On 16 May 2018 the Supreme Court reopened Komenda's case and acquitted him based on new genetic, osmological and odontological evidence. By that time, Komenda had already served 18 out of 25 years of his penalty. He then applied for material compensation in the amount of 811,533.12 PLN (approx. €175,000) and 18 million PLN (approx. €4,000,000) for non-material harm. On 8 February 2021, the court granted the applicant's claim in total with respect to material damage and 12 million PLN (approx. €2,600,000) with respect to non-material harm. It is the highest compensation for wrongful conviction in Polish history. In the press release following the judgment the court stated:

> The amount of compensation for non-pecuniary damage was calculated on the basis of the applicant's suffering, length of incarceration and its conditions, improper treatment of the applicant by fellow inmates and the prison guards, deprivation of contact with the family, young age, many sufferings, physical and psychological violence, experienced fear of his life and health for a crime that he did not commit and the influence of his incarceration on the life and health of the applicant. The court asserted that the extent of the non-pecuniary damage of Tomasz Komenda was particularly significant and the amount of compensation is appropriate, within reasonable limits, and will compensate the pain and sufferings of the applicant and is adequate with regard to modern practices and society's living standard.[77]

Neither the applicant nor the prosecutor appealed the judgment.

9 Conclusions

The development of the provisions and practice regarding compensation for wrongful conviction in Poland in the last 20 years has not been linear and it is hard to define its direction. Even though a new model was introduced in 2015 – with changes concerning the ways in which compensation for the wrongful application of non-custodial preventive measures was awarded, the addition of a

75 Dorota Czerwińska and Artur Kowalczyk, 'Kryteria ustalania związku przyczynowego' (n 61) 153; Katarzyna Wiśniewska, *Model odpowiedzialności* (n 51) 451–452.

76 See the detailed analysis: Wojciech Jasiński and Karolina Kremens, 'The right to claim innocence in Poland' (n 23) 44–54.

77 https://opole.so.gov.pl/komunikat-prasowy-w-sprawie-wniosku-o-odszkodowanie-i-zadoscuczynienie-tomasza-komendy,new,mg,309,311.html,820 (accessed 5 February 2022). The judgment itself was not published, neither was the case number stated in public.

representative of the State Treasury to the proceedings as well as an extension of the claims' limitation period – it was almost totally repealed in 2016. The representative of the State Treasury as a party to the proceedings was, however, reintroduced in 2019. Thus, the changes in the model of compensating wrongful conviction do not follow a logical pattern. One tendency that may be distinguished in practice is a slow but continuous increase in the amount of compensation granted.

An unprecedent level of interest has been witnessed in the media on the issue of compensation for wrongful conviction due to the widely reported case of Tomasz Komenda. Other publicly discussed cases of wrongful convictions have also increased awareness of the topic among the general public.

The legal framework is evaluated in a nuanced way as both advantages and disadvantages of the model are identified. One of the problems concerns awarding compensation under a civil or criminal regime. The current model, based on granting a civil claim by a criminal court in a hybrid procedure, generates practical difficulties.[78] They partially result from the lack of comprehensive knowledge of civil law aspects of pecuniary and non-pecuniary damage by criminal court judges and from ambiguities regarding the extent to which the provisions of the Code of Civil Procedure should be applied during the proceedings discussed. This led some authors to the conclusion that the compensation claims should be heard in regular civil proceedings, like any other civil claim.[79] It was also proposed in the legal doctrine that mixed adjudicating panels, composed of judges sitting in criminal court, judges sitting in civil court and a lay judge, shall be composed in order to provide comprehensive knowledge of both specificity of a criminal conviction and imprisonment and civil aspects of damages claims as well as a guarantee that a social sense of justice is met.[80] However, there are also advantages to the existing model. The judges who sit in criminal courts are familiar with the reality of

78 Łukasz Chojniak, *Odszkodowanie* (n 49) 301; Joanna Misztal-Konecka, 'Zasądzenie odszkodowania i zadośćuczynienia za niesłuszne wykonanie środka zabezpieczającego lub niewątpliwie niesłuszne tymczasowe aresztowanie wykonane w zakładzie psychiatrycznym' (2018) 10 *Prokuratura i Prawo* 5–29; Dariusz Kala, 'Procedura dochodzenia roszczeń z tytułu niesłusznego skazania, tymczasowego aresztowania i zatrzymania' in Arkadiusz Lach (ed), *Dochodzenie roszczeń cywilnych a proces karny* (Wolters Kluwer 2018) 250; Dariusz Świecki, in Dariusz Świecki (ed.), *Kodeks postępowania karnego. Komentarz*, vol. 2 (Wolters Kluwer 2018), 768.

79 Paweł Cioch, *Odpowiedzialność Skarbu Państwa* (n 20) 271; Dariusz Kala, 'Procedura dochodzenia roszczeń' (n 78) 244–250, Dariusz Kala and Maja Klubińska, 'Odszkodowanie i zadośćuczynienie za niesłuszne skazanie oraz niesłuszne stosowanie środków przymusu procesowego – analiza trybu i zasad dochodzenia roszczeń (cz. I)' (2016) 1 *Przegląd Sądowy* 8–14, Joanna Misztal-Konecka, 'Zasądzenie odszkodowania i zadośćuczynienia' (n 78) 26–27.

80 Wojciech Jasiński and Dorota Czerwińska, 'W kwestii optymalnego trybu kompensowania szkód i krzywd wynikających z niesłusznego tymczasowego aresztowania' in Andrzej Sakowicz and Cezary Kulesza (eds), *Ewolucja polskiego wymiaru sprawiedliwości w latach 2013–2018 w świetle standardów rzetelnego procesu* (Wydawnictwo Temida 2 2019) 301–302. The role of the lay judges in compensation cases is also highlighted by Łukasz Chojniak, *Odszkodowanie* (n 49) 309–310.

incarceration and thus have a better understanding of its consequences as well as knowledge regarding evidence which is potentially relevant when establishing the conditions of imprisonment of the applicant. The procedure is free of charge and less formalised than the civil one. What is more, it allows the court to play an active role in gathering evidence. The court's activity might be important for the applicants who are not represented by lawyers and are not capable of presenting all the evidence in favour of their claim on their own initiative.[81] Civil courts also hear a larger number of cases, which lengthens proceedings, whereas the discussed claims should be heard quickly. Thus, criminal courts in fact guarantee proceedings are appropriately fast.[82] Moreover, the criminal court's competence to adjudicate compensation claims is also justified historically and – to some extent – constitutionally, as Article 41(5) of the Polish Constitution expressly mentions a separate guarantee of compensating harms resulting from unlawful deprivation of liberty.[83] It also has symbolic significance since a miscarriage of justice is the most striking example of the violation of individual rights by the state.[84]

These arguments lead to the conclusion that the competence of criminal courts to hear such cases in a hybrid procedure is justified and allows the peculiarities of the compensation claims to be considered.[85] The proposal of mixed adjudicating panels is also worth considering, although it might be difficult to implement for pragmatic reasons.

The other point of criticism is the inconsistent approach to calculating the amount of compensation. Due to regional differences uneven amounts of non-

81 The opponents of the criminal court's competence to hear compensation cases also claim that the civil court is entitled to conduct evidence on its own initiative (Dariusz Kala, 'Procedura dochodzenia roszczeń' (n 78) 246–247). However, in practice it is rather a rare exception, as is stated by Tomasz Woźny, 'Charakter prawny postępowania o odszkodowanie za niesłuszne skazanie, tymczasowe aresztowanie, zatrzymanie' (2004) 8 *Państwo i Prawo* 65; Wojciech Jasiński and Dorota Czerwińska, 'W kwestii optymalnego trybu' (n 80) 296.

82 Wojciech Jasiński and Artur Kowalczyk, 'Czas trwania i sprawność postępowań w przedmiocie odszkodowania za niesłuszne skazanie, tymczasowe aresztowanie i zatrzymanie – w świetle badań aktowych' (2021) 3 *Forum Prawnicze* 70–86; Wojciech Jasiński and Dorota Czerwińska, 'W kwestii optymalnego trybu' (n 80) 297. The cited research showed that proceedings usually last from three to six months once the motion has been filed. In more than 75 per cent of analysed cases the total length of compensatory proceedings in first instance did not exceed nine months.

83 Dariusz Kala, 'Procedura dochodzenia roszczeń' (n 78) 236–241; Paweł Wiliński, 'Odszkodowanie za stosowanie środków reakcji karnej lub przymusu procesowego – w świetle konstytucyjnej gwarancji prawa do odszkodowania' (2012) 1 *Wrocławskie Studia Sądowe* 6; Wojciech Jasiński and Dorota Czerwińska, 'W kwestii optymalnego trybu' (n 80) 287, 298.

84 Wojciech Jasiński and Dorota Czerwińska, 'W kwestii optymalnego trybu' (n 80) 297.

85 A similar view was expressed for example by Łukasz Chojniak, *Odszkodowanie* (n 49) 313; Wojciech Jasiński and Dorota Czerwińska, 'W kwestii optymalnego trybu' (n 80) 297–299. Compare Katarzyna Wiśniewska, *Model odpowiedzialności* (n 51) 532–535. This author supports the criminal court's competence to hear compensation cases but sees the need to regulate the issue properly in the Code of Criminal Procedure.

pecuniary damages are awarded in comparable situations.[86] Although the principle of individualisation of such compensation leads to differentiation of the amounts granted, the sums should not depend on the region or even the court which hears the case. Therefore, creating an exemplary catalogue of circumstances determining the amount of compensation should be considered.[87] However, the idea of creating a formalised set of initial amounts of compensation for typical situations should not be entirely excluded from discussion. Such lump sums could constitute a starting point for the court, subject to modifications depending on individual circumstances, rather than a strict tariff. Such an instrument would provide a clear methodology for the court to follow while providing enough space to include all the peculiarities of the case in the final judgment.

Despite the discussed drawbacks of the model of compensation for wrongful conviction, the system has to be assessed as generally effective and capable of providing full compensation for the harm suffered within a reasonable period of time.[88] The most evident disadvantage, which should be immediately eliminated by amending the law, is the limitation period of one year, which must be evaluated as definitely too short.[89] A longer limitation period would not endanger the interests of the criminal justice system but would serve the purpose of granting as many individuals as possible the compensation they deserve.

Bibliography

PK-P1K Report of the National Prosecutor's Office, <https://www.gov.pl/web/prokuratura-krajowa/sprawozdania-statystyczne-za-2021-rok> accessed 4 May 2022.

Bieńkowska B, 'Glosa do postanowienia Sądu Najwyższego z dnia 5 lutego 1988 r., II KZ 3/88' (1989) 7–12 *Orzecznictwo Sądów Polskich i Komisji Arbitrażowych*

Bulsiewicz A, *Proces o odszkodowanie za niesłuszne skazanie lub oczywiście bezzasadny areszt tymczasowy* (Towarzystwo Naukowe w Toruniu 1968)

Bulsiewicz A, 'Glosa do wyroku Sądu Najwyższego z 13.06.2002 r., V KKN 125/00' (2003) 5 *Orzecznictwo Sądów Polskich*

Chojniak Ł, *Odszkodowanie za niesłuszne skazanie, tymczasowe aresztowanie lub zatrzymanie* (C.H. Beck 2013)

Cioch P, *Odpowiedzialność Skarbu Państwa z tytułu niesłusznego skazania* (Wolters Kluwer 2007)

Czarnecki P, 'Odpowiedzialność Skarbu Państwa za błędy wymiaru sprawiedliwości w sprawach karnych po 1 lipca 2015 r.' (2015) 2 *Internetowy Przegląd Prawniczy TBSP UJ*

86 Katarzyna Wiśniewska, *Model odpowiedzialności* (n 51) 523, 528–529.

87 Katarzyna Wiśniewska, *Model odpowiedzialności* (n 51) 421, 529.

88 Other authors also share this view. See Łukasz Chojniak, *Odszkodowanie* (n 49) 312–313.

89 Łukasz Chojniak, *Odszkodowanie* (n 49) 312; Wojciech Jasiński, 'Odszkodowanie i zadośćuczynienie' (n 14) 68–69; Katarzyna Wiśniewska, *Model odpowiedzialności* (n 51) 523; Wojciech Jasiński, Dorota Czerwińska and Artur Kowalczyk, 'The optimum model of compensation for wrongful detention on remand – a comparative perspective' (2019) 2 *Osteuropa Recht* 280.

Czerwińska D and Kowalczyk A, 'Kryteria ustalania związku przyczynowego oraz rozmiaru szkody majątkowej i krzywdy wynikłej z niesłusznego pozbawienia wolności w świetle badań aktowych' (2021) 11–12*Przegląd Sądowy*

Daszkiewicz W, 'Podstawy prawne wyłączenia odpowiedzialności państwa za szkodę wyrządzoną niesłusznym skazaniem' (1978) 11–12 *Nowe Prawo*

Dudka K and Dobosiewicz B, *Odszkodowanie za niesłuszne skazanie* (Instytut Wymiaru Sprawiedliwości 2012)

Fon V and Parisi F, 'Judicial precedents in civil law systems: A dynamic analysis' (2006) 26 *International Review of Law and Economics*

Gostyński Z and Stefański RA, in RA Stefański and S Zabłocki (eds), *Kodeks postępowania karnego. Komentarz*, vol. 3 (Wydawnictwo ABC 2004)

Hofmański P, Sadzik E and Zgryzek K, *Kodeks postępowania karnego. Komentarz*, vol. 3 (C.H. Beck 2012)

Jasiński W, 'Odszkodowanie i zadośćuczynienie za niesłuszne skazanie, wykonanie środka zabezpieczającego oraz niezasadne stosowanie środków przymusu po nowelizacji kodeksu postępowania karnego' (2015) 9 *Prokuratura i Prawo*

Jasiński W, in J Skorupka (ed), *Kodeks postępowania karnego. Komentarz* (C.H. Beck 2021a)

Jasiński W, 'W kwestii zasadności uregulowania katalogu stron postępowania w przedmiocie odszkodowania za niesłuszne pozbawienie wolności' (2021b) 1 *Ruch Prawniczy, Ekonomiczny i Socjologiczny*

Jasiński W and Czerwińska D, 'W kwestii optymalnego trybu kompensowania szkód i krzywd wynikających z niesłusznego tymczasowego aresztowania' in A Sakowicz and C Kulesza (eds), *Ewolucja polskiego wymiaru sprawiedliwości w latach 2013–2018 w świetle standardów rzetelnego procesu* (Wydawnictwo Temida 2 2019)

Jasiński W, Czerwińska D and Kowalczyk A, 'The optimum model of compensation for wrongful detention on remand – a comparative perspective' (2019) 2 *Osteuropa Recht*

Jasiński W and Kowalczyk A, 'Czas trwania i sprawność postępowań w przedmiocie odszkodowania za niesłuszne skazanie, tymczasowe aresztowanie i zatrzymanie – w świetle badań aktowych' (2021) 3 *Forum Prawnicze*

Jasiński W and Kremens K, *Criminal Law in Poland* (Kluwer Law International B.B. 2019)

Jasiński W and Kremens K, 'The right to claim innocence in Poland' (2020) 4 *Erasmus Law Review*

Kafarski A, 'Postępowanie w sprawach o wynagrodzenie za niesłuszne skazanie' (1959) 1 *Państwo i Prawo*

Kala D, 'Procedura dochodzenia roszczeń z tytułu niesłusznego skazania, tymczasowego aresztowania i zatrzymania' in Arkadiusz Lach (ed), *Dochodzenie roszczeń cywilnych a proces karny* (Wolters Kluwer 2018)

Kala D and Klubińska M, 'Odszkodowanie i zadośćuczynienie za niesłuszne skazanie oraz niesłuszne stosowanie środków przymusu procesowego – analiza trybu i zasad dochodzenia roszczeń (cz. I)' (2016) 1 *Przegląd Sądowy*

Kala D and Klubińska M, 'Odszkodowanie i zadośćuczynienie za niesłuszne skazanie oraz niesłuszne stosowanie środków przymusu procesowego – analiza trybu i zasad dochodzenia roszczeń (cz. I)' (2016) 1 *Przegląd Sądowy*

Kmiecik R, 'Glosa do uchwały Sądu Najwyższego z dnia 11 września 1992 r. (I KZP 27/92)' (1995) 4 *Przegląd Sądowy*

Krasnowska V, 'Państwo płaci, państwo płacą', *Polityka*, 25 May 2021.

Kruszyński P, 'Z problematyki odszkodowania za niewątpliwie niesłuszne tymczasowe aresztowanie', in J Czapska, A Gaberle, A Światłowski andA Zoll (eds), *Zasady procesu karnego wobec wyzwań współczesności. Księga ku czci profesora Stanisława Waltosia* (Wydawnictwo Prawnicze 2000)

Kubec Z, 'O zmianach w przepisach k.p.k. o odszkodowaniu za niesłuszne skazanie lub oskarżenie' (1957) 2 *Nowe Prawo*

Matras J, in K Dudka (ed), *Kodeks postępowania karnego. Komentarz*, Wolters Kluwer 2020.

Ministry of Justice, Response to an interpellation no. 11615, <http://orka2.sejm.gov.pl/IZ6.nsf/main/517F80B7> accessed 5 February 2022.

Misztal-Konecka J, 'Zasądzenie odszkodowania i zadośćuczynienia za niesłuszne wykonanie środka zabezpieczającego lub niewątpliwie niesłuszne tymczasowe aresztowanie wykonane w zakładzie psychiatrycznym' (2018) 10 *Prokuratura i Prawo*

Mrowicki M, *Wznowienie postępowania karnego na podstawie rozstrzygnięcia Europejskiego Trybunału Praw Człowieka* (Biuro Rzecznika Praw Obywatelskich 2020)

Nita-Światłowska B, 'Podmiotowy i przedmiotowy zakres roszczenia odszkodowawczego wynikającego z art. 556 § 1 k.p.k.' (2016) 9 *Przegląd Sądowy*

Nita-Światłowska B, 'Prokuratoria Generalna w postępowaniu karnym' in L Bosek (ed), *Prawo i państwo. Księga jubileuszowa 200-lecia Prokuratorii Generalnej Rzeczypospolitej Polskiej* (Wydawnictwo Sejmowe 2017)

Paprzycki LK, in LK Paprzycki (ed), *Kodeks postępowania karnego. Komentarz*, vol. 2 (Wolters Kluwer 2013)

Peiper L, *Komentarz do kodeksu postępowania karnego i przepisów wprowadzających tenże kodeks z dodatkowemi ustawami, rozporządzeniami i umowami międzynarodowemi w przedmiocie wydania przestępców przy szczegółowem uwzględnieniu przepisów kodeksu karnego i ustawy karnej skarbowej* (Leon Frommer Kraków 1933)

Rajzman H, 'Nowe przepisy o odszkodowaniu za niesłuszne skazanie lub oskarżenie' (1957) 3 *Państwo i Prawo*

Sarnecki P, in L Garlicki, M Zubik (eds) *Konstytucja Rzeczypospolitej Polskiej. Komentarz*, vol. II (Wydawnictwo Sejmowe 2016)

Sąd Okręgowy w Opolu, Press release regarding case of Tomasz Komenda, <https://opole.so.gov.pl/komunikat-prasowy-w-sprawie-wniosku-o-odszkodowanie-i-zadoscuczynienie-tomasza-komendy,new,mg,309,311.html,820> accessed 5 February 2022

Skorupka J, 'Sposób ukształtowania procedury karnej jako element oceny bezstronności obiektywnej (zewnętrznej) sądu' (2021) 7–8 *Palestra*

Stachowiak S, 'Odszkodowanie za niesłuszne skazanie, tymczasowe aresztowanie lub zatrzymanie w kodeksie postępowania karnego' (1999) 1 *Prokuratura i Prawo*

Świecki D, in D Świecki (ed), *Kodeks postępowania karnego. Komentarz*, vol. 2 (Wolters Kluwer 2018)

The Ombudsman, Statement to the Ministry of Justice of 25 April 2014, II.519.1463.2014.PS, <https://bip.brpo.gov.pl/sites/default/files/Do_MS_ws_%20dochodzenia_roszczen_regresowych_%20przys%C5%82ugujacych_Skarbowi_Panstwa.pdf> accessed 5 February 2022

The Statistical Directory of the Justice System, A long-term analysis, <https://isws.ms.gov.pl/pl/baza-statystyczna/opracowania-wieloletnie/download,2853,33.html> accessed 22 November 2022

Waszczyński J, *Odszkodowanie za niesłuszne skazanie i bezzasadne aresztowanie w polskim procesie karnym* (Wydawnictwo Prawnicze 1967)

Wiliński P, *Proces karny w świetle Konstytucji* (Wolters Kluwer 2011)

Wiliński P, 'Odszkodowanie za stosowanie środków reakcji karnej lub przymusu procesowego – w świetle konstytucyjnej gwarancji prawa do odszkodowania' (2012) 1 *Wrocławskie Studia Sądowe*

Wiśniewska K, *Model odpowiedzialności Skarbu Państwa za stosowanie środków penalnych i procesowych wobec jednostki* (Krakowski Instytut Prawa Karnego 2020)

Woźny T, 'Charakter prawny postępowania o odszkodowanie za niesłuszne skazanie, tymczasowe aresztowanie, zatrzymanie' (2004) 8 *Państwo i Prawo*

Table of cases

Guidelines for the judiciary concerning application of Articles 510–516 CCP, 729/58, (1958) Orzecznictwo Sądu Najwyższego, position 34

Resolution of the Supreme Court of 15 September 1999, I KZP 27/99, (1999) 11–12 Orzecznictwo Sądu Najwyższego Izba Karna i Izba Wojskowa, position 79

Decision of the Supreme Court of 20 January 2000, I KZP 46/00, LEX no. 550515

Judgment of the Supreme Court of 13 June 2002, V KKN 125/00, (2002) 9–10 Orzecznictwo Sądu Najwyższego Izba Karna i Izba Wojskowa, position 80

Judgment of the Supreme Court of 4 November 2004, WK 19/04, (2004) Orzecznictwo Sądu Najwyższego w Sprawach Karnych, position 2011

Judgment of the Supreme Court of 7 November 2005, III KK 177/05, (2006) 4 Orzecznictwo Sądu Najwyższego Izba Karna i Izba Wojskowa, position 34

Judgment of the Supreme Court of 1 April 2008, V KK 33/08, (2008) 1 Orzecznictwo Sądu Najwyższego w Sprawach Karnych, position 776

Judgment of the Court of Appeal in Białystok of 26 January 2010, II AKa 7/10, (2010) 10 Prokuratura i Prawo position 31

Judgment of the Supreme Court of 12 June 2012, IV KO 10/12, (2012) 10 Orzecznictwo Sądu Najwyższego Izba Karna i Izba Wojskowa, position 109

Decision of the Supreme Court of 6 May 2014, V KK 384/13, LEX no. 1463434

Decision of the Supreme Court of 22 January 2015, III KK 252/14, LEX no. 1640256

Judgment of the Court of Appeal in Wrocław of 29 December 2015, II AKa 404/15, LEX no. 2039642

Judgment of the Court of Appeal in Wrocław of 19 May 2016, II AKa 336/15, LEX no. 2057773

Decision of the Supreme Court of 24 April 2019, III KK 39/19, LEX no. 2686351

Judgment of the Supreme Court of 26 June 2019, III KK 289/18, LEX no. 2705800

Judgment of the Supreme Court of 15 October 2020, II KK 16/20, LEX no. 3097169

9 Compensation for wrongful convictions in the United States

Meghan J. Ryan *

1 Introduction

The American criminal justice system is disjointed, as there are fifty-two individual jurisdictions[1]—fifty states, the federal system, and the District of Columbia—and each jurisdiction has its own laws and procedures, as well as its own avenues for possibly establishing wrongful conviction. This disjointedness means that it is very difficult to track the number of individuals who have been able to establish that they were wrongfully convicted. The National Registry of Exonerations reports that there have been more than 3,000 exonerations since they were first systematically tracked in 1989,[2] and it is very likely that this figure underestimates the true number of wrongful convictions. Scholars have estimated that anywhere from 0.02 percent to 15 percent of convictions are wrongful in the United States.[3] The sources of these wrongful convictions are manifold, stemming from a variety of issues such as relying on unscientific forensic evidence, coerced confessions, and faulty eyewitness identifications.[4] Wrongful conviction is indeed a serious problem in the United States.[5]

Concerns about possible wrongful convictions have led to a variety of approaches to right these wrongs. Generally, individuals may seek compensation for wrongful

* I thank Karolina Kremens and Wojciech Jasiński for their generous invitation to contribute to this volume and for their excellent work in putting it together. I also thank Jeff Gutman, Jenia Turner, and Jeff Kahn for their generous comments on this chapter, and Jacob Fishman, Tim Gallina, and Hufsa Husain for their helpful research assistance.

1 For the purpose of this chapter, I am not including U.S. territories.

2 See National Registry of Exonerations <https://www.law.umich.edu/special/exoneration/Pages/about.aspx> accessed 9 June 2022.

3 Meghan J. Ryan and John Adams, 'Cultivating Judgment on the Tools of Wrongful Conviction' (2015) 68 *SMU L Rev* 1073, 1075–76.

4 Ibid 1079–1102; see National Registry (n 2).

5 Although the numbers may seem small, it is important to consider them in context. As one commentator has explained:

> It may help to consider the analogy of plane crashes. Roughly 18,000 flights arrive or depart Atlanta's Hartsfield-Jackson airport each week. If five of those planes crashed—roughly.027% of flights—operations at the airport would cease immediately. So, too, would 125 people wrongfully imprisoned annually (.027% of all state court felony convictions) represent a disturbing number of wrongful convictions.

Robert J. Smith, 'Recalibrating Constitutional Innocence Protection' (2012) 87 *Wash L Rev* 139, 143–44.

DOI: 10.4324/9781003229414-10

conviction through three avenues: tort and civil-rights litigation, bills of moral obligation, and wrongful conviction compensation statutes.[6] Each of these paths is fraught with their own difficulties, and not all wrongfully convicted individuals have success in obtaining compensation.

2 Compensation through tort claims, civil rights suits, and moral bills of obligation

Individuals seeking compensation for wrongful conviction might pursue traditional legal avenues for relief, including bringing tort or civil rights suits. They also sometimes seek relief though the democratic process by lobbying the legislature to pass moral bills of obligation. Claimants' success in obtaining compensation through these pathways has often been unsuccessful, but in some of the more egregious cases, claimants have won significant compensation awards. Despite general acknowledgment that compensation via any of these avenues is quite difficult, a recent study suggests—somewhat surprisingly—that about 45 percent of exonerated persons seek compensation through tort or civil rights claims, and about 55 percent of those recover damages either through judgment or settlement.[7] Obtaining compensation through bills of moral obligation, however, is significantly less common.[8]

2.1 Common-law tort claims

Civil litigation in the United States varies by jurisdiction. Through the common-law tort system, wrongfully convicted individuals may be able to sue those who caused them harm. A popular claim that wrongfully convicted individuals make is that of malicious prosecution.[9] Establishing such a claim generally requires proving by a preponderance of the evidence that the individual was exonerated and that someone[10] initiated the proceeding with malice—meaning "without probable cause and primarily for a purpose other than bringing an offender to justice."[11] As one might imagine, this is extraordinarily difficult to establish except in the most

6 For a more thorough discussion of these individual pathways to compensation, see generally Meghan J. Ryan, 'Remedying Wrongful Execution' (2012) 45 *U Mich J L Reform* 261.

7 Jeffrey S. Gutman and Lingxiao Sun, 'Why Is Mississippi the Best State in Which to Be Exonerated? An Empirical Evaluation of State Statutory and Civil Compensation for the Wrongfully Convicted' (2019), 11 *Ne U L Rev* 694, 764, 772. Another study, which examined only exonerations based on DNA evidence, found that about 28 percent of DNA exonerees prevailed in tort or civil rights suits. Innocence Project, *Making Up for Lost Time: What the Wrongfully Convicted Endure and How to Provide Fair Compensation* (2009) 13.

8 Gutman and Sun (n 7) 709.

9 Ryan, 'Remedying Wrongful Execution' (n 6) 280.

10 The *Restatement (Second) of Torts*' articulation of the claim provides that prosecutors cannot be sued for malicious prosecution because they enjoy absolute immunity. RESTATEMENT (SECOND) OF TORTS § 653 cmt e (Am L Inst 1977); see also text to notes 28–29.

11 RESTATEMENT (SECOND) OF TORTS [n 10] § 653; see also Ryan, 'Remedying Wrongful Execution' (n 6) 280; Brandon L. Garrett, 'Innocence, Harmless Error, and Federal Wrongful Conviction Law' (2005) *Wis L Rev* 35. The *Restatement (Second) of Torts* provides that:

extreme cases. Probable cause is a very low standard that prosecutors will be able to establish in most cases of wrongful conviction.[12] Moreover, in a number of jurisdictions, the underlying conviction constitutes conclusive evidence that there was probable cause for the prosecution.[13] Beyond the low probable cause standard, evidence that prosecution was initiated for a nefarious purpose would be quite sparse in most circumstances.[14] Additionally, where the defendant is anyone but a prosecutor, he will most likely argue that he did not actually "initiate" the prosecution.[15] Perhaps one could argue that a police officer in effect initiated prosecution if he deliberately misrepresented information to the prosecutor, which ultimately led to prosecution and wrongful conviction, but this argument will be available in only the more extreme cases.[16] Overall, most wrongfully convicted individuals will be unlikely to prevail on such malicious prosecution claims.

Some additional common-law tort claims that wrongfully convicted individuals have raised include assertions of false imprisonment, intentional infliction of emotional distress, and legal malpractice.[17] It is also difficult for individuals to prevail on these claims due to an inability to prove sufficient intent or causation, and also because of certain privilege defenses.[18] For example, in false imprisonment cases, the confinement would be privileged if there was probable cause for arrest.[19] As in the malicious prosecution context, this is a low bar.[20] With respect to intentional infliction of emotional distress cases, these claims are, even in ordinary circumstances, difficult to establish, and this is made all the more difficult in the context of wrongful conviction.[21] Legal malpractice claims, which are also difficult to establish in ordinary cases, are tough to make out in the wrongful conviction context as well.[22] Proving that the defense attorney's errors actually caused the wrongful conviction is a significant impediment to prevailing on such claims.[23]

A private person who initiates or procures the institution of criminal proceedings against another who is not guilty of the offense charged is subject to liability for malicious prosecution if

(a) he initiates or procures the proceedings without probable cause and primarily for a purpose other than that of bringing an offender to justice, and

(b) the proceedings have terminated in favor of the accused.

RESTATEMENT (SECOND) OF TORTS (n 10) § 653.

12 Ryan, 'Remedying Wrongful Execution' (n 6) 280.

13 Ibid 281; Michael Avery, 'Obstacles to Litigating Civil Claims for Wrongful Conviction: An Overview' (2009), 18 *BU Pub Int LJ* 439, 442.

14 Avery (n 13) 442; Ryan, 'Remedying Wrongful Execution' (n 6) 280–81.

15 Ryan, 'Remedying Wrongful Execution' (n 6) 281.

16 Ibid.

17 Ibid.

18 Ibid 281–82.

19 Ibid 281; Adele Bernhard, 'When Justice Fails: Indemnification for Unjust Conviction' (1999) 6 *U Chi L Sch Roundtable* 73, 86.

20 Ryan, 'Remedying Wrongful Execution' (n 6) 281.

21 Ibid.

22 Ibid.

23 Ibid.

Perhaps the greatest hurdle in claimants prevailing on common-law tort claims where wrongful convictions are at issue is the broad blanket of immunity that most cognizable civil defendants enjoy in this context. In general, any defendants that could otherwise be sued for torts related to wrongful conviction are insulated from suit by some type of immunity.[24] The government—whether state or federal—enjoys sovereign immunity unless it has waived it, which most jurisdictions have done in only particular circumstances.[25] For example, the federal government has waived its sovereign immunity under some circumstances pursuant to the Federal Tort Claims Act, which provides that the government may be held liable for injuries "caused by the negligent or wrongful act or omission of any employee of the Government while acting within the scope of his office or employment, under circumstances where the United States, if a private person, would be liable."[26] This may sound promising, but the federal government has *not* waived its immunity where its employee was acting in a discretionary manner pursuant to a government statute or regulation.[27] Further, individual government actors—including prosecutors, police officers, testifying witnesses, and judges—also benefit from either absolute or qualified immunity, making suits against them untenable in most instances. In fact, the *Restatement (Second) of Torts*' articulation of the elements of a malicious prosecution claim provides not that *prosecutors* could be liable for the tort but instead only that a "*private person*" might be liable for malicious prosecution.[28] A comment to the provision explains that prosecutors cannot be liable for malicious prosecution because "[t]hese officials are protected from civil liability by an absolute privilege that is incident to their official position."[29] Judges also enjoy absolute immunity, which insulates them from liability related to actions carried out in their official capacities. And testifying witnesses are generally immune from suits targeting their testimony.[30] Police officers often enjoy qualified immunity. Although the extent of immunity varies somewhat by jurisdiction, police officers are often immune to suits related to discretionary acts unless the officer committed those acts with malice, in bad faith, or the like.[31] Finally, recognizing that public defenders have limited resources, some jurisdictions have even cloaked these actors with immunity from legal malpractice suits.[32] Altogether, these broad immunity provisions make it extraordinarily difficult for wrongfully convicted individuals to prevail on these common-law tort claims except in egregious circumstances.

24 Ibid 282–83.
25 Dan B. Dobbs, *The Law of Torts* (2000) 715–16.
26 28 U.S.C. § 1346(b)(1) (2013).
27 See 28 U.S.C. § 2680(a); see also Ryan, 'Remedying Wrongful Execution' (n 6) 283 (outlining the federal government's waiver of immunity).
28 Restatement (Second) of Torts (n 10) § 653 (emphasis added).
29 Ibid.
30 Ryan, 'Remedying Wrongful Execution' (n 6) 284. Individuals perjuring themselves could be subject to perjury charges, however.
31 Dobbs (n 25) 579.
32 See, e.g., Dziubak v Mott, 503 NW2d 771, 777 (Minn 1993); see also Ryan, 'Remedying Wrongful Execution' (n 6) 284.

2.2 Civil rights suits

Most claimants seeking compensation through traditional litigation file federal civil rights suits—instead of, or in addition to—common-law tort claims.[33] Through 42 U.S.C. § 1983, federal law provides an avenue to bring suit against individuals who, under the color of state law, have deprived them "of any rights, privileges, or immunities secured by the Constitution and laws."[34] Wrongfully convicted individuals generally pursue such claims by alleging that government actors violated any combination of their Fourth, Fifth, Sixth, and Fourteenth Amendment rights. This includes allegations that an individual was unconstitutionally seized by being subject to prosecution, the prosecution improperly withheld exculpatory evidence, an eyewitness identification procedure was improperly suggestive, the police fabricated evidence, or the individual received ineffective assistance of counsel.[35] As with common-law tort claims, though, it is often difficult to establish prima facie claims under § 1983. Many exonerees were not actually deprived of a right covered by § 1983, and establishing sufficient government culpability in these cases is often difficult as well.[36] Moreover, individuals pursuing these civil rights claims face immunity hurdles similar to those facing common-law tort plaintiffs. Absolute immunity for judges, prosecutors, and testifying witnesses makes these suits difficult to bring. Police officers' immunity—where they are immune from suit unless their conduct violated "clearly established statutory or constitutional rights of which a reasonable person would have known"[37]—also poses a problem. Finally, *Monell* claims—those against municipalities and other local governments—are also often unsuccessful because such entities are not held vicariously liable for their employees' misconduct, so successful claims must usually be based on the local governments' unconstitutional policies that were implemented with deliberate indifference to their consequences.[38]

2.3 Bills of moral obligation

Another avenue for compensation—although one not often taken—is through bills of moral obligation. Legislators draft and pass these laws in response to specific situations in which an individual (or entity) is entitled to compensation. The laws "spring[] from a sense of justice and equity,"[39] but obtaining relief in this

33 Gutman and Sun (n 7) 721.

34 42 USC § 1983 (1996). "States cannot be held liable for damages under § 1983, nor can state officials be sued in their official capacities." Ryan, 'Remedying Wrongful Execution' (n 6) 295.

35 Ryan, 'Remedying Wrongful Execution' (n 6) 288–94.

36 Daniel S. Kahn, 'Presumed Guilty Until Proven Innocent: The Burden of Proof in Wrongful Conviction Claims Under State Compensation Statutes' (2010) 44 U Mich JL Reform 123, 132.

37 Harlow v Fitzgerald, 457 US 800, 818 (1982); City of Tahlequah v Bond, 142 S Ct 9, 11 (2021) (per curiam).

38 Gutman and Sun (n 7) 721.

39 Koike v Bd of Water Supply, 352 P2d 835, 839 (Haw 1960), quoted in Bernhard (n 19) 93.

manner is far from reliable. As might be imagined, wrongfully convicted individuals often lack the political connections necessary to push through these bills of moral obligation. Further, some states—such as Texas and Oregon—constitutionally prohibit bills of moral obligation.[40]

One example of a claimant successfully pursuing a bill of moral obligation is the case of Edward Honaker. After serving a ten-year sentence in Virginia for sexual assault, sodomy, and rape, the state governor pardoned Honaker in 1994.[41] At the time, Virginia did not have a compensation statute for wrongful conviction, but Honaker pursued compensation through a private bill.[42] He was fortunate enough to obtain the interest of an attorney who was an old friend of a state legislator, and that legislator was willing to draft legislation and lobby on Honaker's behalf.[43] After a couple of years and much work advocating for compensation, the Virginia legislature appropriated $500,000 in compensation to Honaker.[44] This sort of success is quite rare, though. Claimants have had much more success pursuing compensation through other means.

3 Wrongful conviction compensation statutes

Obtaining compensation through common-law tort claims, civil rights actions, and bills of moral obligation is exceedingly difficult in many cases, and wrongfully convicted individuals often have greater luck in obtaining compensation through statutes specifically directed at compensating individuals for wrongful conviction and incarceration. Today, most, but not all, jurisdictions in the United States have such wrongful conviction compensation statutes.

In the early 1900s, there was a well-publicized case of an immigrant working in one of Andrew Carnegie's Pennsylvania steel mills who was wrongfully convicted.[45] When the state refused to compensate the man for this injustice, Carnegie himself provided the man—who returned to his native Hungary after exoneration—with a monthly pension.[46] Shortly thereafter, Edwin Borchard, a Yale University law professor specializing in international law, along with others, began working toward passing statutory compensation for wrongful conviction and incarceration. Borchard observed that European nations compensated individuals who were wrongfully

40 See Or Const art IV §24 ("Provision may be made by general law, for bringing suit against the State, as to all liabilities originating after, or existing at the time of the adoption of this Constitution; but no special act authorizeing [sic] such suit to be brought, or making compensation to any person claiming damages against the State, shall ever be passed."); Adams v. Harris Cnty, 530 SW2d 606, 608 (Tex Civ App 1975).

41 Bernard (n 19) 94–95.

42 Ibid 95.

43 Ibid.

44 1996 Va. Acts Assembly H 222 (enacted); Bernard (n 19) 94–95.

45 See Jeffrey S. Gutman, 'Are Federal Exonerees Paid?: Lessons for the Drafting and Interpretation of Wrongful Conviction Compensation Statutes' (2021) 69 *Cleveland St L Rev* 219, 223–24.

46 Ibid 224.

convicted but that similar compensation was exceedingly difficult in the United States.[47] He pointed out that "[a]mong the most shocking of … injuries and most glaring of injustices [committed by states] are erroneous criminal convictions of innocent people" and explained that governments ought to assume the risk of state wrongdoing in this context.[48] Inspired by this grave injustice, Borchard spearheaded the movement within the United States to provide statutory redress for wrongful conviction and incarceration. In 1912, bills for statutory compensation were introduced in both the U.S. House of Representatives and Senate, but those bills died in committee before the House of Representatives or Senate had the opportunity to vote on them.[49]

Despite the inability to pass federal legislation in 1912, the justifications for indemnification remained powerful, spanning both fairness and practical concerns. First, when an individual is wrongfully convicted and punished, the government has broken its compact with the individual that, in exchange for submitting to the criminal law, the government will protect that individual from both crime and the risk of wrongful conviction.[50] Additionally, the government can better bear the cost of wrongful conviction than individuals, and it can spread those costs across the rest of society.[51] Further, if the government does bear this cost, it can better strike the appropriate balance between pursuing criminal offenders and protecting against the risk of wrongful conviction.[52] This might also provide state actors with a greater incentive to be more careful in ensuring that convictions and sentences are just, and it could encourage the state to take the appropriate level of care to prevent such injustices.[53] On top of that, if the government takes responsibility for wrongful convictions, this accountability may inspire greater faith in the criminal justice system.[54] The resulting increased legitimacy of the system could then further compliance with the criminal law.[55]

Considering these moving justifications, the death of the House and Senate bills in 1912 did not mark the end of the story. Some states soon took up the cause. For example, California and Wisconsin passed wrongful conviction compensation statutes in 1913, and North Dakota followed suit four years later. The federal government finally passed an indemnification statute for wrongful conviction in 1938, and most jurisdictions—although not all—have enacted statutes to compensate wrongfully convicted and incarcerated persons.[56] Today,

47 Edwin M. Borchard, 'European Systems of State Indemnity for Errors of Criminal Justice' (1913) 3 *J Crim L & Criminology* 684, 684; also Edwin M. Borchard, 'State Indemnity for Errors of Criminal Justice' (1912) *S. Doc.* Nos. 62–974 (1912).

48 Edwin M. Borchard, *Convicting the Innocent* (Garden City Publishing Co. 1932).

49 Gutman, 'Are Federal Exonerees Paid?' (n 45) 226.

50 See Ryan, 'Remedying Wrongful Execution' (n 6) 298.

51 Ibid 298–99.

52 Ibid 299.

53 Ibid.

54 Ibid.

55 Ibid.

56 Cf. Gutman, 'Are Federal Exonerees Paid?' (n 45) 222 (explaining that the effort to pass a compensation statute at the federal level dates back to 1912 but that this first attempt was unsuccessful).

thirty-nine jurisdictions (including the federal government and the District of Columbia) have such compensation statutes.[57] Their details and generosity vary by jurisdiction, but, generally, experts agree that wrongful conviction compensation statutes are the best avenue by which wrongfully convicted and incarcerated individuals may secure compensation.[58]

3.1 Varying procedures

Depending on the jurisdiction that wrongly convicted and incarcerated the claimant, the path to statutory compensation may vary dramatically. And, often, these statutory schemes are quite complicated. In several jurisdictions, the claimant will take his claim to a traditional court to establish the fact of wrongful conviction and his eligibility for compensation.[59] In many instances, it is a district court within the county that convicted the defendant that decides whether compensation is appropriate.[60] This is often a civil action that may be opposed by the state attorney general or another prosecutor, or the action may go unopposed. Other jurisdictions instead employ an administrative process, requiring the claimant to take his case to a state board or some other actor or entity to resolve the issue. In Alabama, for example, it is the State Division of Risk Management and the Committee on Compensation for Wrongful Incarceration.[61] In California, it is the California Victim Compensation Board.[62] In Connecticut, it is the Claims Commissioner.[63] Some jurisdictions require the claimant to go through both the civil claim and administrative processes, making it more onerous for the claimant to obtain compensation.[64] When held in civil court, the proceedings are ordinarily public and adversarial, and the regular rules of evidence and local rules usually apply. Although evidentiary rules vary by jurisdiction, they often are similar to the Federal Rules of Evidence, with their limitations that only relevant evidence should be admitted and that the reliability of that evidence is important in admissibility decisions.[65] When the compensation question is before other decisionmakers, the

57 See 'Compensating the Wrongfully Convicted' (*Innocence Project*) <https://innocenceproject.org/compensating-wrongly-convicted> accessed 2 November 2021.

58 See Ryan, 'Remedying Wrongful Execution' (n 6) 279 ("As many scholars have explained, ... neither traditional tort actions nor civil rights suits have proven satisfactory in providing compensation for exonerees."); see, e.g. Kahn (n 36) 125 (noting that "[compensation] statutes appear to present the best opportunity for recovery for wrongfully convicted persons").

59 See, e.g., Colo Rev Stat 13-65-102 (2013).

60 See, e.g., Colo Rev Stat 13-65-102(5) (2013); Utah Code Ann § 78B-9-402(1) (2021).

61 Ala Code § 29-2-151 (2001); Ala Code § 29-2-152 (2001).

62 Cal Penal Code § 4901 (2020).

63 Conn Gen Stat § 54-102uu(d) (2016).

64 Justin Brooks and Alexander Simpson, 'Find the Cost of Freedom: The State of Wrongful Conviction Compensation Statutes Across the Country and the Strange Legal Odyssey of Timothy Atkins' (2012) 9 *San Diego L Rev* 627, 637–38.

65 See, e.g., Fed R Evid 402 ("Irrelevant evidence is not admissible."); Fed R Evid 802 (providing that "[h]earsay is not admissible unless" it is specifically allowed by federal

process may or may not be public and adversarial, and different rules of evidence and procedure may also apply.

Ordinarily, publicly funded legal aid is not available for those seeking compensation for wrongful conviction. Instead, claimants may enter into contingent-fee arrangements with lawyers, whereby the attorneys helping them with their claims are entitled to a portion of the proceeds. Additionally, organizations such as the various Innocence Projects around the country, as well as a number of attorneys acting in a pro bono capacity, have helped claimants pursue compensation.[66] And in some jurisdictions, compensation includes reimbursement of attorney's fees as part of the award.[67] While state-provided legal aid is not the norm, some jurisdictions do offer some support to claimants. The California Victim Compensation Board, for example, offers access to legal advocates for assistance with tasks such as completing an application for compensation or finding necessary resources like food and shelter.[68]

Further, jurisdictions vary in the extent to which they allow claimants to appeal determinations on eligibility for compensation and any monetary amounts awarded.[69] Some explicitly provide for appeals, others reject the possibility, and some fail to specify whether an appeal is permitted.[70] However, in a good number of cases, claimants actually settle these suits with the state before a final award amount is reached through the legal process.[71]

Finally, while one could perhaps imagine the state seeking reimbursement from the individuals responsible for the wrongful convictions (to extent the cause could be determined)—whether that be a perjurious witness, an aggressive police officer, or an overzealous prosecutor—in practice this does not seem to happen. Jurisdictions compensating wrongfully convicted and incarcerated individuals must find the funds within their own budgets.

3.2 Grounds for compensation

In addition to a variety of procedures for making out a case for compensation, the grounds for compensation—the eligibility requirements—also vary by jurisdiction. Compensation is generally awarded only if the claimant has been wrongfully convicted and incarcerated.[72] For example, Texas law provides that compensation is appropriate only if "the person has served in whole or in part a sentence in prison under the laws of this state."[73] The means of establishing that the conviction was

statute, other provisions of the Federal Rules of Evidence, or rules prescribed by the U.S Supreme Court).

66 Brooks and Simpson (n 64) 641.

67 See, e.g., FLA STAT § 961.06(1)(a), (c)–(d) (2017).

68 California Victim Compensation Board <https://victims.ca.gov/for-victims> accessed 12 December 2021.

69 See Brooks and Simpson (n 64) 660–61.

70 Ibid.

71 Kahn (n 36) 125.

72 Ryan, 'Remedying Wrongful Execution' (n 6) 296.

73 TEX CIV PRAC & REM CODE § 103.001(a)(1) (2011).

"wrongful," however, vary. Ordinarily this requires a showing that the claimant is factually innocent of the crime for which he was convicted. Jurisdictions differ on how a claimant may demonstrate this fact, however. For example, Ohio law requires a showing "that the offense of which the individual was found guilty, including all lesser-included offenses, was not committed by the individual, or that no offense was committed by any person."[74] Oklahoma law requires a pardon on the ground of innocence or that a court determined the claimant was innocent and thus vacated, dismissed, or reversed the conviction and sentence and provided that there would be no further related proceedings.[75] Similarly, under the federal system, a claimant may be eligible for compensation if "[h]is conviction has been reversed or set aside on the ground that he is not guilty of the offense of which he was convicted ... or ... he has been pardoned upon the stated ground of innocence ...."[76] Maine law, however, requires the claimant to have "received a full and free pardon ... which is accompanied by a written finding by the Governor who grants the pardon that the person is innocent of the crime for which that person was convicted," and, as if that were not enough, it also requires a court finding of the claimant's actual innocence.[77] Not all states require a showing of factual innocence, though. Connecticut, for example, also provides compensation for individuals whose criminal complaint or information was dismissed because of government misconduct.[78]

In addition to variations as to when a conviction might be wrongful, jurisdictions differ as to other eligibility requirements. Sometimes compensation is warranted only when the claimant was wrongfully convicted of a particular criminal offense. For example, Washington compensates for only the wrongful conviction of a felony,[79] and Iowa compensates for only the wrongful conviction of a felony or aggravated misdemeanor.[80] Perhaps this stems from the understanding that greater harms usually flow from the wrongful conviction of more serious offenses. At least one jurisdiction restricts compensation to cases in which the wrongfulness of the conviction was established by DNA evidence[81]—presumably because of the heightened level of reliability that DNA can provide. And several jurisdictions provide that claimants may not recover if the claimant "contributed" to his wrongful conviction, which may very well mean that someone who falsely

74 Ohio Rev Code Ann § 2743.48(A)(5) (2018).
75 Okla Stat tit 51 § 154 (2021)
76 28 U.S.C. S 2513.
77 Me Stat tit 14 § 8241 (1993).
78 Conn Gen Stat § 54-102uu(a)(2) (2016) (providing that an individual is eligible for compensation if he was incarcerated and his "conviction was vacated or reversed and ... the complaint or information dismissed on a ground citing an act or omission that constitutes malfeasance or other serious misconduct by any officer, agent, employee or official of the state that contributed to such person's arrest, prosecution, conviction or incarceration").
79 Wash Rev Code § 4.100.060(1)(a) (2013).
80 Iowa Code § 663A.1(1) (1997).
81 See, e.g., Mo Rev Stat § 650.058 (2021).

confessed may not recover.[82] Perhaps even more importantly, some jurisdictions will not allow compensation if the defendant pleaded guilty to the offense.[83] While not quite as extreme, California law provides that compensation is not allowed if the "claimant pled guilty with the specific intent to protect another from prosecution for the underlying conviction."[84] Additionally, some jurisdictions prohibit compensation where the claimant is serving time for another crime for which he has not established his innocence,[85] and a handful of jurisdictions will cut off compensation payments if an individual is subsequently convicted of a felony.[86] Alabama, for example, provides that "[a] person awarded compensation and subsequently convicted of a felony crime will not be eligible to receive any unpaid amounts from any compensation [previously] authorized."[87] Finally, most jurisdictions have imposed statutes of limitations on bringing these claims for compensation. In Connecticut, for example, a claimant must file his claim within two years of the date his case was dismissed or he was pardoned.[88]

3.3 The standard(s) for compensation

As with the procedures for asserting compensation claims and the grounds on which indemnification may be awarded, jurisdictions vary in the standards of proof required in making the necessary showings for compensation. Preliminarily, a surprising number of jurisdictions do not statutorily set a standard of proof for establishing the right to compensation.[89] Of the jurisdictions that do specify the standard of proof, though, several allow the claimant to recover if he establishes eligibility by a preponderance of the evidence.[90] Numerous other jurisdictions have set a "clear and convincing" standard of proof that the claimant must meet to be awarded compensation. Iowa and Massachusetts, for example, use this onerous standard for a claimant establishing his factual innocence.[91] In the 2017 case of *Nelson v. Colorado*, the U.S. Supreme Court held that Colorado's statute requiring the claimant to establish her actual innocence by this higher standard

82 See, e.g., NY Ct Cl Act § 8-B(5)(d) (2007). In some jurisdictions, establishing that a confession was coerced could relieve a claimant from this restriction. See, e.g., Neb Rev Stat §29-4603(4) (2009).

83 See, e.g., Iowa Code § 663A.1(1) (1997) ("As used in this section, a 'wrongfully imprisoned person' means an individual who [among other things] … did not plead guilty to the public offense charged, or to any lesser included offense ….").

84 Cal Penal Code § 4903(c) (2020).

85 See, e.g., Ala Code § 29-2-161(a) (2001).

86 See, e.g., Tex Civ Prac & Rem Code § 103.154(a) (2015); Va Code Ann §8.01-195.12(A) (2004); Ala Code § 29-2-161(e) (2001).

87 Ala Code § 29-2-161(e) (2001).

88 Conn Gen Stat § 54-102uu(f) (2016).

89 See, e.g., Cal Penal Code § 4903(c) (2020); cf. Brooks and Simpson (n 64) 641 (noting that the California statute fails to specify a burden of proof but that the practice has been to use the preponderance-of-the-evidence standard).

90 See, e.g., Conn Gen Stat § 54-102uu(a)(c) (2016).

91 Iowa Code § 663A.1(2) (1997); Mass Gen Laws ch 1 258D § 1(C) (2018).

before the state would "refund fees, court costs, and restitution" associated with the conviction violates the Due Process Clause of the U.S. Constitution's Fourteenth Amendment.[92] Most courts have found that the *Nelson* Court's narrow holding does not invalidate statutes imposing a clear and convincing standard to establish eligibility in ordinary statutory compensation claims, though.[93] Still, commentators have criticized the higher, clear-and-convincing standard as nearly impossible for claimants to meet. But one limited study has suggested that the burden of persuasion may not actually matter in determining the success of claimants in obtaining compensation.[94] Perhaps this is because so many jurisdictions have rather clear-cut requirements—such as pardons or case reversals—for establishing eligibility.

3.4 Calculating compensation

Calculating the amount of compensation a claimant may receive for wrongful conviction and incarceration also varies by jurisdiction. Often, that amount is based primarily on the number of days or years the claimant wrongfully spent behind bars. At the high end, the District of Columbia's administrative remedy offers compensation at a rate of $200,000 per year incarcerated (plus additional amounts for time spent on parole, probation, etc.).[95] At the low end, Wisconsin offers compensation in an amount up to $5,000 per year incarcerated.[96] A number of jurisdictions provide compensation at the level of approximately $50,000 per year incarcerated (sometimes providing for adjustments for inflation), with some providing greater amounts for years on death row and additional amounts for time spent on parole, as a registered sex offender, or the like.[97] Some jurisdictions offer compensation on a more dynamic basis, pegging the compensation amount to average or median incomes. Maryland, for example, provides compensation on a pro rata basis of the amount of the annual median household wage according to the American Community Survey of the U.S. Census Bureau in the year the claimant's order of eligibility issues.[98]

Some jurisdictions allow for more open-ended determinations of damages awards. For example, New York law provides that, "[i]f the court finds that the

92 137 S Ct 1249, 1252 (2017).
93 See, e.g., United States v. Davis, 16 F4th 1192 (5th Cir. 2021).
94 See Bernhard (n 19) 108 ("[A]lthough many claims (in New York and elsewhere) have been dismissed for failure to meet pleading requirements or to establish innocence, I have not found a single case where that determination was affected by the burden of proof or where the burden was even discussed as claim determinative.").
95 DC Code § 2-423.02 (2021). The claimant is also entitled to additional miscellaneous amounts. Further, the claimant could instead pursue a civil claim under the statute. DC Code § 2-421 (2017).
96 Wis Stat § 775.05 (2021). The Board may petition the legislature for additional funds, however.
97 See, e.g., Ala Code § 29-2-159(a) (2001); Wash Rev Code § 4.100.060(5) (2013); Fla Stat § 961.06(1)(a) (2017).
98 Md Code Ann State Fin & Proc §10-501 (2021).

claimant is entitled to a judgment, it shall award damages in such sum of money as the court determines will fairly and reasonably compensate him."[99] Courts determining what constitutes fair and reasonable compensation usually turn to tort-based damages approaches. This primarily includes assessing lost wages, but it sometimes also includes awarding damages for mental anguish, damaged reputation, and loss of liberty.[100]

Many jurisdictions also have damages caps. For example, New Hampshire limits total damages awards to $20,000,[101] Maine restricts them to a maximum of $300,000,[102] and Florida caps them at $2 million.[103] This means that, for inmates incarcerated for long periods of time, some of those years of wrongful incarceration will go uncompensated.

Beyond monetary compensation, a number of jurisdictions provide additional support for wrongfully convicted and incarcerated individuals. Such additional support includes items such as housing assistance, job training, job-search assistance, mental health services, healthcare, tuition assistance, financial literacy assistance, child support payments, reimbursement for attorney's fees, reimbursement for any fines or costs imposed at the time of judgment, and expungement.[104] In some instances, some of these additional forms of compensation are subject to the overall damages caps.[105]

Compensation amounts may be adjusted, though, under certain circumstances. Some jurisdictions allow requests to the legislature for the provision of additional funds.[106] And some jurisdictions' compensation statutes have claw-back provisions that reduce compensation awards if the claimant has received compensation through other avenues. Nevada's compensation statute, for example, provides that, if the claimant has received compensation for the wrongful conviction from the state or a government entity, the claimant's award under the statute will be reduced or the claimant will be required to reimburse the state for the amount that was covered by this other judgment or settlement.[107] Further, in several jurisdictions, a new felony conviction will result in the state stopping any otherwise owed compensation payments.[108]

3.5 *The practice of compensating for wrongful conviction and incarceration*

Not all exonerees actually seek compensation for their wrongful convictions, and not all who do are successful in recovering. According to a relatively recent study,

99 NY Ct Cl Act § 8-B(6) (2007).
100 See Baba-Ali v. State, 878 NYS2d 555 (NY Ct Cl 2009), rev'd in part, 907 NYS2d 432 (NY App Div 2010).
101 NH Rev Stat Ann § 541-B:14(II) (2018).
102 Me Stat tit 14 § 8242(1) (1993).
103 Fla Stat § 961.06(1)(e) (2017).
104 See, e.g., Conn Gen Stat § 54-102uu(e) (2016); DC Code § 2-423.02(a) (2021).
105 See, e.g., NC Gen Stat §148-84(a) & (c) (2010).
106 See, e.g., Ala Code § 29-2-159(b) (2001)
107 Nev Rev Stat § 41.960 (2021).
108 See, e.g., Ala Code § 29-2-161(e) (2001); Tex Civ Prac & Rem Code § 103.154(a) (2015); Va Code Ann §8.01-195.12(A) (2004).

the percentage of incarcerated exonerees actually filing for compensation varies quite significantly by jurisdiction.[109] In New Hampshire and Montana, 0 percent and 11.11 percent, respectively, of eligible claimants filed claims for compensation during the study period, which was from 1989—when exonerations were first systematically recorded—to May 3, 2017.[110] Low filing rates are often due to statutory hurdles, and, especially in Montana, perhaps the 11.11 percent filing rate should not be surprising considering that, during the time of the study, Montana offered no compensation other than educational aid and required a DNA exoneration for even that.[111] At the other end of the spectrum, one out of one, or 100 percent, of incarcerated exonerees in Vermont filed for compensation, and fifteen out of eighteen, or 88.33 percent, of incarcerated exonerees in Connecticut filed for compensation.[112] Overall, about 52.67 percent of incarcerated exonerees filed compensation claims.[113]

Further, only a certain percentage of filed claims are successful. At the low end, no claimants were successful in Hawaii during the study period,[114] and only 25 percent of filing claimants found success in Iowa.[115] In several jurisdictions, though—Missouri, Nebraska, Tennessee, Utah, and Vermont—100 percent of claimants were successful in obtaining damages for their wrongful convictions.[116] It is worth noting that these states with high success rates do not all have the least onerous proof requirements under the applicable statutes even though, ordinarily, more onerous proof requirements lead to lower success rates.

Overall, approximately 74 percent of claimants were awarded compensation during the study period.[117] When considering the entire number of incarcerated exonerees, however, the success rate plummets to about 38.74 percent; only this smaller percentage of incarcerated exonerees were actually paid.[118] And, on average, those payments were in the amount of $70,154.74 per year incarcerated.[119] But for the awards in states that do not cap damages, this figure would be considerably lower.[120]

4 An evaluation of the U.S. approaches

Most commentators agree that the various mechanisms for compensating individuals for wrongful conviction and incarceration in the United Sates are inadequate. It is often difficult to obtain compensation through traditional means such as common-

109 Gutman and Sun (n 7) 784.
110 Ibid 703, 786–87 Spreadsheet 1.
111 Mont Code Ann § 53-1-214 (2003).
112 Gutman and Sun (n 7) 786–87 Spreadsheet 1.
113 Ibid.
114 Ibid. Just one of the two incarcerated exonerees filed for compensation during the study period.
115 Ibid.
116 Ibid.
117 Ibid.
118 Ibid.
119 Ibid.
120 Ibid. 699.

law tort and civil rights claims due to issues like intent, causation, and immunity. Pushing through a bill of moral obligation is exceedingly difficult, especially for wrongfully convicted individuals who ordinarily lack political power. Even obtaining compensation through statutes precisely directed at wrongful conviction can be difficult, depending on the particular provisions of the statute at issue. Moreover, compensation under these statutes is often capped at inadequate amounts. Commentators generally agree, though, that compensation by statute is the best approach to righting wrongful conviction and incarceration. And, despite the deficiencies of existing statutory compensation schemes, exonerees would likely be in a better position if more states were to adopt compensation statutes for wrongful conviction. Rather than trying to overhaul the entire tort system or other avenues for compensation, improving upon particular statutory provisions related to compensating wrongfully convicted individuals will probably be the most successful and efficient way to improve outcomes for wrongfully convicted individuals.

There are several criticisms of existing statutory compensation schemes. First, sometimes the procedures are quite demanding. Administrative procedures may be the most efficient in getting compensation to exonerees in a timely manner. They may also be more efficient in terms of resources, as civil suits are often expensive. Establishing special administrative processes for compensating wrongfully convicted and incarcerated individuals, though, also expends resources, as it requires special procedures, knowledge, and decisionmakers. Processes that have both administrative and judicial components are the most onerous, though, as they generally decrease the efficiency of the compensation scheme. Overall, the more complicated the process, the less efficient it tends to be.

An even more serious concern about existing compensation schemes is that many of them are too stringent in their eligibility requirements. For example, some states limit compensation to only individuals who were pardoned[121] or to those who were exonerated by DNA.[122] But obtaining a pardon is often political, and there are other reliable bases for exoneration, so it seems odd to privilege pardons and DNA exonerations in this regard. Several jurisdictions limit compensation to those who were convicted and incarcerated based on felony offenses. But wrongful convictions and incarcerations based on misdemeanor offenses are similarly grave wrongs committed by the state. Perhaps compensation should be of a lesser amount in these cases, but exonerees should still be eligible for compensation.

Additionally, a good number of states prohibit compensation where the exoneree contributed to his own conviction, including by falsely confessing or pleading guilty. But the intense pressures of the criminal justice system regularly push innocent people to confess, and, based on the limited data we have, about 12 percent of known wrongful convictions are, at least in part, due to the defendant's false confession.[123] Additionally, more than 95 percent of cases are resolved by

121 Me Rev Stat tit 14 §8241 (1993).

122 Mo Rev Stat § 650.058 (2021).

123 The National Registry of Exonerations shows that, as of 9 June, 2022, 370 out of 3,164 known exonerations were in part due to the defendant's false confession. National Registry (n 2).

plea, and even the U.S. Supreme Court has acknowledged that the U.S. "criminal justice [system] today is for the most part a system of pleas."[124] This is partially because defendants regularly receive significantly harsher sentences if they are found guilty at trial rather than plead guilty and forgo a trial.[125] Considering these facts, it seems unjust to deny compensation for a defendant's contribution to his own conviction, at least by confession or guilty plea. It is difficult to imagine anyone willfully contributing to his own conviction;[126] rather, wrongful convictions are ordinarily the result of *state* errors despite defendants' attempts to escape conviction and minimize their sentences. The intense pressure to plead guilty can easily overwhelm a defendant, and the state often contributes to the stressful nature of the atmosphere producing confessions. Further, tort principles would actually *encourage* innocent defendants to mitigate their damages and thus, in a sense, endorse pleading guilty for a lesser sentence where conviction is a serious possibility. Overall, prohibiting compensation in cases where defendants have contributed to their own convictions by conduct such as falsely confessing or pleading guilty could very well eliminate a broad swath of wronged individuals from eligibility for compensation. Such provisions in statutory compensation schemes drastically limit the ability to truly redress the grievous nature of wrongful convictions.

Perhaps the biggest criticism of existing compensation statutes for wrongful conviction is that most of the awards are inadequate. Commentators generally favor statutory compensation for wrongful conviction over compensation through other avenues because success is higher with the former approach, but many commentators view statutory compensation scheme awards as unsatisfactory in most instances. For example, a relatively recent study shows that the average amounts paid per year incarcerated range from a measly $3,163.25 in Wisconsin, to a larger—but arguably still too low—$130,156.90 in Minnesota, to a much larger $376,864.17 in the District of Columbia, where damages are uncapped under the judicial remedy.[127] If a claimant is successful in a tort or civil rights suit, though, awards can be astonishingly high. In a recent civil rights suit, two exonerated brothers were awarded a total of $75 million in damages after they each spent thirty-one years behind bars (or about $1.2 million each per year incarcerated) for crimes they did not commit.[128] One of the most well-known settlements for wrongful conviction was the $40

124 Lafler v. Cooper, 566 US 156, 170 (U.S. 2012).

125 National Association of Criminal Defense Lawyers, 'The Trial Penalty: The Sixth Amendment Right to Trial on the Verge of Extinction and How to Save It' (2018) 5.

126 As some state statutes indicate, though, one circumstance in which one might willfully contribute to one's own conviction is when this is done to protect a loved one. See, e.g., IDAHO CODE ANN § 6-3502(3) (2021).

127 See Gutman and Sun (n 7) 786–87 Spreadsheet 1.

128 'Two Men Wrongfully Sent to Death Row Awarded $75M in Damages' (15 May 2021) *AP News* <https://apnews.com/article/nc-state-wire-health-1d992026ccbf69fa5d7e617382e9c976> accessed 13 December 2021. At the time of this award, they had also already reached settlements with other defendants, in the amounts of $9 million and $1 million. Ibid.

million awarded to defendants from the notorious "Central Park Five" case in 2014, who collectively spent around forty years behind bars.[129] They thus received about $1 million per year incarcerated. (They later were awarded an additional $3.9 million.)[130] And in 2016, Donald Gates's claim for wrongful conviction and more than twenty-seven years of wrongful incarceration settled for $16,650,000.[131] This amounts to more than $600,000 per year behind bars—much higher than the highest cap amount in any state.

Unfortunately, most jurisdictions have damages caps under their statutory compensation schemes. But when damages calculations have been left to decisionmakers in jurisdictions without damages caps, some fairly large amounts have been awarded to wrongfully convicted and incarcerated claimants. In 2016, for example, the Connecticut Claims Commissioner awarded $4.2 million each to four individuals convicted and incarcerated for about seventeen years for a gang-related murder pursuant to a compensation statute that did not cap damages.[132] This award caused a stir, not only because of its size, but also because the exoneration was based on evidence of prosecutorial misconduct rather than factual innocence. Such significant awards may have a downside, though. After the Claims Commissioner's award, Connecticut amended its statute to limit damages awards to two times the median state household income (although the amended statute does allow the Claims Commissioner to adjust the award by up to 25 percent depending on the facts of the case).[133] Further, awards in excess of $20,000 must now be reviewed and approved by the legislature.[134]

Today, most jurisdictions impose caps on the damages available to claimants, which is the basis for significant criticism of the statutory compensation schemes. These caps tend to be quite low, too. For example, California limits compensation to $140 per day of incarceration (approximately $51,100 per year),[135] Florida caps damages at $50,000 per year (plus fines, costs, and attorney's fees),[136] and the federal government similarly limits damages to $50,000 per year.[137] While it is naturally difficult to assess what would be a fair compensation amount in any case, it seems that $50,000 per year incarcerated would not come close to making a claimant whole again. That individual has lost his liberty, privacy, dignity, wages,

129 Benjamin Weiser, '5 Exonerated in Central Park Jogger Case Agree to Settle Suit for $40 Million' (19 June 2014) *New York Times*; Stephen Rex Brown, 'Central Park Five Received Additional $3.9 Million from the State in 2016' (9 June 2019) *NY Daily News* <https://www.nydailynews.com/new-york/ny-central-park-five-claims-settlement-20190609-u6vryrdhrfefdja6datzkofnf4-story.html> accessed 13 December 2021.

130 Ibid. These exonerees' stories were told in the recent Netflix miniseries entitled *When They See Us*.

131 Jeffrey S. Gutman, 'An Empirical Reexamination of State Statutory Compensation for the Wrongly Convicted' (2017) 82 *Mo L Rev* 369, 375, 427.

132 Ibid. 383.

133 Conn Gen Stat § 54-102uu(d)(2) (2016).

134 Ibid (d)(1).

135 Cal Penal Code § 4904 (2016).

136 Fla Stat § 961.06(1)(a), (c)–(d) (2017). This would amount to about $137 per day.

137 28 USC § 2513(e) (2019). This would amount to about $137 per day.

and most contact with friends and family. He has also likely been subject to gruesome prison conditions, which could include minimal nutritious food, a lack of air conditioning in hot climates, overcrowding, unsanitary conditions, and solitary confinement, which is known to contribute to serious mental health problems.[138] He will also probably face significant hurdles transitioning back into society even though he has been exonerated. A sum of $50,000 per year incarcerated does not begin to make up for these deprivations and impositions.

Understandably, jurisdictions may be concerned about their coffers,[139] and paying out several multi-million-dollar awards to wrongfully convicted and incarcerated persons could very well limit a jurisdiction's ability to do other good and necessary work. But these large awards are compensation for the egregious wrongs the jurisdictions have committed. And perhaps if the jurisdiction is concerned about having to pay out these large awards it can—and *should*—take measures to avoid these wrongs in the first place. Indeed, there are a number of measures jurisdictions can take to minimize the possibility of wrongful conviction and the damages flowing from such a wrong.

There are multiple reasons why wrongful convictions occur, and often several factors lead to such an event.[140] Many of these sources of error can be significantly curtailed, though. For example, according to the National Registry of Exonerations, approximately 23 percent of wrongful convictions were caused at least in part by false or misleading forensic evidence.[141] Today, many judges admit questionable forensic evidence that indeed results in wrongful convictions. Most forensic science evidence—other than DNA evidence—is not rooted in science and has not been proven to be reliable.[142] Further, in several instances, such forensic methods have actually been shown to produce erroneous results. Bite-mark evidence, for example, is roundly criticized by scientific experts, yet judges still admit it in cases as proof of guilt.[143] If a jurisdiction is fearful that high compensation awards for wrongful conviction will drain its coffers, that jurisdiction could pass laws prohibiting reliance on questionable forensic evidence in cases or at least appoint a committee to study such issues in anticipation of legislation. Jurisdictions could also invest in more effectively training judges charged with assessing the reliability of this evidence.[144] Another significant source of wrongful convictions is mistaken eyewitness identifications, which the National Registry estimates

138 See Meghan J. Ryan, 'Framing Individualized Sentencing for Politics and the Constitution' (2021) 58 *Am Crim L Rev* 1747, 1766.

139 See Bernhard (n 19) 96, 106.

140 For a more in-depth examination of the sources of wrongful conviction, see generally Ryan and Adams (n 3).

141 See National Registry (n 2).

142 Ryan and Adams (n 3) 1080–82.

143 Elizabeth Anne Brown, 'Most Agree Bitemark Matching Is Junk Science. Why Is It Still in Courts?' (23 December 2020) *Legal Examiner* < https://www.legalexaminer.com/legal/most-agree-bitemark-matching-is-junk-science-why-is-it-still-in-courts> accessed 13 December 2021.

144 Meghan J. Ryan, 'Understanding Criminal Justice Innovations' (2022) 5 *J L & Innovations* 38, 57–58 (2023).

as leading to about 27 percent of such convictions.[145] Studies show, though, that this figure could be reduced by changing live and photographic line-up procedures to make them less leading to eyewitnesses.[146] Similarly, official misconduct, which has contributed to about 57 percent of known wrongful convictions,[147] could be decreased by improving police and prosecutor training, as well as by changing internal incentives for advancement. Many jurisdictions, for example, evaluate prosecutors by the number of convictions they secure, which encourages prosecutors to seek convictions even if those convictions are inconsistent with the goal of justice in some circumstances.[148] Simply altering the metrics for evaluation could effect a decrease in overzealous prosecutions that lead to wrongful convictions. Also, false confessions have caused about 12 percent of known wrongful convictions.[149] Many of these confessions result from coercive interrogation procedures—a problem that jurisdictions could at least partially address by video-recording the interrogations.[150] These are just some examples of the often cost-effective measures jurisdictions can put into place to cut down on wrongful convictions.[151] This could, in turn, drastically limit the number of wrongful convictions requiring compensation.

Jurisdictions can also take measures to minimize the amount of full compensation for wrongful conviction by limiting the harms flowing from conviction. The United States has a massive over-incarceration problem. There are approximately 2.3 million people incarcerated in the United States, with about 689 per every 100,000 persons behind bars.[152] Indeed, the United States has more people incarcerated on a per capita basis than any other nation on Earth.[153] Further, we tend to impose very long prison sentences, with approximately 10 percent of individuals in prison serving a life sentence.[154] These long prison sentences are in stark contrast to the much shorter criminal sentences imposed in much of the

145 See National Registry (n 2).

146 See, e.g., Jennifer E. Dysart, Victoria Z. Lawson, and Anna Rainey, 'Blind Lineup Administration as a Prophylactic Against the Postidentification Feedback Effect' (2012) 36 *L & Human Behavior* 312.

147 See National Registry (n 2).

148 Meghan J. Ryan, 'Criminal Justice Secrets' (2022) 59 *Am Crim L Rev* 1541, 1568.

149 See National Registry (n 2).

150 'False Confessions & Recording of Custodial Interrogations' Innocence Project, <https://innocenceproject.org/false-confessions-recording-interrogations> accessed 13 December 2021.

151 Other changes to minimize the number of wrongful convictions could require more financial resources. For example, inadequate legal defense, which has contributed to about 27 percent of wrongful convictions, could be minimized by investing more resources in publicly funded defense.

152 Wendy Sawyer and Peter Wagner, 'Mass Incarceration: The Whole Pie (2020)'(Prison Policy Initiative <https://www.prisonpolicy.org/reports/pie2020.html> accessed 13 December 2021.

153 Ibid.

154 Ben Miller and Daniel S. Harawa, 'Why America Needs to Break Its Addiction to Long Prison Sentences' *Politico* 3 September 2019 <https://www.politico.com/magazine/story/2019/09/03/why-america-needs-to-break-its-addiction-to-long-prison-sentences-227999>.

world.[155] Not only are many individuals imprisoned and for long periods of time, but American prison conditions are often horrendous. It is not unusual to find severe overcrowding, unsanitary conditions, a lack of nutritious food, and the use of solitary confinement, which is known to contribute to mental health problems.[156] All of these factors—the overuse of imprisonment, for long periods of time, under terrible conditions—contribute to assessments of compensation when compensation awards are not artificially capped by statute. In addition to addressing the sources of wrongful conviction, addressing the results flowing from that conviction could mitigate the effect of compensation awards on jurisdictions' coffers. And in the case of limiting imprisonment, it would actually help replenish jurisdictions' coffers, as long sentences significantly deplete jurisdictions' resources.[157] For example, as one commentator has noted: "U.S. prisons spend $16 billion per year on elder care alone. Billions of dollars are diverted to prisons to care for the elderly who would pose no real risk if released when that money could be going to our schools, hospitals, and communities."[158] Fiscally conscious jurisdictions, then, would be well advised to examine their incarceration practices.

While jurisdictions might understandably fear large compensation awards, they may take reasonable measures to avoid such awards. Capping damages is the easy way out. Instead, asking juries, judges, and other decisionmakers to determine compensation awards based on what will make the claimant as close to being whole again as possible through a monetary award could possibly serve as a useful deterrent for actors within the system acting unfairly in determining whether convictions and sentences are just. This deterrent effect is likely diminished, though, by the time lag between the sources of wrongful conviction and the subsequent compensation, as well as the distinct funding sources for police departments, prosecutors' offices, and compensation awards.[159] Still, decisionmakers should be aware that there are consequences not only for the individual at issue but also for the jurisdiction if someone is wrongfully convicted and incarcerated. This most egregious wrong should indeed have appreciable consequences for the jurisdiction.

To truly effect change, though, and improve upon compensation for wrongfully convicted individuals, something beyond financial incentives is probably necessary. Naturally, politics plays an important role in shaping statutory compensation schemes, and convicted persons often have very little political power. Additionally, once someone is incarcerated, he often loses most of his connections with the outside world. Indeed, prisons are often in remote locations, inmates' abilities to communicate with their friends and family are often significantly limited, and there is very little reporting of what goes on behind prison walls.[160] Convicted persons

155 Marc Mauer, 'Long-Term Sentences: Time to Reconsider the Scale of Punishment' (2018) 87 *UMKC L. Rev.* 113, 127.
156 Ryan, 'Framing Individualized Sentencing' (n 138) 1766.
157 Miller and Harawa (n 154).
158 Ibid.
159 For an interesting discussion of how judgments and settlements affect (or fail to affect) police department policies and actions, see generally Joanna C. Schwartz, 'How Governments Pay: Lawsuits, Budgets, and Police Reform' (2016) 63 *UCLA L Rev* 1144.
160 Ryan, 'Criminal Justice Secrets (n 148).

are seen as "others"; we often have the mentality of locking them up and throwing away the key. Once an inmate is released—even if his conviction has been declared wrongful—reintegration into society is often difficult. And because society has moved on, it is challenging to get the public to relate to and have sufficient empathy for the plight of the wrongfully convicted person. But this is likely key to amassing the political power necessary to improve upon existing wrongful conviction compensation statutes. Putting a relatable face on the problem of wrongful conviction may perhaps be the greatest motivator in producing change.

Bibliography

'Compensating the Wrongfully Convicted' Innocence Project <https://innocenceproject.org/compensating-wrongly-convicted> accessed 2 November 2021.

'False Confessions & Recording of Custodial Interrogations' Innocence Project, <https://innocenceproject.org/false-confessions-recording-interrogations> accessed 13 December 2021.

Restatement (Second) of Torts § 653 (Am L Inst 1977).

'Two Men Wrongfully Sent to Death Row Awarded $75M in Damages' (15 May 2021) *APNews* <https://apnews.com/article/nc-state-wire-health-1d992026ccbf69fa5d7e617382e9c976> accessed 13 December 2021.

Avery M, 'Obstacles to Litigating Civil Claims for Wrongful Conviction: An Overview' (2009), 18 *BU Pub Int LJ* 439.

Bernhard A, 'When Justice Fails: Indemnification for Unjust Conviction' (1999) 6 *U Chi L Sch Roundtable* 73.

Borchard E, 'State Indemnity for Errors of Criminal Justice' (1912) *S. Doc.* Nos. 62–974 (1912).

Borchard E, 'European Systems of State Indemnity for Errors of Criminal Justice' (1913) 3 *J Crim L & Criminology* 684.

Borchard E, *Convicting the Innocent* (Garden City Publishing Co. 1932).

Brooks J and Simpson A, 'Find the Cost of Freedom: The State of Wrongful Conviction Compensation Statutes Across the Country and the Strange Legal Odyssey of Timothy Atkins' (2012) 9 *San Diego L Rev* 627.

Brown E, 'Most Agree Bitemark Matching Is Junk Science. Why Is It Still in Courts?' (23 December 2020) *Legal Examiner* <https://www.legalexaminer.com/legal/most-agree-bitemark-matching-is-junk-science-why-is-it-still-in-courts> accessed 13 December 2021.

Brown S, 'Central Park Five Received Additional $3.9 Million from the State in 2016' (9 June 2019) *NY Daily News* <https://www.nydailynews.com/new-york/ny-central-park-five-claims-settlement-20190609-u6vryrdhrfefdja6datzkofnf4-story.html> accessed 13 December 2021.

California Victim Compensation Board <https://victims.ca.gov/for-victims> accessed 12 December 2021.

Dobbs D, *The Law of Torts* (2000).

Dysart J, Lawson V, and Rainey A, 'Blind Lineup Administration as a Prophylactic Against the Postidentification Feedback Effect' (2012) 36 *L & Human Behavior* 312.

Garrett B, 'Innocence, Harmless Error, and Federal Wrongful Conviction Law' (2005) 2005 *Wis L Rev* 35.

Gutman J, 'An Empirical Reexamination of State Statutory Compensation for the Wrongly Convicted' (2017) 82 *Mo L Rev* 369.

Gutman J, ' 'Are Federal Exonerees Paid?: Lessons for the Drafting and Interpretation of Wrongful Conviction Compensation Statutes' (2021) 69 *Cleveland St L Rev* 219.

Gutman J, and Sun L, 'Why Is Mississippi the Best State in Which to Be Exonerated? An Empirical Evaluation of State Statutory and Civil Compensation for the Wrongfully Convicted' (2019), 11 *Ne U L Rev* 694.

Innocence Project, *Making Up for Lost Time: What the Wrongfully Convicted Endure and How to Provide Fair Compensation* (2009).

Kahn D, 'Presumed Guilty Until Proven Innocent: The Burden of Proof in Wrongful Conviction Claims Under State Compensation Statutes' (2010) 44 *U Mich JL Reform* 123.

Mauer M, 'Long-Term Sentences: Time to Reconsider the Scale of Punishment' (2018) 87 *UMKC L. Rev.* 113.

Miller B and Harawa D, 'Why America Needs to Break Its Addiction to Long Prison Sentences' *Politico* 3 September 2019) <https://www.politico.com/magazine/story/2019/09/03/why-america-needs-to-break-its-addiction-to-long-prison-sentences-227999>.

National Association of Criminal Defense Lawyers, 'The Trial Penalty: The Sixth Amendment Right to Trial on the Verge of Extinction and How to Save It' (2018).

National Registry of Exonerations <https://www.law.umich.edu/special/exoneration/Pages/about.aspx> accessed 9 June 2022.

Ryan M, 'Remedying Wrongful Execution' (2012) 45 *U Mich J L Reform* 261.

Ryan M, 'Framing Individualized Sentencing for Politics and the Constitution' (2021) 58 *Am Crim L Rev* 1747.

Ryan M, 'Criminal Justice Secrets' (2022) 59 *Am Crim L Rev* 1541.

Ryan M, 'Understanding Criminal Justice Innovations' (2022) 5 *J L & Innovations* 38 (2023).

Ryan M and John Adams, 'Cultivating Judgment on the Tools of Wrongful Conviction' (2015) 68 *SMU L Rev* 1073.

Sawyer W and Wagner P, 'Mass Incarceration: The Whole Pie (2020)' Prison Policy Initiative <https://www.prisonpolicy.org/reports/pie2020.html> accessed 13 December 2021.

Schwartz J, 'How Governments Pay: Lawsuits, Budgets, and Police Reform' (2016) 63 *UCLA L Rev* 1144.

Smith Robert J, 'Recalibrating Constitutional Innocence Protection' (2012) 87 *Wash L Rev* 139.

Weiser B, '5 Exonerated in Central Park Jogger Case Agree to Settle Suit for $40 Million' (19 June 2014) *New York Times.*

Table of Cases

Adams v. Harris Cnty, 530 SW2d 606, 608 (Tex Civ App 1975)

Baba-Ali v. State, 878 NYS2d 555 (NY Ct Cl 2009), rev'd in part, 907 NYS2d 432 (NY App Div 2010)

City of Tahlequah v Bond, 142 S Ct 9, 11 (2021) (per curiam)

Dziubak v Mott, 503 NW2d 771, 777 (Minn 1993)

Harlow v Fitzgerald, 457 US 800, 818 (1982)

Koike v Bd of Water Supply, 352 P2d 835, 839 (Haw 1960)

Lafler v. Cooper, 566 US 156, 170 (U.S. 2012)

Nelson v. Colorado, 137 S Ct 1249, 1252 (2017)

United States v. Davis, 16 F4th 1192 (5th Cir. 2021)

10 European standard of compensation for wrongful convictions

Małgorzata Wąsek-Wiaderek

1 Introduction

The aim of the chapter is to establish and assess, based on the European Court of Human Rights (ECtHR) case law, the common European standard of compensation for wrongful conviction. Although in many European countries state liability for wrongful conviction was not questioned when the Convention for the Protection of Human Rights and Fundamental Freedoms[1] was drafted in 1950, it took almost four decades to acknowledge the right to claim compensation as the European standard (in 1988 in Article 3 of Protocol No. 7 to the ECtHR).

An in-depth analysis of the ECtHR case law concerning the application of Article 3 of Protocol No. 7 allows us to draw the conclusion that this provision offers little chance of enhancing and developing European standards of compensation for wrongful conviction. This is mainly due to the weakness of this right, which is limited by many conditions and leaves a very wide margin of interpretation to national law.

However, the right to compensation for damages caused by the unlawful execution of the penalty of imprisonment could also be derived from the original text of the Convention: from Article 5 para. 5. As transpires from recent case law of the ECtHR, this provision may be invoked to claim compensation for damages stemming from a conviction with the penalty of imprisonment imposed in criminal proceedings affected by serious shortcomings classified as "flagrant denials of justice". It is argued in this chapter that the scope of application of both normative sources of the right to compensation varies and does not overlap.

Paradoxically, Article 5 para. 5 of the Convention seems to offer a more efficient and easily accessible right to compensation, but its application has very limited scope, concerning only unlawful "detention after conviction" imposed in proceedings affected by serious shortcomings. Under certain conditions, this provision may also be invoked to claim compensation for damages caused by unlawful execution of confinement to a psychiatric institution of a person who, due to their mental condition, cannot be held criminally responsible for an offence.

1 Hereafter referred to as "Convention" or "ECHR".

DOI: 10.4324/9781003229414-11

The two normative grounds for compensation discussed have a common characteristic. They both provide a right to compensation after a previous finding of a miscarriage of justice (Article 3 of Protocol No. 7) or "unlawfulness of detention" (Article 5 para. 5 of the Convention). This is one of the reasons why it is hard to argue that the European standard of compensation for wrongful conviction may really contribute to raising the national standards in this regard. Even if the Strasbourg Court was willing to play an active role in shaping the scope of the right to compensation for wrongful conviction, the subsidiary character of this right, which always depends on a previous finding of a miscarriage of justice or unlawfulness of detention, makes its role very complicated. This analysis proves that the ECtHR is only prepared to condemn states for a violation of Article 3 of Protocol No. 7 in exceptional cases, namely in cases where the lack of a legal basis in national law for claiming compensation for wrongful conviction is obvious.

2 The right to compensation under Article 3 of Protocol No. 7

The original text of the Convention on Human Rights and Fundamental Freedoms, adopted in 1950, did not provide for the right to compensation for wrongful conviction. Moreover, it did not even define the notion of "wrongful conviction". Only in 1984 did the Member States of the Council of Europe adopt Protocol No. 7 to the Convention,[2] which, upon its entry into force in 1988,[3] enlarged the catalogue of human rights as set in the ECHR by a few additional procedural guarantees, including the right to compensation for wrongful conviction. To date, the Protocol has been ratified by almost all Member States of the Council of Europe, except Germany, the Netherlands and the UK.[4]

Article 3 of Protocol No. 7 states as follows:

> When a person has by a final decision been convicted of a criminal offence and when subsequently his conviction has been reversed, or he has been pardoned, on the grounds that a new or newly discovered fact shows conclusively that there has been a miscarriage of justice, the person who has suffered punishment as a result of such conviction shall be compensated according to the law or the practice of the State concerned, unless it is proved that the nondisclosure of the unknown fact in time is wholly or partly attributable to him.

The right to compensation for wrongful conviction is almost identically drafted in Article 14 para. 6 of the International Covenant on Civil and Political Rights

2 Protocol No. 7 to the Convention for the Protection of Human Rights and Fundamental Freedoms (ETS No. 117).

3 Pursuant to Article 9 para. 1 of the Protocol, it shall enter into force on the first day of the month following the expiration of a period of two months after the date on which seven Member States of the Council of Europe have expressed their consent to be bound by the Protocol. This requirement was fulfilled on 1 November 1988.

4 See, current status of ratifications: https://www.coe.int/en/web/conventions/full-list?module=signatures-by-treaty&treatynum=117

(ICCPR), adopted more than two decades earlier than Protocol No. 7. Both provisions refer to a "miscarriage of justice" as a key prerequisite for compensation for wrongful conviction, without providing a definition of this notion. The only difference concerns the scope of reference to national law. While Article 14 para. 6 of the ICCPR provides that a person shall be compensated "according to law", in Article 3 of Protocol No. 7, reference is made to "the law or the practice of the State concerned". There is no doubt, however, that the aim of both texts was to leave the regulation of the substantive and procedural aspects of the right to compensation to national law. The Human Rights Committee (HRC) stressed, with reference to this issue, that it is for states to enact legislation ensuring that compensation, as required by this provision, can in fact be paid and that the payment is made within a reasonable period of time.[5] Thus, both rights to compensation, as provided in the ICCPR and European legislation, have the same scope of application.

As transpires from Article 3 of Protocol No. 7, the right to compensation for wrongful conviction is dependent on cumulatively fulfilling a few conditions.[6]

The first is that a person is convicted for a criminal offence. It is a common view that the term "criminal offence" shall be interpreted in the same way as the notion of "criminal charge" used in Article 6 of the ECHR.[7] The Explanatory Report to the Protocol is silent on this issue; so is the case law as it now stands. As is rightly argued by some authors, Article 3 may also apply to those disciplinary and administrative sanctions that fall within the scope of Article 6.[8] It should be stressed regarding this issue that, in accordance with the well-established case law of the ECtHR, not all disciplinary sanctions fall within the ambit of the "criminal part" of Article 6 of the ECHR. *Engel* criteria shall be applied in every case concerning disciplinary sanctions, i.e. 1) classification of an act under domestic law, 2) scope of the norm and purpose of the penalty and 3) nature and severity of the penalty.[9]

It is worth noting that some Member States, while signing the Protocol or upon depositing documents of its ratification, made declarations that Article 3 will apply only to offences, procedures and decisions qualified as criminal by national law.[10]

5 General Comment No. 32 – Article 14: Right to equality before courts and tribunals and to a fair trial, CCPR/C/GC/32, published on 23 August 2007.

6 Kees Flinterman mentions seven conditions (Kees Flinterman, 'Compensation for Wrongful Conviction' in Pieter van Dijk, Fried van Hoof, Arjen van Rijn, Leo Zwaak (eds), *Theory and Practice of the European Convention on Human Rights* (Intersentia 2018) 978–979), while Stefan Trechsel sets nine (Stefan Trechsel, with the assistance of S. J. Summers, *Human Rights in Criminal Proceedings* (Oxford University Press 2009) 375–379).

7 Flinterman, 'Compensation for Wrongful Conviction' (n 6) 978; Trechsel, *Human Rights in Criminal Proceedings* (n 6) 375.

8 Flinterman, 'Compensation for Wrongful Conviction' (n 6) 978; Christoph Grabenwarter, *Europäische Menschenrechtskonvention* (C.H. Beck 2009) 410.

9 *Engel and Others v the Netherlands*, App. no. 5100/71, 5101/71, 5102/71 and 5370/72 (ECtHR, 8 June 1976).

10 Such reservations or declarations were made by: Austria, France, Germany (declaration made at the time of signature), Italy and San Marino. See Reservations and Declarations for Treaty No. 117 – Protocol No. 7 to the Convention for the Protection of Human Rights and Fundamental Freedoms (ETS No. 117), published at: https://

Hence, they were also assuming that the notion of a "criminal offence" under Article 3 of Protocol No. 7 may be interpreted broadly, in the manner applied under Article 6 of the Convention.

The second condition of the right to compensation is that a person is convicted by a final judgment. The Explanatory Report to the Protocol specifies this notion by stating that a decision is final

> if, according to the traditional expression, it has acquired the force of res judicata. This is the case when it is irrevocable, that is to say when no further ordinary remedies are available or when the parties have exhausted such remedies or have permitted the time-limit to expire without availing themselves of them.

Thus, "wrongful conviction" within the meaning of this provision does not occur if a conviction had not acquired the res judicata character. Neither does it happen if a person was charged with having committed an offence, but was not brought to trial due to the expiry of the statutory time limit for investigation.[11] Damages stemming from detention on remand applied in the course of criminal proceedings which subsequently ended by acquittal are also excluded from the scope of application of the discussed provision.[12] While applying Article 3 of Protocol No. 7, no differentiation shall be made between various forms of convictions. This provision applies to all final convictions, also those imposed as a result of various forms of plea bargaining. However, as rightly noted by S. Trechsel,[13] in cases of convictions willingly accepted by the accused, a subsequent acquittal would be rather unusual. On the other hand, the discussed provision does not apply to decisions different from convictions, even if they confirm commission of an offence by the accused and provide a basis for penal reaction comparable to punishment. In particular, Article 3 of Protocol No. 7 does not apply to cases where a state inflicted harm on a person by issuing an administrative decision or another act, without finding his individual guilt after a trial in a court of law, for instance by applying collective deportation.[14] Furthermore, doubts may be raised with reference to the application of this provision to decisions imposing psychiatric detention on perpetrators of criminal acts who cannot be found guilty due to mental conditions. As will be discussed later in this chapter, compensation for unjustified execution of such a

www.coe.int/en/web/conventions/full-list?module=declarations-by-treaty&numSte=117&codeNature=0

11 Decision in the case of *Dimitar Nakov v the Former Republic of Macedonia*, App. no. 68286/01 (ECtHR, 24 October 2002); Decision in the case of *Marios Georgiou v Greece*, App. no. 45138/98 (ECtHR, 13 January 2000).

12 Para. 22 of the Explanatory Report to Protocol No. 7 to the Convention for the Protection of Human Rights and Fundamental Freedoms.

13 Trechsel, *Human Rights in Criminal Proceedings* (n 6) 375.

14 Decision in the case *Sanet Soyupova v Russia*, App. no. 37957/15 (ECtHR, 19 April 2016).

security measure may, in certain circumstances, be claimed under Article 5 para. 5 of the Convention.

The third condition which must be fulfilled to claim the right to compensation under Article 3 of Protocol No. 7 is that a convicted person "suffered punishment". There is nothing in this provision determining what kind of punishment must be suffered. It seems reasonable to argue that it covers all kinds of punishments whose execution may result in moral or financial damage. Thus, the right to compensation under Article 3 of Protocol No. 7, unlike under Article 5 para. 5 of the Convention, is not limited to damages caused by deprivation of liberty suffered by a convicted person. From a comparative perspective, it is also worth mentioning that the right to compensation provided in Article 14 para. 6 of the ICCPR concerns all kinds of punishment, not only imprisonment, although the drafting history of this provision and the reservations made by some states may suggest a different view.[15]

The subsequent, fourth condition of the right to compensation is that the notion of "wrongful conviction" may apply only to a person who was convicted by final judgment, but this conviction has subsequently been reversed, or he has been pardoned. Article 3 of Protocol No. 7 does not require that a subsequent decision be in the form of "final acquittal". Instead of this, the words "reversion" or "pardon" are used. This could be justified by the fact that in European countries final conviction may be quashed by various decisions with an effect equal to acquittal but not necessarily having a form of final acquittal.[16] According to the Explanatory Report to the Protocol, its intention was that "States would be obliged to compensate persons only in clear cases of miscarriage of justice, in the sense that there would be acknowledgement that the person concerned was clearly innocent".[17] However, as stated in the *Allen v. UK* judgment, references to the need to demonstrate "clear innocence", contained in the Explanatory Report, must now be considered to have been overtaken by the Court's intervening case law on Article 6 para. 2 of the Convention.[18] Hence, all kinds of domestic decisions with effect equal to acquittal may constitute the prerequisite for finding that a miscarriage of justice has occurred in the case.

15 Jamil Ddamulira Mujuzi, 'The Right to Compensation for Wrongful Conviction/Miscarriage of Justice in International Law' [2019] 8 *International Human Rights Law Review* 221.

16 For instance, in the UK a conviction may be quashed as "unsafe" with the effects equal to acquittal. It happens "where the fresh evidence renders the conviction unsafe, but the court could not say that no fair-minded jury could properly have convicted" – Hannah Quirk, 'Compensation for Miscarriages of Justice: Degrees of Innocence', [2020] 1 *Cambridge Law Journal* 5. See also *Allen v UK*, App. no. 25424/09 (ECtHR [GC], 12 July 2013). Critically on the system of compensation for wrongful conviction in England and Wales: Carolyn Hoyle, Laura Tilt, 'Not Innocent Enough: State Compensation for Miscarriages of Justice in England and Wales' [2020] 1 *Criminal Law Review* 29–51.

17 Para. 25 of the Explanatory Report to Protocol No. 7.

18 See *Allen v UK* para. 133.

The issue of “factual innocence” as a condition for claiming compensation for wrongful conviction was also analysed by the HRC in *Dumont v. Canada.*[19] In this case, the HRC did not take a firm and clear position as to whether the compensation mentioned in Article 14 para. 6 of the ICCPR depends on establishing the applicant’s innocence. However, even though the applicant’s innocence had not been established by the domestic courts and he was acquitted due to the lack of evidence of his guilt,[20] the HRC found a violation of Article 2 para. 3 in conjunction with Article 14 para. 6 of the Covenant, since the applicant had been deprived of an effective remedy to enable him to establish his innocence, as required of the state party, allowing him to obtain compensation for wrongful conviction.

Article 3 of Protocol No. 7 clearly does not cover the situation where, in the subsequent criminal proceedings conducted after a final conviction, as a result of a retrial or examination of an extraordinary appeal, the convict is sentenced to a lesser penalty than already served. As a result, it should be assumed that financial and moral damage resulting from serving a penalty wrongly performed in the light of a later final conviction is not covered by the right to compensation guaranteed in Article 3 of Protocol No. 7.

Yet another condition limiting the scope of Article 3 of Protocol No. 7 is the following: a reversion or pardon must be issued on the grounds that “a new or newly discovered fact” shows conclusively that there has been a miscarriage of justice, that is, some serious failure in the judicial process involving grave prejudice to the convicted person. Therefore, if the conviction has been reversed or a pardon has been granted on some other ground, Article 3 of Protocol No. 7 does not apply.[21] For instance, misapplication of the substantive criminal law which was a basis of conviction, subsequently revised by an acquittal judgment based on the reassessment of evidence which had already been used and known to the court in the original proceedings, does not fall within the scope of Article 3 of Protocol No. 7.[22] Furthermore, the reassessment of evidence which was taken into consideration in the original trial resulting in the conviction of the applicant cannot be considered as “a new or newly discovered fact” within the meaning of Article 3 of Protocol No. 7, even if this new approach to the evidence results in the revision of the final judgment.[23]

In many national criminal justice systems, final conviction may be quashed, and a person may be acquitted, as a result of a cassation appeal which is based on

19 *Dumont v Canada*, Comm. 1467/2006, U.N. No. CCPR/C/98/D/1467/2006, A/65/40, Vol. II (2010), Annex part. V, point “Q” at 153 (HRC, 16 March 2010).

20 The Court of Appeal of Quebec acquitted the applicant “in view of the fact that the new evidence which has come to light would not permit a reasonable jury acting on correct instructions to find the appellant [the author] guilty beyond all reasonable doubt”. See para. 23.3 of the views of the HRC.

21 Para. 23 of the Explanatory Report to Protocol No. 7.

22 Decision in the case *Herbert Bachowski v Poland*, App. no. 32463/06 (ECtHR, 2 November 2010).

23 *Matveyev v Russia*, App. no. 26601/02 (ECtHR, 3 July 2008) paras. 42–44.

serious breaches of the law (both substantive or procedural) but not on "new or newly discovered facts".[24] Such a final conviction reversed due to serious procedural errors occurring during the criminal proceedings is not interpreted as being "a miscarriage of justice" which could be covered by Article 3 of Protocol No. 7. As will be argued later in this chapter, damages stemming from this kind of "miscarriage of justice" may, under certain conditions, be subject to compensation under Article 5 para. 5 of the Convention. Furthermore, a pardon granted as a measure of clemency cannot bring about the right to compensation.[25] However, the term "a new or newly discovered fact" shall be understood as also including new evidence, such as, for instance, new witness testimony providing an alibi for the convict.[26]

Yet another limitation of the scope of this provision stems from the wording that the right to compensation may not be provided when it is proved that the nondisclosure of the unknown fact in time after final conviction is wholly or partly attributable to the convict. It is rightly underlined in the literature that if, besides the convicted person, others are also responsible for non-disclosure of the unknown fact, it would not be fair to put the blame for that solely on the convict. Thus, in such cases, partial compensation shall be granted.[27]

As stressed in the Explanatory Report, in all cases in which the above preconditions are satisfied, compensation is payable "according to the law or the practice of the State concerned". This means that the law or practice of the state should provide for the payment of compensation in all cases to which the provision applies. However, it is not required under Article 3 of Protocol No. 7 to give a right to compensation if not all prerequisites mentioned in this provision were fulfilled. As an example of such a situation, the Explanatory Report indicated a case "where an appellate court has quashed a conviction because it had discovered some fact which introduced a reasonable doubt as to the guilt of the accused and which had been overlooked by the trial judge".[28] Hence, as already mentioned,

24 In Poland and some European countries cassation appeal is available against a final and enforceable judgment. However, typically this measure may be brought before a judgment becomes final. See, Stephen C. Thaman, 'Appeal and Cassation in Continental European Criminal Justice Systems. Guarantees of Factual Accuracy, or Vehicles for Administrative Control?' in Darryl K. Brown, Jenia I. Turner, Bettina Weisser (eds), *The Oxford Handbook of Criminal Process* (Oxford University Press 2019) 949–950.

25 See Trechsel, *Human Rights in Criminal Proceedings* (n 6) 377. The same interpretation is applied with reference to Article 14 para. 6 of the ICCPR. Cf Mujuzi, (n 15) 222.

26 Trechsel, *Human Rights in Criminal Proceedings* (n 6) 378. On the understanding of the notion of "new facts and evidence" under the Polish rules on reopening of criminal proceedings: Karolina Kremens, Wojciech Jasiński, 'The Right to Claim Innocence in Poland' (2020) 4 *Erasmus Law Review* < www.erasmuslawreview.nl/tijdschrift/ELR/2020/4/ELR-D-20-00029.pdf> accessed 20 January 2022.

27 Flinterman, 'Compensation for Wrongful Conviction' (n 6) 979.

28 Para. 25 of the Explanatory Report to Protocol No. 7 to the Convention for the Protection of Human Rights and Fundamental Freedoms.

the reversal of a conviction which is not final in the course of appellate proceedings cannot be classified as "a miscarriage of justice".

The case law of the ECtHR on Article 3 of Protocol No. 7 is relatively modest. Until the end of November 2022, in only one case did the ECtHR find a violation of the right to compensation provided in this provision.[29] The applicant, Mr Poghosyan, was a classic victim of wrongful conviction. His conviction for rape and murder, based on his testimony and confession obtained under duress, was subsequently reversed due to the disclosure of new facts and evidence. The applicant was granted compensation for pecuniary damages caused by his conviction in civil proceedings initiated under national law. However, Armenian law, as applicable at the material time, did not offer a legal basis for compensation of non-pecuniary damages suffered as a result of miscarriages of justice. This was contested by the applicant before the ECtHR under various provisions of the Convention (Articles 13, 6 and 5 para. 5). The Court decided to examine the complaint regarding this issue under Article 3 of Protocol No. 7 and underlined that, while this provision guarantees payment of compensation according to the law or the practice of the state concerned, it does not mean that no compensation is payable if the domestic law or practice makes no provision for such compensation. Furthermore, the Court stressed that "the purpose of Article 3 of Protocol No. 7 is not merely to recover any pecuniary loss caused by a wrongful conviction but also to provide a person convicted as a result of a miscarriage of justice with compensation for any non-pecuniary damage such as distress, anxiety, inconvenience and loss of enjoyment of life".[30] Since such compensation was not available to the applicant, the ECtHR found a violation of Article 3 of Protocol No. 7 and decided to adjudicate EUR 30,000 of compensation for non-pecuniary damages suffered by the applicant.

One additional important procedural issue was also clarified by this judgment. The Court rejected as inadmissible *ratione personae* the complaint brought together with the applicant by his mother, Ms Baghdasaryan, arguing that only the direct victim of a wrongful conviction is entitled to bring an application under Article 3 of Protocol No. 7.

Although the discussed provision clearly states that a person shall be compensated "according to the law or the practice of the State concerned", it does not leave that state full freedom while regulating the scope of compensation. As transpires from the judgment in the *Poghosyan and Baghdasaryan v. Armenia* case, both pecuniary and non-pecuniary damages shall be covered by compensation offered in the domestic law. On the other hand, ECtHR case law does not prohibit the contracting states from making the award of compensation dependent upon the ability of the person concerned to show damage resulting from the breach, nor does it refer to any specific amounts.[31] However, the Court has a competence to examine whether the compensation awarded is arbitrary

29 *Poghosyan and Baghdasaryan v Armenia*, App. no. 22999/06 (ECtHR, 12 June 2012).
30 *Poghosyan and Baghdasaryan v Armenia*, App. no. 22999/06 (ECtHR, 12 June 2012), para. 51.
31 Decision in the case of *Emanuel Camilleri v Malta*, App. no. 16101/18 (ECtHR, 19 October 2021).

or unreasonable. To assess this issue, the ECtHR also takes into account whether the claim for compensation was carefully examined by the domestic court, having regard to all relevant circumstances of the case, including the applicant's personal situation, the nature of the criminal case against them, the length of suffering the punishment as well as personal after-effects.[32]

However, as transpires from case law, a broad margin of appreciation is left for the domestic courts with this regard since, until the end of November 2022, no violation of Article 3 of Protocol No. 7 has been found due to an unreasonably low amount of compensation granted. All complaints concerning this issue were found inadmissible as manifestly ill-founded.

3 The relationship between the right to compensation under Article 3 of Protocol No. 7 and Article 5 para. 5 of the Convention

The right to compensation for wrongful conviction is closely connected with the right to compensation for unlawful deprivation of liberty set out in Article 5 para. 5 of the Convention. Although the relationship between these concepts is not clear-cut, a few differences are self-evident. First, Article 5 para. 5 of the Convention may concern only a penalty consisting of deprivation of liberty, while Article 3 of Protocol No. 7 may be invoked with reference to damages caused by all forms of punishment suffered by a person wrongfully convicted. Moreover, while the latter provision indicates several conditions which must be fulfilled to receive compensation, Article 5 para. 5 of the Convention sets only one, that the deprivation of liberty must be unlawful, i.e. executed "in contravention of the provisions of this article". As transpires from the jurisprudence of the ECtHR, the right to compensation under this provision arises if a breach of one of its other four paragraphs has been established, directly or in substance, either by the Court or by the domestic courts.[33] Hence, to bring a case within the scope of application of Article 5 para. 5 of the Convention, it suffices that a domestic court has found a violation of the right indicated in one of the preceding paragraphs of Article 5 of the Convention. Such violation does not have to invoke *expressis verbis* or directly Article 5 of the ECHR, since a violation must be established "in substance".[34]

On the other hand, the rights guaranteed by both provisions have some common characteristics. They both require that the right to compensation must be not only theoretically available but also accessible in practice to the individual concerned. Moreover, it must be effective and provide compensation for both pecuniary and non-pecuniary damages that a person has suffered due to execution of a sentence which should not have been enforced against him. Hence, under

32 *Shilyayev v Russia*, App. no. 9647/02 (ECtHR, 6 October 2005) para. 21; see also a decision in the case of *Laetitia Morgenthaler v Luxemburg*, App. no. 3883/14 (ECtHR, 4 November 2014) para. 22.

33 *N.C. v Italy*, App. no. 24952/94 (ECtHR [GC], 18 December 2002) para. 61.

34 *Salmanov v Slovakia*, App. no. 40132/16 (ECtHR, 20 January 2022) para. 76.

both discussed provisions, the ECtHR in general has a right to assess the amount of compensation granted by the domestic organ.[35]

The term "detention", used in Article 5 para. 5 of the Convention, also applies to the "detention of a person after conviction by a competent court", as indicated in Article 5 para. 1 (a) of the Convention. The latter provision applies to two kinds of detention. Firstly, it concerns detention pending appeal against a conviction, applied prior to final adjudication of the case but after conviction by the first-instance court. The Strasbourg Court underlined that the phrase "after conviction" cannot be interpreted as being restricted to the case of a final conviction.[36] Furthermore, Article 5 para. 1 (a) of the Convention covers the execution of a penalty of imprisonment following final conviction of a defendant. Only in the latter case, i.e. suffering damages caused by enforcement of an unlawful penalty of imprisonment following a final judgment, can the compensation claimed under Article 5 para. 5 of the Convention be classified as "compensation for wrongful conviction".

Although Article 5 para. 1 of the Convention does not specify requirements which make "a detention after conviction" lawful, it clearly makes reference to the domestic law by providing that it should be applied "in accordance with a procedure prescribed by law". Thus, if a person has suffered punishment because of a final conviction to a penalty of imprisonment and subsequently this conviction is revised or changed due to a serious procedural error, such person has a right to compensation under Article 5 para. 5 of the Convention, provided that the penalty of imprisonment originally imposed and executed exceeded the penalty imposed in the proceedings aimed at correcting this serious procedural error. Summarizing, the right to compensation under Article 5 para. 5 of the Convention may be invoked in cases where final conviction appeared to be manifestly wrong but not due to new facts or newly disclosed evidence, but for the reason of serious procedural errors subsequently removed by extraordinary appeal measures.

35 With reference to the right to compensation under Article 5 para. 5 of the Convention, see, *inter alia, Salmanov v Slovakia*, App. no. 40132/16 (ECtHR, 20 January 2022), para. 81. With regard to Article 3 of Protocol No. 7, see the Decision in the case of *Emanuel Camilleri v Malta*, App. no. 16101/18 (ECtHR, 19 October 2021) paras. 35–38.

36 Pursuant to Polish law and the law of many other European countries, such detention is considered as "the lawful arrest or detention of a person effected for the purpose of bringing him before the competent legal authority on reasonable suspicion of having committed an offence" withing the meaning of Article 5 para. 1(c) of the Convention. Such interpretation is also consistent with the wording of Article 6 para. 2 of the Convention. However, the ECtHR's jurisprudence is constant on this issue and provides that "detention after conviction" covers also detention applied in the course of examination of an appeal against a judgment convicting a defendant, i.e. before the conviction became final. See, *inter alia, Ruslan Yakovenko v Ukraine*, App. no. 5425/11 (ECtHR, 4 June 2015), para. 45. See also, Edwin Bleichrodt, 'Right to Liberty and Security' in Pieter van Dijk, Fried van Hoof, Arjen van Rijn, Leo Zwaak (eds), *Theory and Practice of the European Convention on Human Rights* (Intersentia 2018) 451.

In the *Shulgin v. Ukraine* case, the final conviction of the applicant appeared to be partly unlawful because of the mistakes of the national courts, which, while recognizing the lack of evidence with reference to one charge brought against the applicant (i.e. extortion), failed to reflect this finding in the operative part of the final judgment by acquitting the applicant regarding this charge. In the framework of the cassation proceedings initiated a few years later, the sentence of imprisonment imposed on the applicant was reduced from seven to five years. As was underlined by the ECtHR, the miscarriage of justice in this case was established by the Supreme Court of Ukraine in the cassation proceedings, referring to the charge of serious procedural error. Moreover, the original final conviction had resulted in an additional two years' imprisonment, already served by that time. For this reason, the prerequisite of the right to compensation in the form of "unlawfulness" of "a detention after conviction" was established in this case.[37] Despite this, the applicant's claim for compensation was refused by the domestic courts on the grounds that his conviction had been quashed as unlawful only in part, i.e. only with reference to the charge of extortion, but not in its entirety. The ECtHR established this approach to be excessively formalistic and found a violation of Article 5 para. 5 of the Convention.

It is emphasized in the case law of the ECtHR that not all procedural errors occurring in criminal proceedings and resulting in the subsequent change of a final judgment shall be classified as making "detention after conviction" unlawful. Article 5 para. 1 (a) of the Convention does not imply that the Court must subject the proceedings leading to the conviction to comprehensive scrutiny and verify whether they fully complied with all the requirements of Article 6 of the Convention. However, "the detention of a person after a conviction which was itself the result of a flagrant denial of justice, that is, which was imposed in proceedings conducted manifestly contrary to the provisions of Article 6, cannot be considered as lawful within the meaning of Article 5 § 1".[38] For the purpose of Article 5 para. 5 of the Convention, mere mistakes are to be distinguished from a flagrant denial of justice undermining not only the fairness of a person's trial, but also the lawfulness of the ensuing detention. Detention following a conviction imposed in manifestly unfair proceedings amounting to a flagrant denial of justice is unlawful and automatically implies a breach of Article 5 para. 1 of the Convention.[39]

In the *Gruber v. Germany* case, the Court refused to accept that the applicant's conviction amounted to a flagrant denial of justice. In the applicant's submissions, the domestic courts had considered an unlawful criterion as an aggravating factor in fixing his sentence, which had resulted in a longer (and therefore executable) term of imprisonment. The Court underlined that such an error of law, even if committed by domestic courts, concerned only one of numerous aspects relevant

37 *Shulgin v Ukraine*, App. no. 29912/05 (ECtHR, 8 December 2011) paras. 52–55.

38 See, *Karl-Heinz Gruber v Germany*, App. no. 45198/04 (decision ECtHR, 20 November 2007).

39 *Shulgin v Ukraine*, App. no. 29912/05 (ECtHR, 8 December 2011) paras. 52–55; *Norik Poghosyan v Armenia*, App. no. 63106/12 (ECtHR, 22 October 2020) para. 32.

in fixing the applicant's sentence and cannot be considered as having infringed the basic requirements of Article 6 of the Convention. Therefore, the conviction of the applicant was not contrary to Article 5 para. 1 (a) of the Convention.

The jurisprudence of the Court provides for other examples of "detention after conviction" amounting to flagrant denial of justice. In *Vasilevskiy and Bogdanov v. Russia,*[40] the first applicant stayed in detention for longer than he should have because the sentencing courts did not count the time he had spent in pre-trial detention towards the overall duration of his sentence, in breach of the applicable domestic provisions. The second applicant was incited by the police to commit drug offences for which he was subsequently convicted. With reference to both applicants, flagrant denials of justice were established by domestic courts. Moreover, they were both granted compensation for unlawful detention after conviction under national law. However, the applicants considered the amounts of compensation unsatisfactory, and this was the subject matter of their successful complaints to the ECtHR.

As already mentioned, under Article 5 para. 5 of the Convention the Court is also entitled to assess whether the amount of compensation granted by the domestic authorities is arbitrary. Recognizing the wide margin of appreciation of the Member States regarding this issue, as well as the subsidiary character of Article 5 para. 5 of the Convention, the Court underlined that compensation for detention imposed in breach of the provisions of Article 5 must be not only theoretically available but also accessible and enforceable in practice. Therefore "a right to compensation for damage suffered which sets the levels of that so low as no longer to be 'enforceable' in practical terms would not comply with the requirements of that provision".[41] Being aware of the difficulties in assessing the exact amount of damages, especially for non-pecuniary damages, the Court underlines three aspects. First, that a violation of Article 5 para. 5 of the Convention must be assessed in the light of the monetary redress afforded at the domestic level. Second, that due account shall be made of its own practice under Article 41 of the Convention in similar cases.[42] Third, that the factual elements of the case, such as the duration of the applicant's detention, shall be taken into consideration.[43] The compensation granted under national law may be lower than that usually fixed by the ECtHR in similar cases. Moreover, it may consider the standard of living in the country concerned. Applying all these criteria in *Vasilevskiy and Bogdanov v. Russia*, the Court found that compensation for non-pecuniary damages granted to the applicants, which amounted respectively to EUR 7.00 and

40 *Vasilevskiy and Bogdanov v Russia*, App. no. 52241/14 and 74222/14 (ECtHR, 10 July 2018).

41 *Vasilevskiy and Bogdanov v Russia*, App. no. 52241/14 and 74222/14 (ECtHR, 10 July 2018) para. 22.

42 *Selami and Others v the Former Yugoslav Republic of Macedonia*, App. no. 78241/13 (ECtHR, 1 March 2018) para. 102.

43 *Vasilevskiy and Bogdanov v Russia*, App. no. 52241/14 and 74222/14 (ECtHR, 10 July 2018) para. 23.

EUR 2.70 per day of wrongful deprivation of liberty, was contrary to Article 5 para. 5 of the Convention.[44]

4 Compensation for "wrongful imposition" of security measures in the framework of criminal proceedings

A separate issue which should be discussed with reference to compensation for "wrongful conviction" concerns damages resulting from unjustified application of special security measures on persons of unsound mind who are unable to be criminally responsible for their criminal acts but who at the same time present a risk of reoffending and for this reason are considered "dangerous" to society. Article 3 of Protocol No. 7 clearly states that only a person "convicted" has a right to compensation for damages resulting from "suffering punishment". A security measure of confinement to a mental institution cannot be classified as a type of "punishment", although it brings about suffering equal or even more severe than a penalty of imprisonment. Hence, for some authors, damages caused by measures imposed on persons of unsound mind, like confinement to a psychiatric hospital, even if subsequently assessed as wrongfully imposed due to new or newly discovered facts, cannot be addressed by relying on Article 3 of Protocol No. 7.[45] Unfortunately no answer to this difficult problem is provided by the case law of the ECtHR. The opposite opinion with regard to this issue is reasoned by referring to the general purpose of this provision, which should not differentiate between suffering stemming from punishment and other forms of reaction to an offence, bringing equal consequences for a person found to be a perpetrator of a criminal act.[46] Indeed, compulsory confinement may be based on a wrongful finding that a person of unsound mind has committed a criminal act and, as a person "dangerous" to society, requires the application of a security measure. As in the case of a conviction, the new or newly discovered facts or evidence may prove that initiation of the criminal proceedings against a person of unsound mind, finding him to be a perpetrator of a criminal act and imposing on him a measure of compulsory confinement constituted a miscarriage of justice.

It should be stressed, however, that damages caused by unlawful confinement to a psychiatric institution may, under certain conditions, be claimed by invoking Article 5 para. 5 of the Convention. As transpires from the standing case law of the ECtHR, detention of a person of unsound mind, as a form of reaction to commission of a criminal act, may be assessed as "lawful" only if it fulfils three minimum conditions: firstly, a person must reliably be shown to be of unsound

44 The ECtHR granted to each applicant EUR 5,000 as just satisfaction for non-pecuniary damage.

45 Flinterman, 'Compensation for Wrongful Conviction' (n 6) 376.

46 Piotr Hofmański, in Leszek Garlicki (ed.), *Konwencja o ochronie praw człowieka i podstawowych wolności. Komentarz, tom II* (Wolters Kluwer 2011) 644. I share this view. See, Małgorzata Wąsek-Wiaderek, 'Niesłuszne skazanie w świetle Europejskiej Konwencji Praw Człowieka i Podstawowych Wolności' in Łukasz Chojniak (ed.), *Niesłuszne skazania – przyczyny i skutki*, (C.H. Beck 2017) 21.

mind; secondly, the mental disorder must be of a kind or degree warranting compulsory confinement; thirdly, the validity of continued confinement depends upon the persistence of such a disorder.[47] With regard to the second condition, it is stressed that the detention of a person of unsound mind may be necessary not only where the person needs therapy, medication or other clinical treatment to cure or alleviate his condition, but also where he needs control and supervision to prevent him, for example, causing harm to himself or other persons. However, in all circumstances, the "detention" of a person as a mental-health patient will be "lawful" for the purposes of Article 5 para. 1 (e) only if effected in a hospital, clinic or other appropriate institution authorized for that purpose. This rule applies even where the illness or condition is not curable or where the person concerned is not amenable to treatment.[48]

While assessing these three conditions of lawful detention, one cannot overlook the potential risk posed by the release of such a person. Without doubt, this risk shall be examined with due regard to social harm to the community of the criminal act committed by a person of unsound mind. As is underlined in the case law, with the passage of time and the developments in the factual basis for the assessment, the possible risk of reoffending may become less significant. Therefore, when extending the execution of a security measure, domestic courts shall duly examine whether a person still represents an imminent danger to others or to himself. Lack of diligent examination of this issue and adequate reasoning for continued detention may result in a finding by the Court that the execution of a security measure was contrary to Article 5 para. 1 (e) of the Convention.[49] A medical diagnosis establishing the necessity of compulsory confinement in a psychiatric institution shall be updated. The ECtHR stated that a diagnosis delivered a year and six months earlier cannot reliably show the necessity for confinement. Therefore, psychiatric detention enforced on the basis of such medical expertise is unlawful.[50]

Moreover, it is also stressed that a refusal to release a person placed in compulsory confinement may become incompatible with the initial objective of the security measure contained in the conviction judgment if the person concerned is

47 See, *inter alia, Stanev v Bulgaria*, App. no. 36760/06 (ECtHR [GC], 17 January 2012), para. 145; *Kallweit v Germany*, App. no. 17792/07 (ECtHR, 13 January 2011), para. 45. See also: Bleichrodt (n 36) 462; M. Wąsek-Wiaderek, 'Healthcare and Human Rights Requirements as Regards Detainees with Psychiatric Disturbances' in Piet H.P.H.M.C. van Kempen, Maartje J.M. Krabbe (eds) *Mental Health and Criminal Justice/*Santé mentale et justice pénale. *International and Domestic Perspectives on Defendants and Detainees with Mental Illness/*Perspectives internationales et nationales sur les prévenus et les détenus atteints de maladie mentale (Eleven Publisher 2021) 176–177.

48 *Rooman v Belgium*, App. no. 18052/11 (ECtHR [GC], 31 January 2019) para. 193; *Strazimiri v Albania*, App. no. 34602/16 (ECtHR, 21 January 2020) paras. 117–124.

49 See, *inter alia, Nawrot v Poland*, App. no. 77850/12 (ECtHR, 19 October 2017) paras. 73–76.

50 *M.B. v Poland*, App. no. 60157/15 (ECtHR, 14 October 2021) paras. 65–66.

detained due to the risk that he may reoffend but, at the same time, is deprived of the measures – such as appropriate therapy – that are necessary in order to demonstrate that he is no longer dangerous to society.[51] Accordingly, the lack of treatment suited to the person's state of health may allow for establishing that execution of a security measure in a psychiatric institution was not lawful and therefore contrary to Article 5 para. 1 (e) of the Convention.

Security measures applied to a perpetrator of a criminal act who cannot be found guilty are usually imposed for an indefinite period of time with an obligation to verify the necessity of confinement at regular intervals. Therefore, in such cases, the unlawfulness of the application of security measures usually stems from inappropriate examination of the validity of continued confinement.

In all the cases discussed above of the wrong application of a security measure, a violation of Article 5 para. 1 of the Convention could constitute a prerequisite for requesting compensation for unlawful psychiatric detention. Therefore, if domestic law does not afford an enforceable right to such compensation for breaches of Article 5 para. 1 of the Convention, this itself constitutes a violation of its Article 5 para. 5.[52]

To sum up, wrongful application of security measures may constitute a miscarriage of justice within the meaning of Article 3 of Protocol No. 7. However, serious doubts have been voiced as to the opportunity to apply this provision to damages stemming from the application of such measures. On the other hand, the manner of the execution of psychiatric confinement may be assessed as unlawful within the meaning of Article 5 para. 1 of the Convention. A person affected by such a measure has a right to compensation guaranteed by Article 5 para. 5 of the Convention.

5 Conclusions

Although Protocol No. 7 has been in force for three decades, the jurisprudence of the ECtHR on the right to compensation for wrongful conviction is relatively modest. To date, only in one case did the ECtHR find a violation of this provision. As was argued in this chapter, the right to compensation provided therein is dependent on many strict conditions, so that it is almost impossible to find a country in Europe offering a lower standard with regard to this issue. However, even if drafted as a minimum standard, this provision may have a considerable impact on the application of domestic laws on compensation for wrongful conviction. After all, the ECtHR has a competence to assess whether the amount of compensation granted by a domestic court is appropriate and not arbitrary. So far, it has been used very carefully, since no violation of Article 3 of Protocol No. 7 has been found on this basis. However, it seems that it is precisely through the competence to assess the amount of awarded compensation that the Strasbourg

51 *Rooman v Belgium*, App. no. 18052/11 (ECtHR [GC], 31 January 2019) paras. 210, 242.

52 *Strazimiri v Albania*, App. no. 34602/16 (ECtHR, 21 January 2020) para. 136.

Court may play an important role in shaping the European standard of the right to compensation.

The second conclusion which may be drawn from the above analysis is that the notion of "miscarriage of justice", mentioned in Article 3 of Protocol No. 7, shall not be associated exclusively with wrongful conviction based on new or newly discovered facts or evidence. A "miscarriage of justice" may also be the result of a serious breach of substantive or procedural law occurring during criminal proceedings. As was presented in this chapter, damages caused by a final conviction amounting to a flagrant denial of justice may be compensated relying on Article 5 para. 5 of the Convention, but only with reference to those suffered as a result of the enforcement of a penalty of imprisonment.

Bibliography

Bleichrodt E, 'Right to Liberty and Security' in Pieter van Dijk, Fried van Hoof, Arjen van Rijn, Leo Zwaak (eds), *Theory and Practice of the European Convention on Human Rights* (Intersentia 2018).

Flinterman K, 'Compensation for Wrongful Conviction' in Pieter van Dijk, Fried van Hoof, Arjen van Rijn, Leo Zwaak (eds), *Theory and Practice of the European Convention on Human Rights* (Intersentia 2018).

Grabenwarter CH, *Europäische Menschenrechtskonvention* (C.H. Beck 2009).

Hofmański P, in Leszek Garlicki (ed.), *Konwencja o ochronie praw człowieka i podstawowych wolności. Komentarz, tom* II (Wolters Kluwer 2011).

Hoyle C, Tilt L, 'Not Innocent Enough: State Compensation for Miscarriages of Justice in England and Wales' [2020] 1 *Criminal Law Review*.

Kremens K, Jasiński W, 'The Right to Claim Innocence in Poland' (2020) 4 *Erasmus Law Review* < www.erasmuslawreview.nl/tijdschrift/ELR/2020/4/ELR-D-20-00029.pdf> accessed 20 January 2022.

Mujuzi JD, 'The Right to Compensation for Wrongful Conviction/Miscarriage of Justice in International Law' [2019] 8 *International Human Rights Law Review*.

Quirk H, 'Compensation for Miscarriages of Justice: Degrees of Innocence' [2020] 1 *Cambridge Law Journal* 2020.

Thaman SC, 'Appeal and Cassation in Continental European Criminal Justice Systems. Guarantees of Factual Accuracy, or Vehicles for Administrative Control?' in Darryl K. Brown, Jenia I. Turner, Bettina Weisser (eds), *The Oxford Handbook of Criminal Process* (Oxford University Press 2019).

Trechsel S, with the assistance of Summers SJ, *Human Rights in Criminal Proceedings* (Oxford University Press 2009).

Wąsek-Wiaderek M, 'Healthcare and Human Rights Requirements as Regards Detainees with Psychiatric Disturbances' in Piet HPHMC van Kempen, Maartje J.M. Krabbe (eds) *Mental Health and Criminal Justice/Santé mentale et justice pénale. International and Domestic Perspectives on Defendants and Detainees with Mental Illness/Perspectives internationales et nationales sur les prévenus et les détenus atteints de maladie mentale* (Eleven Publisher 2021).

Wąsek-Wiaderek M, 'Niesłuszne skazanie w świetle Europejskiej Konwencji Praw Człowieka i Podstawowych Wolności' in Łukasz Chojniak (ed.) *Niesłuszne skazania – przyczyny i skutki* (C.H. Beck 2017).

Table of cases

Allen v UK, App. no. 25424/09 (ECtHR [GC], 12 July 2013)
Dimitar Nakov v the Former Republic of Macedonia, App. no. 68286/01 (decision, ECtHR, 24 October 2002)
Emanuel Camilleri v Malta, App. no. 16101/18 (decision, ECtHR, 19 October 2021)
Engel and Others v the Netherlands, App. no. 5100/71, 5101/71, 5102/71 and 5370/72 (ECtHR, 8 June 1976)
Herbert Bachowski v Poland, App. no. 32463/06 (decision, ECtHR, 2 November 2010)
Dumont v Canada, Comm. 1467/2006, *U.N.* No. CCPR/C/98/D/1467/2006, A/65/40, Vol. II (2010) Annex part V, point "Q"
Laetitia Morgenthaler v Luxemburg, App. no. 3883/14 (ECtHR, 4 November 2014)
Marios Georgiou v Greece, App. no. 45138/98 (decision, ECtHR, 13 January 2000)
Matveyev v Russia, App. no. 26601/02 (ECtHR, 3 July 2008)
M.B. v Poland, App. no. 60157/15 (ECtHR, 14 October 2021)
Nawrot v Poland, App. no. 77850/12 (ECtHR, 19 October 2017)
N.C. v Italy, App. no. 24952/94 (ECtHR [GC], 18 December 2002)
Norik Poghosyan v Armenia, App. no. 63106/12 (ECtHR, 22 October 2020)
Kallweit v Germany, App. no. 17792/07 (ECtHR, 13 January 2011)
Karl-Heinz Gruber v Germany, App. no. 45198/04 (decision, ECtHR, 20 November 2007)
Poghosyan and Baghdasaryan v Armenia, App. no. 22999/06 (ECtHR, 12 June 2012)
Rooman v Belgium, App. no. 18052/11 (ECtHR [GC], 31 January 2019)
Ruslan Yakovenko v Ukraine, App. no. 5425/11 (ECtHR, 4 June 2015)
Salmanov v Slovakia, App. no. 40132/16 (ECtHR, 20 January 2022)
Sanet Soyupova v Russia, App. no. 37957/15 (ECtHR, 19 April 2016)
Selami and Others v the Former Yugoslav Republic of Macedonia, App. no. 78241/13 (ECtHR, 1 March 2018)
Shilyayev v Russia, App. no. 9647/02 (ECtHR, 6 October 2005)
Shulgin v Ukraine, App. no. 29912/05 (ECtHR, 8 December 2011)
Stanev v Bulgaria, App. no. 36760/06 (ECtHR [GC], 17 January 2012)
Strazimiri v Albania, App. no. 34602/16 (ECtHR, 21 January 2020)
Vasilevskiy and Bogdanov v Russia, App. no. 52241/14 and 74222/14 (ECtHR, 10 July 2018)

11 In quest of the optimum model for compensating wrongful convictions[1]

Wojciech Jasiński and Karolina Kremens

1 Introduction

Effective protection of human rights demands not only their recognition in the domestic legal systems, but also operative enforcement mechanisms. In practice, this means that legal instruments must be available to individuals allowing them to prevent possible violations of human rights or to remedy them if violations occur. The remedies are of particular importance. They not only aim to compensate the victim for the damage that occurred, but also have a wider impact on shaping the overall perception of how individuals are treated by the state and how the state responds to its malfunctioning. This in turn is crucial for building confidence in state policies and actions.

The role of effective remedies should be emphasized especially in situations where violations of human rights are particularly grave. This is certainly the case when a person has been wrongfully found guilty of committing a criminal offence and deprived of liberty. In such a case the person is deprived of one of the core human rights, i.e. the right to personal liberty. Moreover, when detained the possibility of exercising other human rights is also limited. The consequences of such deprivation, regardless of the time spent in incarceration, often have far-reaching and devastating consequences for the future of the wrongfully convicted person.

Certainly, the best way to overcome this problem is to eliminate miscarriages of justice. However, none of the criminal justice systems is flawless. Moreover, even if objective obstacles could be neutralized, there are still situations where wrongful convictions occur even though the criminal justice system acted with due diligence. False testimonies, forged documents or simply undiscovered exculpatory evidence are factors that cannot be eliminated even in a perfectly shaped machinery of justice. Numerous procedural safeguards which are in place in domestic and international legal systems are helpful but cannot guarantee the infallibility of the court. Considering the risks inherent in undertaking justice there is a pressing

1 This chapter has been developed as part of the project Compensation for Wrongful Deprivation of Liberty. Theory and Practice (Registration No. 2017/26/E/HS5/00382) financed by the National Science Centre, Poland.

DOI: 10.4324/9781003229414-12

need to adopt effective remedies applicable in cases where breaches of the right to liberty, including wrongful convictions, take place.

There are various factors that determine the efficiency of the remedy. They concern both the scope of its application and accessibility ('entry requirements') as well as various procedural guarantees which may also undermine the possibility of being awarded adequate compensation. The legal provisions specifying the criteria relevant for taking compensation decisions are also essential.

The starting point in the discussion about awarding compensation for wrongful conviction is, however, the term 'wrongful conviction' itself. It might at first glance seem clear, but the in-depth analysis, as well as observation of legal provisions and their functioning, prove that there are important controversies as to how it should be understood.

Apart from the discussion on what constitutes a wrongful conviction, it is important to analyse the relation between the finding that a conviction is wrongful and the right to compensation. There is no automatism here. Besides the existence of damage and a causal relationship between the damage and the wrongful conviction, there might also be other eligibility criteria limiting the right to compensation in practice such as various time limits including a statute of limitations or formalities of the procedure. Also the procedure for claiming compensation is important since the level of its complexity may affect the availability of the compensation and its perception by the wrongfully convicted person.

Another issue is the amount of compensation a person can claim and obtain. Even if the definition of wrongful conviction is not discriminatory and the procedure is accessible, too low or arbitrarily awarded damages undermine the effectiveness of the scheme. Clearly, calculating compensation is not effortless. Nonetheless a transparent and adequate method of estimation must be adopted. The European Court of Human Rights (ECtHR) emphasizes that one of the principles is that deprivation of liberty should not be arbitrary.[2] The same pertains to the compensation scheme. It should be emphasized that the latter has not only a remedial function but also plays a preventive role. Therefore, it has to be tailored in such a way that it guarantees effective protection of personal liberty. The amount of compensation, or extent of other forms of remedies, remains an important piece of that puzzle.

This chapter addresses the following issues. First, the notion of wrongful conviction and other elements of eligibility for compensation will be addressed (section 2). This is followed by a discussion focusing on the procedural aspects of compensatory proceedings (section 3) and methods of calculating compensation (section 4). The chapter ends with general conclusions regarding the optimal compensation scheme.

2 See Wojciech Jasiński, 'The limits of interference with the right to liberty, privacy, property and privilege against self-incrimination in criminal proceedings – European standards' in Jerzy Skorupka (ed.) *Model of Acceptable Interference with the Rights and Freedoms of an Individual in the Criminal Process* (Beck 2019) 435–436.

2 The notion of wrongful conviction and eligibility for compensation

2.1 Understanding of the notion of 'wrongful conviction'

The crucial issue in the discussion about compensation for wrongful conviction is what is understood by the 'wrongful conviction'. As M. Naughton rightly points out, wrongful conviction is commonly understood as a situation where an innocent person is convicted for a criminal offence he or she did not commit.[3] However, since the guilt is attributed according to a procedure designed by law, the question arises as to exactly what it means that the person did not commit a crime. In a democracy based on rule of law the criminal justice system is founded on two important assumptions. According to the first one every individual is presumed innocent until proven guilty. The second one entails that guilt can be proved only in a fair trial. The latter concept includes procedural rules such as publicity of proceedings, equality of arms or privilege against self-incrimination. The adjudicator also needs to meet the standard of institutional guarantees such as independence, impartiality and establishment by law. If the guilt is proven in accordance with the fair trial rules the individual can be convicted and, in consequence, deprived of liberty. However, accepting the above principles also means that the wrongful conviction does not need to refer to actual innocence but may also be understood as a situation where the conviction occurred even though the presumption of innocence was not correctly rebutted in the court of law applying both relevant substantive and procedural law provisions.[4] In other words, since a criminal court applies a formal procedure and this procedure implies a certain evidentiary standard to prove guilt, there might be cases in which the presumption of innocence could not be rebutted, yet the actual innocence of the accused has not been proven. Therefore, the individual does not necessarily have to prove actual innocence to quash the conviction. Often it is the lack of convincing evidence of guilt that suffices. Certainly, this does not mean that the actual innocence is irrelevant. However, the adherence to procedural rules that have to be followed in order to rebut the presumption of innocence is of primary importance in criminal proceedings. The question that can be asked as a result is whether in all cases where the conviction resulted from wrongful rebuttal of presumption of innocence it should also be labelled as wrongful.

A sole reference to the necessity of observing procedure allowing the presumption of innocence to be rebutted is not enough to fully grasp the concept of wrongful conviction. In some situations, even strict adherence to substantive and procedural rules may result in convicting a person who at the moment of conviction seemed guilty and was proven guilty, but because of newly discovered facts after the conclusion of the trial it is obvious that the person should not have been found guilty. In such situations domestic legal systems usually allow the reopening of the proceedings and quashing of the conviction. Certainly, it would be

3 Michael Naughton, *Rethinking Miscarriages of Justice. Beyond the Tip of the Iceberg* (Palgrave Macmillan 2012), 15–16.

4 See Naughton (n 2), 14–36.

unreasonable to protect the *res judicata* and block the chance of correcting the flawed judgment just for the sake of stability of legal rulings. As observed above, the judicial procedures do not guarantee infallibility, so creating an opportunity to correct mistakes resulting from insufficient knowledge at the time of passing the judgment is fully justified. This, however, means that the choice between a narrower concept of wrongful conviction equated with convicted persons who are factually innocent and a wider one encompassing all who were not proven guilty in accordance with the relevant legal provisions allowing the presumption of innocence to be rebutted is not an either/or choice. Even if the latter is adopted there still might be cases of wrongful conviction that fall outside the scope of this.

Moreover, even if the answer to the question of whether in all cases where the conviction is a result of wrongful rebuttal of the presumption of innocence it should also be labelled as wrongful is generally positive, another issue that pops up is if all types of errors that occur in the criminal proceedings and result in wrongful rebuttal of the presumption of innocence lead to a wrongful conviction. The answer to this does not have to be positive. Only some types of errors, reaching a certain level of gravity in terms of their character and actual or potential impact on conviction, might be perceived as leading to a wrongful conviction. In this case various factors may come into play. They might be related not only to the fact that an error occurred or to the error itself, but also to the attribution of the error to a certain person. Obviously, that may be of importance since the victim may contribute to a wrongful conviction. In general the crucial thing is the establishment of an optimum equilibrium between the stability of the legal system (finality of judgments) and its ability to correct miscarriages of justice.

Another relevant problem is that not all domestic legal systems, including the ones investigated in this volume, apply the term 'wrongful conviction'. Thus, the understanding of what constitutes 'wrongful conviction' that warrants compensation demands analysis of interpretations of other similar concepts. In England and Wales the law uses the term 'miscarriages of justice'. In Spain, the wrongful convictions may fall under the category of either 'judicial error' (*error judicial*) or 'abnormal functioning of the administration of justice' (*funcionamiento anormal de la Administración de Justicia*). The Italian Code of Criminal Procedure uses the phrase 'judicial error' (*errore giudiziario*), but its definition expressed in Article 643(1) indicates that it can be understood as a wrongful conviction. In the USA, the alternative paths of obtaining compensation to claims based on wrongful conviction compensation statutes such as common-law tort claims and civil-rights litigation do not refer expressly or exclusively to 'wrongful conviction'. Instead, such concepts as malicious prosecution, false imprisonment, intentional infliction of emotional distress and legal malpractice as well as the violation of Fourth, Fifth, Sixth and Fourteenth Amendment rights or their combination are used.[5] Similar claims can be raised in England and Wales.[6] In Germany and Poland too the law does not explicitly use the notion of wrongful conviction, although the title of the

5 Cf. Chapter 9.
6 Cf. Chapter 1.

relevant chapter of the Polish Code of Criminal Procedure refers to 'compensation for wrongful conviction'. Nonetheless, the Polish statutory requirements for obtaining compensation clarify, at least to a certain extent, what is understood as a wrongful conviction.

The different terminology used in the countries analysed and the lack of a straightforward definition of wrongful conviction make the comparison and assessment of systems complicated. Nonetheless, there are patterns that can be identified. The main tension is between allowing compensation to be granted only to those who are actually innocent, or to a broader category of persons whose guilt has not been proved according to the law.

On the one hand, in the USA the general rule is that the person has to prove actual innocence, although the evidentiary threshold varies among US jurisdictions. A similar approach is currently adopted in England and Wales. Here, the law stresses that there has been a miscarriage of justice in relation to a person convicted of a criminal offence if and only if the new or newly discovered fact shows beyond reasonable doubt that the person did not commit the offence.[7] This provision was introduced as late as 2014, so more than 25 years after the adoption of the statutory scheme for compensation, which originally was not explicitly that restrictive. It was introduced in order to reverse the Supreme Court ruling in *R (Adams) v Secretary of State for Justice,*[8] whereby not only obvious cases of actual innocence qualified as a miscarriage of justice, but also situations where the fresh evidence was such that, had it been available at the time of the trial, no reasonable jury could properly have convicted the defendant. The lawmaker's reaction proves that there are serious controversies in England and Wales over the understanding of the term 'wrongful conviction'.

A much broader concept of wrongful conviction has been adopted in the Continental law countries. In Italy, to be eligible for compensation the final conviction must be quashed in the judicial review procedure and a person has to be acquitted or the proceedings against him or her must be discontinued. A similar solution has been adopted in Spain, where an extraordinary revision procedure should be initiated resulting in quashing the conviction and acquitting the convicted person. In Germany and Poland, the judicial decision convicting a person must be overturned in extraordinary proceedings initiated after the decision became final. The convicted person has to be subsequently acquitted or the proceedings must be discontinued. In the Netherlands, wrongful conviction is understood as a conviction that has been overturned after the extraordinary procedure of revision. Similarly in Norway, the convicted person has to succeed in reopening proceedings and obtaining acquittal. The only major difference is that the reopening of the case is decided by the extra-judicial body – the Norwegian Criminal Cases Review Commission – while the subsequent procedure is conducted before the criminal court. The situation is slightly different in the case of

7 Subsection 1ZA section 133 of the Criminal Justice Act.

8 [2011] UKSC 18. This judgment in turn differed substantially from the former approach of the House of Lords, which was not unanimous – cf. Chapter 1.

Lithuania, where the liability of the state is based on the unlawfulness of the conviction. As a consequence, the person alleging the wrongful conviction can claim compensation in cases of errors of law that took place during his or her criminal proceedings.

Therefore, the common approach is that Continental countries do not demand actual innocence to be demonstrated during proceedings. What suffices is that the conviction is quashed, acquitting the individual regardless of the grounds, or the procedure is discontinued in another permissible way. As A. Albrecht observes, the current version of the German Code of Criminal Procedure (StrEG), as opposed to the earlier ones, no longer differentiates between acquittals based on proved innocence and those based on a lack of sufficient evidence of guilt.[9] Moreover, the law in these systems allows the conviction to be questioned not only on the basis of new or newly discovered evidence, but to some extent on the basis of errors of law, regardless of whether substantive or procedural. Usually, catalogues of such errors are limited.[10] It can be expressed as a *numerus clausus* or, as in the case of Poland, more broadly as every gross violation of law, if it could have had a significant impact on the content of the ruling.

In some of the countries analysed (Germany, Norway, Poland) the law allows compensation to be granted not only to persons who were acquitted or against whom the proceedings were discontinued but also when the penalty was just mitigated. However, this option can only be applied if the person served a longer custodial penalty (alternative measure involving deprivation of liberty) than the one ordered after the second trial.

2.2 *Other eligibility criteria for compensation for wrongful conviction*

In none of the countries that were researched is the identification of the conviction as wrongful enough to obtain compensation. There are other important factors that determine the eligibility for compensation. This rule is expressly stated in Spanish law, providing that revocation or annulment of judicial decisions does not entail *per se* a right to compensation.[11]

Some of the restrictions relate to the criminal act committed, criminal proceedings which resulted in conviction and the prior criminal record of the convicted person. In the USA, numerous examples of such provisions can be found within various wrongful conviction compensation statutes. In some of the US states compensation can be awarded only to those convicted of felonies or to those convicted of aggravated misdemeanours. Limitations relate also to the type of evidence enabling the establishment of the wrongfulness of conviction, e.g. DNA evidence. Some of the states exclude the possibility of obtaining compensation if

9 Cf. Chapter 2 ('any remaining doubts about the guilt of the person concerned are no longer to the detriment of the convicted person, but to the detriment of the state treasury').

10 Cf. Chapters 3, 4 and 5.

11 Article 292.3 LOPJ.

the claimant pleaded guilty to the offence for which he or she was wrongfully convicted or, as in the case of Florida, entered a plea of *nolo contendere* to any violent felony.[12] In some cases the individual is also ineligible for compensation if before, apart from wrongful conviction he or she was convicted for a different criminal offence and served a sentence. Such restrictions are characteristic of the USA. Of course, one has to bear in mind that, at least theoretically, there are other ways to get compensation than the wrongful conviction compensation statutes available in the USA.[13] However, the analysis of the legal instruments designed to compensate wrongful convictions clearly indicates that their scope is substantially limited in comparison to European countries.

Another relevant issue in claiming compensation is the finality of the conviction that is qualified as wrongful. Although the systems of appeals differ significantly among the states analysed, there is a widespread consensus that the compensation for wrongful conviction can be granted if the initial conviction is final and subsequently quashed or in any other way its effects are neutralized (e.g. by pardon) and there is no subsequent judgment of conviction.[14] There is no identifiable common scheme for quashing a conviction that is followed in all the states analysed. However, it generally takes place within the scope of extraordinary proceedings allowing the judgments which are final and enforceable to be changed. In Italy, Spain and the Netherlands these are called revision procedures (*revision, recurso de revision, herziening*), in Germany reopening of the proceedings (*Wiederaufnahme eines durch rechtskräftiges Urteil abgeschlossenen Verfahrens*) and in Poland either cassation, reopening of proceedings or extraordinary complaint (*kasacja, wznowienie postępowania, skarga nadzwyczajna*). In England and Wales these are the appeal out of time, pardon or other specific types of appeals listed in section 133 Criminal Justice Act 1988.

The requirement of finality of the conviction is nonetheless not always absolute. Some countries where the legal provision that is a basis for claiming compensation does not explicitly contain the condition of finality do not preclude the possibility of claiming compensation even if the conviction was passed in a first instance court, but the convicted person was later exempted from criminal liability and suffered harm (Spain). Moreover, the plurality of avenues for claiming compensation could be relevant. If the domestic provisions allow more than one way of claiming compensation then the scheme designed exclusively to remedy wrongful conviction might be excluded, but other options might still be open. This is the case in Poland, where the compensation scheme designed to compensate wrongful conviction prescribed in the Code of Criminal Procedure is applicable if the final conviction has been quashed. But the general liability of the state based on unlawfulness provided in the Civil Code is, at least theoretically, available also in

12 § 961.04(1) Victims of Wrongful Incarceration Compensation Act (Florida Statutes, <www.leg.state.fl.us/statutes/index.cfm?App_mode=Display_Statute&URL=0900-0999/0961/0961.html> accessed 20 July 2022). Cf. Chapter 9.

13 Cf. Chapter 9.

14 Unless the domestic legal system allows for compensation in cases where the subsequent penalty of imprisonment is shorter than the one already served.

cases where the non-final conviction was issued in breach of the law and caused harm to a convicted person.

Another condition for claiming compensation is the actual incarceration of the convicted person. While some states do not attach, at least at the level of explicit statutory provisions, any relevance to it (Italy, Germany and Spain), others make it a formal requirement that enables the convict to claim compensation (the Netherlands, Poland and the USA). However, in the latter case the plurality of avenues allowing persons to claim compensation might be of importance. Poland may serve as a good example. As in situations where the conviction is not final, if the judgment was not enforced the scheme provided in the Polish Code of Criminal Procedure is not available, but the general rules of state liability based on civil law could be invoked.

All the states analysed also take into account, at least to some extent, whether the convicted person caused or contributed to his or her conviction. There are various situations which can be qualified as such, including false confessions and concealment of exculpatory evidence. However, the wording and interpretation of the relevant provisions differ. In England and Wales, the person is eligible for compensation 'unless the non-disclosure of the unknown fact was wholly or partly attributable to the person convicted'.[15] In Italy, there is a reference to malice or gross negligence (*dolo o colpa grave*).[16] Similar provisions are in place in Spain (*conducta dolosa o culposa*)[17] and in Germany (intentionally or by gross negligence – *vorsätzlich oder grob fahrlässig*).[18] The civil law regime in Lithuania also acknowledges the limitation of the state's liability in cases where the wrongfully convicted person contributed to his or her conviction. In Norway there is provision for the compensation to be reduced or cease to be payable if the person charged had without reasonable grounds refused to testify or withheld relevant information about the case or otherwise contributed to the conviction.[19]

Other limitations of the right to claim compensation cover various situations where the conviction is wrongful but its duration is credited to another custodial measure. Some of the national laws expressly acknowledge such an exception. Italian law provides that a person is not eligible for compensation when the term of imprisonment has already been deducted from the sentence to be served for another crime.[20] Similarly in Germany the law excludes the possibility of awarding compensation in cases where the conviction was wrongful, but the deprivation of liberty is credited to custodial correctional measures.[21] Such provisions tend to

15 Section 133 of the Criminal Justice Act.

16 Article 643(1) of the Italian Code of Criminal Procedure.

17 Article 295 LOPJ.

18 § 5(2) StrEG. Note that this provision expressly states that the wrongfully convicted person is nevertheless eligible for compensation if he or she profited from the right to silence or did not lodge an appeal.

19 § 446 of the Norwegian Code of Criminal Procedure.

20 Article 643(3) of the Italian Code of Criminal Procedure.

21 § 5 (1) no. 2 StrEG.

avoid situations where the time spent in incarceration counts double, both influencing the execution of other custodial sentences and resulting in compensation.

2.3 Conclusions

The accessibility and fairness of the compensation scheme is shaped by the principles and rules of state liability as well as additional eligibility criteria. In this respect the most important decision that has to be taken is whether only the actually innocent person or a wider category of persons not proven guilty in a court of law (subject to possible limitations) should be qualified as wrongfully convicted person. International law seems to support the narrow interpretation of who is wrongfully convicted.[22] However, as is rightly pointed out by the ECtHR in the case of *Allen v. UK*, the requirement of proving actual innocence has to be verified in the light of the contemporary understanding of the presumption of innocence.[23] Yet the differentiation between the 'force' of acquittals based on whether they stem from clear evidence indicating that a person did not commit a criminal offence or not is not allowed.[24] Certainly, there is no automatism between being acquitted and being eligible for compensation for wrongful deprivation of liberty. The ECtHR rightly points out that the refusal of compensation for wrongful detention does not in itself constitute a violation of the presumption of innocence.[25] However, if the presumption of innocence is to be treated seriously as a fundamental principle shaping the relation between the individual and the state and an indicator as to how to place the risk of malfunctioning of the system of justice then there is no convincing reason to support the view that only those who prove their innocence should be eligible for compensation. Clearly, the proceedings regarding the state liability (usually civil or civil-like) for the wrongful deprivation of liberty are not governed by the same rules as criminal proceedings. Therefore, at least in theory there is nothing wrong in claiming that it is possible, in contrast to criminal trial, to introduce a requirement for the convicted person to prove innocence to get compensation. However, this position ignores the relationship between compensating miscarriages of the criminal justice system and the fundamental importance of presumption of innocence in a democratic society. If it is assumed that only those whose guilt was established in a fair criminal trial can be punished, there is no justification for differentiating between defendants who are innocent according to the law. Allowing such a differentiation to be introduced through the back door undermines the legal position of the individual and burdens him or her with the consequences of unjustified, as it turns out *ex post*, actions of the criminal justice system authorities. Moreover, this also undermines the legitimacy of the criminal justice system, which is based on strict rules allowing

22 Article 14 para. 6 of the ICCPR and Article 3 of Protocol No. 7 to the ECHR. See also the Explanatory Report to the Protocol No. 7.

23 *Allen v. UK*, App no 25424/09 (ECtHR, 12 July 2013), § 127–133.

24 See e.g. *Sekanina v. Austria* App no 13126/87 (ECtHR, 25 August 1993), § 30–31.

25 *Cheema v. Belgium*, App no 60056/08 (ECtHR, 9 February 2016), § 23.

conviction only if the prosecution proves guilt. The presumption of innocence as a basic guarantee of the legal status of the individual *vis-à-vis* the state places the risk on the side of the state and reversing that logic in the compensation proceedings is not justified. Doing justice is inherently fraught with risk and the whole society rather than the individual who ought not to have suffered harm should take this burden. Otherwise a person whose innocence was not rebutted according to the fair trial rules, but was deprived of liberty, will need to bear the burden of the failure of the criminal justice system. If we assume that it is better to let the crime of a guilty person go unpunished than to convict the innocent, then it also seems justified to say that it is better to compensate a person who was acquitted but whose actual innocence cannot be proved, than to leave this person without any redress for the time spent in jail.

Turning to other eligibility criteria, in the first place the limitations of the right to compensation based on the type of offence committed or specific type of new evidence allowing the initial conviction to be questioned or on whether a person pled guilty or confessed should be questioned. It is rightly emphasized by M. Ryan[26] that such criteria are discriminatory and there is no justified reason to uphold them. In the case of confessions and guilty pleas, such limitations ignore the fact that in practice they are not as voluntary as many would like them to be. Lack of legal expertise of suspects and defendants, lack of effective legal representation or the systemic pressure on people to enter guilty pleas cannot be simply ignored by saying that if the suspect or defendant chose to admit to committing a crime or accepted the verdict he or she also voluntarily waived the right to compensation if the conviction turned out to be wrongful. This is not to say that the voluntary confession should not be taken into consideration by the authority deciding on granting compensation. It should be an important factor in deciding *in concreto* whether the compensation is to be granted but not in determining the eligibility of compensation in general.

Another highly discriminative factor used in some jurisdictions in the USA is a subsequent conviction for a criminal offence (in various forms). In this case the basic misunderstanding is that it is not the person wrongfully convicted who should be evaluated but the conviction itself. The compensation is paid because the conviction was wrongful and not because one considers that the person wrongfully incarcerated is good or bad. The fact that someone was convicted for a different criminal offence does not in any way influence the evaluation of another conviction as wrongful. If we allow such a global assessment the criminal justice system will be absolved from taking responsibility for even the most shameful errors just because the person wrongfully convicted is not a model citizen. By labelling a person as a criminal an excuse is found not to pay for what was determined as a violation of one of the most important values – personal liberty. Moreover, a consequence of accepting such a global assessment is also an unjustified differentiation between the gravity of the violations of personal liberty. It turns out that in the case of some wrongfully convicted people – those having a

26 Cf. Chapter 9.

criminal record – their personal liberty counts for much less than that of others. It is hard to see any convincing reasons to introduce such a distinction, taking into account that all people are equal and their personal liberty should be equally protected. Last but not least, it is worth noting that a previous conviction is treated during a criminal trial as highly prejudicial information. It should be treated in exactly the same way in the compensation proceedings, so there is equally no reason to allow the decision makers to base their judgments on whether they think a person deserves praise for abiding by the law in general or a reprimand for not doing so.

The above critique of eligibility criteria does not mean that all limitations of the right to compensation should be assessed negatively. As mentioned in section 2.2 of this chapter, in some jurisdictions there is a requirement for the finality of the conviction before it can be overturned and the procedure for claiming compensation initiated as well as the requirement for the execution of the imprisonment sentence. These conditions, depending on the national law regulating the system of appeals and execution of sentences, seem justified. It is reasonable from the systemic perspective to pay compensation only where the ordinary appeal measures accessible to the individual failed to eliminate potential errors. This rule is widely accepted in cases of constitutional complaints or human rights protection procedures (e.g. in front of the ECtHR), where the exhaustion of ordinary remedies is a condition of reaching for an extraordinary one. The condition of the sentence being enforced is also acceptable since it is the wrongful deprivation of liberty that the person should be protected from in the first place. Of course, other consequences of conviction, even if not enforced, may also be harmful to some individuals (e.g. loss of reputation for public persons). However, in such a case domestic legal orders usually allow victims to bring claims based on other grounds and accessible via other avenues. So it is not unreasonable to limit the accessibility of a specific scheme allowing to award compensation for wrongful conviction only to situations where a person was in fact deprived of liberty, as it is the most serious harm, at least generally speaking, the individual may suffer from a wrongful conviction.

A more problematic limitation of the right to compensation, but commonly adopted in the countries analysed, is the contribution of the wrongfully convicted person to his or her conviction. This limitation as such is not arbitrary. However, as usual, the devil is in the detail. On the one hand, it seems justified to claim that a person who concealed the true perpetrator and got himself or herself convicted for the criminal offence of that person should not be compensated for wrongful conviction if the relevant exculpatory evidence was known only to him or her and not revealed during the trial. However, accepting this claim does not mean that every time the person confesses or exercises his or her right to silence it automatically amounts to a ban on receiving compensation for wrongful conviction. M. Ryan rightly points out that the confessions might be coerced[27] or the accused's lack of sufficient legal knowledge may be abused by the investigating

27 Cf. Chapter 1.

authorities and result in a false confession. All cases where the defendant fails to exercise all possible actions in order to avoid conviction should certainly not be lumped together. There are several reasons for a cautious approach. First, it is easy to judge the situation *post facto* having knowledge and experience that the convicted person, especially if not represented by a lawyer, might not have had during the trial. Second, often there can be different defence strategies adopted in the criminal case and there is always room for error, which does not necessarily need to be attributed to the defendant. Third, the right to silence and the right to adduce evidence are rights which the person is free to exercise in a criminal trial. It does not mean that the exercise of this freedom cannot be evaluated in compensation proceedings, as opposed to criminal proceedings where, for example, exercising the right to silence cannot be treated as an aggravating factor. Compensation proceedings is a separate issue, where the rules of criminal procedure are not directly applicable. However, as A. Albrecht rightly points out,[28] the details of the case and the reasons why the convicted person acted in a certain way to defend his or her innocence are very important and should be considered by the authority deciding on compensation. Introducing detailed provisions defining in which situations the compensation is limited or the claim is to be rejected might seem tempting. Such an effort was made in Germany, where § 5 (2) sentence 2 StrEG states that the exercise of the right to silence or a failure to lodge an appeal are not legitimate reasons for denying compensation. However, one needs to be aware that there will always be cases not covered by even the most detailed legislation. Therefore, it seems that some discretion has to be left to the authorities deciding on compensation. A margin of appreciation may of course lead to controversial rulings excessively limiting the state's liability, as proved by the Italian example.[29] However, it is doubtful whether such a risk can be eliminated.

3 Procedure for claiming compensation

3.1 Procedural regime and authority deciding on the claim

The ICCPR and ECHR provide little guidance as to how the compensatory proceedings should be carried out at the national level. Focusing on other issues the international conventions as well as international human rights bodies and courts, in particular the ECtHR, are also silent as to which authority should be responsible for delivering the decision on compensation for wrongful conviction. This gives for the states leeway to prescribe the specific procedure and environment in which the right to compensation shall be requested. As a result, there is a range of models and options in the researched countries.

Most of the countries explicitly declare that their systems are generally based on one of three competing legal regimes, making it easy to divide them into three

28 Cf. Chapter 2.
29 Cf. Chapter 3.

separate groups. The first one establishes the compensatory proceedings under the criminal law regime regulated almost entirely in the respective codes of criminal procedure. This applies to Italy,[30] the Netherlands[31] and Poland.[32] The second group of researched countries regulates the compensatory procedure within the civil system. This happens in Lithuania[33] and in some parts of the USA.[34] The administrative path has been chosen by several other states including Norway,[35] Spain[36] and England and Wales.[37] Germany evades this tripartition by offering a combination of criminal and administrative regimes.

The authority that is called to decide on the compensation for wrongful conviction and the amount to be paid to the individual is a natural consequence of the legal regime chosen by each state. Accordingly, three possible options can be identified.

Those countries that have chosen the criminal regulations to govern the compensatory proceedings not surprisingly vest the competence to decide on the issue in the hands of the criminal court. In Italy and the Netherlands, it is the appellate court that overturned the conviction. In the latter case it is even the same panel of three judges that quashed the conviction. In Poland the situation is slightly different as the decision is made by the regional court of the circuit where the judgment of conviction was issued by the court of first instance. It is, therefore, not the same court as the one whose ruling led to finding a person innocent. All three countries seem to agree that the decision on compensation should be taken by the court of higher instance, presumably by more experienced judges.

The primary authority to decide on compensation in Lithuania is a civil court employing the regular civil procedure. The decision as to whether the court of higher instance hears the case depends on the value of the filed claim (the value has to exceed €40,000, however the claim for the award of non-pecuniary damage is not included in this amount). In those US states that follow the civil law regime a district court in the county in which the person was convicted decides on the

30 Article 643–646 of the Italian Code of Criminal Procedure.
31 Article 529–539 of the Dutch Code of Criminal Procedure.
32 Article 552–558 of the Polish Code of Criminal Procedure.
33 Article 6.271–6.273 of the Lithuanian Civil Code
34 Note that since the US system is fragmented due to the federal character of that country each state adopts a different compensatory regime. The civil law regime is often established, although the law of some states also provides for an administrative or civil-administrative regime. Cf. Chapter 9.
35 Sec. 444–451 of the Norwegian Code of Criminal Procedure (note that despite regulating the procedure within Code the procedure is purely administrative and the court has almost no role).
36 This is regulated by separate legal act: Law on the Common Administrative Procedure of the Public Administrations: Ley 39/2015, de 1 de octubre, del procedimiento administrativo común de las Administraciones Públicas. Spanish Official Journal (BOE) no 236, 2 October 2015. Permalink ELI: <https://www.boe.es/eli/es/l/2015/10/01/39/con> accessed 20 July 2022.
37 Section 133 of the Criminal Justice Act (similarly to Norwegian case, even if procedure is regulated within the English law on criminal procedure the system is described as 'purely administrative' – cf. Chapter 1).

compensation. But in some other states the administrative authority that decides on the case takes the form of an independent board, commission or single commissioner.

Similarly, the countries that have chosen exclusively the administrative path naturally transfer the competence to decide on compensation to administrative authorities. In the case of Norway, it is *Statens Sivilrettsforvaltning* (State Civil Law Administration, SCLA), a governmental body also responsible for decision-making in such areas as guardianship and legal aid. Since the SCLA is also seen in Norway as the authority responsible for strengthening the rule of law and ensuring the rights of the individual,[38] that puts the issues on compensation for wrongful conviction in the appropriate place. It should not go unnoted that until 2004 (that is before the creation of the famous Norwegian Criminal Cases Review Commission (NCCRC) and allocation of the decision on reopening criminal proceedings to their competence) the decision was made by the criminal court that was hearing the case after its reopening and making a new determination on the guilt. It is perceived that transferring the decision to a centralized administrative body was both to better ensure the legal security of the accused, as well as a desire to make the processing of compensation claims more efficient and less resource-intensive.[39] Nonetheless, the wrongfully convicted person, if dissatisfied with the amount awarded by the SCLA, may take the compensation case to a court for a civil trial suing the state.

In the case of Spain and England and Wales the decision is made entirely within the Ministry of Justice. In the former case, the decision-maker is the Minister of Justice. And in the latter case the question of whether there is a right to compensation is determined by the Secretary of State but the question of the amount of compensation is made by the Independent Assessor.[40]

However, the reality appears to be more complicated. In addition to setting a firm legal regime for claiming compensation within one of the systems (criminal, civil or administrative), some of these countries also decided to provide alternative paths for the wrongfully convicted person to obtain compensation. For example, in Lithuania besides the general right to claim for compensation in the civil law regime under tort law, there is an extrajudicial administrative procedure available that allows the former convict to request compensation directly from the Ministry of Justice.[41] However, this is only possible in cases where the harm is considered relatively low (the compensation offered may not exceed €10,000 in pecuniary damages and €5,000 in non-pecuniary damages).[42] On the other hand, in

38 Cf. Chapter 6.

39 Cf. Chapter 6.

40 Note that the system has been changed twice in recent history in 2006 and 2018 – cf. Chapter 1. None of these changes affected the administrative nature of compensatory proceedings maintaining the Secretary of State as the decision-maker.

41 Cf. Chapter 7 (note that the extrajudicial procedure is also available to those unlawfully arrested, unlawfully detained or those against whom the unlawful procedural coercive measures have been exercised).

42 Cf. Chapter 7.

Norway, where the usual path is in fact an administrative one, in high-profile cases covered by the media the Minister of Justice may step in and award higher compensation than the one offered.[43] This also happens in the Netherlands, where the state may engage in an out-of-court settlement with the wrongfully convicted person based on the general civil liability of the state.[44]

Finally, an interesting mixed system is rooted within the German law providing for a two-step procedure involving a combination of criminal and administrative regimes. The first step conducted within the regulatory regime of criminal procedure focuses on whether there are grounds for the obligation to compensate (*Grundverfahren*). The second step, devoted to the assessment of compensation, is designed as an entirely judicial administrative procedure (*Betragsverfahren*).[45] These examples show that the frameworks set for deciding on compensation claims are not only differ between states but are also more divergent internally than one would expect.

3.2 Compensation claim – who can apply and how it should be done

The important element of each system in claiming compensation for wrongful conviction is the procedure that allows the wrongfully convicted person to file such a request. On the one hand, this depends on who the person eligible to claim compensation is and, on the other hand, what formal requirements must be met by such an individual to successfully trigger the proceedings. Both issues will be discussed below.[46]

The right to apply for compensation in all the countries researched belongs foremost to the person who was wrongfully convicted. However, all systems recognize that others who were to some extent dependent on the wrongfully convicted person may also be eligible for compensation if that person is deceased and the compensation was not granted before their death. However, the specific categories of eligible claimants are prescribed distinctively in the jurisdictions researched. For example, in Italy it is the spouse, the next of kin, an affine to the first degree or a lineal relative by adoption who can apply for compensation.[47] In Germany it can be awarded to persons to whom the wrongfully convicted person was obliged to provide maintenance if they have been deprived of maintenance because of the prosecution measure.[48] And in Poland the person to whom the

43 Cf. Chapter 6.

44 Cf. Chapter 5.

45 Both regimes are regulated jointly within the Gesetz über die Entschädigung für Strafverfolgungsmaßnahmen (Act on Compensation for Punitive Measures; StrEG), Bundesgesetzblatt (Federal Law Gazette; (abbr. BGBl) 1971 I, 157); available at <http://www.gesetze-im-internet.de/streg/> accessed 26 December 2021.

46 Note that besides the personal grounds to file application for compensation there are the general grounds for compensation which are described in detail above – cf. Section 2.2.

47 Article 644 para. 1 of the Italian Code of Criminal Procedure.

48 § 11 StrEG

wrongfully convicted person was obliged to provide maintenance by law (spouse, children, parents, etc.) is eligible.[49] If the maintenance did not result from a legal obligation, the damages may be provided if 'considerations of equity' speak in favour of granting them but only if such financial support was permanent.

There are, however, limitations on the eligibility of persons other than the wrongfully convicted person to receive non-pecuniary damages. Some states resolve this straightforwardly. In Poland and the Netherlands those for whom the wrongfully convicted person was financially responsible can only apply for pecuniary damages.[50] However, this issue raised a broad legal debate in the Lithuanian system that included contradicting interpretations by the highest national courts on the eligibility of secondary victims to claim compensation for damage.[51] It was eventually recognized that the secondary victims are fully entitled to pecuniary damages but there are some limits on non-pecuniary damages. The depth with which this analysis took place was probably a consequence of regulating compensatory proceedings under the tort law which in Lithuania is a part of civil proceedings that certainly tend to focus more on the descendants and their rights than within the criminal law framework.

The second issue in relation to accessibility to compensatory proceedings concerns the obstacles standing between the eligible person and the decision awarding compensation. As the procedure itself is usually conducted before the authority that will take over the course of proceedings conducted *ex officio* as soon as the request has been filed, this relates to the formal requirements at the start of the process. This applies to the prescribed formalism of application, i.e. the requirements that must be met by the applicant to trigger the process. And as such requirements might be demanding it is also important to establish whether the applicant is eligible for legal aid if not capable of covering the costs of legal representation themselves. Finally, the time limits within which the applicant must operate might be an important factor that restricts the number of possible applications.

Certainly, all the countries researched agree that the proceedings in the case of compensation for wrongful conviction are not initiated *ex officio* and demand action by the interested party. In all cases this necessitates filing a written application with the authority competent to grant the compensation. An interesting exception in that regard is Norway, where the claim must be filed with the police district that investigated the case, and only with the opinion delivered by the relevant police department is the application transferred to the SCLA, where the proceedings are continued.[52]

49 Article 556 § 1 of the Polish Code of Criminal Procedure.

50 Article 556 § 1 of the Polish Code of Criminal Procedure. See also similar provision in Dutch law – Article 539 Section 1 in conjunction with Article 533 Section 6 of the Dutch Code of Criminal Procedure.

51 See two cases of Lithuanian Supreme Court analysed in Chapter 7 *A G and R G v the Republic of Lithuania*, Supreme Court of Lithuania, 5 February 2014, case No 3K-3–4/2014 and *R T and others v the Republic of Lithuania*, Supreme Court of Lithuania, 30 September 2016, case No 3K-3–399–687/2016.

52 Cf. Chapter 6.

The comparative study has shown a tendency among jurisdictions to deformalize the way in which the application is filed. Most states require only basic information concerning the name of the applicant with his or her signature supported at most by documents that are deemed useful to prove eligibility for compensation (e.g. Poland, Italy and the Netherlands). In other cases (e.g. Spain and Lithuania) the requirements seem to be set a bit higher[53] but still within the general requirements of other administrative or civil claims. It is also possible that the differences in the wording and practices used might not be that significant. On the other hand, England and Wales have taken simplification so far that the application can be completed online. Although the application form may appear quite lengthy (13 pages), the information requested in it is evaluated as straightforward and only occasionally challenging.[54] But even in Germany, where the application should indicate details of the claim in more concrete terms, enabling the competent judicial administrative authority to immediately enter an initial examination of the claim, the case law provides that the applicant may supplement the claim on a later occasion. This means that the claim just has to be raised within the prescribed time and not further substantiated.[55]

Another issue that arises is whether the applicant is asked to assess the precise value of compensation he or she is entitled to in the initial request. No common approach among jurisdictions can be identified. In some, the applicant must indicate at least in general terms the amount that he or she wants to receive (e.g. England and Wales) and in others a specific calculation must be made by the applicant who is bound by his or her request despite being subsequently able to modify such calculation (e.g. Spain). In Poland the applicant is neither forbidden nor obliged to indicate the amount of damages, although the court may request clarification on the matter to facilitate the proceedings.[56] And in Germany such indication is never requested as the amount of compensation (for non-pecuniary harm) is fixed, as it is calculated based on the duration of the imprisonment within the first step of the proceedings (*Grundverfahren*).[57]

But even if the application requirements are generally considered to be quite low, there might still be claimants who are unable to prepare an application and, even more importantly, effectively represent their interests during compensatory proceedings. Therefore, a valid question is whether the law provides legal aid for those eligible to apply for compensation. The answer to this question is affirmative for the majority of states considered (Germany, Lithuania, the Netherlands, Poland, Spain, Norway and Italy), but some are entirely silent on the issue (England and Wales and the USA). However, in the USA, as the problem of wrongful convictions is so widely discussed and gets a great deal of media attention, there are many different options open to claimants to obtain the legal advice, like many

53 See, for example, in case of Spain Article 66.1 (c) LPAC. Cf. Chapter 4.
54 Cf. Chapter 1.
55 Cf. case law cited in Chapter 2.
56 Cf. Chapter 8.
57 See also § 7 (3) StrEG. Note that the final word on how much the person will be compensated always belongs to the awarding authority (cf. Section 4).

pro bono organizations, such as the Innocence Project, helping those seeking compensation or the possibility to pay the lawyer only upon a successful win.[58] Interestingly, there is also no common rule on whether compensatory proceedings are free of charge.[59]

Another factor to be taken into consideration in the application for compensation is time. The right to file a claim is not limitless and states tend to regulate the possibility to do so usually starting from the moment when the wrongful conviction is finally confirmed. Nor do countries have a common standard in this regard. Probably the most rigid regime is found in the Netherlands, where the request must be filed within three months of the reviewed verdict being given.[60] However, the upcoming reform states that this surprisingly short statute of limitations will be replaced by a five-year-long timeframe, which will make it the longest period among the European countries researched in this study.

In the USA most states have adopted a two-year deadline from the moment the person is acquitted, pardoned or released or from the date the person obtained a certificate confirming his or her right to claim compensation. However, the deadlines provided by state law vary in length – short ones (1 year) or longer ones (5, 10 years) –and there are even cases where there is no statute of limitations.[61] In England and Wales the right to claim compensation expires two years from the date when the conviction was reversed or the individual was pardoned. In Italy the time limit is also two years from when the judgment quashing the conviction or other relevant decision being a title to claim damages became final.[62] In Poland, Germany and Spain the claim will be rejected if submitted after one year.

Depending on the modalities of the national compensatory scheme, there might also be shorter time limits to submit claims for compensation. For example, in Spain in order to obtain confirmation that there was a judicial error (*error judicial*) the application has to be lodged within three months of the date from which the right could be exercised. In Germany, although the eligible person must apply within a six-month limit,[63] the clock starts with the notification made by the public prosecutor's office.[64]

In some countries there is a certain amount of flexibility in observing the time limits. In England and Wales, a delayed application for compensation is to be treated as if it had been made within the prescribed statute of limitations if the Secretary of State considers that there are exceptional circumstances which justify

58 Cf. Chapter 9 (note that some states offer broader support for claimants including legal help or even food and shelter while others don't).
59 E.g. in Poland they are whereas in Norway they are not.
60 Cf. Chapter 5.
61 Compensation statutes: a national overview <https://www.law.umich.edu/special/exoneration/Documents/CompensationByState_InnocenceProject.pdf> accessed 20 July 2022.
62 Article 645(1) of the Italian Code of Criminal Procedure.
63 § 10 (1) sentence 1 StrEG.
64 § 10 (1) sentence 4 StrEG.

doing so.[65] Also in Poland, if the motion for compensation went beyond the statute of limitations it will be rejected only if the representative of the state treasury raised this issue during the trial. Moreover, the court may also continue to hear the case even if such an objection was raised, if the court finds it against the rules of social conduct, that is where extraordinary and justified circumstances such as serious illness or mental disorder of the claimant made it impossible to submit a claim in time.

3.3 The conduct of the proceedings and the right to appeal

One of the issues that attracts particular attention in discussions on the compensatory proceedings is the set-up in which they are carried out and how their outcome is supervised. Certainly, whether proceedings are held during a hearing open to the public or conducted *in camera* (in chambers) sometimes without any opportunity for the parties to participate in the proceedings remains a valid topic in the discussion on the ways in which control over this type of proceedings should be conducted.

The approach to these issues appears to be predetermined by the chosen legal regime regulating compensatory proceedings, that is judicial or non-judicial procedure. Thus, those states that have chosen a criminal or civil procedure, making the court the decision-maker concerning compensation, provide a formula where the case is heard in open court, during a public and oral hearing, as, for example, in Poland and Lithuania. On the other hand, the states that decided to vest the decision-making process in administrative, that is nonjudicial hands, provide for written procedure held *in camera*. That is the case in England and Wales, Norway and Spain.

The judicial–nonjudicial distinction and its relation to the nature of the conduct of proceedings is probably best seen in the German system, where, due to the duality of the compensatory proceedings being shared between the criminal court and judicial administrative authority, the approach towards the publicity of the proceedings is twofold. When eligibility for compensation is determined in step one (*Grundverfahren*) the hearing takes place in accordance with the general rules of criminal process, that is orality, immediacy and publicity.[66] However, when the proceedings move to the administrative regime for the decision concerning the compensation as such (*Betragsverfahren*), no hearing takes place and proceedings are held *in camera* in a written form. A similar situation is found in the USA. Those US states that entrust the compensatory powers to the civil court provide for a public and adversarial trial following the regular evidentiary rules as available in each jurisdiction. And when the administrative body decides on the issue the process may not become either public or adversarial.[67]

65 Section 133(2A) of the Criminal Justice Act.

66 Cf. Chapter 2 (noting that in practice the court rarely decides such cases during hearing).

67 Cf. Chapter 9.

But there are certainly exceptions to this duplex. In the case of Italy, despite the proceedings being held before the criminal court the law provides that they will be held *in camera*, and the presence of the parties is merely optional.[68] This resolution received criticism from the ECtHR, which, surprisingly, has to date not had an impact on Italian law.[69] Some concerns in that regard are raised by the Dutch system, where the oral and public hearing is held only when it is deemed necessary by the court. If the outcome of the case appears to be confirming the applicant's expectations, the oral hearing is unnecessary.[70] But the most problematic in the context of the transparency of the proceedings is the practice of obtaining out-of-court settlements in lieu of regular court proceedings, the details of which are not made public.[71] Although, as the authors of Chapter 5 suggested, this practice might be advantageous to both the claimant and the government; the complete lack of information on the amount of awarded damages as well as circumstances taken into consideration when making the decision appears to be an attempt to bypass the existing system of compensating wrongfully convicted persons.

The second important element of the supervision of the scheme of compensatory proceedings is the right to appeal the decision that awards the compensation. The countries researched differ in the availability of such an instrument. In this case, the legal regime of compensatory proceedings seems not to predetermine the legal path that the appeal will take.

At one end of the spectrum is the Netherlands, which makes no provision for a right to appeal the decision concerning compensation for wrongful conviction.[72] But the majority of states do offer some form of judicial review. In Lithuania, Italy and Poland the appeal is heard by the court of higher instance from the previously chosen legal regime – civil or criminal. This is also true for the USA; the civil court of appeal hears the case at least in those states that clearly provide for a right to appeal decisions on compensation.[73] On the other hand, in Germany and Spain, where decisions are made by the administrative authorities, the law has designed distinct paths. In the former case the applicant is entitled to bring a civil action against the decision made during the *Betragsverfahren* before the civil regional court.[74] Spain continues to follow the administrative regime, allowing the dissatisfied claimant to file an appeal with the administrative chamber of the National Court.[75] Technically, a judicial review is also available in England and Wales, however the discretion in decision-making offered by the system makes it difficult

68 Cf. Article 127 of the Italian Code of Criminal Procedure and Chapter 3.
69 *Lorenzetti v. Italy* App no 32075/09 (ECtHR, 10 April 2012). Cf. Chapter 3.
70 Cf. Chapter 5.
71 Cf. Chapter 5.
72 Article 445 of the Dutch Code of Criminal Procedure.
73 Cf. Chapter 9 (noting that in some other states the right of appeal is explicitly excluded and in some others unspecified).
74 § 13 StrEG.
75 Cf. Chapter 4 on the position of National Court (Audiencia Nacional) in the court structure of Spain.

to challenge the decision.[76] And even in the case of Norway, where the decision of the SCLA is not subject to appeal,[77] the dissatisfied applicant may bring the case before a civil court.[78]

Finally, when the decision on the wrongful conviction becomes final and compensation is eventually awarded the question remains as to who will take the financial responsibility for damages. All the researched states provide for the state to take full financial responsibility. In the majority of jurisdictions the law provides for the state to subsequently claim recourse against the person who caused the wrongful conviction (e.g. Poland, the Netherlands). Various exemptions, however, may in fact limit that option (e.g. the USA). But even in the former case where the law straightforwardly provides for the opportunity of recourse claim, these rules are almost never used in practice. This is probably due to the problem of finding enough evidence and proving that the individual person (judge, prosecutor, police officer or expert witness) was exclusively responsible for a wrongful conviction. The requirements for making such persons accountable for the miscarriage of justice are also set quite high.[79]

3.4 Conclusions

The diversity of the researched systems of compensation for wrongful conviction makes it almost impossible to extract from these models one standard procedural regime that could be considered as common. The lack of any guidance on the part of international law is probably the reason for this situation. However, one trend can be identified. The research shows that there is a clear tendency to move towards the administrative procedure. Obviously not all states are going in the same direction at the same speed. But whereas in Spain, Norway, England and Wales and some US states the administrative path is the one that is presumed to be the usual procedural regime, other countries have made significant moves towards adopting at least some administrative-like options. This applies to Germany (the second stage of the proceedings being entirely administrative), Lithuania (allowing this option for low claims) and the Netherlands (out-of-court settlements negotiated and decided by the Ministry of Justice even in high-profile cases). However, although it is uncertain whether this is just a coincidence or that states really are slowly moving decision-making processes towards the government or independent administrative bodies, it seems that only Poland and Italy are reluctant to introduce similar options. Moreover, whether the usual administrative route is really better than the strict civil and criminal law regimes decided in courts is hard to tell since it depends on many different factors incorporated in each of the chosen systems.

76 Cf. Chapter 1.

77 Section 449 first paragraph CPA. Cf. Chapter 6 (noting that SCLA can reconsider the decision either *ex officio* or upon the applicant's request 'if there is new and significant information of importance for the outcome of the case').

78 Section 449 second paragraph CPA.

79 Cf. Chapter 5.

The study of the compensatory proceedings did show a consistent approach among the researched states to provide for a broad acknowledgement of the right to compensation not only of the wrongfully convicted person but also to his or her dependents. This right does not only concern those most obvious persons like descendants but rather extends to all those whose living expenses were covered by the claimant. The scope of the right to compensation covers eligibility to demand non-pecuniary damages which are elaborated in the law or the case law.

Some of the factors that can discourage the eligible person from seeking compensation for the wrongful conviction he or she experienced are the requirements that he or she encounters upon entry into the system. When designing the system of compensating wrongfully convicted persons it should never be forgotten that such a claim is not like any other claim but results from an identified and confirmed mistake on the part of the state that resulted in an extremely harsh measure, namely incarceration. Making the procedure for wrongfully convicted persons the same as for any other claimant seems to be at odds with the state obligations in relation to that matter. Therefore, the procedure should be deformalized, and the researched states appear to recognize the necessity to do so. The tendency is to set the application requirements at a fairly low level, usually not demanding too many details, although what is demanded from the claimant certainly varies. It is worth other countries considering the system adopted in England and Wales using a web form. It forces the applicant to provide all the essential elements of the claim and prevents the situation arising where the application might be rejected due to the lack of an element that was mistakenly not included by the claimant. The flip side is that the necessity to apply for compensation on a web form raises additional concerns and might be also a limiting factor. Even though the availability and accessibility of electronic devices that can be used for that purpose in society is increasing there are still those that have limited access to the internet. And, more importantly, in the case of those who were detained for a longer period, which is often the case of those wrongfully convicted, their capabilities with regard to such tools might be somewhat restricted.

This is also the reason why the assessment of the compensation provided in the application, whether concerning pecuniary or non-pecuniary damages, should not be conclusive. Even if the claimant is asked to provide his or her expectations in written form there should always be leeway to assess the requested amount of compensation and grant a lower or higher amount if necessary. As the following section will show there are various ways of calculating compensation and countries differ significantly in that regard. The deciding authority – as the comparative analysis suggests – should have the competence to ask for additional supporting material confirming the demanded compensation or even to recalculate the damages independently from the request in the light of other similar cases. Additionally, setting longer procedural time limits for the compensation claim might help to raise the number of such requests. Therefore, attempts to extend these deadlines should be welcomed with appreciation. A good example might be the Dutch reform giving wrongfully convicted person a five-year-long timeframe to make up his or her mind whether or not to apply for such compensation.

But even if the law's requirements are set at a very low level, preparing the application may be beyond the competence of the eligible individual. If we are thinking about wrongfully convicted persons who spent years in prison it is unrealistic to expect them to have the means and resources to prepare an application and successfully represent themselves in the proceedings. Thankfully the majority of the states researched recognize the need to provide such individuals with legal aid and this should be considered as the basic desired standard regardless of the legal regime chosen for deciding on compensation for wrongful conviction. Other initiatives, such as NGO support and lawyers working pro bono, as available in some states, should be welcomed but cannot effectively supersede an efficient system of legal aid available to the wrongfully convicted persons.

Certainly, there are some elements that speak against moving towards the administrative framework. Although the assumed lower formality and flexibility of this type of proceedings may seem to be an advantage, the administrative system for compensating wrongfully convicted persons has obvious shortcomings. These relate to the transparency of the proceedings in particular. While the judicial regime, regardless of whether civil or criminal, provides clear and established rules on the proceedings being made public those countries that have chosen the administrative regime (e.g. Norway or England and Wales) do not find it necessary to give the public insight throughout the proceedings. On the other hand, as observed in the Dutch system, the outcome of the secret out-of-court negotiations may be beneficiary to the claimant. This, nevertheless, raises questions as to the reasons behind the decision taken and the amount of compensation awarded making it impossible to compare the outcome of similar cases. In such instances also public scrutiny of the outcome of the proceedings is impossible which does not make for a sense of social justice. As a result, the study does not provide a straightforward answer to the superiority of one particular legal system nor even one legal regime under which the compensatory proceedings should be conducted.

4 Calculating compensation

4.1 Criteria for calculating compensation

Another crucial element of effective compensation schemes is the proper calculation of compensation. Even if the compensation scheme is accessible in terms of legal conditions and the procedure is 'user friendly', awarding inadequate compensation undermines the effectiveness and legitimacy of the remedy for wrongfully convicted persons. What can be seen from the analysis of various jurisdictions is that the task of calculating the amount of just satisfaction for a person who has been wrongfully convicted is complicated. In the case of damages awarded for material harm there is less controversy because the harm suffered is relatively measurable. It is more difficult to calculate non-material harm, where the criteria for calculating compensation and their application in practice are unclear. Therefore, it is worth analysing how the law and relevant authorities (courts, administrative bodies) deal with that issue.

Generally, there are two approaches to calculating compensation. The first one leaves the method of calculation of the compensation to the respective judicial or administrative authority (depending on the jurisdiction). In this case the law either does not provide any guidance as to how to assess the amount of compensation or there are only very general provisions. The second approach involves introducing more detailed criteria or guidelines.

A good example of the first approach is the Norwegian Criminal Procedure Act, which provides only that the compensation for non-pecuniary loss 'shall be determined according to the circumstances of the particular case'. In the case of pecuniary loss there is no similar provision. However, in practice the rules of tort law are applied.[80] Another system that does not specify the method of calculating compensation is Poland. Since the compensation claim is considered a civil claim the relevant provisions of civil law apply. However, the Polish Civil Code is almost silent on how to calculate compensation. It only states that the pecuniary damage shall equate to both the substantial loss suffered and the loss of reasonably expected profits.[81] There is no similar provision referring to non-pecuniary damage. In practice the appellate courts and the Supreme Court tried to standardize the approach to calculating compensation. However, these guidelines are extremely general, just listing the variety of factors that need to be analysed or offering a universal but hardly useful indication that the compensation should be 'compensatory in nature, and thus must represent an appreciable economic value, not excessive in relation to the harm suffered'.[82] A similar approach can also be found in some US jurisdictions. For example, in the State of New York damages should be fair and reasonably compensate the wrongfully convicted person. In this case also the tort-based approach to calculating damages is adopted in practice.[83] Dutch law is also very concise. The Dutch Code of Criminal Procedure states that calculating the amount of compensation has to be done with the application of the principle of fairness. The living conditions of the wrongfully convicted person should also be taken into account when determining the damages. In practice, at least to some extent, the leeway of judges is limited by a general agreement drafted by Dutch criminal judges which refers to compensation for pretrial detention (*Oriëntatiepunten voor straftoemeting en LOVS-afspraken*), among other things. Although the document is not formally a source of law it stipulates that the compensation should be calculated as €130 for any day spent in custody at a police station and €100 when detained on remand. This serves as a point of reference in deciding on the damages for wrongful conviction.[84] In the case of Spain there is also no explicit guidance on calculating the compensation. This is a consequence of the lack of explicit provisions regarding this type of miscarriage of justice. However, the statutory provisions on the judicial error or irregular functioning of

80 Cf. Chapter 6.
81 Article 361 § 2 of the Polish Civil Code.
82 post. SN z 12.8.2008 r., V KK 45/08, OSNwSK 2008, Nr 1, poz. 1638.
83 Cf. Chapter 1.
84 Cf. Chapter 5.

the administration of justice make a reference to rules adopted in cases of compulsory insurance and social security. As a result, in practice the criteria and amounts of compensation related to damage caused in traffic accidents as specified in respective statutes are taken into account.[85] However, since they do not include all damage typically caused by wrongful convictions, the general criteria applicable in cases of wrongful detention on remand are also relevant, i.e. the time for which the individual was deprived of liberty as well as personal and family consequences. These general guidelines have been developed by the Spanish Supreme Court, which underlines the necessity for an overall assessment of various factors related both to the wrongfully convicted person (e.g. age, state of health, profession) and to the incarceration and its consequences.[86] Slightly more detailed provisions are in place in Italian law. It is provided that a person is entitled to compensation of an amount proportionate to the length of imprisonment and the personal and family consequences resulting from the conviction.[87] Italian scholars stress that the compensation should be assessed globally in an equitable manner (*diritto a un'equa riparazione*).[88] Since it is not a civil liability of the state, its specific rules of calculating compensation are not directly applicable. Of course, this does not mean that the amount of compensation can be arbitrary. The court has to give adequate reasons for its decision. However, the global character of the assessment makes the judicial discretion wider.

The alternative approach is based on more detailed criteria that should be considered by the authority calculating damages or a specific criterion that determines the amount of compensation. One of the systems adopted is based on a daily or yearly rate. This solution is quite common in the USA. The amounts range from thousands of dollars to tens of thousands of dollars a year. In the case of daily rates they range from $50 in Iowa to $140 in Florida.[89] Frequently, the yearly or daily rates are not the only relevant criterion. In several states additional costs such as attorney or court fees are paid to the wrongfully convicted person. In some states the increase in the cost of living is also taken into account. Moreover, even if there are fixed sums of money provided, the authority deciding on compensation is sometimes authorized to grant an additional sum where appropriate, depending on the circumstances of the case (e.g. in Alabama). Moreover, some US jurisdictions explicitly provide an additional sum of money for time spent on death row or for time being registered as a sex offender.

Some US states provide different points of reference in calculating compensation than a yearly or daily rate. In Connecticut the amount per year is calculated based on anywhere between 75 and 200 percent of the median local household

85 Cf. Chapter 4.

86 Cf. Chapter 4.

87 Article 643(1) of the Italian Code of Criminal Procedure.

88 Cf. Chapter 3.

89 Compensation statutes: a national overview <https://www.law.umich.edu/special/exoneration/Documents/CompensationByState_InnocenceProject.pdf> accessed 20 July 2022.

income, in Virginia it is 90 percent of the local per capita personal income, and in Utah the monetary value of the average annual nonagricultural payroll.

A different solution has been adopted in England and Wales to provide general criteria relevant in assessing the amount of compensation.[90] The assessor deciding on compensation

> must have regard in particular to (a) the seriousness of the offence of which the person was convicted and the severity of the punishment suffered as a result of the conviction, and (b) the conduct of the investigation and prosecution of the offence.

This list is not exhaustive, but indicates the main circumstances that should be taken into account. Moreover, Section 133A(3) provides for possible deductions that can be made. They may be justified either because of 'any conduct of the person appearing to the assessor to have directly or indirectly caused, or contributed to, the conviction concerned' or 'any other convictions of the person and any punishment suffered as a result of them' or both these criteria. In exceptional circumstances, the assessor may determine that the amount of compensation payable is to be a nominal amount.

A similar level of preciseness of the relevant criteria can be found in Lithuanian law. In that case the liability is of a civil character and is regulated by the Civil Code. The general rule is that the damage has to be fully compensated. Therefore in cases of pecuniary damage the compensation covers both *damnum emergens* and *lucrum cessans* that can be proved by the claimant. On the other hand, in the case of non-pecuniary damage the following factors have to be taken into consideration: the consequences of the damage sustained, the gravity of the fault of the person by whom the damage is caused, his or her financial status, the amount of pecuniary damage sustained by the victim and any other circumstances of importance for the case, likewise to the criteria of good faith, justice and reasonableness.[91]

In addition to the two models described above there is also a third, mixed approach adopted in Germany. The German compensation scheme combines the criteria based on fixed rates and general criteria for calculating compensation. On the one hand, there is a minimum threshold of €25 of material harm that has to be reached in order to be compensated. On the other hand, there are no explicit statutory provisions as to how the compensation exceeding €25 should be calculated. However, in practice in such a case the general rules governing damages for pecuniary loss derived from civil law are applied.[92] In the case of non-material harm § 7 (3) StrEG provides for a fixed lump sum of €75 for each day or part thereof of executed deprivation of liberty, regardless of the circumstances of the individual case.

90 Section 133A of the Criminal Justice Act.
91 Cf. Chapter 7.
92 Cf. Chapter 2.

4.2 Compensation caps

Along with the adopted method of calculating compensation, the existence of compensation caps is also very important. They have been adopted in some of the US states. The amount of the statutory caps differs significantly, ranging from tens of thousands to several million dollars.[93] The caps have also been adopted in England and Wales, providing a compensation limit for a specific type of miscarriage of justice.[94] That limit is £1 million in a case in which a person has been detained for at least ten years and £500,000 in any other case. Moreover, the total amount of compensation for a person's loss of earnings or earnings capacity in respect of any one year must not exceed the earnings compensation limit, which is 1.5 times the median annual gross earnings according to the latest figures published by the Office of National Statistics at the time of the assessment.

4.3 Alternatives to monetary compensation

All the systems researched have adopted monetary compensation as the most suitable remedy for wrongful conviction. In most of them it is a one-off payment. Some states allow the payments to be periodic (e.g. Germany). However, it is worth underlining that in some US jurisdictions compensating wrongfully convicted persons in monetary form may be supplemented by other types of remedies. These are educational aid (e.g. tuition waivers), housing assistance, job training, child support payments and health services.[95] These are certainly interesting options that aims at neutralizing the risk that the money given to wrongfully convicted persons will not help them in the long run.

4.4 Conclusions

The analysis of the provisions and practices regarding the calculation of compensation for wrongful conviction leads to the conclusion that it is much less problematic to remedy the material damage than non-material damage. In the first case either directly or indirectly the civil law principles of compensating material damage are applied. The harm suffered is in general quantifiable, as it usually refers to lost wages or other income as well as lost profits. Of course, that is not to say that there are no challenges. The general idea of remedying material damage is that the person should be placed in the same position as he or she would have been in if the damage had not occurred. However, what this means exactly is a matter of controversy. In several countries (England and Wales, Poland and Germany) the debate concerns, for example, the possibility of deducting living costs during incarceration from the total income lost by the person wrongfully deprived of liberty. On the one hand, it can be said that lost incomes should not be repaid in total (save taxes) as the person, if not incarcerated, would have needed to spend

93 Cf. Chapter 1.
94 See Section 133A(5) of the Criminal Justice Act.
95 Cf. Chapter 9.

some part of it on satisfying his or her basic life needs.[96] On the other hand, however, demanding reimbursement of such costs might be questioned. The first issue is what costs should be deducted. In Poland a progressively critical approach to the scope of such costs can be observed. Although from the mid-20th century onwards the courts claimed that the cost of the convicted person's and his or her family's maintenance, upbringing and education of children, culture, entertainment and other needs could be deducted, recently this line of reasoning has been abandoned. This is definitely right, because such an approach was simply unfair. Not only are people who are incarcerated unable to spend the money they would potentially have earned on the above-mentioned needs, which in many cases has to be covered from other resources, but they are not given them back in the compensation for pecuniary damage. However, in many judicial decisions in Poland other costs, namely those satisfying the person's basic needs in jail, are still being deducted.[97] The latter is not purely a Polish phenomenon, as a similar approach can also be seen in England and Wales and Germany.[98] This may seem reasonable if the fundamental assumption in calculating compensation is that the real financial situation of the wrongfully convicted person is to be compared with a hypothetical one that would have existed without that person being incarcerated. However, such an approach is also criticized by scholars in Poland as morally unacceptable.[99] The state is obliged to protect the dignity of convicted persons, including by providing necessary maintenance, so the claim for their reimbursement is not grounded. Moreover this claim is only made for wrongfully convicted persons, for correctly incarcerated prisoners the state treasury always bears all the costs. In such a case deducting the living expenses from the compensation granted for wrongful conviction is not justified and violates the equality principle.[100]

Another potential problem in relation to material damage, especially long-term wrongful conviction, is the changing purchasing power of the money over time. A recent study conducted in Poland demonstrates that there is no uniform approach to how that indicator should be acknowledged in the calculation made by the court.[101] Although it may sound like a technicality, the need for a uniform and fair approach in that matter is quite obvious, as the lack of a proper calculus may lead to a significant reduction in the value of the compensation sum.

96 See e.g.: *R. (on the application of O'Brien) v Independent Assessor* [2007] UKHL 10; [2007] 2 A.C. 312.

97 See: Anna Błachnio-Parzych, 'Odszkodowanie z tytułu braku możliwości wykonywania pracy w czasie niesłusznego pozbawienia wolności a dyferencyjna metoda ustalania szkody w orzecznictwie Sądu Najwyższego' (2021) 4 *Forum Prawnicze* 25.

98 Cf. Chapters 1 and 2.

99 Katarzyna Wiśniewska, *Model odpowiedzialności Skarbu Państwa za stosowanie środków penalnych i procesowych wobec jednostki* (Krakowski Instytut Prawa Karnego Fundacja 2020), 225–226.

100 See: Błachnio-Parzych (n 96), 35.

101 Dorota Czerwińska and Artur Kowalczyk, 'Kryteria ustalania związku przyczynowego oraz rozmiaru szkody majątkowej i krzywdy wynikłej z niesłusznego pozbawienia wolności w świetle badań aktowych' (2021) 11–12 *Przegląd Sądowy*, 155–156.

A really hard nut to crack is the task of determining how the non-pecuniary damage should be estimated. As H. Quirk rightly points out, even though the statutory guidance in that respect was adopted in England and Wales (Criminal Justice Act 1988, s133(4A)), it is still unclear how the calculation is being made.[102] It is not a coincidence that in some countries the legal doctrine and the case law promote the idea that the calculation of damages should be made globally or based on equity. This seems to be a way of avoiding the necessity to do the precise arithmetical calculation, which in the case of non-pecuniary damages is almost impossible anyway. Personal liberty, reputation and suffering cannot simply be converted into money. Of course, both in legislation and in practice there are clear efforts to at least enumerate the relevant criteria that should be assessed while calculating the amount of compensation and limit the discretionary power of the authorities hearing compensation claims. Nonetheless, even if the law or the case law of such authorities offers some guidance, there are remarkable disparities in the amount of compensation granted to wrongfully convicted persons. This was confirmed in the empirical research conducted in Poland[103] and in other countries (e.g. Spain).[104]

Tackling this problem is not easy. A solution adopted in some countries (e.g. Germany) is a fixed daily lump sum. Such an approach undoubtedly has some advantages. As argued in Poland and in Germany it promotes equality but, as rightly pointed out by A. Albrecht, it does not take into account the social status of the person wrongfully incarcerated.[105] This system protects some of the wrongfully convicted persons from an underestimation of the amount of compensation for non-material harm they deserve, as it does not allow less than a certain amount of money to be given. However, there is also criticism of this system. For example, in Spain it is argued that 'moral damage cannot be assessed daily'.[106] This is certainly true. Having one uniform rate for every day of detention not only ignores the specific aspects of deprivation of liberty related to the person incarcerated but also adopts a fiction that every single day in jail weighs the same. Moreover, if not accompanied by the possibility of adjusting the basic payable amount, lump sums disfavour those whose trauma and its consequences related to imprisonment are particularly grave. Moreover, even if the lump sums operate flexibly, controversies may arise as to what constitutes a 'regular' inconvenience related to imprisonment, as opposed to what constitutes an irregularity deserving extra compensation above the fixed sum.

It is doubtful whether such dilemmas can be solved. However, in this case a different approach from a focus on the criteria of calculating compensation might be more productive. In all of the European countries that were analysed the compensation is calculated either by the state administration or judges, often

102 Cf. Chapter 1.
103 Cf. Chapter 8.
104 Cf. Chapter 4.
105 Cf. Chapter 2.
106 Supreme Court Judgment (Administrative Bench) 20 December 2019 Cassation no. 3847/2018.

sitting in a single formation. This solution is not the best protection against incorrect or biased decisions. Therefore it is worth focusing not only on how the decision is made but also who makes it. The transfer of the power to grant compensation to authorities that are detached from the executive or judicial power, are collective and composed of people with different backgrounds and social sensitivities is worth consideration. Such solutions were adopted in England and Wales and Norway in respect of the determination of wrongful convictions (Criminal Cases Review Commissions) and serve as a good example of how the problem can be tackled. Introducing collectivity and diversity on the panel deciding on compensation may help analyse cases more thoroughly and better adjust the amounts of compensation.

What definitely should be criticized are caps limiting the amount of compensation adopted in some jurisdictions. Usually they are defined as a certain maximum sum of money or a reference is made to a certain indicator (the median annual gross earnings according to the latest figures published by the Office of National Statistics at the time of the assessment in England and Wales). Except for the protection of the national budget it is difficult to find any convincing reasons for their existence. There is also no clear justification for why the caps are as they are. In the USA they differ significantly from state to state, which is in itself proof of their arbitrariness, as the average living standards are not that diverse. It is also symptomatic that the amounts of compensation for wrongful conviction granted in civil cases in the USA can be counted in millions of dollars and are not limited by statutory caps, while compensation statutes provide them.[107] Moreover, those who are able to prove particularly serious harm (both pecuniary and non-pecuniary) are simply left with partial compensation at best. Their legitimate interests are disregarded just because they are too high according to arbitrarily set standards. This violates the principle of equality, because the harm suffered by some people is not valued in the same manner as for others. Equally arbitrary is the provision in England and Wales which allows the amount of compensation to be a nominal amount.[108] As H. Quirk rightly points out, this provision may be highly discriminatory against 'those who are not "ideal victims"'[109] and therefore do not deserve as much sympathy as others.

Summing up, it is clear that the calculation of compensation for wrongful conviction is not an easy task. It is relatively uncomplicated in the case of pecuniary harm. The biggest problem is the estimation of the extent of non-pecuniary damage. In many jurisdictions there is a remarkable disparity in the amounts of compensation granted to wrongfully convicted persons. To avoid divergent case law in some legal systems objective indicators, usually based on daily (yearly) rates, were adopted. They can only be accepted however if accompanied by a prerogative of a competent authority to adjust the rate to the circumstances of the individual case. This may unfortunately neutralize the standardization at which

107 Cf. Chapter 9.
108 s.133A(4).
109 Cf. Chapter 1.

rates are aiming, but nonetheless it is a path worth pursuing. Of course, one needs to be aware that the adoption of flexible rates is not a perfect remedy for divergent decisions on the amount of compensation. Nonetheless the reduction of existing divergences in the amounts of compensation would certainly be a step in the right direction.

A very worrying phenomenon is that the full compensation of damage caused by wrongful conviction is not ensured in all the states analysed. The existence of various caps limits the possibility of getting just redress and impairs the effectiveness of the compensation system. These limitations are arbitrary and seem to free the state from assuming liability for particularly grave miscarriages of justice. Arguing that their role is to protect taxpayers from excessive claims of wrongfully convicted persons is hardly convincing. Apart from reasons related to equality, the number of compensation claims for wrongful conviction awarded each year in the jurisdictions analysed is not big enough to have an impact on the state treasuries.

5 Concluding remarks

There are three main issues that are crucial for the system of effective remedy for wrongful conviction. The first one is the understanding of the term wrongful conviction adopted in the domestic legal system and the existence of additional eligibility criteria curtailing the right to compensation. These two elements predetermine the accessibility of the compensation scheme. The second issue is the procedure for claiming compensation. The choice of who decides on claims and how it is done is not a mere technicality. The length of proceedings and the potential difficulties which the victim of a wrongful conviction encounters are profoundly important in assessing whether the compensation scheme serves its purpose. Finally, the adopted method of calculating compensation is of great significance, as arbitrary decisions or the awarding of excessively low damages undermine the effectiveness and legitimacy of the compensation scheme.

The global assessment of the jurisdictions analysed indicates that with reference to the first of the above issues there is a visible trend in the common law countries examined (USA and England and Wales) to curtail the right to compensation, both by adopting a narrow understanding of what constitutes a 'wrongful conviction' and by adding (in the USA) further unjustified eligibility criteria. As argued in section 2.3. of this chapter, taking into account the role of the presumption of innocence as a fundamental principle governing the position of the individual vis-à-vis the state, these limitations are not justified. Similarly, the protection of individual liberty and the principle of equal treatment militate against introducing eligibility criteria not related to the wrongfulness of the conviction itself. However, that does not mean that the wrongfulness of the conviction automatically results in granting compensation. All the states analysed allow the quashing of convictions in extraordinary proceedings and on limited grounds (particularly the discovery of new evidence) and only then can compensation be claimed. Moreover, further limitations are being introduced, among which the convicted person's contributory negligence plays a very important role. Such restrictions are generally acceptable, although their application should be carefully verified in each case. As can be noted, the operation of contributory negligence (see section 2.2 of this chapter) may be controversial in practice. Here too, however, a reference to fundamental values determining state responsibility for wrongful convictions and the role of compensating wrongful convictions for the legitimacy of the criminal justice system should be a general guidance in solving difficult cases.

Not surprisingly, the compensation procedures adopted in the countries analysed differ significantly. There is no identifiable pattern which can be related to legal families or Eastern–Western Europe oppositions. In most cases the provisions in force are rooted in the peculiar historical development of the legal systems. The research does not provide any strong evidence that one of the adopted models is superior, in terms of accessibility or efficiency, over the others. Neither the administrative nor the judicial model, regardless of the type of court, is in itself better suited to deal with compensation cases. Although the administrative model might seem more efficient and to offer more uniform decisions compared with the judicial one, both efficiency and uniformity can also be guaranteed in a court, provided the legal framework is carefully drafted. The independence of the authority deciding on compensation is also a potentially important factor. If the compensation decisions are vested in the hands of an administrative body, there might always be concerns about whether the interests of the state treasury are being overweighted in the reasoning process. Judges may seem more independent and better suited to adjudicating compensation cases. However, wrongful convictions are decisions taken by judges, so other judges deciding in such cases might be perceived as not fully independent. Consequently, none of the solutions is ideal. Another important consideration is the transparency of the compensation scheme. A potential problem with the administrative model, as well as out-of-procedure settlements, is that the decisions are taken *in camera*. Open court proceedings usually better serve the transparency of the system. However, the public character of the proceedings is not the only relevant factor. What is equally important is that the decisions given in compensation cases are accessible and reasoned. If this is so, even an administrative procedure conducted *in camera* may be transparent enough to legitimize the compensation scheme.

In all of the states analysed there is an obvious trend to limit the formalities of the procedure. The wrongfully convicted person is not overburdened with formal requirements when submitting the claim to a relevant authority. Legal aid is available for those claimants that need legal assistance and cannot afford it. Moreover, the authorities deciding the compensation cases are offered *ex officio* powers allowing them to overstep the boundaries of compensation claims if necessary. These solutions deserve appraisal as they facilitate seeking justice in cases where a fundamental right to liberty has been violated. The only concern that can be raised from the perspective of the accessibility of compensation schemes relates to the time limits for submitting claims for compensation. In the majority of cases, they are relatively short. There is certainly room for improvement here in order to guarantee that no legitimate claim is declined just because a short time limit expired. Apart from limited formalism a widespread trend to allow the relatives of deceased wrongful convict to claim compensation can be observed. Some restrictions for dependents of the wrongfully convicted person concern the scope of their right, which exclude the possibility of requesting non-pecuniary damages.

Last but not least, the issue of how the compensation is calculated is crucial. There are two main problems related to the calculation of compensation – arbitrariness and lack of uniformity. Certainly the rectifying of the miscarriages of justice cannot be based on arbitrary decisions. Nor do arbitrary disparities between compensation sums granted in individual cases serve the purpose of legitimizing the system. What is clear is that all the countries examined struggle with these problems. The estimation of damages is not an easy task, especially in the case of non-material harm. None of the adopted solutions, whether based on a global assessment of damage or on a fixed sum for each day or year spent in jail, is optimal. It is doubtful whether such a system exists. However, it is worth considering the efforts aimed at limiting the disparities between compensations granted based on the adoption of fixed sums coupled with additional adjustment criteria. Moreover, entrusting the power to decide on the amount of compensation to authorities detached from the executive or judicial power, acting collectively and being composed of people of different backgrounds and social sensitivities is also worthy of consideration.

Not only should the damages be calculated fairly, but the calculation should also not be limited by arbitrarily adopted caps. They introduce unequal protection of personal liberty and leave people who suffered particularly serious harm only partially compensated.

Finally, it is worth emphasizing that in several states – Poland, Italy, Spain and Germany – compensation for wrongful conviction is treated not merely as a statutory privilege granted to wrongfully convicted persons but an important consequence of basic constitutional principles of modern liberal democracies – protection of personal liberty and state liability for causing harm to individuals, including liability for miscarriages of justice. Although in most of the above countries the constitutional provisions are general and leave the legislator quite substantial leeway in implementing these principles, their existence nonetheless indicates clearly the axiological presuppositions on which the state and, in particular, the legitimacy of the justice system are founded. This axiology is not a specificity of the above states, but should, even without explicit constitutional provisions, be shared by other liberal democracies. Therefore, a fairly drafted compensation scheme acknowledging the state's liability for compensation for wrongful conviction, free from arbitrary limitations and unjustified eligibility criteria or excessive formalities, with a transparent and reasoned decision-making process should not be perceived as a generously granted privilege but a simple consequence of the adherence to the fundamental values of the modern state taking individuals and liability for miscarriages of justice seriously.

Bibliography

Błachnio-Parzych A, 'Odszkodowanie z tytułu braku możliwości wykonywania pracy w czasie niesłusznego pozbawienia wolności a dyferencyjna metoda ustalania szkody w orzecznictwie Sądu Najwyższego' (2021) 4 *Forum Prawnicze* 25–36

Compensation statutes: a national overview, <https://www.law.umich.edu/special/exoneration/Documents/CompensationByState_InnocenceProject.pdf>

Czerwińska D and Kowalczyk A, 'Kryteria ustalania związku przyczynowego oraz rozmiaru szkody majątkowej i krzywdy wynikłej z niesłusznego pozbawienia wolności w świetle badań aktowych' (2021) 11–12 *Przegląd Sądowy* 148–166

Jasiński W, 'The limits of interference with the right to liberty, privacy, property and privilege against self-incrimination in criminal proceedings – European standards' in J Skorupka (ed.) *Model of Acceptable Interference with the Rights and Freedoms of an Individual in the Criminal Process* (Beck 2019)

Naughton M, *Rethinking Miscarriages of Justice. Beyond the Tip of the Iceberg* (Palgrave Macmillan 2012)

Wiśniewska K, *Model odpowiedzialności Skarbu Państwa za stosowanie środków penalnych i procesowych wobec jednostki* (Krakowski Instytut Prawa Karnego Fundacja 2020)

Table of cases

[2007] 2 A.C. 312

[2011] UKSC 18

A G and R G v the Republic of Lithuania, Supreme Court of Lithuania, 5 February 2014, case No 3K-3-4/2014

Allen v. UK, App no 25424/09 (ECtHR, 12 July 2013)

Cheema v. Belgium, App no 60056/08 (ECtHR, 9 February 2016)

Lorenzetti v. Italy, App no 32075/09 (EctHR, 10 April 2012)

R. (on the application of O'Brien) v Independent Assessor [2007] UKHL 10; [2007] 2 A.C. 312.

R (on the application of Adams) v Secretary of State for Justice [2011] UKSC 18

R T and others v the Republic of Lithuania, Supreme Court of Lithuania, 30 September 2016, case No 3K-3-399-687/2016

Postanowienie Sądu Najwyższego z 12.8.2008 r., V KK 45/08, OSNwSK 2008, Nr 1, poz. 1638

Sekanina v. Austria, App no 13126/87 (ECtHR, 25 August 1993)

Supreme Court Judgment (Administrative Bench) 20 December 2019 Cassation no. 3847/2018

Index

Page numbers in bold refer to tables. Page numbers followed by 'n' refer to notes.

For Product Safety Concerns and Information please contact our EU
representative GPSR@taylorandfrancis.com
Taylor & Francis Verlag GmbH, Kaufingerstraße 24, 80331 München, Germany

www.ingramcontent.com/pod-product-compliance
Lightning Source LLC
LaVergne TN
LVHW021122300926
849160LV00010B/831
* 9 7 8 1 0 3 2 1 3 4 7 6 5 *